Neo-Nazi Postmodern

Neo-Nazi Postmodern

Right-Wing Terror Tactics, the Intellectual New Right, and the Destabilization of Memory in Germany since 1989

Esther Elizabeth Adaire

BLOOMSBURY ACADEMIC
LONDON • NEW YORK • OXFORD • NEW DELHI • SYDNEY

BLOOMSBURY ACADEMIC
Bloomsbury Publishing Plc, 50 Bedford Square, London, WC1B 3DP, UK
Bloomsbury Publishing Inc, 1359 Broadway, New York, NY 10018, USA
Bloomsbury Publishing Ireland, 29 Earlsfort Terrace, Dublin 2, D02 AY28, Ireland

BLOOMSBURY, BLOOMSBURY ACADEMIC and the Diana logo are
trademarks of Bloomsbury Publishing Plc

First published in Great Britain 2024
This paperback edition published 2025

Copyright © Esther Elizabeth Adaire, 2024

Esther Elizabeth Adaire has asserted her right under the Copyright,
Designs and Patents Act, 1988, to be identified as Author of this work.

For legal purposes the Acknowledgments on p. vi
constitute an extension of this copyright page.

Cover image: Commémoration de la mort de Rudolf Hess en 1991 © Chip HIRES/Getty

All rights reserved. No part of this publication may be: i) reproduced or transmitted in any form, electronic or mechanical, including photocopying, recording or by means of any information storage or retrieval system without prior permission in writing from the publishers; or ii) used or reproduced in any way for the training, development or operation of artificial intelligence (AI) technologies, including generative AI technologies. The rights holders expressly reserve this publication from the text and data mining exception as per Article 4(3) of the Digital Single Market Directive (EU) 2019/790.

Bloomsbury Publishing Plc does not have any control over, or responsibility for, any third-party websites referred to or in this book. All internet addresses given in this book were correct at the time of going to press. The author and publisher regret any inconvenience caused if addresses have changed or sites have ceased to exist, but can accept no responsibility for any such changes.

Every effort has been made to trace the copyright holders and obtain permission to reproduce the copyright material. Please do get in touch with any enquiries or any information relating to such material or the rights holder. We would be pleased to rectify any omissions in subsequent editions of this publication should they be drawn to our attention.

A catalogue record for this book is available from the British Library.

A catalog record for this book is available from the Library of Congress.

ISBN: HB: 978-1-3504-1712-0
PB: 978-1-3504-1713-7
ePDF: 978-1-3504-1714-4
eBook: 978-1-3504-1715-1

Typeset by Integra Software Services Pvt. Ltd.

For product safety related questions contact productsafety@bloomsbury.com.

To find out more about our authors and books visit www.bloomsbury.com
and sign up for our newsletters.

Contents

Acknowledgments	vi
List of Abbreviations	vii
Introduction: Postmodern Terrorism	1
1 SKINS Reunification and the Neo-Nazi Scene	9
2 COUNTERMEMORY The Reactionary Historicism of the New Right	39
3 BUNDESWEHR Right-Wing Extremism in the German Armed Forces	67
4 LEADERLESS RESISTANCE Failings in Counterterrorism from the NPD to the NSU	99
5 VOLK PEGIDA, the AfD, and the Disruptive Tactics of the New-New Right	133
Epilogue: Confronting the Present	163
Notes	168
Sources	237
Select Bibliography	239
Index	247

Acknowledgments

This book was partly funded by the Randolph L. Braham Fellowship, awarded to me by the CUNY Graduate Center in 2022.

There are also a number of individuals who deserve mention, here. I would first like to thank those who mentored me years ago at Goldsmiths, University of London, and who are responsible for giving me a solid grounding in all manner of theoretical and historical frameworks upon which I still rely in order to make sense of the world: Mischa Twitchin, John London, Ben Levitas, Rosie Kennedy, Benno Gammerl, Jan Plamper, and especially my former advisor Alex Watson, without whom I would not know how to be a historian at all. I would also like to thank Daniel Wildmann at Queen Mary University, whose class on antisemitism was foundational to me.

At CUNY I must acknowledge professors Julia Sneeringer, Ben Hett, Samira Haj, and Dagmar Herzog for their continual guidance and encouragement. Particularly heartfelt thanks are owed to Andreas Killen for keeping me sane throughout my doctoral studies.

Thank you to all my colleagues throughout the world of academia and beyond who have provided me with thoughtful feedback, inspiration, and reassurance over the years: Yanara Schmacks, Rebecca Irvine, Marybeth Tamborra, Marta Millar, Gavriel Rosenfeld, Frank Hentschker, Ninad Pandit, Evan Spritzer, Liz Fink, Nada Ayad, Christopher Molnar, Eric Langenbacher, Raymond Patton, Emil Kerenji, and Leah Wolfson. Thank you especially to Michelle Kahn and to Rabea Rittgerodt, both of whom read an earlier manuscript of this book and provided valuable support. Thank you, also, to my patient editor Rhodri Mogford and to everyone at Bloomsbury.

Much gratitude is owed to my family for putting up with my intellectual provocations for several decades now, and to all the friends whose mirth and understanding prove a continual source of solace through trying times: Nadine Sadler, Skye Savage, David Grunner, Noah Merenfeld, Anna Müller, Emily Olsen, Anne Tastad, Seth Pollack, and Chloe Pye. Thank you especially to my dearest friend Simon Horton for absolutely everything.

Finally, I would not have been able to complete this book without Steve Remy, whose surprise marzipan treats on my laptop keyboard helped keep me from despair and whose devotion, empathy, and tireless encouragement I do not take for granted.

List of Abbreviations

AfD	Alternative für Deutschland
BfV	Bundesamt für Verfassungsschutz
BKA	Bundeskriminalamt
CDU	Christlich Demokratische Union
DA	Deutsche Alternative
DMZ	Deutsche Militärzeitschrift
DVU	Deutsches Volksunion
FAP	Freiheitliche Deutsche Arbeiterpartei
FAZ	Frankfurter Allgemeine Zeitung
GdNF	Gesinnungsgemeinschaft der Neuen Front
GDR	German Democratic Republic
KKK	Ku Klux Klan
KSK	Kommando Spezialkräfte
LKA	Landeskriminalamt
NA	Nationale Alternative
NPD	Nationaldemokratische Partei Deutschlands
NSU	Nationalsozialistischer Untergrund
NSDAP	Nationalsozialistische Deutsche Arbeiterpartei
PDS	Partei des Demokratischen Sozialismus
PEGIDA	Patriotische Europäer gegen die Islamisierung des Abendlandes
REP	Die Republikaner
SA	Sturmabteilung

SED	Sozialistische Einheitspartei Deutschlands
SPD	Sozialdemokratische Partei Deutschlands
VAPO	Volkstreue außerparlamentarische Opposition
ZOG	Zionist Occupation Government

Introduction: Postmodern Terrorism

In May 2020, a police raid on the property of a soldier in the second company of the Kommando Spezialkräfte (KSK)—the special forces command of the German Army (the Bundeswehr)—led to the unraveling of a doomsday conspiracy plot, replete with hoarded weaponry, ammunition, enemy hit-lists, and body bags, organized by a network of neo-Nazis within the elite command.[1] Nordkreuz, a right-wing extremist paramilitary group made up of armed forces veterans, serving officers, and KSK soldiers who communicated using the encrypted messaging app Telegram, had facilitated meetings, gun competitions, and Nazi-esque ceremonies on the property located in the eastern state of Mecklenburg-Vorpommern. Codenamed "Day X," in a nod to the notorious neo-Nazi bible *The Turner Diaries*, the plot would have seen enemy politicians as well as foreign workers and refugees rounded onto trucks and taken to a secret location where they were to be disposed of—a pre-emptive strike against the liberals and migrants who ostensibly sought to bring about Germany's cultural collapse.[2] While journalists abroad asked whether these disturbing revelations indicated some weakness in Germany's admirable culture of memory and historical consciousness, Nordkreuz saw themselves as crusaders against an obstinate moral conformity that threatened to abolish what remained of a German national identity already suppressed by guilt and defeat since the end of the First World War.[3]

The fantasy was neo-Nazi postmodern: a paranoiac alternate universe in which trust in liberal democratic structures has broken down entirely. Like those on the political left who first, in the 1970s and '80s, read the heady cultural critiques of Jean-François Lyotard, Michel Foucault, and Jean Baudrillard and could not, thereafter, un-see the relations of power which seem to everywhere guide our cultural values and systems of knowledge, right-wing extremists in Germany, the United States, and elsewhere have long guarded their own mistrust of governing structures—only, on their side of the looking glass, the enemy is a hegemonic liberal order which controls everything from immigration to what's sayable and unsayable in public discourse.[4] For those who jump into this black rabbit hole, what's seen and learned therein becomes an object of intense fixation. While in the United States this mistrust has culturally specific roots in the reactionary response to the Civil Rights movement as well as the deceptions of the Vietnam War—influences which produced the notorious neo-Nazi and antisemite William Luther Pierce's 1978 *The Turner Diaries*, a dystopian fiction in which whites have become a subjugated race[5]— in Germany the far right's postmodern critique aims its sights at cultures of remembrance and historical reckoning.[6] It is this stifling discourse of moral conformity and eternal guilt, the far-right argument goes, that has allowed Germany to become a subjugated nation, bowing to pressure from the European Union to take in more than its share of migrants and trading the nation's rich history of cultural traditions for multiculturalism in perpetual atonement for the crimes of National Socialism.

The KSK scandal came amidst a global wave of unrest concerning structural racism within police forces and other government institutions, as well as increased far-right paramilitary activity in the United States, and therefore seemed to speak of a frightening new radicalization threatening numerous countries.[7] In Germany, however, the presence of a shadow army within the nation's armed forces was but the latest and most grim evidence of what counterterrorism experts and anti-fascist activists alike had known since the National Socialist Underground (NSU) scandal of 2011, in which it was discovered that an active network of neo-Nazis had gone ignored for over a decade by the security services, leading to the murder of nine men with migrant family backgrounds. Namely, decades of government malfeasance and refusal to acknowledge the growing strength, coherence, and paramilitarism of a vast far-right network had enabled a right-wing extremist terror spree unlike anything seen in Germany since the days of the Weimar Republic.[8] Both the 2011 and the 2020 scandals recall earlier events from the years encompassing the reunification of East and West Germany (known in German as the *Wende*, or "turnaround" years), in which waves of neo-Nazi skinheads—galvanized by both economic despair in the eastern states and a renewed sense of nationalism overall—led attacks on migrants and Germans with foreign backgrounds, threatening the moral foundations of the Federal Republic. As this book will argue, those foundational events of the early 1990s were dealt with far from adequately at the time, laying faulty groundwork for both political and legislative reckoning with right-wing extremism for decades to come.

While the Federal Government and security services such as the Bundesamt für Verfassungsschutz (BfV), Germany's domestic intelligence bureau, have known about so-called "isolated" instances of far-right radicalism within the German military, the police, and society at large for decades, they have consistently rejected inquiries into any broader infiltration of state institutions by neo-Nazis or far-right actors.[9] Moreover, this growing neo-Nazi scene has since the 2010s become entangled with circles of the far-right intellectual milieu known as the Neue Rechte—the New Right—a crowd which once eschewed association with skinheads and neo-Nazis but now marries violent street protest with ethnopluralist ideology, a politics of racial exclusion that adopts its language from their French counterparts, the Nouvelle Droite.[10] Groups like Patriotische Europäer gegen die Islamisierung des Abendlandes (PEGIDA), parties like the Alternative für Deutschland (AfD), and more recent and difficult-to-categorize movements like Querdenker, represent the integration of previously disparate factions within the world of the far-right: in particular, a marriage between those who see themselves as conservative intellectuals and those who see themselves as patriotic shock troopers, as well as the mainstreaming of ethno-nationalist politics and post-truth—or right-wing postmodernist—attacks on liberal democracy.

It has taken the liberal political order far too long to wake up to the groundswell of reactionary opposition to Germany's culture of memory, which takes the form of the mainstreaming of illiberal politics and violence against migrants and foreigners as well as an epistemological attack on historical facts and commonly held truths, a result of this marriage of neo-Nazis and Neue Rechte ideologues. This opposition has been brewing on the political fringes and in the intellectual circles of the Neue Rechte since before reunification, with much earlier West German roots in a right-wing pushback against the student movement of 1968 and the *Historikerstreit* (historian's dispute) of the 1980s, the latter of which produced relativizing trends that would lead some public intellectuals down the path of Holocaust denial, an early and extreme post-truth development.[11] The overarching aim of this book is to demonstrate that none of the instances of far-right terror herein are separable from the slow eradication of historical certainties in public discourse—a major facet of right-wing postmodernism.

In 1996 the late historian Walter Laqueur predicted that terrorism was about to make a postmodern turn. The new "Postmodern Terrorism," he wrote, would increasingly come to be characterized by small groups and so-called "lone wolf" actors who, possessing ever greater technological skill, would be better able to evade detection by working alone. His prediction is worth quoting at length:

> In the future, terrorists will be individuals or like-minded people working in very small groups, on the pattern of the technology-hating Unabomber, who apparently worked alone sending out parcel bombs over two decades, or the perpetrators of the 1995 bombing of the federal building in Oklahoma City. An individual may possess the technical competence to steal, buy, or manufacture the weapons he or she needs for a terrorist purpose; he or she may or may not require help from one or two others in delivering these weapons to the designated target. The ideologies such individuals and minigroups espouse are likely to be even more aberrant than those of larger groups. And terrorists working alone or in very small groups will be more difficult to detect unless they make a major mistake or are discovered by accident.[12]

This describes precisely the tactic of "Leaderless Resistance" that was calculatingly put into practice by right-wing extremist groups from the mid-1980s onwards, from Aryan Nations in the United States to the NSU in Germany. Originally pioneered by Ku Klux Klan (KKK) leader Louis L. Beam, "Leaderless Resistance" comprises a terror structure designed to misleadingly give the impression of attacks perpetrated by "lone wolf" actors rather than a coherent terror group with a leader and a chain of command.[13] By the mid-1990s the lone wolf misnomer seemed to characterize most high-profile far-right terror attacks, perhaps most famously Timothy McVeigh and Terry Nichols' attack on the Alfred P. Murrah Federal Building in Oklahoma City in the United States.[14] Yet its enduring significance as a terror tactic is that it relied upon manufacturing a sense of indeterminacy of what can be seen and understood—i.e., the ostensibly pathological lone wolf actor masks a much wider community of white supremacist and far-right groups, militias, and cells. Emphasizing the use of uncertainty as a terror tactic, Laqueur further predicted that these new self-led terrorists would come to harness information warfare/infoterror in the form of disinformation campaigns aimed at political destabilization, and that some of the distributors of such disinformation might even believe their own "aberrant ideologies."[15]

Writing before the age of Web 2.0, let alone social media, Laqueur did not quite foresee how acute an epistemological turn infoterror would later take—i.e., the manner in which the far-right, in particular, has taken advantage of algorithmically distorted information environments in order to conduct subversive campaigns against social stability and recruit new members *en masse*.[16] Nevertheless, his classification of a "postmodern" form of terrorism that weaponizes information predicted that terror would come to take aim at society's given forms and structures, throwing them into chaotic relativity. This is a step which, as countless intelligence and counterterrorism experts have noted in recent years, goes far beyond familiar, Cold War-era forms of subversion and sedition.[17] Moreover, as Peter Gill and Mark Pythian point out, the relevance of postmodernism for the intelligence analyst is that intelligence itself "is about the production of knowledge," and it therefore makes sense to apply a postmodernist framework to the study of terrorism that "emphasizes the significance of new information technologies in reshaping and subverting modernist methods of generating knowledge."[18] Laqueur's reference to Ted Kaczynski, the Unabomber, already hinted at the role that an overly mediated society might soon play in future forms of terrorism, with the far-right increasingly coming to mistrust the truth content of mainstream media technologies while also weaponizing society's increasing reliance on online spaces in order to conduct their disinformation campaigns.[19]

The new far right's assault on liberal conceits and historical certainties calls to mind a passage from Ernst Jünger that is often quoted by Neue Rechte pundits such as Götz Kubitschek, who styles himself as the leader of a dark enlightenment, originally written during an interwar era ensnared between nihilism and futurism:

> Our hope rests in the young people who suffer a rise in temperature because the green purulence of disgust consumes them; in the souls of *grandezza* whose bearers we see creeping along like sick people between rows of feeding troughs. It rests in the uprising that opposes the reign of bourgeois comfort and that calls for explosives, weapons of destruction, to be directed against the world of forms so that the living space may be swept empty for a new hierarchy.[20]

Jünger did not originally imbue these words with far-right sentiment; written during the Weimar Republic's twilight years against a backdrop of democratic instability and economic despair, they mainly express a visceral discontentment with liberal apathy. And yet, as this book will demonstrate, the German Neue Rechte has appropriated this creed precisely due to its political ambiguity—a small example of the movement's broader effort to muddy the political binaries that liberal democracy has for so long taken for granted. Certainly, to characterize these aims as postmodern is not necessarily to argue that they are wholly new or recently formed concepts. Rather, the development that this book aims to describe is one in which a genealogy of older right-wing grievances and paranoias has merged, since reunification, with the new anxieties of the post-1989 era, in particular anxiety over a growing culture of commemoration in Germany. Moreover, preexisting far-right obsessions have found new outlets in the technologies and epistemologies of the post-1989 era, which have themselves become weapons of terror.

Since the 1950s the Neue Rechte has guarded a German conservative intellectual tradition from Goethe and Heidegger to the writers of the interwar conservative revolution such as Jünger and Carl Schmitt. Leaders of the postwar West German Neue Rechte like Armin Mohler mostly reproduced interwar texts of a racist, *völkisch*, and antisemitic nature while calling for a new German nationalism based on "pre-political," Enlightenment-era notions of national identity. Yet during the 1970s this reactionary milieu discovered new common ground with mainstream conservative figures like the philosopher Hermann Lübbe, who voiced concern over the influence of left-wing, extra-parliamentary opposition, contextualizing the broader student movement of '68 alongside terrorist organizations such as the Red Army Faction (RAF). By the 1980s a distinct intellectual reactionary scene had formed with, in its midst, a cabal of nominally conservative historians—most famously Ernst Nolte, who was drifting ever further toward the far-right. Building on the revisionist arguments he had made during the 1986–7 *Historikerstreit*,[21] Nolte transgressed even further during the 1990s into all-out revisionism and even Holocaust denial, casting doubt upon commonly acknowledged facts about the Holocaust and framing popular acceptance of the Holocaust's factuality as uncritical liberal dogma.[22]

In a distinctly right-wing postmodernist turn, the Neue Rechte of the 1990s and beyond has successfully weaponized anxiety concerning the knowability of facts, from its attack on the liberal media to its online disinformation campaigns in recent years.[23] While other nations, for example the United States and Britain, have experienced their own post-truth climates in which concepts such as "alternative facts" and "fake news" abound to discordant effect (a development referred to by the RAND corporation as "Truth Decay"),[24] in Germany historical memory is the specific target of the Neue Rechte's campaign of infoterror precisely because memory of the Holocaust is synonymous with a central and terrible truth about German history and identity. Throughout the 1990s and into the new millennium, the Neue Rechte increasingly aimed its rhetorical ammunition at the stability of historical truth and the German culture of remembrance by engaging in historical revisionism, now joined by neo-Nazi foot soldiers who took their grievances to the streets, violently protesting historical exhibitions and publicly commemorating Nazi "heroes." In weaponizing memory, the Neue Rechte is able to call the very basis of the Federal Republic's self-image into question; attacks on European integration, on asylum policies, and on the perceived liberal hegemony of the German media all begin and end with the claim that the Holocaust is used as a "moral cudgel" by liberal politicians and historians.[25]

This post-mnemonic shift could not have occurred without the defection of left-wing intellectuals and politicians to the ranks of the Neue Rechte during the 1990s and onwards, who brought with them a new language of postmodernist critique with which to take aim at the discursive power of the media. Scornful critique of the "telecratic masses"—imported to the Neue Rechte by left-wing apostates such as the dramatist Botho Strauß[26]—occurred concurrently with the far right's embracing of new communications technologies which became a subversive alternative to traditional media. As Kathleen Belew has documented in the US context, throughout the late 1980s and the 1990s a previously diffuse white supremacist and neo-Nazi scene now found commonality on the unregulated and encrypted bulletin board systems of a nascent internet.[27] The White Power movement, as it became known, cohered its ideology around alternative understandings of history and contemporary political events as well as shared doctrines like Beam's "Leaderless Resistance"—a tract which ended up on the hard drives of some of Germany's most notorious neo-Nazi terrorists, notably the NSU. While experts have written on the relationship between online communication and right-wing terrorism in the German context, few have thought about the connection between the new organizational tactics of a militant neo-Nazi International and the weaponization of the internet as a form of political destabilization.[28] Even fewer have noted this global connection in the German context.[29]

This book reveals the connection between the evolving terror tactics of an increasingly organized neo-Nazi underground and the Neue Rechte's growing crusade against the stability of truth via information warfare—the far right's harnessing of epistemic chaos for politically disruptive ends.[30] Some chapters will trace the link between historical revisionism and post-truth claims, while others will trace the evolution of the neo-Nazi underground from the skinheads of the *Wende* years to the terror networks of the NSU and their close relationship with the far-right Nationaldemokratische Partei Deutschlands (NPD)—an important precursor to PEGIDA and the AfD. This book also makes revelatory and urgent observations regarding the role played by the Bundeswehr, Germany's armed forces, within the German far right's own culture of memory as well as the shameful failings in counterterrorism exhibited by Germany's Defense Ministry and its intelligence services. From a new generation of militant ideologues who combine violent street protest with intellectual posturing to the self-described "electronic shock troops" of online forums and their campaigns of disinformation, the unfolding link between various factions and iterations of the far-right traced throughout this book is the subversion of historical memory, which the Neue Rechte targets precisely because of its discursive power.

1

SKINS

Reunification and the Neo-Nazi Scene

In January 2015, several months before the onset of a refugee crisis which would ferociously catalyze an already burgeoning partnership between Germany's right-wing extremist networks and the Euro-skeptic AfD party, Afghani-German film director Burhan Qurbani debuted a fictionalized portrait of neo-Nazi youth that touched upon subtle, emotional themes of memory and forgetting seldom evoked in political debates over the years to come.[1] In *Wir sind jung, wir sind stark*, Qurbani portrays in cold, monochromatic tones the psycho-social world of a group of young East German neo-Nazis whose industrial town succumbs to economic liquidation alongside a migration wave of Vietnamese and North African workers, both developments at least partially the result of reunification. Endeavoring to comprehend the emotional drive behind the waves of anti-foreigner violence that swept Germany during the *Wende* years (specifically, in this case, the brutal 1992 attack on a housing estate for asylum seekers that was carried out by neo-Nazis in the town of Rostock-Lichtenhagen to the rancorous encouragement of thousands of local bystanders), Qurbani locates the source of this outpouring of grievance at a point of tension between melancholic inability to recall the GDR as it rapidly collapses and fades into memory, on the one hand, and on the other an impulse to simply obliterate what remains. After committing suicide by jumping from the balcony of his apartment on the eighth floor of a drab Rostock *Neubaukomplex*, the character Philip leaves behind a note in which he expresses a growing inability to recall his own past: "Every day, I lose a day, a week, a month … My memories are dissolving."[2] Underpinning the economic

---

Parts of this chapter are based on an earlier article published by the author as "'This Other Germany, the Dark One.' Post-Wall Memory Politics Surrounding the Neo-Nazi Riots in Rostock and Hoyerswerda" in *German Politics and Society*, Vol. 37, No. 4 (Winter 2019/2020), pp. 43–57.

despairs of his family and peers, he writes, is the sense that his town and his former nation are being erased entirely, subsumed within the Federal Republic and its Western, democratic imperatives: "How can you keep on going," he asks, "if you no longer have a past?" Later, armed with Molotov cocktails outside of a housing estate for asylum seekers, other characters express a nihilistic surplus of memory—a longing to break into the future and efface the discredited edifices of the GDR. As the character Robbie exclaims before hurling a *Molli* through the window of an apartment, referring as much to his personal, romantic grievances as to the present situation he finds himself in: "Fuck the past. Let's just destroy everything."[3]

The film shrewdly locates the origins of recent, similar displays of right-wing extremist strife in the *Wende* years, demonstrating that the anti-migrant violence of the late 2010s and early 2020s is rooted, at least in part, in unresolved anger from the early 1990s. While public debates concerning the popularity of the AfD have often raged over whether Germans in the eastern states have properly imbibed the same culture of memory as those in the western states, Qurbani's film is a rare example of an onlooker seeking to understand the nature of East German memory itself, which during the years of reunification resembled a memory of the present in collapse.[4] However, the film is also a continuation of other media-driven and popular efforts to analyze the inner world of the young, troubled, and usually East German neo-Nazi. Since the NSU revelations of 2011 made grim celebrities of Uwe Mundlos, Uwe Böhnhardt, and Beate Zschäpe—the notorious Thuringian terror trio who, over the course of a decade, evaded authorities while committing several bank robberies, numerous small-scale bomb attacks, and ten murders—a fascination with the disrupted and fragmentary landscape of East German youth emerging from the wreckage of totalitarianism has tended, narratively speaking, to isolate the lone skinhead in an oppressive world of personal grievances. Fundamental as personal grievances are for comprehending what motivates an individual to join up with a far-right gang or network, these popular narratives have tended to underestimate—or ignore entirely—the importance of the broader network itself as a space for far-right socialization. This includes both ideological indoctrination and training in the fundamentals of terror: building of improvised explosive devices (IEDs), use of firearms, and organizational strategy.

As this chapter will show, debates which took place over the problem of "the East German neo-Nazi" in the early 1990s laid some faulty foundations on which political discourse surrounding this topic would continue to be built over the following decades, inhibiting common understandings of *where* contemporary right-wing extremism originates from in Germany—geographically, socially, and ideologically. This discourse, which in a broad sense attempted to isolate the phenomenon of neo-Nazi violence to the eastern states alone, also contributed to a limited understanding of right-wing extremist tactics in Germany which were, at the time, becoming ever more integrated within a growing international terror movement. In both the media and parliamentary debates throughout the early 1990s the misnomer of the "lone wolf" actor, the trope of the disaffected East German youth, and the suggested lack of any meaningful connection between neo-Nazi youth and the political and intellectual far-right all amounted to the underestimation of an organized and ideologically coherent neo-Nazi terror scene in Germany with important ties to the United States, the UK, and other European nations. By the time of the NSU revelations in 2011 and, later, the Bundeswehr scandal of 2020, this long persisting limited understanding of such networks had proved fatal again and again.

Furthermore, the underestimation of neo-Nazi terror networks has rested, in Germany, atop a discursive minefield concerning the relationship between East and West. In the first few years of German reunification, unease about the consequences and even the feasibility of uniting two politically and culturally distinct Germanys seemed to receive grim validation in the face of several outbreaks of extreme right-wing violence directed at foreign workers and migrants, much of it situated in the eastern states. The outbreaks of neo-Nazi aggression against foreigners and asylum seekers in the eastern towns of Hoyerswerda, in 1991, and Rostock-Lichtenhagen, in 1992, were, at the time, the most violent demonstrations of right-wing extremism to occur in Germany since the end of the Third Reich. In the Federal Republic, whose postwar political culture had, since the later half of the 1960s, come to be defined by a tumultuous process of reckoning with the past, neo-Nazi phenomena signified the re-emergence of vehement racist nationalism that had long been considered worked through or historicized in official public narratives. Underpinned by this political culture of memory, discourse surrounding the events in Hoyerswerda and Rostock often hinted that reunification had ushered in some ugly remnants of a totalitarian past that elsewhere in Eastern Europe was finally being dismantled, but in Germany had merely been annexed. As *Der Spiegel*'s 2012 retrospective of the events in Rostock-Lichtenhagen put it: "There it was again, this *other* Germany, the dark one."[5]

This reflexive tendency to split Germany in half has persisted in both journalistic and political discourse long after reunification. The metaphor of good, democratic Germany wrestling with its dark *Doppelgänger* has a wide utility because it can be applied in more than one sense: an allusion to the "*other* Germany" might be a reference to the GDR (which for four decades was quite literally another Germany) or it might evoke the Nazi past, depending on the context. The metaphor can also be employed in a deliberately vague manner that alludes to both these things at once. For example, the "totalitarian" model for comprehending both the Nazi and the Communist pasts became, in the years that followed reunification, a rhetorical crutch when used by journalists and politicians alike; a convenient way both to demonize East Germans collectively and in so doing exculpate West Germany from any sense of responsibility— either for inviting and fostering an anti-foreigner climate or for the resurgence of German nationalistic fervor that swelled in the wake of the Berlin Wall's collapse.

In this context, common understandings of totalitarianism (what it does to a society; what its major political components consist of) as put into discursive play by politicians such as Helmut Kohl, West Germany's Chancellor throughout the years of reunification, were framed by Germany's "divided memory"—i.e., the extremely different ways in which East and West Germany each dealt with the Nazi past.[6] In contrast to an ostensibly healthy historical consciousness, entailing a reckoning with guilt and responsibility that had developed in several phases throughout the existence of the Federal Republic, the GDR's state-imposed narrative of anti-fascism came to be exposed as part and parcel of doctrinal totalitarian ideology.[7] Much of the discourse surrounding the right-wing extremism supposedly endemic to the so-called "new states" that rejoined Germany in 1991 therefore concerned cultures of memory and the popular claim that East Germans had not yet expelled ethno-nationalist aggression from their national psyche—in fact, it may have only grown more savage, repressed for forty years under the "mask" of anti-fascism.[8] The Germany that had failed to confess its historical sins, the Germany that had walled itself in for forty years and had therefore not experienced the same waves of post-colonial migration as West Germany, now resembled a defeated ethno-state in need of reeducating.

This narrative—which also did much to discredit the genuine anti-fascism of East German activists and politicians following reunification[9]—relied on an implicit claim that Western, democratic society had successfully overcome fascist, nationalist, and right-wing extremist tendencies in general. Yet, while the numerous examples of neo-fascist and ultranationalistic fervor that swept Eastern Europe after the collapse of the Soviet Bloc can be attributed to causes unique to the struggles and resentments of Eastern Europeans who lived under communism, right-wing extremism was also experiencing success in the Western world during these years.[10] In the United States, 1991 saw David Duke, former chief of the KKK, win 38.8 percent of the vote in his run for Louisiana governor, followed by a notable yet dismal presidential bid in 1992.[11] (The growth and global reach of US-based white supremacy would soon, as later chapters of this book discuss, have great implications for the direction that German right-wing extremism took in the 1990s.) The early 1990s also saw unprecedented successes for Western European far-right parties which typically ran on anti-EU platforms and utilized ethno-nationalist sentiments in their appeals to their respective political bases, for example the British National Party; the Front National in France; the Lega Nord in Italy; Sweden's Sverigedemokraterna (only just founded in 1988); Austria's Freiheitliche Partei Österreichs; the secessionist Vlaams Blok in Belgium; and in Germany the Republikaner (REP) party, which began as a West German organization but soon gained strong favor in the eastern states, as discussed below.[12] These examples demonstrate that both East and West were experiencing far-right responses to shifting global alliances and emerging political and economic unions such as the EU, albeit in their own unique contexts.

The various fallouts of reunification did, indeed, introduce West Germans to a culturally distinct East German neo-Nazi scene which had been brewing in the final years of the GDR, the origins of which this chapter will explore. However, it made little sense to lump East Germany in, via intellectual discussions concerning the post-totalitarian personality which often trickled down to mainstream media, with other neo-fascist phenomena that were occurring elsewhere in Eastern Europe—especially as, unlike those other former communist states, East Germany had the unique distinction of having been absorbed into the Western, liberal-democratic Federal Republic. Rising racist aggression was a problem for the newly reunified Germany as a whole, as much attributable to the influence of long-established West German far-right political parties as to the problem of "troubled youth" (a choice phrase of the times) in the eastern states. And yet in response to the outbreaks of anti-foreigner violence in Hoyerswerda and Rostock, political and journalistic discourse often caricatured rhetorical images of *Ossi* skinhead neo-Nazis, framing right-wing extremism as a uniquely East German problem.

There were various, often pathologizing, explanations for this apparent phenomenon: one was the narrative about disaffected youth, which sometimes tried to draw attention to the social and economic injustices occurring in the eastern states at the behest of Kohl's privatization initiative, but just as often emphasized the hooliganism that arose from the boredom and stagnation of life in the GDR. Moreover, the political response to right-wing extremism ultimately demonstrated the anti-migration sentiments of mainstream West German conservatism: when racist attacks finally turned fatal in the West German town of Mölln, in Schleswig-Holstein, Kohl's CDU government responded not by toughening its stance on violent hate crimes, but by reforming Germany's asylum laws, thereby capitulating to the extremists. As this chapter will show, siphoning blame for racist violence (often framed euphemistically as "xenophobia"—a fear of outsiders) when it occurred in the eastern states and, in turn, treating similar occurrences in the western states as anomalous, isolated tragedies within an otherwise healthy culture of remembrance in the end masked a political ambivalence toward foreignness and migration that was becoming ever more mainstream throughout the Federal Republic. In addition, such tactics cemented discursive norms regarding the memory divide between East and West which would continue to obfuscate debate over the issue of right-wing extremism in Germany over the next few decades.

The GDR Skinhead Scene

In the years following the fall of the Berlin Wall and subsequent collapse of the Soviet Bloc, Eastern Europe saw the gradual emergence of various groups and movements of a radical right, or neo-fascist nature, ranging from underground social milieu to fringe political parties. While such movements in newly sovereign nations like Hungary, Bulgaria, Romania, Belarus, and Poland exhibited traditional characteristics of the radical right (nationalism, antisemitism, racism, etc.), they were also rooted in a distinct anticommunism which arose during the Bloc's years of political and economic disintegration, and which provided a nationalist identity politics with which to both throw off the mantle of communism *and* reject Western, democratic hegemony.[13] Scholarly debate over the origins of this neo-fascist wave, and the degree to which right-wing extremist activity in Eastern Europe occurs in communication or solidarity with similar movements in the West, has largely concluded that anti-Westernism and anti-democracy are so integral to the political project of these movements that neo-fascisms in the East must be understood within their specific historical context, distinct from the aims and origins of those in the West.[14]

Yet for the reasons discussed above, the case of the former GDR was unique. Several high-profile instances of anti-foreigner aggression in the early years of reunification prompted commentators at the time to deliberate between two major explanatory frameworks for the growth of a violent right-wing extremist scene in the new states, broadly speaking: either that it was a product of conditions in the GDR, or, conversely, that it was a result of reunification.[15] Moreover, while in the first decade of reunification right-wing extremism in the eastern states was thought to be limited to fringe movements rather than political parties,[16] experts have long since established that a skinhead and neo-Nazi milieu which had formed autonomously in the GDR soon merged, during the *Wende*, with West German influences and became part of what Gideon Botsch refers to as a politically oriented, "pan-German 'national opposition.'"[17] Much of the discourse surrounding outbreaks of neo-Nazi violence in the eastern states during the early years of reunification was shaped by the political ambitions of Kohl's Federal Republic as well as West German perceptions of itself in comparison to its totalitarian double. Notably, both sides of the old debate concerning whether East German skinheads were a product of the GDR or a result of reunification tended to rely upon a psycho-social interpretive framework which, while calling attention to urgent issues like the dissolution of the GDR's economy following reunification, nevertheless failed to take seriously the neo-Nazi scene as an organized, terrorist structure—and failed to consider the complicity of Western actors and influences.[18] Though salient, political debates over the economic disenfranchisement of East Germans proved blind to the true scope and organizational scale of the far-right scene, not only in the eastern states but in Germany as a whole. The developments and revelations of our past two decades, however, highlight how sorely the strength and coherence of neo-Nazi networks have been underestimated, despite the public outrage that attacks on foreigners rightly provokes. The covert formation of the Thuringia-based NSU terror cell during the *Wende* years is perhaps one of the most striking justifications for a re-conceptualization of the neo-Nazi scene in the eastern states and its relationship to a broader, pan-German network of right-wing extremists.[19]

The sociological arguments produced during the 1990s that concerned the meaning of East German racism, which tended to focus on explaining the structures which constituted "foreignness" within the GDR's autocratic society, were not entirely without merit and remain in many ways instructive.[20] One popular argument—by no means incorrect—reasoned that a preexisting ambivalence toward foreigners during the GDR increased due to the systemic upheaval of the East German state during its collapse in 1989/90, leading to a "specific East German xenophobia" that persisted throughout the 1990s and beyond.[21] This argument is often further compounded by the observation that foreigners had comprised less than 1 percent of the GDR's population.²² This statistic can, of course, be interpreted to mean various things—one being the slightly dubious claim that long-standing SED party discourse had supposedly fashioned the GDR as a bounded ethno-national community, another being that the GDR's closed border itself counted as *de facto* xenophobia.²³

In any case, statistics and paradigms of "foreignness" alone do not explain how an anti-establishment scene that identified itself with the politics and aesthetics of fascism arose in an avowedly anti-fascist state. As Botsch points out, the GDR state stringently forbade the existence of official political opposition in obvious contrast to the Federal Republic, which has had to contend with some notable far-right opposition parties attempting to gain democratic representation—for example, the NPD, founded in the 1960s, and the REP, founded in the 1980s.²⁴ What seems to have proven the actual turning point for the growth of a neo-Nazi subcultural scene in East Germany was, in fact, the erosion of the GDR's political and cultural edifices from 1975 onwards. As the Leipzig-based social scientist Wolfgang Brück observed, the newfound ability to form autonomous youth subcultures led, during the 1980s, to the crystallization of a right-wing extremist scene composed of various elements ranging from apolitical, violent youths, to a few outspoken extremists who were deeply opposed to the SED state as well as to socialism and communism generally. These individuals tended, later on, to become local ringleaders.²⁵

Apart from these outspoken ringleaders, unlike West German examples of right-wing extremism that existed before 1989, right-extremist elements in the GDR were limited to a social milieu almost exclusively of young men who, rather than being politically organized around any nationalist agenda, existed mainly as a subcultural scene composed of football hooligans as well as skinheads who had been ousted from the largely anarchist punk scene.²⁶ Broadly speaking, the genesis of skinhead neo-Nazi culture in East Germany runs more or less parallel with the bifurcation of skinhead subculture from the broader punk scene in Western Europe and the United States. As skinheads became a distinct subset, the skinhead look became synonymous with angry boys who engaged in vandalism and misdemeanor, often brandishing or daubing swastikas for provocative effect, though sometimes out of genuine conviction.²⁷ In both the West and the GDR, the skinhead style of dress—a closely shaved head, bomber jacket, turned-up stovepipe jeans (if available, in East Germany) and combat boots—emerged as an off-shoot of the much more diverse/less uniform punk style, though skins were typically not so much bounded by a shared love of punk music as by a shared love of violence; a shaved head often signified that one was up for a fight.[28]

There are, however, some important contextual differences between East and West. For one thing, in Western Europe and the United States the broader neo-Nazi and far-right network had much more in common with long-established ultraconservative—and in the United States, paramilitary—trends which had little if anything to do with youth subcultures; if and when skinhead punks became neo-Nazis, these tended to be localized cases.[29] The now-legendary ousting of neo-Nazis from the US punk scene—perhaps best exemplified by The Dead Kennedys' 1981 single "Nazi Punks Fuck Off"[30]—is illustrative of only one small facet of a growing right-wing extremist scene in the United States which shared (and still does share) a far deeper genealogy with groups like the KKK than it does with alternative music.

In East Germany, on the other hand, punks, skinheads, and neo-Nazis came into being—and into conflict with one another—in a context directly related to conditions within an increasingly stagnant socialist state. With official opposition parties strictly forbidden, unauthorized youth scenes provided some sense of autonomy and affective solidarity. Yet while punks espoused a left-wing or anarchist ethos adopted from Western influences, other dissident youths in the GDR—the ones who would become neo-Nazis—felt deep disgust for anything remotely leftist. Moreover, the tension between these groups was exacerbated by Stasi efforts to suppress the growth of autonomous youth movements. While many skins could be classed as mere hooligans with no particular politics to speak of (in a sense, being apolitical and adrift was the whole point), some began to espouse right-wing ideas, even calling for German reunification long before the Berlin Wall fell.[31] The subsequent provocation and aggression which swelled between the anti-fascist punk scene and skinhead neo-Nazi gangs proved useful for the overall smearing of both groups by Stasi officials.[32]

Neo-Nazi activity had, in fact, occurred sporadically in the GDR as an extreme form of anti-state resistance since the 1950s. As historian Harry Waibel has noted, the stifling authoritarian atmosphere of the GDR had a particular effect upon young people, whose personal grievances against the state found taboo expression in the provocative display of swastikas and the adoption of xenophobic attitudes.[33] The Stasi did not often make its findings on neo-Nazi activity public, most likely in the interests of maintaining the official narrative of fascism's defeat by communism. However, by the 1980s the increasing presence of volatile youth on East German streets had become a conspicuous reality. In 1986 the Interior Ministry of the GDR noted a sudden growth in displays of neo-Nazi sentiment amongst skinheads and football hooligans, estimating a total number of 800 individuals (350 in Berlin alone) spread across thirty-six groups, with a further 1,500 youths who exhibited "extreme-rightist tendencies."[34] One significant group was the Lichtenberg Front, which had emerged from the fan club of Berliner Fußballclub Dynamo and which later re-named itself the 30 January Movement after the date of Adolf Hitler's rise to power in 1933.[35] Another was the Ostkreuz skinheads, who had split off from the East Berlin punk scene.

For a time, the Stasi found the emergence of skinhead gangs to be an opportune means for dealing with punks, who—committed above all to individual autonomy—were proving a destabilizing threat to the East German state. In *Stirb nicht im Warteraum der Zukunft*, music journalist Tim Mohr documents the many ways in which the GDR's punk community, bounded by a love of music imported from the West as well as by shared frustration with the claustrophobia of life in the GDR, subverted state structures by absconding from their state-prescribed vocations and finding alternative means of survival in squats. For a few years, the Stasi attempted to smear the punk scene in general as neo-fascist. Once these smear tactics proved ineffective, the Stasi "seem to have tried to convince themselves that neo-Nazism was a Western problem"—a capitalist import that had crept in, like contraband, alongside other Western cultural influences like Levi jeans and rock-and-roll music.[36] But as Mohr and multiple scholars note, the violent clashes between punks and neo-Nazi skinheads which occurred in 1987 at the Zionskirche—home to a Christian youth club which had become a notorious refuge for opposition groups in East Berlin—can be considered a pivotal moment in the growth of an autonomous neo-Nazi scene.[37] The events of October 17, 1987, when dozens of skins ambushed a punk concert at the Zionskirche demonstrating their violent rejection of punk's anarchist origins, marked the arrival of a coherent East German neo-Nazi scene bounded by anti-leftist rage.[38] Since the Stasi officially denied the existence of neo-Nazis in the anti-fascist GDR, the East German media reported on these events as having been engineered by Western forces. This narrative—which effectively allowed for the skinhead instigators to walk free—suited the Stasi well, as it enabled them to simultaneously "shift the blame across the Wall" and tar punks with the brush of fascism.[39]

Initially, targeting anarchists and anti-fascists had been the *raison d'être* of East German skins. Yet what really united these angry youths in their antipathy was the precarity of life in a stagnant socialist state that could provide neither material comforts nor a meaningful sense of national identity. After the fall of the Wall, bored, frustrated, and indigent youths began to look toward potential reunification not only as a new future under bounteous capitalism, but as restorative of a German national identity unimpeded by the state-imposed tenets of socialism. Following his sojourn through the collapsing Soviet Bloc, journalist Paul Hockenos described exactly these ambivalent political sentiments as expressed by a group of taciturn adolescents he encountered in the East Berlin district of Hellersdorf in December 1989:

> No, they said, they hadn't been following the events in Romania. Yes, they agreed, the opening of the Berlin Wall was a fine thing, even if it was only the first step to ousting the communists once and for all. As for politics, they didn't have much use for them, and none of them identified with any of the political parties, East or West. At the same time, they all considered themselves to be "right wing," which translated first into being anti-communist and second into wanting the reunification of Germany. Finally, they said, they could be "proud to be Germans again."[40]

Political listlessness made these young men a prime target for right-wing extremist recruitment tactics based on emotion and affect rather than the lofty rhetoric of mainstream politics. Recalling his encounter a few years later in 1994, Hockenos observed that the xenophobic aggression which had seemingly spilled from the new states of a reunified Germany could partly be attributed to the expectation (which was by no means held by everyone in East Germany)[41] that a transition to capitalism would raise the living standard in East Germany to something comparable to the West going unfulfilled. The East German neo-Nazi scene would therefore come to forge new allies in the western states; in fact, representatives of long-standing West German far-right parties made first contact, seeing in the restless, agitated East German youth an opportunity to recruit new foot soldiers to their cause.

Western Alliances and Anti-Foreigner Violence during the *Wende*

After the fall of the Berlin Wall on November 9, 1989, both Germanys experienced a surge in far-right extremist violence the likes of which had not been seen since the days of the Third Reich and which would continue throughout the *Wende* period to the deep concern of many. Just as East German authorities had tried in the late 1980s to view neo-Nazism as a Western import, West German politicians largely tended throughout the early 1990s to characterize the rise in anti-foreigner violence as a problem stemming from the new states alone. Yet while politicians and the media alike relied on convenient and simplifying theories about totalitarianism and a lack of historical reckoning that depicted East Germany as a hotbed of repressed fascist aggression (as discussed further below), none of these events are explicable without knowledge of the complicity of West German right-wing extremists.

Although contact between West German far-right parties and the East German neo-Nazi scene had been sporadic during the years of the GDR, from late 1989 onwards—with imminent reunification already widely speculated upon— parties such as the REP, the NPD, the Deutsche Volksunion (DVU), and the neo-Nazi Freiheitliche Deutsche Arbeiterpartei (FAP) ruthlessly disseminated propaganda materials in the GDR to a new audience who would soon parrot their slogans.[42] The REP began establishing district associations throughout the GDR as early as January 1990, with calls for immediate reunification of the GDR and the Federal Republic met by strong approval at their inaugural meetings.[43] (One West German journalist observed, in early 1990, that "the Republikaner's chances of political success in the near future appear to be even greater in the GDR than in the FRG".[44]) The tactics and political base of each of these parties varied somewhat; the REP's approach—which rested on a deeply xenophobic, anti-immigrant platform—strove for political legitimacy, while parties such as the NPD made inroads within far more underground spaces such as "Anti-Antifa Ostthüringen," which would later become the Thüringer Heimatschutz— the neo-Nazi *Kameradschaft* (fellowship) which produced the NSU terror cell.

In addition, new alliances with West German neo-Nazis such as the notorious Michael Kühnen and Christian Worch, who in 1984 founded the Gesinnungsgemeinschaft der Neuen Front (GdNF), a right-wing extremist group that has been responsible for acts of terror,[45] provided the subcultural neo-Nazi scene in the GDR with new means of mobilization and a structural coherence which spurred its evolution into a political movement. Taking a cue from their antifa adversaries, some groups forged bases in squat houses in the East Berlin districts of Friedrichshain, Prenzlauer Berg, and Lichtenberg. One such dwelling at 122 Weitlingstraße in Lichtenberg became a particular hub of activity. Taken over by the Lichtenberg Front/30 January movement in February 1990, the Weitlingstraße house was frequented by allies from West Germany—notably Kühnen, Worch, and their cohort—and also from the Austrian Volkstreue außerparlamentarische Opposition (VAPO), who trained the *Ossi* neo-Nazis in rudimentary terror tactics, provided financial support, and participated with them in small-scale acts of violence.[46] Recruits from the

GDR also traveled to the leadership meetings of the GdNF, which took place in Groningen, in the Netherlands (approximately sixty miles from the German border). Here the German movement surrounding Kühnen met with their Dutch counterparts, many of whom claimed to be the grandsons (and in one case even the widow) of members of the Dutch division of the SS. The recruits also met with notorious US-based white supremacist Gary "Gerhard" Lauck, whose writings on such topics as the *Protocols of the Elders of Zion*, the struggles of the SA and the Wehrmacht, and the "lie" of the genocide of European Jews became the core ideological doctrine of this movement. (Alternative facts, as Chapters 2 and 3 will show, had long been the ideological basis of the postwar far-right and would go on to find new ways of resonating with an evolving audience over the next several decades.) Lauck was also crucial to the import of banned Nazi paraphernalia and propaganda, such as copies of *Mein Kampf*, into Germany; his own journal, *National Socialist Battle Cry (NS-Kampfruf)*, was by this point being translated into six languages.[47] The neo-Nazi scene was quickly becoming international as well as pan-German, with allies in Austria, the Netherlands, the UK, the United States, and throughout Scandinavia.[48]

The movement at 122 Weitlingstraße, by now consisting of around 600 "members and close sympathizers," soon changed its name to Nationale Alternative (NA) and even managed, in March 1990, to become included in the party register of the GDR, though it was excluded from the Volkskammer elections of March 18.[49] Women—often the girlfriends and wives of NA members—were also welcome within the movement, though they had to join the ancillary Deutsche Frauenfront, an offshoot of the GdNF, rather than being considered full-fledged members of the NA.[50] By the end of 1990, the NA had dissolved following a police raid of the Weitlingstraße property during which numerous weapons were confiscated, and then a split with GdNF over Kühnen's recently confessed homosexuality.[51] Yet the NA remains a significant milestone in the evolution of organized neo-Nazi terror in Germany. Established as one cell in a much larger network presided over by Kühnen and Worch, the one-time NA split and merged with other cells, or formed new ones. Many former members of NA went on to join Kühnen and Worch's Deutsche Alternative (DA), originally founded in Bremen in 1989; others joined the Freundeskreis Revolutionärer Volkssozialisten and the Kameradschaft Sozialrevolutionärer Nationalisten.[52]

West German far-right influences had quickly flooded into an already worsening atmosphere of violence in the GDR, which varied between brutal, sometimes fatal attacks on individuals by small gangs of neo-Nazis, and large-scale riots targeting the homes of asylum seekers. From late 1989 onwards groups of predominantly young, male neo-Nazis perpetrated violent attacks on Jewish landmarks, leftist squats and cultural projects, and on individuals of foreign origin. On December 7, 1989, a Jewish cemetery in East Berlin was vandalized.[53] Throughout the following year, mobs of neo-Nazis marched through East German towns, defacing Soviet landmarks and beating anyone who looked to be of non-German origin.[54] Neo-Nazis held demonstrations, notably the marches through Dresden and Leipzig led by the movement surrounding Kühnen, which took place during the Volkskammer elections of March 1990 as well as during the ratification of the reunification treaty in August later that year and again at the establishment of the new *Länder* in October.[55]

Throughout 1990, as new waves of guest workers and refugees arrived in Germany, mobs of right-wing extremists perpetrated frequent attacks against immigrants living in both the East and the West, stoked by the rhetoric of parties like the REP ("The boat is full! Stop the asylum fraud" read one of their 1990 campaign posters). In October, 200 skinheads rioted through Berlin Mitte armed with baseball bats and other blunt objects, resulting in the brutal assault of a young Turkish man.[56] The violence reached a crescendo when, on November 24 in Eberswalde, Brandenburg—less than two months after Germany had officially reunified—a group of somewhere between forty and fifty neo-Nazis attacked a *Kneipe* popularly frequented by immigrant workers, injuring several and killing 28-year-old Angolan contract worker Amadeu Antonio Kiowa—the first such fatality in the newly reunified Germany.

Amadeu's death marked a discernable shift away from leftists being the predominant target of East German neo-Nazi violence to contract workers and asylum-seekers.[57] In 1991, racially motivated attacks in the new Federal Republic soared from 270 in the previous year to 1,480, averaging around thirty per month and including 338 cases of arson.[58] In March one hundred youths torched a settlement of Romany people in the town of Eisenhüttenstadt, near the Polish border. In June around thirty skinheads stoned a home for refugees in Pirna, near Dresden, chanting "*Heil Hitler*" and "*Ausländer raus*" ("foreigners out"). In July, in Großenhain, Saxony, the home of a Vietnamese person was petrol bombed.[59] The city of Magdeburg, Saxony-Anhalt, experienced near-constant threat of neo-Nazi violence as new arrivals of asylum seekers were greeted by angry neo-Nazi protests—to which local police turned a blind eye. As one refugee present at such a demonstration exclaimed, "When skinheads come, policemen run."[60] The one year anniversary of reunification in 1991 was marked by demonstrations of antagonism toward asylum seekers as well as Roma migrants, as police raided twenty hiding locations of suspected undocumented migrants throughout East and West, and housing barracks for refugees were targeted with arson in Rostock, in Hannover, and on the island of Rügen.[61] These manifestations of a new racist nationalism threatened to challenge the notion, in the eyes of the global media, that Germany had overcome the Nazi past. As one *New York Times* article claimed, "a poll taken this month found that 21 percent of eastern Germans and 38 percent of Westerners now have some sympathy for 'radical rightist tendencies.'"[62]

Those with "radical rightist tendencies" had also begun seizing opportunities for the socialization of a pan-German neo-Nazi scene. A significant example of this is the annual Rudolf Hess march, the first of which occurred in Wunsiedel, Bavaria, in 1988, and which still occurs in some locations today. On August 17, 1987, former Deputy Führer to the Third Reich Rudolf Hess was found dead by hanging in the reading room of Spandau military prison, where he had been imprisoned for forty-six years. A somber mythology had already developed around Hess in the years preceding his suicide; after the release of architect Albert Speer and former Hitler Youth leader Baldur von Schirach in 1966, he came to be known as the "loneliest prisoner in the world"—as neo-Nazi magazine *Zentralorgan* put it in 1988.[63] Hess's continued and isolating imprisonment drew inspiration from many; UK punk band the Angelic Upstarts even devoted a politically divisive song to Hess titled "Lonely Man of Spandau," the chorus of which was a plea to release the geriatric Nazi on humanitarian grounds: "Let him go, let him go / He ain't got so long to go."[64] Hess had also long been the center of various conspiracy theories surrounding his confounding solo flight to Scotland in 1941; a particular theory favored by neo-Nazis was that, rather than committing treason, Hess had embarked on this mission with Hitler's knowledge and authorization.[65]

But it was Hess's death in 1987 that provoked the annual memorial marches, which were organized and enthusiastically attended by neo-Nazis. As Fabian Virchow has pointed out, the marches, which grew in importance into the 1990s, "contributed to the unity of an otherwise quarrelsome extreme-right milieu."[66] The first memorial march on August 17 in Wunsiedel, the town of Hess's burial, drew a modest crowd of 120; by 1990 the event had grown in meaning and magnitude, attracting around 1,000. Following a state-mandated ban on the event, the organizers moved to Bayreuth in 1991, where 1,500 neo-Nazis—a mix of skinhead youths and older sympathizers—marched through the city. By 1992 Hess marches were occurring in cities all over the recently united Germany, in both western and eastern states.

The demonstrations provided a particular touchstone for neo-Nazi youths in the eastern states, for whom it was their most exciting and anticipated yearly event in otherwise drab and economically stricken towns. Brandishing signs with slogans such as "His spirit lives in us"—as they did in Rudolstadt, Thuringia, in 1992—neo-Nazis decked out in their traditional drip of bomber jackets and combat boots were accompanied by representatives from the FAP, the DA, the DVU, the NPD, and other groups like the Austrian VAPO and even the Russian Pamyat (Память; Memory, an antisemitic and historical revisionist group).[67] Typically, the marchers moved in the direction of local government buildings such as embassies or town halls, where they would then clash with crowds of antifa counter-demonstrators. In this manner the marches almost always brought chaos and aggression into town centers; in locations as far apart as eastern Berlin, Hamburg, Munich, and Vienna, nightfall signaled the start of drunken vandalism and small-scale arson attacks on the homes of foreigners.[68]

"Deutschland den Deutschen": Hoyerswerda and Rostock

Although regular outbreaks of violence against foreigners were occurring throughout Germany, until September 1991 nothing matched the explosion of uncontrolled racist aggression which began in the town of Hoyerswerda, Saxony, and which continued for several months. Hoyerswerda had developed during the GDR in the 1970s from a small village of only 7,000 inhabitants to an "industrial barracks" of 70,000 workers who were initially enticed to this "cultural no-man's land" by the state's promises of comfortable modern living in a settlement of *Neubauten*.[69] Residents of Hoyerswerda were fatally dependent upon the nearby power plant and coal mines for their livelihoods; a town which already in the final, stagnant years of the GDR saw high suicide and crime rates, the liquidation of local industry following reunification caused dire unemployment, and a pervasive atmosphere of hopelessness. Added to this atmosphere was a drab social scene; Hoyerswerda featured no clubs or cinemas, and only three *Kneipen*. The town's small community of foreign workers from Mozambique, Angola, and Vietnam—who had arrived from these "socialist brother countries" in the 1980s—were joined, following reunification, by 230 applicants for political asylum from conflict-torn places like Romania, Turkey, Yugoslavia, Senegal, and Ghana. Housed in a twelve-story residential complex on Thomas-Müntzer-Straße, these migrants experienced not only unemployment and boredom but outright hostility from "native" locals, who spat and cursed at them on the streets.[70]

Between September 17 and 23, the foreign residents of Hoyerswerda experienced waves of violence led by skinhead neo-Nazis. Local gangs began by attacking Vietnamese market stall owners before directing their ire toward the asylum hostel on Thomas-Müntzer-Straße, which they besieged, armed with rocks, bottles, and Molotov cocktails. News of the swelling rage in Hoyerswerda spread throughout Saxony over the following days, and soon over 100 neo-Nazis from the nearby cities of Dresden, Leipzig, and Guben arrived to lend a hand.[71] The skinheads were then joined by jeering local residents (news reports estimate that at its peak the crowd reached 600), with local law enforcement nowhere to be found.[72] Finally unable to guarantee the safety of the 150 Romanian and Vietnamese hostel residents—and unwilling to intervene with force—local authorities had them evacuated toward Pirna in a caravan of busses. (The migrant camps on the outskirts of Pirna to which these people were taken soon themselves became targets of violence once their location was discovered.[73]) Hoyerswerdians of all ages—women with babies, groups of teenagers, men with beer bottles—sprawled on the lawn outside of the hostel as if at a picnic, cheering for the removal of the migrants as smiling police officers lazily kept watch over the scene. The local news station interviewed the gleeful onlookers, who triumphantly declared their town *"ausländerfrei"* (foreigner-free).[74] It is clear that in Hoyerswerda, the aggression of skinhead youths exemplified the overt and collective grievances of the townspeople as a whole, fed up with the prospect of sharing their already meager social welfare and shrinking job opportunities with foreigners. Official statements given by some of the eighty-three skinheads who were, finally, taken into police custody expressed more than just adolescent joy in the violation of taboos; foreigners, they argued, had to be "kicked and trampled on until they realized that they weren't wanted here."[75]

These events cemented the notion within German public discourse that the eastern states were a region uniquely hostile toward foreigners. Yet the violence quickly spread throughout the country, amplified by the encroaching anniversary of reunification day, which the far-right celebrated with displays of German nationalism. Lending an apocalyptic mood to run-up to the anniversary, radio stations began their morning news broadcasts by listing attacks which had taken place the evening before. Most major newspapers and tabloids ran special issues addressing the riots and the spread of skinhead culture in Germany, framed as an issue stemming from eastern states like Saxony in particular. One *Spiegel* cover featured a scene of angry skinhead boys giving fascist salutes and raising their middle fingers, the headlines reading "Violence against Foreigners" and "Hate," this word covering half the page in bold, red text; inside, the main feature editorial bore the title "Rather Die than go to Saxony."[76] The imagery, the headlines, and the political rhetoric of these weeks framed the violence as an issue stemming from angry, disaffected youths from the eastern states, with some officials ruminating on whether reunification had been misguided. Condemning the violence, politicians evoked memories of Nazi terror in an expression of concern over the direction that the reunified Germany was headed. Günter Apel, then-Commissioner for Foreigners in the city of Hamburg, stated that the violence was "roughly the worst thing to happen on German soil" since the November Pogroms of 1938 and remarked that the "united Germans" were proving to be the "ugly Germans."[77] While the leaders of other Western nations—most notably British Prime Minister Margaret Thatcher—expressed anxieties over German reunification that were rooted in the memory of Germany's militaristic quest for global power in the first half of the twentieth century, West German politicians were more fearful of an imminent confrontation with their totalitarian other.[78] To the West German mindset, the economic strength and respectable geopolitical position the country had regained throughout the postwar period were synonymous with a story of successful democratic rehabilitation. As the German tabloids presented it, any latent nationalism that might resurface as a result of reunification had until now been safely compartmentalized in the East.

Between 1991 and 1992 right-wing extremist attacks increased across Germany almost 75 percent, from 1,483 to 2,584, including seventeen fatalities.[79] As in 1991, the violence peaked in the eastern states during the summer months of 1992. On August 22, hundreds of neo-Nazis descended upon the *Sonnenblumenhaus*, a hostel for asylum seekers in the Lichtenhagen district of the city of Rostock, Mecklenburg-Vorpommern, setting the building ablaze with Molotov cocktails and attacking residents in a riot which lasted several days. As in Hoyerswerda, many gleeful spectators joined the riots in Rostock-Lichtenhagen, which grew to a crowd of an estimated 3,000.[80] As they launched their petrol bombs through the windows of the hostel straight into the living rooms of terrified residents, the ringleaders chanted *"Deutschland den Deutschen, Ausländer raus"* ("Germany for the Germans, foreigners out") to the jocular intonations of the crowd.[81] Like Hoyerswerda, Rostock had rapidly expanded during the 1970s into an industrial shipping town of "sprawling, soulless and shoddy" housing estates.[82] Like elsewhere in the eastern states, the almost quarter of a million residents suffered gravely from mass unemployment and the shutting down of industry following reunification; by August 1992, the unemployment rate for the state of MV had reached 17 percent, with some polls estimating that in Rostock almost half the population was out of work.[83] As in Hoyerswerda, the development of the violence in Rostock was seemingly spontaneous, with a local group of skinheads attacking the asylum shelter with rocks and beer bottles, the bloodthirsty atmosphere swelling as other gangs arrived on the scene followed by the mass crowds who cheered and encouraged the throwing of petrol bombs. Yet as Hockenos recalls, "the ground had also been prepared beforehand" by organized, far-right groups who circulated leaflets with the heading "Rostock will Stay German." The day before the attack on the *Sonnenblumenhaus*, the local *Ostsee Zeitung* had "as much as announced what was in the works."[84]

The violence continued throughout August 23 and 24, with police and fire services initially taking little action. On August 24, 500 youths turned their attention to another nearby hostel which mostly housed Vietnamese workers, which they stormed and set fire to. By August 25 as many as 1,000 people were taking part in the rioting while nearly 2,000 bystanders watched; by this stage, the mostly Romanian Roma and Vietnamese residents were being bussed to safety in neighboring towns, as around 500 riot police stood guard over the scene.[85] Yet human rights group Helsinki Watch (today known as Human Rights Watch) reported that these police withdrew as soon as the petrol bombs started to fly, and it seemed evident to the television reporters and journalists who were present that they had received orders not to intervene.[86] The violence finally came to an end several days later only with the aid of 1,600 riot police who had been brought in from other states, and the failure of the East German police remained a talking point long after. As Helsinki Watch reported:

> The police in East Germany have been unable or unwilling to guarantee the safety of foreigners living within their jurisdiction. The shocking failure of the police in Rostock to intervene when Vietnamese were trapped in a burning building is only the most recent in a long series of police failures to protect foreigners in danger.[87]

Moreover, public opinion in MV seemed to reflect the police's apparent ambivalence toward foreigners and a view that migrants were being housed in eastern states to the detriment of "native" residents. Despite the fact that numbers of foreigners had on the whole *decreased* since reunification owing to large amounts of workers returning to their home countries, the common perception that asylum rights in Germany were now being abused persisted, with many bystanders expressing support for the skinheads.[88] One local woman, the resident of a Rostock *Neubau* project, told the Berlin *Tageszeitung*, "[The rioters] aren't Nazis. These are our children, normal Germans who aren't going to put up with these foreigners here any longer."[89] The CDU mayor of Rostock, Klaus Kilimann, was eventually forced to resign after having blamed the outbursts of racist violence on "the uncontrolled influx of foreigners" into Germany; a parliamentary report into events in Rostock deemed that Kilimann had failed to fulfill his responsibilities to residents of the city.[90] Yet despite parliamentary agreement that officials in the eastern states had broadly failed to live up to the democratic standards of a reunified nation that was ostensibly embracing a multicultural image, as Hockenos points out, Kilimann was "simply reiterating the line of his more experienced colleagues in Bonn."[91] The eastern states were becoming a convenient scapegoat to avoid discussion of ongoing right-wing extremist violence against foreigners in Germany as a whole.

The Politics of Memory and "the Other Germany"

While the international media characterized the riots in Rostock "as images of terror reminiscent of the Nazi era,"[92] in Germany they triggered a fierce debate in the press and in the Bundestag over the question of whether they could be explained by a variety of factors unique to East German culture and history. Chancellor Kohl, for one, absurdly insisted that the riots had been planned and directed by former Stasi members "as if they were generals," while neglecting to voice any sympathy for the victims.[93] Although outbreaks of neo-Nazi violence continued throughout the early 1990s in both the eastern and western states, the meaning-making involved in media discourse and in political debates surrounding such events was markedly different depending on location.

When a group of teenage skinheads in the West German town of Hünxe threw Molotov cocktails into the home of a Lebanese family on the anniversary of unification in October 1992, and when, in November, the house of a Turkish family in Mölln was bombed killing a woman, her niece, and her granddaughter, West German politicians theorized that these were "isolated incidents" committed by perpetrators who came from "broken homes."[94] While the German public responded, however mawkishly, with an outpouring of grief in the form of silent, candle-lit vigils—and Turkish and Lebanese populations with angry protests—CDU politicians tended throughout the early 1990s to brush aside outbreaks of neo-Nazi extremism aimed at foreigners and asylum seekers as anomalous within a dominant culture of remembrance and guilt particular to the Federal Republic. Kohl himself largely brushed off the entire topic as a non-issue, concerned that the media's fixation on violence in the eastern states would undermine the success story of his reunification campaign.[95] Meanwhile other CDU politicians treated identical events in the eastern states as endemic to the former GDR, and even SPD politicians adopted a condescending didacticism in their discussion of the "East German problem."

For their part, political and journalistic commentators were quick to frame anti-foreigner aggression as an alarming new problem resulting from reunification, for it could not be ignored that this explosion of neo-Nazi terror seemed to be situated mostly in the eastern states and seemed therefore to represent a growing social problem of angry, disaffected youth emerging from a former Socialist state. The violence also signified the uncovering of an "other Germany" which had not yet confronted the crimes of Nazism.[96] Anxiety about the resurgence of this other, shadow Germany abounded in media reports surrounding the events in Hoyerswerda and Rostock, betraying a sense that a past loudly claimed by West German politicians to be precisely that—past—in fact still persisted uncomfortably in public memory. Moreover, the metaphor of the other Germany held a potent double meaning; in postwar West German discourse, this notion had come to signify both the National Socialist past *and* the GDR—which, as commonly understood, had continued to practice totalitarianism after 1945.[97] Reunification therefore posed a dilemma for West German national memory and identity in that a Germany long considered regressive, a false Germany, had to somehow be incorporated into the cultural identity of the Federal Republic.

There is indeed much truth to the claim that East Germany did not educate its citizens in the realities of antisemitic and other forms of racial persecution during the Holocaust. Whereas in West Germany by 1989 the memory of National Socialism had largely been consolidated into commemorative practices which acknowledged the Holocaust as the central crime of the Nazi era, in the GDR a state-imposed ethos of anti-fascism had circumscribed the way in which fascism was remembered. Shaped by a Marxist interpretation of fascism's causes and origins that was based on economics and class consciousness rather than on acknowledging the effluence of racist antisemitism, the official East German narrative about National Socialism celebrated communist victory over fascism and left no room for reckoning with racial hatred.[98] State-imposed "anti-fascism" in the GDR therefore amounted to little more than an ideological sheen and, in the early years of the state's existence, sensationalist show trials of former and suspected Nazis.[99] However, it is possible to overstate or misinterpret the significance of this. Widely read studies of GDR memory culture in the early

1990s tended to be written precisely within the context of contemporaneous skinhead and neo-Nazi aggression, which was therefore also presented as a uniquely East German phenomenon connected to an ostensible lack of reckoning with the Nazi past which had (not) occurred in the GDR. This proved a convenient scapegoat for West German politicians who could not stomach the reality that a right-wing extremist network had been growing in both Germanys and, like these two states, was now forging its own unity and coherence.[100]

In his 1993 article "On the Psychological Processing of the Holocaust in the GDR," psychiatrist Hans-Joachim Maaz—who, also of East German origin, was often called upon to comment in the pages of news publications such as *Der Spiegel*[101]—offered his clinical assessment of the denazification process in the GDR, which he argued had only occurred at the political and legal level, not the psycho-social.[102] Responding to outbreaks of neo-Nazi aggression seemingly endemic to the eastern states, Maaz argued that aggressive, fascist tendencies had been repressed under the "mask" of socialism in the GDR and were now at risk of emerging in the new Federal Republic. Emphasizing what he understood as structural similarities between the two authoritarian regimes of National Socialism and the Soviet Union, Maaz controversially argued that fascist "character deformations" were to be found in many residents of the former East Germany, owing to decades of repressive education and a failure to work through the Nazi past.

Maaz's central hypothesis was that "'Anti-fascism' is the expression of a psychological defense—and projection process"—a process designed to forget the Holocaust by transferring emotional attachment to Nazi rule with what he called the "Stalinist principle." By laying claim to the humanistic ideals of socialism, Maaz argued, the GDR was able to perhaps "appease" guilt but never profess it in the same manner as the Federal Republic. For Maaz, this was

> a comprehensive, collective exculpation of the East Germans, the disadvantageous consequences of which are not only to be seen in the development of a new totalitarian regime, but above all in the ongoing and unrecognized inner-psychic conflict between the social mask of obedience and conformity and a latent, pent-up willingness to use violence as a result of authoritarian upbringing.[103]

Maaz claimed to have seen expressions of this pent-up violence among his psychiatric patients, though notably he gave no specific details from any case study and his assertions therefore mostly read as vague conjecture, pathologizing his subjects with the claim that expressions of fascist aggression are caused by internal distress alone. Citing the disaffection and resentment of those in former

GDR states as the emotional fuel for neo-Nazi violence, Maaz avoided any material explanation of how such resentment from within a formerly socialist state could turn into racism and hatred of those seeking asylum in Germany, relying only on his perception that a deep psychological repression of fascist tendencies had occurred.

Other vocal commentators took a similar view which, while swapping psychological for sociological language, nevertheless also argued that anti-fascism was essentially the GDR's version of fascism with regard to the social duties it inscribed within a more or less homogenous society. For Christoph Classen, broad public approval of the "highly homogenized, predominantly morally based construct aimed at internal consensus and external demarcation"[104] that was state-imposed anti-fascism sufficed as "evidence of the continuity of those anti-liberal mentalities and value orientations, ... that currently form such an explosive social sounding board for right-wing extremism and xenophobia in the East."[105] However, urgent as these observations felt in the 1990s, this approach fell into the trap of imposing a homogenizing (and pathologizing) understanding of GDR society. As Botsch points out, there did exist oppositional anti-fascist movements in the GDR which, far from resembling anything akin to groupthink, were engendered by anger at "the discrepancy between, on the one hand, the anti-fascism inseparable from official doctrine and, on the other hand, the way the Stasi was thought to have winked at far-right attacks on other opposition elements" (such as the Stasi campaign to smear the punk scene with the brush of neo-Nazism and simultaneously look the other way during events such as the clashes at the Zionskirche).[106]

The importance of a separate and repressive culture of memory in the GDR notwithstanding (of which there has been produced insightful studies which detail individual strategies for preserving one's private memories within a system of enforced public memory),[107] there was, in the early 1990s—and still remains—a danger that this kind of commentary can be used to discredit all forms of anti-fascism. In the wake of the unrest in Hoyerswerda and Rostock, the duplicity of the term anti-fascism as a discursive signifier was often appropriated to questionable degree in the urgent outpouring of political debate that followed. In a parliamentary proceeding that followed the events in Hoyerswerda in 1991, CDU politician Johannes Gerster went as far as to blame East Germany for outbreaks of neo-Nazi violence that were also occurring in the *western* states, arguing that "there is a very important, GDR-specific reason for why we are dealing with right-wing extremism across the board"—namely, that a regime which had denied its right-wing extremist past through the state narrative of anti-fascism had therefore created a repressed subculture of right-wing extremism now surfacing in the present:

> Especially in the peculiar situation of the new federal states, there is no question that where there existed a supposedly anti-fascist state—and [because], therefore, any kind of right-wing extremism was denied—these right-wing extremist dregs will come out. Many people in the former GDR, which presented itself as international but was in fact closed, naturally find it very difficult to get along with foreigners and strangers.[108]

For one thing, this ignored the reality that long-established far-right parties and terror groups from the western states had just as much to do with the nationwide growth of the neo-Nazi scene following reunification. Moreover, explanations such as Gerster's seemed to imply that racial hatred is innate, occurring "naturally" through influences as benign as mere lack of exposure to races other than one's own, and that it is *tolerance* that must be learned through the establishing of a multicultural society.

Yet, rather disappointingly, the excuse that "native" inhabitants of the former East Germany were simply unaccustomed to the presence of foreigners in their midst proved popular across the political spectrum. Following Gerster's remarks, Dietmar Matterne of the SPD seemed to concur, evoking the clichéd adage "*Tal der Ahnungslosen*" (Valley of the Clueless) to describe Hoyerswerda and its inhabitants:

> Unfortunately, the depressing events in the Saxon town of Hoyerswerda are not accidental. They are certainly not over, and not limited to this city. In this completely synthetic city of Socialism, located in the "Valley of the Clueless"—for those who might be present here from the western areas and unaware, that's what regions where western television and radio could only be received relatively poorly were called—not far from the Polish border, much accumulates in the way of intolerance and xenophobia.[109]

As well as avoiding any real soul-searching concerning the ways in which racism is learned and taught (either generally or in relation to popular conceptions of what constitutes "Germanness"), and also assuming that "western television and radio" are always ideologically and morally pure influences, this narrative unwittingly provided an opening for some rather obscure opinions that were beginning to gain traction from the pundits of the Neue Rechte.

In 1993, reflecting on Hoyerswerda and Rostock as well as other outbreaks of neo-Nazi violence occurring in the eastern states, Klaus Rainer Röhl—the former editor of far-left magazine *konkret* (and ex-husband to Red Army

Faction terrorist Ulrike Meinhof) who now contributed to far-right journals—published a scathing article in the pages of the *Frankfurter Allgemeine Zeitung* on what he called the *Lebenslüge* (grand delusion) of anti-fascism. In response to politicians from the far-left PDS party evoking anti-fascism as an urgent form of praxis against right-wing radicals, Röhl accused German politicians and intellectuals of being "blind in the left eye," ignorant of anti-fascism's "role as an instrument of domination."[110] Suspicious, also, of the manner in which the specter of National Socialism was so widely evoked by journalists and politicians in the wake of Hoyerswerda, Rostock, and the 1993 arson attack on a Turkish family home in Solingen (located in the West; discussed below), Röhl asked—in a decidedly paranoiac fashion—who really stood to "gain" from neo-Nazi phenomena:

> Current events such as the mounting attacks on accommodation for foreigners are extraordinarily convenient for this old Communist propaganda [i.e., anti-fascism]. One must look closely, when [PDS party politician Gregor] Gysi summons the threat of impending fascism after each new arson attack in front of the television cameras. *Cui bono* Rostock, Hoyerswerda and Solingen?[111]

Röhl, a recent defector from the far-left and new addition to the growing intellectual milieu of the Neue Rechte, was here employing what would become a well-worn Neue Rechte tactic of moral equivalency and historical relativism. Röhl's suspicion of anti-fascism (GDR-style or otherwise) illustrates the extreme end of what grew into an obfuscating political and intellectual battle over not only the social and cultural origins of right-wing extremist violence in the former East, but also the significance of neo-Nazi presence in reunified Germany, and *which* German culture of memory this phenomenon belonged to—the Federal Republic or the GDR. As Chapter 2 will discuss, the implicit and calculating question raised by the Neue Rechte was: Are Nazis far-right, or far-left?

The memory of National Socialism itself was, it must be said, evoked with much sensation during parliamentary debate and in journalistic reporting. SPD politician Ottmar Schreiner, in a well-meaning attempt to urge that the CDU party curb their own xenophobic rhetoric against foreigners, cautioned parliamentarians "to think of the line from Bertolt Brecht, which is now more topical than ever: 'The womb is fertile still from which that crept'"[112]—implying that an innate fascist tendency in German culture is ever ready to be reborn. In the wake of Rostock, *Der Spiegel* evoked a past yet to be overcome, lamenting that "the 'ugly German'" had surfaced once again, "stomping with a Hitler-saluting arm through the republic and through the media."[113] Yet, in questioning whether unifying the two Germanys had been misguided and premature, it seemed to be the present that now needed to be overcome:

> The unmastered German reunification stokes resentment everywhere. The East Germans feel like second-class citizens, the West Germans tremble for their estate. "Marauding anxieties," according to Social Democrat Wolfgang Thierse, "seek their victims among the weakest, the foreigners."[114]

Certainly, the West German, far-right REP party—which in 1992 briefly became the second strongest party in Bavaria, threatening a potential entrance into the Bundestag and into the EU Parliament—capitalized on the anxieties of both easterners and westerners by offering a convenient scapegoat in foreigners, particularly asylum seekers. But while Social Democrats and the sensationalizing media struggled to make sense of this resurgence in racially motivated violence and displays of nationalism, Kohl's CDU party—who, after all, had been the architects of reunification—came up with their own solution which targeted the problem of right-wing extremism and the apparent *Ausländerproblem* ("foreigner problem") on an equal basis.

Escalating Violence and Asylum Reforms

The Kohl government did not act decisively against neo-Nazi attacks on foreigners and asylum seekers until, in late 1992, one of them turned fatal. On November 22, 25-year-old skinhead Michael Peters and 19-year-old Lars Christiansen perpetrated an arson attack on the adjoining homes of two Turkish families—the Arslan and the Yılmaz families, who were related—in the town of Mölln, Schleswig-Holstein, near Hamburg. The resulting deaths of 14-year-old Ayşe Yılmaz, 10-year-old Yeliz Arslan, and their 51-year-old grandmother Bahide Arslan had a considerable impact on the German public's mindset with regard to the apparently interrelated issues of migration and right-wing extremism. According to a poll conducted in the aftermath, 33 percent of those surveyed had, before the Mölln arson attack, held "sympathy" for right-wing extremist tendencies "owing to the foreigner problem." In the aftermath, the figure shrank to 12 percent. Moreover, before the Mölln attack only 39 percent of Germans had agreed with the statement "Asylum is a human right," whereas after Mölln the number rose to 61 percent.[115] It would seem that the fatal outcome of the Mölln attack—and, most definitely, the ages of the victims—provoked this moderate level of sympathy from presumed *Biodeutscher*.

The Turkish community in Germany had, meanwhile, been protesting in waves throughout 1992—a year in which racist attacks doubled, from the previous year, to 2,280 (including 701 arson attacks and 600 beatings), many of which targeted Turks.[116] While these protests went largely ignored by officials and received scant coverage in the media, in the aftermath of the Mölln attack tens of thousands of people joined the Turkish community in demonstration, which was vocally supported by Turkey's government and its ambassador in Bonn. It seems to have taken this largely peaceful participation from the German public as a whole to provoke acknowledgement from the Federal Government; in Hamburg, a funeral procession for the victims was attended by 20,000 members of the public and, however perfunctorily, by foreign secretary Klaus Kinkel.[117] The global attention and condemnation garnered by the Mölln attack also pressured the government into taking some legislative action toward curbing right-wing extremism in Germany.[118]

Finally, after almost an entire year of rampant far-right violence culminating in these three preventable deaths, the executive branch of the Federal Government began to crack down. On November 28, 1992, Interior Minister Rudolf Seiters announced the banning of a neo-Nazi group located in Bielefeld known as the Nationalistische Front.[119] This move was followed a month later in December by the banning of the Nationale Offensive, which operated throughout Bavaria and was led by former FAP chairman Michael Swierczek, as well as Kühnen's DA movement, which by now had affiliate organizations throughout Germany although the main stronghold had relocated to Cottbus, where it was said to have amassed more members than the local branch of the SPD.[120] Racist attacks across Germany did indeed see an overall slight decrease in 1993 to a nevertheless disturbing total of just over 2,000 instances, though for the first part of the year foreigners continued to experience the same degree of aggression as they had in 1992.[121]

However, although the deaths of Turkish women and children had brought a sense of urgency to the growing problem of neo-Nazi activity in Germany, the so-called *"Ausländerproblem"* also remained a priority for Kohl's CDU. In May 1993 the Federal Government resolved to amend Article 16 of the *Grundgesetz* (the Basic Law) which had up til then granted the absolute right to asylum in Germany—at the time, the most liberal asylum laws in Europe. The new law stipulated that asylum would be granted only in the event of political persecution in the applicant's home country, and only if the migrant in question had not entered Germany from a "safe third country"—a virtually unavoidable option for many refugees who make often treacherous journeys to reach the

EU.¹²² This decision was presented, perversely, as a way to curb racist violence by way of quelling the resentments of Germans who opposed recent waves of migration.¹²³ As well as seeming to give "an acceptable face to racism,"¹²⁴ as the center-left critique argued, subsequent acts of legislation also seemed to capitulate to the grievances of those in the eastern states who blamed asylum seekers for their poor quality of life. Following the German legislature's passing of the amendment to Article 16, it passed further laws revising welfare benefits for asylum applicants including their access to government-assisted housing, food, and clothing.¹²⁵

A mere three days after the passing of this new asylum law, a watermark moment occurred in the history of racist violence in the new Federal Republic which cemented, within the Turkish community in particular, a rising combination of vulnerability and anger. On the night of May 28–29 in the city of Solingen, North Rhine-Westphalia, four young, male skinheads between the ages of sixteen and twenty-three targeted a family home with petrol bombs, setting fire to the upper level and killing three young girls—Saime Genç, aged 4; Hülya Genç, 9; and Gülstan Öztürk, 12 years old—and two women, Hatice Genç, who was 18, and Gürsün İnce, aged 27. The Solingen arson attack triggered widescale demonstrations from Germany's Turkish population immediately. Initially the protests were peaceful; during the day of May 30, around 2,000 Turkish-Germans marched through Solingen, voicing outrage about the attack as well as the lackluster initial response of local police, who early on insisted that the attack had been carried out by a sixteen-year-old lone wolf. "I don't believe it," one young Turkish man told reporters, no doubt thinking of how widespread, how frequent, and how organized racist attacks had become in Germany. "Other people must have been behind him."¹²⁶ Sure enough, further investigation eventually pinned the attack on the gang of four—Felix Köhnen, Christian Reher, Christian Buchholz, and Markus Gartmann, a member of the nationalist DVU party—who had initially met one another at a martial arts club which was said to be a local hub for far-right activity. The club, which effectively served as a training facility for a neo-Nazi terror cell, was run by a man named Bernd Schmitt, an expert in special forces combat training who had since 1987 offered a "protection service" for far-right luminaries such as leaders within the FAP and the REP parties, as well as renowned visitors from the United States such as Lauck. Schmitt was also, it turns out, a paid informant for the North Rhine-Westphalian state intelligence services—an early instance of the bungled informant program which would come to light much later during the NSU trials of the 2010s (discussed in Chapter 4).¹²⁷

By the evening of May 30, the peaceful demonstrations had morphed into an angry riot. Five hundred mostly young Turkish men vandalized and set fire to businesses in the city center, daubing store fronts with slogans like "Kill Fascism" and "Nazis Out," shattering bus shelters, and burning tires and mattresses. The following day an estimated 1,000 rioters continued to rampage through Solingen, eventually congregating at police headquarters and pelting the building with stones, with further civil disobedience occurring in Cologne, Hamburg, and Bonn.[128] While representatives from Turkish organizations urged to "stay cool and maintain the tradition of German-Turkish friendship,"[129] many demonstrators expressed the view that it was time for active resistance against a growing culture of racial hatred which targeted a demographic who were just as much German as they were Turkish. As some demonstrators pointed out, in spite of the CDU's long-standing opposition to granting dual citizenship to children born of Turkish parents in Germany, Germany was the only home the youngest victims had ever known. "Born here, burned here" read one chillingly succinct banner flown by protesters who had gathered at the Solingen house, which had been draped with a Turkish flag and wreathed with flowers.[130] "Out of Anger, Now Resistance" became a popular picket sign. These were, moreover, the first major responses led by a minority population following seventeen months of racist aggression which had totaled an excess of 3,000 separate attacks.

By June 2 the violence had subsided enough for memorial services to take place in Solingen and also in Cologne, the latter of which was attended by Federal President Richard von Weizsäcker and several government ministers. Chancellor Kohl, however, opted not to attend. To the utter disgust of many, Kohl remarked that he did not wish to participate in the "condolence tourism" of other politicians.[131] Weizsäcker, for his part, notably broke with the Federal Government's portrayal, soon to be disproved, of the murder of five women and children as "a nonpolitical act by a single sociopath." Speaking outside of Cologne's largest mosque to a tense, restless crowd, Weizsäcker rightly asserted that the attacks in Solingen, in Mölln, and throughout the country over the past year and a half were

> not unrelated, isolated atrocities. Rather, they spring from a climate generated by the extreme right. *Even criminals acting alone do not emerge from nothing* ... Right-wing extremist violence, however mindless, is politically motivated ... When youths become arsonists and murderers, the fault does not lie entirely with them, but with all of us who influence their upbringing—families and schools, clubs and communities, and us politicians.[132]

Weizsäcker intuited what the German-Turkish community already knew: that in Germany there is no such thing as a lone-wolf neo-Nazi.

Chancellor Kohl, meanwhile, could not spare the time to attend any memorial services or to acknowledge the reality of a growing neo-Nazi terror network in Germany, which, finally reunified under democracy, could begin to detach itself from too much association with its past. Kohl could not risk the renewed soul-searching that an acknowledgment of Nazi aggression in the present might inspire, as he was busy forging his own national memory project—central to which was an amnesiac insistence on Germany's unwavering historical commitment to the democratic ideals of the Enlightenment. For East Germans, this project entailed an almost total liquidation of all geographical and cultural markers of the GDR, especially in the newly reinstated capital of Berlin. For Germans of Turkish origin as well as for refugees and asylum seekers, this meant the continued downplaying of their daily persecution. And—as the next chapter will argue—for the growing intellectual milieu of the Neue Rechte, it meant the legitimization of an alternate memory of Germany during the Second World War.

2

COUNTERMEMORY

The Reactionary Historicism of the New Right

In a 1996 exclusive interview with *Foreign Affairs*, German historian Ernst Nolte weighed in on the fire-bombings and xenophobic attacks against asylum seekers which had caused such a soul-searching national crisis a few years before. "When someone throws burning material into a house, they don't necessarily want to kill a human being, but could have completely other intentions," he reasoned—intentions such as venting social frustration, no less legitimate an act of protest than the left-wing student demonstrations of 1968. "And to characterize it as attempted murder," Nolte concluded, "seems highly questionable to me."[1] Once widely praised for advancing scholarly understandings of fascism,[2] Nolte, since triggering the 1986–7 *Historikerstreit* with his infamous revisionist essay published in the pages of the *Frankfurter Allgemeine Zeitung* (in which he claimed that the Holocaust unfolded as a response to Soviet terror),[3] had by the mid-1990s become a guiding ideologue for the intellectual Neue Rechte. The sentiments he articulated to *Foreign Affairs* are but one of many expressions Nolte gave throughout the 1990s of seething mistrust over mainstream narratives about both the past and the present, which moved him ever further away from the domain of acceptable liberal discourse. Nolte's increasingly radical views were echoed by several prominent figures of the Neue Rechte such as Heimo Schwilk, Ulrich Schacht, and Rainer Zitelmann, whose revisionist narratives combined "horseshoe" comparisons between left- and right-wing radicalism, doubt over established facts concerning the Holocaust, and insistence that it was time for the yoke of historical guilt to be removed from around Germany's neck so that, now reunified, it might flourish into a "self-assured nation."[4]

While the previous chapter touched upon the instability and insufficiency of German discourse about the past when it came to confronting nationalist violence in the present, this chapter deals with how the meaning of history was publicly debated during the 1990s, out of which developed a distinct far-right countermemory that today forms the ideological basis of the Neue Rechte. In a trend referred to here as right-wing postmodernism, historical revisionism and an increasingly paranoiac view of the liberal media came to characterize much of the Neue Rechte's critique of national identity in the newly reunified Germany. Much like the original, left-leaning postmodernist critiques of power—most of which rely upon the observation that truth and power are linked discursively—the far-right challenge to commonly accepted historical truths was at its core a challenge to perceived hegemonic liberal power structures.[5] Throughout the *Wende* period, as the Kohl government negotiated Germany's new position in a post-Communist world of rapidly shifting global relations, a series of public debates on all manner of topics from immigration to the economy each in effect held the same issue at stake: German identity and the role of historical guilt in shaping it. For many ideologues of the Neue Rechte, reunification was therefore a pivotal opportunity for a drastic reshaping of German national identity as well as domestic and foreign policy, especially in light of Germany's centralized position in the newly consolidated European Union. Significantly, the death of Marxism that was symbolized by the collapse of "real existing socialism" (*real existierender Sozialismus*) sparked momentum amongst prominent figures of the Neue Rechte who felt it was high time for an end to the perceived leftist media hegemony which, since 1968, had ostensibly kept at bay a German desire for both power and sovereignty by imposing its uncompromising discourse of guilt.[6] Tracing the genealogy of this essential tenet of far-right thought is a prerequisite for comprehending the murkier impulses of today's far-right in Germany and elsewhere (the subject of Chapter 5), a key tactic of which is a challenge to the stability of facts.

The *Historikerstreit* of the late 1980s had been the main precedent for many of the relativist arguments which continued to be put forth by increasingly extreme ideologues (who, in several important instances, did not all originate from the right wing of the political spectrum)—especially comparisons between Nazism and communism, which for the Neue Rechte became part of its broader attack on the political left, which it accused of having near-totalitarian control over the German media. While liberal historians such as Hans Mommsen and more left-leaning public intellectuals like Jürgen Habermas were widely perceived to be the sober, well-reasoned victors of the *Historikerstreit* debate (the bulk of which had unfolded in the pages of *FAZ* throughout the winter of 1986–7), conservative pundits such as Nolte were only emboldened by this fierce reckoning with what they viewed as an ahistorical, liberal mainstream unwilling to ask challenging questions concerning the meaning—and the very factuality—of twentieth-century European history.[7]

Moreover, following reunification and the unsteady merging of East German intellectuals and politicians into the political sphere of the Federal Republic, fears of a resultant, deepening left-wing chokehold on public discourse and historical memory intensified amongst conservative and liberal ideologues alike. Playing the role of knowledgeable former insiders, one-time campaigners for democracy in the GDR such as theologian Steffen Heitmann and politician Wolfgang Templin contributed to fears concerning the newly consolidated Partei des Demokratischen Sozialismus (PDS, today known as Die Linke), which was formed out of the dissolved East German SED. In the process, these former leftists turned themselves into ideal bedfellows of those on the intellectual right who decried the PDS as "anti-western" and "neocommunist,"[8] a continuation of the smear campaign against earnest anti-fascist activism. The backdrop to this, as seen in the previous chapter, was an across-the-board discrediting of what had been East Germany's own culture of memory and historical narrative about itself which the emergence of new memories, once suppressed, only emphasized in the post-'89 period. In a shift which has been referred to by Aleida Assmann as the "postmodern stage" in the ever-changing interplay between history and memory, the 1990s and beyond can be characterized as an epoch in which there accrued a sense of the plasticity of both historical narratives and subjective memories produced by the revelation that "what had been presented and passed as objective history" in the East "turn[ed] out to have been a biased construction of political memory."[9]

This dawning new awareness did not only result in a discrediting of the East German interpretation of history—it also made possible the forking of memory into separate tangents in accordance with radically different political values. As Assmann writes:

> After 1989, with the thawing of frozen memories and the opening of archives, both memory and history took on a new force that carried them into the center of the public arena … The experience of a fundamental change of values exposed the contingence of earlier accounts of the past. In such situations both history and memory become self-reflexive; a sense is developed of their constructedness by discovering that memory has a history and that history itself is a form of memory.[10]

In other words, history is not merely composed of empirical facts and figures. History largely comprises narratives that fall in and out of favor over time according to the manner in which groups, collectivities, and nations construct and identify with historical periods or events—narratives alternatingly preserved or dismantled in such edifices as public memorials, commemoration ceremonies, and educational curricula. While historians had been confronting and reassessing these truisms and their implications for several decades already,[11] the post-'89 period saw the public begin to harness the political salience of forgotten, suppressed, or divisive memories. For liberals, the newfound value and utility of memory lay in its capacity to foster a collective sense of civic duty (toward, for example, drawing lessons from the past and applying them to the present). Meanwhile the far-right was able to constellate an alternate set of memories that had ostensibly been suppressed by a mainstream, collectively agreed-upon narrative about the past. To be clear, this separate, far-right countermemory was nothing new: the Neue Rechte had since the 1950s insisted upon German victimhood rather than German guilt, the honor of the Wehrmacht, and the salvageability of a German conservative tradition (toward which, as discussed later in this chapter, the CDU did not count). However, what made this taboo narrative much more alluring to a growing crowd of adherents in the 1990s was the added postmodern observation that memory holds potent discursive power.

Increasingly in the years following reunification the Neue Rechte came to encompass a complicated new milieu that eschewed classic, binary political distinctions—an early precursor to today's Querdenken ("lateral thinking") movement. Although the Neue Rechte had existed on the fringes of West German conservatism throughout the postwar era, what was doubly "new" about the way in which this intellectual circle grew and changed during the 1990s was that established conservative figures like Nolte, Schacht, and Schwilk were now taking their lead from a disgruntled subsection of the liberal intelligentsia from both East and West Germany—i.e., those who will be referred to in this chapter as "left-wing defectors," such as Templin, Heitmann, writers Martin Walser and Hans Magnus Enzensberger, and the playwright and dramatist Botho Strauß.[12] While a significant part of the Neue Rechte's reorientation during the 1990s can be characterized by mainstream conservatives like Nolte drifting ever further to the right, some of the most controversial, revisionist, and divisive articles which made their way into the public sphere during this time were penned by authors who had formerly been considered left-leaning. The most impactful such example of this was Strauß' chaotic screed titled "Anschwellender Bocksgesang" ("The Swelling of the Goat Song"), which was published in the pages of *Der Spiegel* in 1993 to much controversy and which the Neue Rechte appointed as their new founding testament (as discussed below). This development is strikingly concordant with today's apparent fragmentation of the traditional left-right political binary: the confounding new reality that certain ideas which have historically been associated with the far-left are now finding favor on the far-right, the reasons for which will be discussed further in Chapter 5.

In 1996 the federal intelligence services' annual report into ongoing threats to national democracy (the *Verfassungsschutzbericht*) noted that historical revisionism concerning National Socialism and the Holocaust was increasingly becoming a threat to domestic security in its capacity as an emboldening intellectual weapon of the far-right. While an explosion of Holocaust denial that took place in the early 1990s may seem at first glance like an extreme fringe phenomenon, this challenge to historical fact was emboldened by strands of conservative rhetoric which, intentionally or not, comprised enough of a challenge to historical memory as to become woven into the fabric of far-right thought. In ways apparent to most Germans, the 1990s on the one hand saw a culture of ethically earnest commemoration grow into full fruition, with numerous, ambitious memorial projects in both the western and the "new states" comprising an ever more consolidated politics of responsibility (*Verantwortungspolitik*) being taken on at the level of high politics as well as amongst civilians, activists, and artists (discussed further below). However, this heightened historical consciousness was muddied by Chancellor Kohl's own project of normalization—as exemplified by his plans to de-center the Nazi era, emphasize national triumphs, and situate Germany squarely within the history of Western democracy in a new permanent exhibit at the Deutsches Historisches Museum, for which he hired noted Neue Rechte historian Michael Stürmer as an advisor. Within the Neue Rechte itself—which received its first ever mention by the German intelligence services in the *Verfassungsschutzbericht* of 1995—there was fervent pushback against the emerging culture of historical consciousness in the form of several revisionist tropes that can be understood, together, as components of a unique, far-right countermemory: German victimhood during the allied bombings, 1945 as a year of defeat, and "horseshoe" theories of totalitarianism which compare Nazi and Soviet terrors with the aim of relieving Germany of its particular share of guilt and downplaying the Holocaust. Moreover, the intellectuals of the Neue Rechte were not the only ones harnessing the discursive power of memory. The Wunsiedel Committee which organized the Rudolf Hess neo-Nazi marches throughout the eastern states was, by the mid-1990s, contributing to the far-right memory landscape, having expanded its annual rally into an entire "Month of Memory."[13] As will be discussed in Chapter 3, the 1990s saw neo-Nazis violently organizing against historical exhibitions and memory projects which affronted the far right's alternate narratives about the Nazi past.

As Svetlana Boym once observed in the Russian context, the immediate years following German reunification and the collapse of the Soviet Union saw countermemory, once a civilian tactic against state-imposed official forms of commemoration, warp into a tactic of the new European far-right. Countermemory, which under the Soviet state had "resided in finding blemishes in the official narrative of history or even in one's own life,"[14] was deployed in the 1990s in much the same way, this time as a challenge to liberal narratives of history. While the neo-conservative Pamyat (*Память*; "memory") movement in Russia "lamented the destruction of traditional Russian culture,"[15] employing nostalgia for a lost Russian community in aid of an ethnically defined nationalism, the German Neue Rechte similarly merged longing for a strong German national identity with revisionist historical narratives and opposition to migration, as well as opposition to integration within the EU. In many ways both phenomena foretell the far-right memory politics of our current moment: in Russia, nostalgia for Stalin is at an all-time high and goes hand-in-hand with autocratic nationalism; in Germany, as discussed in the final chapter, the AfD have married virulent opposition to a German "cult of guilt" (*Schuldkult*) with Euroscepticism and racist campaigns against migration.

Assimilating Memory: From Countermonuments to Countermemory

The early-to-mid 1990s saw an intensified culture of historical consciousness in Germany which was not entirely uniform across the political, cultural, and social sectors. On the one hand, a grassroots movement led by artists and local historians from both the East and the West who earnestly sought to grow a German culture of commemoration had since the 1980s conceptualized new forms of remembrance that would avoid the universalizing tendencies of classical monuments—a dilemma critiqued by Martin Broszat in 1985 as the "mythologization of memory."[16] Seeking an aesthetic form which would compel viewers or passers-by to actively engage in remembering as opposed to passively commemorating through traditional monuments, a handful of artists devised conceptual "countermonuments"—a kind of anti-commemoration aimed at dislodging a static past and bridging the gulf between younger generations of Germans and the dwindling memory of fascism.[17] Jochen and Esther Gerz's slowly sinking obelisk titled "Monument Against Fascism," constructed in 1983 in Hamburg; Horst Hoheisel's 1985 subterranean Aschrott Fountain, in Kassel; and Norbert Radermacher's film slide projections in the Neukölln district of Berlin all subverted the affectless conventions of the typical statue or plaque, facilitating a jolting out of the mundane present via unexpected encounters with history.[18]

In addition to these public countermonuments, a new culture of Holocaust education as exemplified by projects such as the Topographie des Terrors—a museum, place of remembrance, and documentation center located in the excavated building foundations of Gestapo and SS headquarters in Berlin—reflected a similar site-specific approach that situated history within present-day surroundings.[19] As Frank Biess has recently recalled in a rebuttal to Dirk Moses' controversial accusation that German memory culture comprises little more than a dogmatic "catechism,"[20] these countermonuments and exhibitions gained importance as a critique of the inefficacy of memorialization in Germany when it came to linking past atrocity with contemporary forms of racism. One example of a corrective to this dilemma is Renata Stih and Frieder Schnock's "Places of Remembrance," unveiled in June 1993, which drew attention to everyday acts of oppression via the placing of signposts around the historically Jewish Schöneberg district of Berlin which described the gradual social ostracism, legal disenfranchisement, and eventual deportation of Jews between 1933 and 1939—and explicitly invoked the Solingen arson attack of the previous month.[21]

On the other hand, the artists who designed Holocaust memorials in late 1980s and early 1990s had very different goals than the politicians who commissioned them. The consolidation of a growing culture of memory with a post-1989 commitment to the politics of responsibility produced a handful of grand-scale memorialization projects such as the Memorial for the Murdered Jews of Europe (*Denkmal für die ermordeten Juden Europas*) in Berlin-Mitte (a design competition for which was launched in 1994, though the project was not completed until 2004), as well as the revamping of the site of Buchenwald concentration camp following reunification, both of which became mired in political drama and entangled with Chancellor Kohl's project to present to the world a forward-facing Germany that had settled its debts with the past.[22] These memorials, while outwardly well-meaning, masked an underlying conservative project of normalization which often skewed toward outright revisionism. In a far cry from the countermonument project of artists and historians who wished to further integrate mnemonic practices into German civic life, some conservative politicians and historians engaged in alternate narratives that redeemed German culture and denied the complicity of average Germans in Nazi atrocity. Perhaps no historical memory project best exemplifies Kohl's quest for normalization than the "Witnessing German History" exhibit which opened in 1995, on the eve of the fiftieth anniversary of the end of the Second World War, at the Deutsches Historisches Museum. The exhibit, curated with the input of CDU politician and historian Christoph Stölzl and Neue Rechte historian Michael Stürmer, simultaneously de-centered the twelve-year period of National Socialism and re-framed the narrative of Hitler's rise to power so that Germany was no longer the aggressor, but the victim. In this ultimately redemptive narrative, Germany was "seized" by Hitler in 1933 and "occupied" by the Nazi regime in a sharp diversion from the true course of German history which was, in Stölzl's words, a "river of the Enlightenment" "flowing through the history of the West," from Luther to Kant to Kohl.[23]

Though the average museum visitor may scarcely have recognized this, the exhibit was the culmination of well over a decade's worth of conservative historical revisionism which had gained steady support from CDU politicians and center-right public forums such as *FAZ*. In response to the leftward political shift which took place in West Germany in the 1970s—not to mention confrontations with leftist terror groups such as the RAF which emerged from the student movement of '68—reactionary conservatives had carved out an intellectual milieu in the pages of *FAZ* and in the ranks of the CDU party, which had regained power in 1982. Conservative German historians such as Stürmer, Andreas Hillgruber, and Klaus Hildebrand—the original instigators of the *Historikerstreit*—gained popularity for their reactionary interpretations of German history which eschewed theories of universal guilt and complicity, relying on a "horseshoe" totalitarian model for explaining the Third Reich.[24] Relativist comparisons between Hitler's regime and Soviet terror made it possible to annex the twelve years of National Socialism as an unfortunate diversion from Germany's true democratic path. This interpretation was situated within broader conservative narratives of German history which capitalized upon contemporary leftist challenges to the by now-outdated *Sonderweg* ("special path") theory, which espoused that Germany's rapid technological advancements during the age of industry had fatally combined with its continuation of authoritarianism, leaving the nation uniquely predisposed to National Socialism.[25] Both Stürmer and Hildebrand, for example, radically adapted criticisms of the *Sonderweg* theory in order to stake their own anti-*Sonderweg* thesis that Imperial Germany had not been so undemocratic as historians previously maintained, attempting to prove that the *Kaiserreich* had experienced moments in which it approached parliamentary democracy.[26] Stürmer's main interpretive flourish was to emphasize Germany's geopolitical position in *Mitteleuropa*, precariously confronted on either side by a revanchist France and an aggressive Russia—an idea which would capture the imagination of a post-1989 Neue Rechte keen to steer Germany into a prosperous and sovereign direction as opposed to one oriented toward the United States and beholden to the EU.[27]

Several landmark moments of scandal about which a considerable amount of scholarship has already been written map the evolution, throughout the 1980s, of a new milieu which formed between these well-known academics and the more reactionary figures of the Neue Rechte: the publishing, in *FAZ*, of the "Heidelberg Manifesto" in 1981;[28] SPD chancellor Helmut Schmidt's comments, in the same year, that German foreign policy will no longer be "held hostage" to Auschwitz;[29] the Bitburg affair of 1985, which prompted questions concerning the mournability of German soldiers;[30] and finally the *Historikerstreit* of 1986–7. While the infamous dispute is largely considered to have been "won" by a contingent of historians who, in addition to opposing relativist arguments about Nazism and Stalinism, also insisted that the Holocaust should not be compared with other genocides, those on the reactionary right—like Nolte, Stürmer, Hillgruber et al.—did not confine their lines of argument to the Letters section of *FAZ*, nor was *their* dispute settled by any historical reckoning that might have occurred as a result of reunification.[31] As historian Stefan Berger pointed out long ago, the *Historikerstreit* did not end in the 1980s but merely continued by other means following reunification, which precipitated efforts on the far-right to establish a nationalist historiography under the auspices of searching for "normality."[32] Throughout the 1990s, intellectual heavyweights from within mainstream conservatism joined ranks with increasingly reactionary voices from the Neue Rechte as well as disgruntled apostates from the left and center, who all espoused one thing in common: a distinctive rebuttal to the so-called culture of guilt that had manifested in the form of Holocaust memorials, yearly commemoration speeches, and museum culture.[33]

One major component of far-right countermemory that had already been present since the founding of the Federal Republic concerned a rehabilitation of the Wehrmacht in commemorative culture, subsumed within a larger project to treat the entire postwar era as one of Allied occupation which had imposed upon Germany the mentality of a defeated nation. Following reunification, conscripts, volunteers, and veterans of the Bundeswehr, Germany's postwar armed forces, increasingly became a target audience for these deeply revisionist trends. While Chapter 3 of this book will cover the Bundeswehr's own post-reunification far-right crisis (as well as the earlier antecedents to this crisis) in detail, it is worth noting here already the ways in which a revisionist approach to German military history contributed to a relativizing discourse concerning historical memory and historical fact, beginning in the early 1990s. In 1993 left-wing parliamentarians reported that the Bundeswehr's monthly postil *Information für die Truppe: Zeitschrift für Innere Führung* ("Information for the Troops: Magazine for Internal Leadership"), which circulated 55,000 annual copies within army barracks,[34] had in the previous year allowed contributions from Neue Rechte ideologues such as revisionist historian Alfred Schickel and the journalist Clemens Range, who has served as editor for far-right revisionist publications *Mut* ("Courage") and the *Preußische Allgemeine Zeitung* ("Prussian Daily Paper") as well as authoring several books on the history of the Bundeswehr.[35] Citing *Historikerstreit* instigator Hillgruber as well as the Bundeswehr's own serial work *Das Deutsche und der Zweite Weltkrieg* ("Germany and the Second World War"), Schickel, in his February 1992 editorial titled "Nations United in the Fight against Germany, Italy and Japan,"[36] both re-wrote the narrative of German defeat in 1945 and argued for the rehabilitation of the Wehrmacht in historical memory.[37] Taking liberties with the extent to which the infamous Morgenthau Plan had impacted the nature of Allied occupation and the denazification of Germany between 1945 and 1949, Schickel painted a picture of a postwar West Germany shaped by American colonial practices following what he described as the "unconditional surrender" of the Wehrmacht:

> The "re-education" of Germans envisaged by the victors had to accomplish how this future liberal-democratic Germany should be striven for and achieved. Roosevelt's Treasury Secretary Henry Morgenthau had a concept drawn up for this in the late summer of 1944, which was then largely implemented after the war and included a review of the Germans' past.[38]

The absurdity of Schickel's claim that the Morgenthau Plan (which, proposed in 1944 by United States Secretary of the Treasury Henry Morgenthau Jr., had called for the almost total liquidation of German industry and which was ultimately rejected by both the United States and Britain) was "largely implemented" nevertheless allowed Schickel to then call into question the moral basis of the re-education of German society following twelve years of Nazi rule, as well as present-day Germany's entire conception of its past, its memory, and democratic identity.[39] In addition, the term "re-education" (*Umerziehung*), which Schickel placed in scare quotes, increasingly came to be used by the Neue Rechte as a buzzword aimed at undermining commonly accepted historical narratives; the above quotation appeared within a subsection sarcastically titled "Eradicate Political Pestilence through Re-education." Yet above all else, Schickel especially critiqued the "unconditional surrender" (a phrase repeated *ad nauseum* throughout the editorial) of the Wehrmacht, which he framed as being deeply unfair to Germany as a whole and the Wehrmacht in particular: "*Even* the military opposition to Hitler," he wrote, "that emerged with the assassination attempt of July 20, 1944 was not accepted in Washington as a possible negotiating partner for a conventional armistice agreement" (emphasis added).[40]

Schickel's attempted revision of a "victors of history" narrative—which had, he argued, shaped West Germany's role within the postwar global order—aligned with fears expressed by other Neue Rechte writers that a grand new victors' narrative taking shape in the wake of Soviet collapse might subsume Germany's chance to finally develop its own narrative autonomy and political self-assurance. The editorials contributed by journalist Clemens Range to *Information für die Truppe* in 1992 married together various anxieties of the immediate post-reunification years that all seem to stem from an imperative, imagined or not, that Germany conform to a homogenous liberal-democratic political identity within the solidifying European Union. An article from March of that year, printed under "Topical Issues" and titled "Perspectives on the New Migration of Peoples," warned readers about the "the impending migration of peoples" from former Soviet Bloc territories, as well as former Yugoslavia, to their own hometowns. Citing a then-recent polemic written by Jan Werner, deputy chairman of the Berlin REP, titled *Die Invasion der Armen: Asylanten und illegale Einwanderer* ("The Invasion of the Poor: Asylum Seekers and Illegal Immigrants"), Range cautioned that "[f]or many people in these mostly economically ruined countries, Germany in particular is considered the promised land," and warned—though vaguely—of the potential "security policy tensions" and "domestic social unrest" that this might provoke.[41] Yet Range also expressed optimism regarding certain political developments within former Soviet territories. His June 1992 article praised new military policies underway in post-Soviet Hungary—which, having held its first democratic elections in April 1990, was building new defense strategies under the rule of the nominally center-right, though nationalist, Hungarian Democratic Forum (Magyar Demokrata Fórum).[42] Range's interest in the Hungarian pursuit of military independence rather than alliance with NATO (which it has since joined) echoes the more extreme sentiments of other Neue Rechte military experts such as former paratrooper-turned journalist Heimo Schwilk, who in his reportage during the 1991 Gulf War expressed a desire to see Germany become a venerated global competitor to the United States, lamenting that Germans—according to his interactions in the press pool in Riyadh—are seen as "hypercritical, moralistic, and undependable" peaceniks.[43]

In these ways, historical revisionism had begun to play an instrumental role within far-right hopes for Germany's future, its foreign policy, and its national identity. Nevertheless, these discursive links were apparently too subtle to raise much alarm amongst CDU parliamentarians. The significance of Schickel and Range's editorials appearing in a standard Bundeswehr monthly was downplayed by government officials; when Range's article on immigration was brought to the attention of the defense ministry via a small inquiry filed by the PDS party in 1993, Parliamentary State Secretary of Defense (PStS) Bernd Wilz firmly stated that "The Federal Government resolutely rejects the claim that *Information für die Truppe* 'propagates xenophobia,'" and that in addition "the Federal Government protests against the defamation of the Bundeswehr in this question." Moreover, Range's editorial on increased migration was considered to be based on "publicly available information" about migration and its possible consequences. "It is not to be inferred from this," Wilz's argument went, "that fear of immigrants is being fueled."[44] No concern was made over the fact that the "publicly available information" cited by Range was, in fact, a polemical work by a representative of the REP—a party that continued to push a radical right-wing platform based on stirring up fear of increased migration.[45]

It must be said that Chancellor Kohl himself did not share the same aims as the increasingly extreme Neue Rechte, which tended to hold him in disdain for signing away hopes of German national sovereignty. Despite Kohl's efforts at normalizing Germany's past,[46] the CDU remained steadfast in its mission to integrate Germany within the nascent European Union. Kohl, alongside French President François Mitterrand, was a main architect of the convergence of EU member state economies under the Maastricht Treaty, which came into force on November 1, 1993. And yet, despite his role in shaping German economic integration, Kohl's personal historical advisors—such as Stürmer—skewed in the direction of a new German nationalism. Already by 1990, liberal West German intellectuals were noting the "hinge" that connected conservatism and right-wing extremism, with *FAZ* serving as an important forum where the mainstream met the reactionary.[47]

In any case (as Chapter 3 of this book will explore in depth), Germany's new military commitments within shifting global alliances following reunification came to be central to Kohl's conceptualization of a "normal" nation successfully integrated amongst global democratic powers. For Kohl as well as the Neue

Rechte, this involved the reworking of memory. An exemplification of this is the Neue Wache ("New Guard") memorial on Berlin's Unter den Linden. Originally built as a guardhouse after the Napoleonic Wars, it then served as a First World War memorial, and subsequently a Communist memorial to the victims of fascism. In 1993 Kohl rededicated the Neue Wache to all "Victims of War and Tyranny," describing it as a monument to "reconciliation."[48] To much controversy, Kohl added a bronze casting of a *pietà* by Expressionist artist Käthe Kollwitz, the Christian symbolism of which seemed to imply a message of redemption. Stripped of any specific historical context, the Neue Wache became a location for individuals to lay wreaths, at the base of the Kollwitz bronze, dedicated with the names of SS officers who had died in the Second World War and whose families considered to be victims also.[49]

Left-Wing Defectors and Right-Wing Postmodernism

Conservatives and long-standing right-wing reactionaries were not the only ones challenging Germany's growing culture of memory in the early 1990s; during these years the Neue Rechte increasingly came to be characterized by former leftist intellectuals defecting to the ranks of the reactionary right. The early 1990s saw the Neue Rechte milieu joined by individuals such as the dramatists Botho Strauß and Peter Handke (the latter of whom became an outspoken sympathizer of Serb nationalism during the Balkans conflicts);[50] novelist Martin Walser; former GDR dissident Wolfgang Templin; author and critic Hans Magnus Enzensberger; and Brigitte Seebacher-Brandt, widow of former SPD Chancellor Willy Brandt.[51] Many of these figures had been involved in the student protests of 1968 and yet had come to view '68 as the demise of free thinking in Germany, which, they argued, had since been dominated by a hegemonic discourse of guilt.[52] Left-wing defectors to the Neue Rechte also brought with them concerns borrowed from the predominantly leftist school of postmodernism, imparting an updated conceptual framework to the classic paranoias and obsessions of the right *apropos* of an increasingly media-driven age.

As Jay Julian Rossellini explored in depth in his 2000 work *Literary Skinheads?*,[53] these figures provoked widespread confusion and controversy during the early-to-mid 1990s with their contributions in a couple of edited anthologies which skewed toward ultra-nationalism and a paranoiac distrust of the media: Werner Weidenfeld's 1993 *Deutschland, eine Nation* ("Germany, one Nation") and Heimo Schwilk and Ulrich Schacht's 1994 *Die selbstbewusste Nation* ("The Self-Assured

Nation"), which in particular received notable attention and academic scorn for its conspiracy theorist undertones.⁵⁴ The contributors to these anthologies dabbled in by now-familiar Neue Rechte themes such as horseshoe theories of totalitarianism, 1945 as a year of defeat, and the desire for Germany to throw off the mantle of historical guilt in order to become a venerated global power—i.e., a "self-assured nation." Those contributors who were established Neue Rechte figures (such as editors Schacht and Schwilk) situated their understanding of German national identity within the same intellectual genealogy as the interwar Conservative Revolution, citing Carl Schmitt, Ernst Jünger, and George Sorel as their ideological forebears, along with postwar figures such as Armin Mohler, as well as Alan de Benoist of the French Nouvelle Droite. (Mohler's seminal 1950 anthology on the Conservative Revolution exhaustively reproduced materials of a *völkisch*, racist, and antisemitic nature, and demonstrated the author's sympathetic alignment with such tracts.⁵⁵) The inclusion of nominally conservative, centrist, and left-leaning authors in this anthology scrambled traditional political distinctions and contributed to a wider moral panic about national identity that was playing out in the pages of the German media.

In the context of reunification and the collapse of "real existing Socialism" the Neue Rechte also welcomed left-wing defectors to their ranks as proof of the ultimate illegitimacy of left-wing ideologies. Both the conservative historian Nolte and former editor of *Die Welt* Rainer Zitelmann argued that continuing to distinguish between left and right in fact made little sense; that the NSDAP itself had always contained "strong leftist features"; and that German reunification should result in the establishment of a truly "democratic German right" distinctive from the CDU, which the Neue Rechte viewed as a liberal technocratic sham.⁵⁶ Rebuking the postwar taboo against hard right politics in Germany, in his contribution to *Deutschland, eine Nation*, Zitelmann claimed that it is the left who have failed to come to terms with the past as evidenced by their "forced 'mourning work' and political commitment," behaviors compounded by the recent "trauma" of the GDR's collapse.⁵⁷

These lines of argument continued in Schwilk and Schacht's 1994 *Die selbstbewusste Nation: "Anschwellender Bocksgesang" und weitere Beiträge zu einer deutschen Debatte* ("The Self-Assured Nation: 'The Swelling of the Goat Song' and other Contributions to German Debate"), which remains a defining anthology of the Neue Rechte in the mid-1990s for the ways in which it demonstrates an instrumental hybridization of traditional political binaries. In a defense still proffered by the ideologues of the far-right today, the contributors to *Die selbstbewusste Nation* took pains to portray themselves *not* as right-wing extremists—nor, even, did they all consider themselves conservative (though many did). Rather, the Neue Rechte at this time fashioned itself as a "free thinking" and apolitical class of intellectual elites who refused to parrot liberal historical narratives which, they argued, had become not only mainstream but hegemonic, in Germany.

The principal essay of *Die selbstbewusste Nation*, referenced in the anthology's full title, was penned by the former radical left-wing dramatist Botho Strauß, best known for his adaptations of the works of Maxim Gorky, who wrote in distinctly postmodernist language of a German nation hopelessly controlled by media consumerism. "Anschwellender Bocksgesang"—which translates literally as "The Swelling of the Goat Song" ("goat song" being the original, ancient Greek term for tragedy)[58]—was initially published in 1993 in the pages of *Der Spiegel* as part of a commissioned series on the new national mood, along with two other essays by left-leaning writers Martin Walser and Hans-Magnus Enzensberger. Enzensberger's essay "Views of Civil War" cast doubts upon the post-'89 "New World Disorder,"[59] as he labeled it, by highlighting the potentially interminable nature of new global conflicts wrought by Western interventionist policies. Walser's "German Concerns" was more of a confessional rant about conformity amongst the German intellectual elite ("They tell you that you can't be the way you are if you still want to belong").[60] While both essays caused a minor stir for the challenge they presented to the legitimacy of liberal democracy (felt by many Germans to be a hard-won historical triumph), neither was as inflammatory as Strauß' "Anschwellender Bocksgesang," which hit such a chord with the Neue Rechte that Schwilk and Schacht reprinted it in *Die selbstbewusste Nation*, curating the entire anthology around responses to this essay.[61] Today it remains significant as an exegesis on media-driven liberal moral conformity, a position which galvanizes the far-right now more than ever.

Strauß' essay was part crusade against a "dominant" liberal narrative of history (which, he felt, was built on postwar economic success alone), part celebration of what he viewed as the right's far more authentic connection to a myth-history of origins—in his words, the "proto-political," which often denotes rubrics of national belonging such as ethnicity or religion. Ruminating on the medieval association of "left" with witchcraft or social outsiders, Strauß lamented that modern leftist politics had become a "masquerade," while to associate with the right is now the true act of rebellion: "It is a different act of rebellion: against the total domination of the present, which seeks to rob and eradicate the individual of any figment of an unenlightened past, of what has become historical, of mythical time." Strauß connected the left to an empty, technocratic modernity obsessed with its own moral validity. The right, by contrast, has no such totalitarian aims; denying any connection between the traditional right and contemporary neo-Nazism, Strauß evoked the far-right system of countermemory that conveniently annexes the Nazi era while at the same time using the same mystical language that was once characteristic of the *völkisch* movement:

> In contrast to the left—which parodies a history of salvation—the right does not envision a future world empire, does not need utopia, but seeks reconnection to the long time [*die lange Zeit*], the unwavering; is in its essence *deep of memory* and to that extent an enlistment into the religious or proto-political … The right in this sense is as far removed from the neo-Nazi as the football fan is from the hooligan, and even more so: The destroyer within the right's sphere of interest becomes its worst, most bitter enemy. (Of course: might the children who we neglect become our enemies?)[62]

The ongoing vandalisms and racist attacks being perpetrated by neo-Nazis, he argued, were "by no means militant acts of counter-enlightenment" as feared, but petty taboo-breaking which threatened to undermine the right's larger ambitions. Strauß saw himself as the true counter-enlightenment, which invokes the forces of *Angst* and *Geist* over rationalism to much grander ends than the destructive acting-out of "neglected children." (Yet in a severe misuse of Rene Girard's *Violence and the Sacred* Strauß also reminded his reader, in a stand-alone sentence formatted as such for dramatic effect, that "Racism and xenophobia are 'fallen' cult passions that originally had a sacred, order-creating meaning".[63]) The pervasive media, however, with its excessive coverage of every neo-Nazi crime, eagerly "nurtures" the problem. Consumers of this cynical "infotainment" are paralyzed by their own "linguistic powerlessness"—a censorship induced by hegemonic liberal discourse which becomes internalized as self-censorship by the "telecratic public" who are "educated, but not free thinkers."[64]

The postmodern condition—specifically, a media-saturated landscape which turns citizens into consumers, as first diagnosed by Jean-François Lyotard and further described by Jean Baudrillard—seems to have had considerable effect on Strauß and those who riffed with him in the essays within *Die selbstbewusste Nation*. "Bocksgesang" was peppered with Baudrillardian terms like "simulacra," which Strauß used to describe the nature of historical representation in the German media and conjure the impression of a German public snared in the mimetic influence of repetitive images and slogans. While one gets the feeling that these terms are often thrown in for effect (and one of vagueness and obscurantism, at that), Strauß's angst over what he referred to as an "overly mediated society" responsible for the uncritical proliferation of "guilt politics" in Germany made clear that he attributed tremendous discursive power to the liberal media, which has apparently stultified all possibility of "free thinking"—an idea that especially inspired editors Schwilk and Schacht in their own contributions to *Die selbstbewusste Nation*. Schacht, in his essay "Stigma and Concern: German Identity after Auschwitz" warned of a "discourse apartheid" perpetrated by those in control of the German "media democracy"—which he described as "the blockwarden system of West German PC society and its PC commissars."[65] The use of the Nazi-adjacent term "block-warden" (*Blockwart*) not only aimed at a chipping away of linguistic taboos but also, as Rosellini has pointed out, depicted "political correctness" as liberal democracy's own form of fascism.[66]

One major facet of the intellectual Neue Rechte can therefore be described as right-wing postmodernism characterized by the increasing relativization of historical narratives and appropriation of linguistic signifiers, engaged in by both mainstream conservative intellectuals as well as pundits who were distinctly of the Neue Rechte.[67] One effect of this, as already demonstrated, was the fragmentation of any hard line between conservative and "brownshirt" politics. An important case in point is *FAZ*, which, at least in its culture section, increasingly published *feuilletons* of a nationalist and revisionist nature during the *Wende* period. It should be noted that few, if any, right-wing intellectuals of the 1980s/90s (or even the present day) would identify themselves as postmodernist thinkers, not merely due to the Marxist origins of several of the most prominent French postmodernists. Postmodernism had largely been met with fury and ire by the intellectual right, who abhorred the idea that what is taken to be truth might be in some ways socially and politically determined. And yet, relativization of historical narratives is precisely a key component to right-wing postmodernism: the ability to make historical arguments based on new discourses that, in Germany, resulted from a conservative power shift in the early 1980s.[68] Out of the broader postmodernist critique of growing technologies, consumerism, and affectless commercialization emerged a right-wing version of this concern, namely that mainstream media narratives were beginning to exert too much influence over the shaping of social realities. Schwilk, in fact, had argued as far back as 1991 that thanks to the destruction of meaning undertaken day after day by television[69]—in addition to the stultifying effects of tabloid publications such as *Bild* and even *Spiegel*—all distinctions "between left and right, between art and kitsch, art and commerce" were being eroded.[70] The vagueness of this argument in terms of whether or not Schwilk thought of this development as entirely a bad thing was, moreover, half the point.

The association of a prescriptive, "PC" media hegemony with the political left is one facet of the Neue Rechte's broader rhetorical strategy of relativization between left and right politics—specifically, relativization of their extremes, Nazism and communism. While this may seem paradoxical given the undeniable right-wing disposition of the Neue Rechte, the main function of this relativization is to attack the left while rehabilitating the hard right from historical associations with Nazism; creating a loop, or horseshoe, from one extreme to the other closes off any trail of causation between interwar Conservatism and the Nazi party—again, annexing the inconvenient Nazi era. In addition, the Neue Rechte attributes "left" not only to the generation of '68, to factions like the Greens, or to anti-fascist activists; the entire Bonn republic—including the CDU—was lambasted as having been a "time from which sorrow, shame and timorousness arose," in the words of Seebacher-Brandt in her contribution to *Die selbstbewusste Nation*.[71] Klaus Rainer Röhl, who had defected from the left long ago, portrayed the Bonn political class as quislings who had sold out to the United States; the reeducation efforts of the Allies in the years of occupation had laid the foundations for a political culture of German self-hatred.[72] Former GDR dissidents Steffen Heitmann and Wolfgang Templin, both of whom had marched for democracy in the months before the fall of the Wall, cast blame at the Bonn republic for failing to confront the GDR dictatorship.[73] And Schacht and Schwilk—who in a few years would expand upon many of their arguments in a volume co-written together titled *Für eine Berliner Republik* ("For a Berlin Republic")—propose, in their conceptualization of the "self-assured nation" that Germany should become, that the nation retreat into myths of honor and tradition as a firmament against loss of affect in the postmodern era.[74]

The Reshaping of Political Distinctions Post-GDR

The apparent apostasy of several prominent left-leaning public intellectuals to the reactionary right caused arguably much more of a media stir than the existence of the Neue Rechte itself, in the mid-1990s, triggering a general sense of political confusion and epistemic chaos. For more than a year after *Spiegel*'s initial publication of Strauß' polemic, German newspapers and magazines were filled with the responses of horrified '68ers. The general hysteria is best summed up by the words of former SPD Secretary Peter Glotz, who wrote: "Botho Strauß is a dangerous madman ... One had hoped that this kind of farrago had been washed away by the bloodbath of 1945."[75] *Der Spiegel*'s editors, on the other hand, confessed their awareness of the panic they had caused by publishing an "afterword" to the 1993 essays by Enzensberger, Walser, and Strauß, defending the muddling of left-right binaries as a search for new values in a changing world:

> What is on the right and what is on the left, some have always known very well—and some know better than others. The writer Martin Walser has long since renounced such templates ... Has *Der Spiegel* lost its left-wing, left-liberal grounding too? As much or as little as the entire critical intelligentsia, which has been on the lookout for new values and orientations since the abrupt end of the well-ordered, bipolar East-West world.[76]

Conscious, perhaps, of its own role in the intellectual stultification of the masses, *Der Spiegel* agreed enthusiastically to play a hand in the collapsing of political distinctions. Meanwhile the ensuing chaos worked very much in favor of the Neue Rechte's destabilizing agenda: as the sowing of absolute distrust in the media was one of the major aims of left-wing defectors and right-wing postmodernists at this time, and the doubt now cast upon nominally liberal publications like *Spiegel* played right into this trap.

Yet *Spiegel* was not the only liberal forum that engaged in this new kind of lateral politics (here one might even apply the term *Querdenken*—"lateral thinking"—a concept which has gained much significance in recent years, as discussed in Chapter 5 of this book)—especially when it came to commissioning pieces by former GDR intellectuals, with the aim of rapidly historicizing the failed socialist state and assimilating its memory within a West German narrative. Citizens of the "new states" had little chance to preserve the cultural and geographical markers of the former GDR state during the *Wende* period. This swift eradication of urban sites of memory included the changing of communist street names; removal of socialist realist public artworks from the Berlin area; the removal of statues (most controversially, perhaps, the replacement of a statue of Karl Marx outside Humboldt University with that of nineteenth-century historian Theodor Mommsen); and the demolition of the Palast der Republik in 1995.[77] Accompanying this assimilation of GDR historical memory (narratively framed as a mirror totalitarianism finally laid to rest) was a trend for inviting former GDR intellectuals and activists to speak on their experiences inside the Soviet satellite state. Former dissident-turned freelance GDR historian Wolfgang Templin provides an example of, in Rosellini's words, "the tenuous position of oppositional figures from the East who attempt to speak to the entire nation from a position of moral superiority."[78]

Templin—who in 1988 had been forced to defect to the Federal Republic as he was wanted for dissident activities including publication in underground journals and participation in civil rights protest—embarked post-reunification on a career built around shaping public perception of the GDR. A founding member of Alliance 90 and one-time Green candidate for state elections in North-Rhine Westphalia, Templin was also a research assistant for the Federal Commission of Stasi Records, established in 1990, and occupied a similar position at the Mauermuseum from 1994 to 1996. Yet also in 1996, after long deliberation, Alliance 90 and the Greens ejected Templin from their coalition party over an interview he had given in 1994 to *Junge Freiheit*, the notorious right-wing radical newspaper. While Templin expressed to *JF* a distaste for the newspaper's frequent relativization of the crimes committed at Auschwitz, the gist of his interview was that both the far-left and the far-right shared fundamental views regarding "the national question," and that a democratic discussion should take place between the two camps. He also appeared to defect from his own political milieu, calling for an end to left-wing "stereotyped thinking" (*Lagerdenken*).[79] For fellow Alliance 90/Greens spokespeople Marianne Birthler and Ludger Volmer, responding in 1994 to Templin's interview, his indiscretion was especially unacceptable because it appeared to support *JF*'s tireless (and tiresome) campaign for social acceptance.[80] Sure enough, in an example, perhaps, of the "changing values" of the times, at a 1995 public discussion which took place at the office of the Greens in Weißensee, Berlin, on the topic of whether the former GDR dissident should still belong to the party, Templin argued that *JF* was not a right-wing extremist publication but merely "conservative," and firmly within "the democratic-liberal spectrum."[81]

Templin's mistake seems to have been in assuming that his oppositional activities against the East German SED made him enough of a martyr of totalitarianism that he could bridge the abyss between those on the left, who oppose fascism, and those on the right, who claim to oppose political and moral hegemony. In the *Wende* years, while still viewed publicly as a dissident hero and important figure in both the roundtable discussions and the formation of Alliance 90, Templin, having pored for weeks over his personal files at the newly opened Stasi archives, theatrically opted to publish these for all to see in the pages of *Die Zeit*.[82] Accompanying these facsimiles was a riveting editorial written by *Die Zeit* reporters which dramatized the emotions and memories recalled by Templin as he read through his Stasi file: the shame and guilt he felt upon discovering his initial declaration of commitment as a Stasi informer; recollections of his naïve belief that he could oppose the system from within.[83]

Clearly, hubris has a large part to play in the formation of such a divisive public figure as Templin. As Antifaschistische Initiative Moabit (AIM) dryly reported from the 1995 meeting at Weißensee:

> W. Templin sees himself as a "representative of a political minority" and points out that the new ideas of the minority have always influenced the majority—whatever that means. He views himself as a theorist, who was prophesied to show the non-thinking left-wing masses the way out of their dark little room.[84]

Templin certainly attempted to position himself as such, contributing articles to anthologies—including the notorious *Die selbstbewusste Nation*—which situated him within a growing motley circle of fellow left-wing defectors, established figures of the Neue Rechte, and ambivalent personages in between. The primary drive of these articles is Templin's wish for a second *Historikerstreit* which would focus not on the Third Reich but on the GDR.[85] Though the Neue Rechte's revisionist anthologies of the mid-1990s failed to incite said debate, any need for such a thing had already been obviated by the normative treatment of GDR history in mainstream discourse during the *Wende* period.

As is clear, nominally leftist ideologues were prized amongst the Neue Rechte of the 1990s for their potential to legitimate the relativization of left- and right-wing totalitarianism owing, precisely, to their apostate status. This is a trend not so dissimilar to tactics displayed by the milieu surrounding later far-right parties such as the AfD, which remains tied to a surviving and ever more radical Neue Rechte intellectual elite. The Neue Rechte has continued to find legitimation from the occasional left-leaning apostate—a notorious example in more recent decades being former SPD member Thilo Sarrazin and his 2010 publication *Deutschland schafft sich ab* ("Germany Abolishes Itself"—a "*Spiegel* Best Seller!" according to the cover), one of the earliest anti-immigration texts of the twenty-first century to focus specifically on the supposed "incompatibility" of Islam with Western culture.[86] Though this later argument focuses on Islamic religious culture, it nevertheless is rooted in the ideology of "ethnopluralism"[87] which was introduced into German far-right discourse from the French Nouvelle Droite by Henning Eichberg in his 1978 text *Nationale Identität: Entfremdung und nationale Frage in der Industrie Gesellschaft* ("National Identity: Alienation and the National Question in Industrial Society").[88] While Eichberg had ties to the Nouvelle Droite going back to the 1960s, in Germany he published throughout various anarchist, left-leaning, and ecological publications.[89] Eichberg, along with the more definitively far-right Armin Mohler, can be considered foundational to the direction the Neue Rechte later took during the 1990s, claiming apoliticism and "free thinking" while harking back to the interwar Conservative Revolution as well as to folkloric, *völkisch* ideology. As the Neue Rechte became increasingly radical in its stance on German memory and history—throwing off ideological taboos and political binaries with much catharsis—it also became progressively brazen in espousing ethnically defined ideas about German national identity.

The *FAZ*, Historical Revisionism, and National Identity

By 1996 the BfV had begun to consider both "Intellectualization efforts in right-wing extremism" and historical revisionism as threats to national security, adding a section on each to that year's *Verfassungsschutzbericht*.[90] The 1995 report had also touched upon these areas, mentioning the Neue Rechte for the first time ever; however, this subsection was brief and labeled an "Annex" at the very end of a larger section on far-right publishing houses responsible for the dissemination of an internationally growing body of Holocaust denial literature.[91] Considering the German Neue Rechte to be nowhere near as organized, coherent, or socially rooted as the French Nouvelle Droite, the BfV had in 1995 characterized the Neue Rechte as a fringe group with no support from well-known academics.[92] This was somewhat of an oversight given the increasing role of mainstream conservative forums such as the *FAZ* and a growing number of lowbrow military magazines in facilitating discourses of a historical revisionist nature in years prior to 1995, as well as the support lent by famed historians such as Nolte to fringe "scholarship" that questioned the factuality of the Holocaust. Nevertheless, by 1996 the Neue Rechte had its own section in the annual *Verfassungsschutzbericht*—as did historical revisionism, which had previously been subsumed within a section dedicated to "international aspects of German right-wing extremism" that referred solely to prominent revisionists who were living abroad (though some were of German origin), such as the Toronto-based Ernst Zündel and the notorious American neo-Nazi Gary Lauck.[93]

With revisionism now considered a growing, determined movement with many frontrunners based in Germany and writing for German publications, the BfV's 1996 report acknowledged the increasingly thin line between conservative and right-wing extremist discourse in Germany:

> Sometimes the boundaries between conservative ideas, on the one hand, and extremist ideological elements on the other are deliberately blurred in order to spread extremist critique of the existing political conditions in Germany in the

sense of feigning common ground. Protagonists couch their ideas in hints and use the systemic critical approaches of democratic theorists. To this end, they take up the discourses and topics of public debate, especially if these can be expanded in line with their long-term goals (e.g., criticism of the social influence of [political] parties). Another characteristic of this tactic is the fact that the authors largely refrain from naming their long-term goal and, from their right-wing extremist point of view, from making plain their consequential demand to surmount the system.[94]

The BfV thus demonstrated that it was aware of what was at stake, though the language of the report nevertheless makes plain that it considered this blurring of lines between conservatism and extremism to be a tactic *only* employed by the far-right—not a phenomenon equally engaged in by conservatives. (To the BfV's credit, the report does note the Neue Rechte's duplicitous appropriation of "critical approaches" commonly associated with the liberal-left). However, mainstream conservative publications such as *FAZ* had also been legitimizing Neue Rechte voices by allowing them editorial space in its pages throughout the early-to-mid 1990s. Moreover, new publications which emerged on newsstands in the mid-1990s, such as *Deutsche Militärzeitschrift* ("German Military Magazine"—more on this in the next chapter), targeted a heterogenous new readership formed of conservatives, army veterans, and right-wing extremists eager to embrace the taboos of militarism and traditionalism.

The breakdown of mainstream conservatism is just as characteristic of the muddying of established political positions in the 1990s as the phenomenon of left-wing defectors. Certain CDU representatives, for example, became exceedingly concerned about the entrance of Neue Rechte ideas and language into mainstream political discussion, and literary critics were quick to note the links between polarizing figures like Strauß, publications such as *FAZ*, and revisionist historians such as Nolte—who by the early 1990s had begun to dabble in all-out Holocaust denial.[95] As the 1995 BfV report had noted, the "movement" for Holocaust denial was achieving international notoriety around this time; it was in this same year that the infamous British denialist David Irving first attempted to sue historian Deborah Lipstadt for libel, after her 1993 book *Denying the Holocaust: The Growing Assault on Truth and Memory* had named him as a leading instigator.[96] (In 2000 the dispute reached its absurd apotheosis with a court trial in which Lipstadt was forced to prove that the Holocaust had happened in order to defend herself.[97]) Nolte, too, went the way of Irving by finding himself warmly accepted amongst a growing international cadre of post-truthers. Nolte's 1993 monograph *Streitpunkte: Heutige und künftige Kontroversen um den Nationalsozialismus* ("Points of Dispute: Current and Future Controversies about National Socialism") had been reviewed well in antisemitic, denialist publications such as the notorious US-based Institute for Historical Review, which praised Nolte for his respectful attitude toward other revisionist scholars who question the factual validity of the Holocaust.[98] The following passage from *Streitpunkte* demonstrates how far Nolte—once a widely respected historian—had wandered from commonly accepted historical truths:

> The widely held opinion that any doubts concerning prevailing views regarding the "Holocaust" and its six million victims must be regarded as the expression of a malicious and inhumane outlook, and, if possible, forbidden … must be rejected as an attack against the principle of scholarly freedom.
>
> Questions [raised by revisionists] about the reliability of witnesses, the value of documents as evidence, the technical feasibility of certain operations, the credibility of statistical figures, and the weighing of circumstances are not only permissible, but, on scholarly grounds, are unavoidable—and every attempt to suppress certain arguments and evidence by ignoring or prohibiting them must be regarded as illegitimate.[99]

And yet, *FAZ* continued to print laudatory articles on Nolte written by other proponents of horseshoe theories of totalitarianism such as Eckhard Jesse (who nevertheless granted that Nolte's work was "at odds with the *Zeitgeist*") and to honor Nolte on his seventieth birthday.[100]

FAZ also engaged in blurring the lines of acceptability between mainstream conservative politics and reactionary conservatism. For example, throughout the summer and autumn of 1993 *FAZ* serialized the diaries of Ernst Jünger, who has always represented for the Neue Rechte an "alternative" history of German conservatism (Jünger himself remained a contributor to the Letters section of *FAZ* until his death).[101] In addition, throughout the Balkans crisis, *FAZ* frequently published opinion pieces and Letters to the Editor theorizing reasons for the breakup of Yugoslavia, a popular one being the inherent instability of multi-ethnic states, as well as explicitly racist cartoons depicting the Federal Republic as Noah's Ark flooded with refugees—many of whom appear drunk or violent, wielding knives.[102] *FAZ* also published the endeavors of CDU politicians who took a hard line on immigration to separate themselves from the excesses of the Neue Rechte. CDU politician Wolfgang Schäuble attempted to distance the pro-European CDU from the Neue Rechte and its "anti-Western *Sonderweg*" by attributing its ideas and vocabulary to the far-left—a deceitful and nevertheless easy tactic, given the recent furor over left-wing apostates—while himself defending "the national as a protective community [*Schutzgemeinschaft*]."[103]

Some CDU commentators cited *FAZ* as the main artery through which radical right ideas were beginning to trickle into conventional conservativism, warning that the Conservative Revolution of the Weimar era had found its grandchildren in the present-day Neue Rechte. Friedbert Pflüger, a CDU spokesman notable for his support for disarmament, penned a 1994 text titled *Deutschland driftet* ("Germany is Drifting"), in which he drew attention to the polar flip that German politics seemed to have taken following reunification, noting that during the height of the Cold War it was the political right which championed Western alliances and a commitment to NATO. By contrast, the Neue Rechte of the 1990s increasingly expressed anti-American sentiments and argued for Germany's non-Western geopolitical position—specifically, as the economic seat of *Mitteleuropa*.[104] Historian Hans-Peter Schwarz, famed for his two-volume biography of Konrad Adenauer, argued exactly this in his 1994 work *Die Zentralmacht Europas. Deutschlands Rückkehr auf die Weltbühne* ("The Central Power of Europe: Germany's Return to the World Stage"), which, as the title suggests, situated the newly reunified Germany at the center of a new European order.[105] Nonetheless, that Chancellor Kohl was the architect of this new order demonstrates a notable schism between established conservative intellectuals like Schwarz and the more radical figures of the Neue Rechte, who preferred to frame Germany's emerging global position in pre-Enlightenment, ethnic terms, eschewing the Western democratic orientation forged by postwar statesmen such as Adenauer and indeed Kohl.

By 1994 *FAZ* had become known for its taboo-testing *feuilletons* written by notable ideologues of the Neue Rechte, for whom anti-Westernism and disdain for the German "cult" of historical guilt went hand in hand. Take for example journalist Eckhard Fuhr's editorial, in which the author claimed that Germany's Western ties are a form of penance which has fostered a national identity of self-flagellation. For Germany to attain self-assurance, Fuhr concluded, the sanctity of Western allyship must be broken:

> Negative nationalism fed by an almost libidinous relationship to Germany's guilty history—the terrible fascination with National Socialist crimes, the anti-German Germanness—turns aggressively against anyone who regards "ties to the West" as merely a simple and reasonable fact, rather than the basis for a new therapeutic national cult. ... There is no reason to carry "the West" before you like a monstrance [*eine Monstranz*]. And it is foolish to taboo as "anti-Western" all questions that reach beyond the status quo of Western self-image.[106]

Seeking an end to the overbearing piety of Western allyship, Fuhr and many on the Neue Rechte sought recourse to a Schmittian geopolitics in which Germany is viewed as "the hegemonic power in Europe," as *FAZ* editor Frank Schirrmacher expressed it in an interview with *Foreign Affairs*, alluding to visions of a German-Slavic alliance that would rest on pre-Enlightenment, ethnic definitions of identity.[107]

The language of religion and morality have become common fixtures of Neue Rechte critiques of German memory culture, most recently exemplified by Rolf Peter Sieferle's 2017 *Finis Germania* ("The End of Germany," dramatically rendered in Latin), which prophesized apocalyptic visions of national decline caused by over-fixation on Germany's past. Describing Auschwitz (which he put in quotation marks, echoing Nolte's "Holocaust") as "the last myth of a thoroughly rationalized world," Sieferle condemned the supposed catechism that Germany is beyond redemption; that its original sins are hereditary, unique, and absolute.[108] Other writers before Sieferle had made the same argument, albeit with less religious overtones but nevertheless hinging on the notion of a moral burden worn like a sackcloth. Rainer Zitelmann, editor of daily broadsheet *Die Welt*, accused prominent mentor figures of the '68 generation such as Günter Grass, Hans-Ulrich Wehler, and Jürgen Habermas of "wield[ing] a 'fascism cudgel,' enforcing a moralistic and 'politically correct' version of history that emphasizes the uniqueness of Nazi crimes so as to suppress German national pride."[109] The core of Zitelmann's reactionary historical revisionism can be found in his 1987 text *Hitler: Selbstverständnis eines Revolutionärs* ("Hitler: The Self-Perception of a Revolutionary"), in which he portrays Hitler as a social modernizer. This in turn allows Zitelmann to challenge "special path" theories of German history precisely because he does not view Nazism as the worst historical divergence of all—instead it was the Bonn Republic, with its Western orientation, which led Germany on a detour away from its national interests. Initially written as his doctoral thesis, the text slowly gained traction in the early 1990s and was eventually given positive reviews in *FAZ* for "aptly criticiz[ing] German self-hatred," and has since been reissued numerous times.[110] The chokehold this self-hatred allegedly has on Germans, according to Zitelmann and his cohorts Nolte, Schwilk, and Schacht, makes it heretical to oppose the Maastricht treaty on European Unity and the arrival of immigrants into Germany.[111]

In April 1995 *FAZ* would play a determining role in the flourishing of the Neue Rechte by allowing Zitelmann, Schwilk, Schacht, Röhl, and former CDU politician Alfred Dregger to take out a full-page campaign in far-right countermemory titled "Appeal May 8, 1945—Against Forgetting." Ten years before, on the fortieth anniversary of German surrender, Federal President

Richard von Weizsäcker had made history with a speech before the Bundestag in which he redefined May 8 not only as an anniversary of sorrow and defeat, but as the end of National Socialist terror, memorably proclaiming: "May 8th was a day of liberation. It freed us all from the inhuman system of National Socialist tyranny."[112] Though Weizsäcker's speech had, in fact, dwelt at length on topics of German suffering after the war, it also directly acknowledged the severity and unprecedented nature of the Holocaust in a manner that no German head of state had previously done, before a Bundestag which still contained individuals who had been involved in the Nazi regime.[113] By the fiftieth anniversary in 1995, May 8 had become very much enshrined in the national consciousness as a day of liberation from National Socialism, an optimistic framing which allowed statesmen like Kohl to speak of a better future (as exemplified by his new exhibit at the Deutsches Historisches Museum). The Neue Rechte, however, managed to find fault with this framing, arguing that the characterization of May 8 as a day of liberation was "one-sided"—that it ignored the Allied destruction of Germany and the expulsions of Germans from the East. Zitelmann, Schwilk et al. began their brief but sizeable advertisement in *FAZ* with a quote from former Federal President Theodor Heuss, followed by the signatures of around 300 people, including university professors, politicians, and military personnel (including twelve Bundeswehr generals):

> "This date, May 8, 1945, essentially remains the most tragic and questionable paradox for each of us. Why? Because we have been redeemed and destroyed in one." The paradox of May 8, which the first Federal President of our Republic, Theodor Heuss, characterized so aptly, is increasingly receding into the background. The media and politicians have unilaterally characterized May 8 as "liberation." There is a risk of forgetting that this day not only marked the end of the Nazi reign of terror, but also the beginning of expulsion terror [*Vertreibungsterror*] and new oppression in the East and the beginning of the division of our country. A view of history that conceals, suppresses, or relativizes these truths cannot be the basis for the self-image of a self-assured nation, which we Germans in the European family of nations must become in order to rule out comparable catastrophes in the future.[114]

The appeal, quoted here in its entirety, caused outrage across the board, and even prompted Kohl to sever his personal ties with co-author Dregger, who planned to speak on May 8 at a counter-commemoration in Munich.[115] That twelve Bundeswehr generals had been among the 300 signees also did not go unnoticed. As *Der Spiegel* acknowledged, Dregger had performed a dress-rehearsal for his Munich speech (which in the end did not go ahead) three weeks prior at the Verband Deutscher Soldaten (Association of German Soldiers), in Heilbronn, calling on "all Germans" to defend themselves against the "one-sidedness of our national masochists" and evoking the memory of Allied bombing campaigns.[116]

The Neue Rechte version of history tapped into the powerful emotions of grievance, resentment, and vengeance—a potent tactic which resonated in particular with a growing culture of militarism throughout the far-right scene in Germany. Presenting far-right militants with a useable historical narrative—one which mourned the Allied bombing campaign over Dresden, restored May 8, 1945, as a day of defeat, and rehabilitated the memory of the Wehrmacht—the self-styled intellectuals of the Neue Rechte demonstrated the instrumental value of historical revisionism to the dissemination of their ideology and the growth of their movement beyond niche academic circles. For example, the BfV report of 1996 acknowledges the link between the Dresden narrative and minimization of the Holocaust:

> An event that is always used to relativize German war crimes is the air raid on Dresden on 13/February 14, 1945. In the *Deutsche Wochen-Zeitung/Deutscher Anzeiger* [German Weekly Newspaper/German Gazette] a headline on this topic read: "Dresden—No Summit of Inhumanity?—The Holocaust in the German Cultural Metropolis." The choice of words here was explicitly equated with the mass extermination of the Jews.[117]

But neither the BfV nor the Federal Government seemed concerned to investigate the circulation of these ideas within the Bundeswehr itself.

In the late 1990s and early 2000s revisionist narratives found considerable salience in magazines marketed toward military veterans and enthusiasts, and in a slew of new far-right publications, think tanks, and publishing houses. Neo-Nazi magazine *Junge Freiheit*, for example—which granted interviews to figures such as Templin, Nolte, Schwilk, Schacht et al.—transformed itself, during the late 1990s, from underground student rag to self-described journal of culture and politics.[118] Soon, an increasingly multifarious demographic of new far-right adherents in Germany gave rise to new leaders of the intellectual Neue Rechte such as Karlheinz Weissmann and Götz Kubitschek, who together in 2000 founded the think tank Institut für Staatspolitik and who would go on to forge important strategic ties between the ideological arm of the far-right and its violent, neo-Nazi counterpart. As the next chapter will show, revisionist and anti-migrant trends within the literature of Germany's armed forces reflected a growing market for similar publications aimed at a wider civilian readership and fringe political scene—and would give neo-Nazi protest groups a new purpose and direction in which to channel their aggression.

3

BUNDESWEHR

Right-Wing Extremism in the German Armed Forces

Late in 1997 the German armed forces—the Bundeswehr, an institution which had been at the heart of (West) German prospects for orientation within global democratic alliances throughout the postwar era—became embroiled in a media scandal which suggested right-wing extremist stirrings within its ranks. As was first revealed in the pages of *Der Spiegel* in early December 1997 and then corroborated in even greater detail days later by a special episode of NDR's *Panorama* program, on January 24, 1995, then-65-year-old Manfred Roeder, a convicted neo-Nazi terrorist, had given a lecture at the Bundeswehr's Hamburg leadership academy on the invitation of Colonel Norbert Schwarzer.[1] Roeder had recently completed eight years of a thirteen-year prison sentence for sedition, as well as for orchestrating a bomb attack on an exhibition about Auschwitz which took place in Esslingen, in 1980; arson attacks on asylum centers for refugees in Zirndorf, Lörrach, and Hamburg, in which several asylum seekers were killed; and leadership of a right-wing extremist network known as Die Deutsche Aktionsgruppen.[2] Yet in 1995 he was invited to give a talk before Bundeswehr soldiers about his new organization known as the "Deutsch-Russische Gemeinschaftswerk—Förderverein Nord-Ostpreußen" ("German-Russian Joint Venture Association for the Promotion of North-East Prussia")—which, devoted to the resettling of so-called ethnic Germans from Russia, had been classified in the 1993 *Verfassungsschutzbericht* as a right-wing extremist organization.[3] *Panorama* discovered in the course of its investigation that Roeder, who presented his "joint venture" in East Prussia as a humanitarian aid mission, had at the approval of Lieutenant General Hartmut Olboeter received around 20,000 Deutschmarks worth of material from the Bundeswehr, including three decommissioned vehicles and other military-grade equipment.[4]

Following *Panorama*'s much discussed December 1997 special, several other (less severe) scandals involving right-wing extremism within the Bundeswehr appeared in the tabloid press.[5] Yet what made the Roeder scandal particularly concerning was his eminence: having served at the helm of a series of neo-Nazi protests against a traveling exhibition which exposed the crimes of the Wehrmacht on the eastern front during the Second World War, Roeder was at the time known to the general public for leading an arson attack on the exhibition when it had reached the city of Erfurt in January 1996.[6] Having also begun a campaign, in the summer of 1997, as parliamentary candidate for the far-right NPD party in Stralsund, Mecklenburg-Vorpommern, the discovery of his appearance at the Bundeswehr's leadership academy barely two years prior was disquieting, to say the least.[7]

This scandal produced much political fallout encompassing a slew of requests for information filed by center-left politicians on far-right activity within the Bundeswehr and responses from the executive body of the Federal Government which often verged on defensive relativization. Speaking before the Bundestag in Bonn on December 7, 1997, then-Defense Minister Volker Rühe opened a scheduled debate about these matters with a lengthy and instrumental speech that blurred the line between situating the Bundeswehr within postwar, West German commitment to democratic values and claiming that German military history as a whole can be overwhelmingly characterized by instances of liberal victory. "The value system of our Basic Law is the orientation and yardstick for [the Bundeswehr's] understanding of tradition [*Traditionsverständnis*],"[8] he asserted—referring, by "*Traditionsverständnis*," to former SPD Defense Minister Hans Apel's *Traditionserlass* (Tradition Decree) of 1982, which had ordered all serving officers and soldiers to hold a "critical commitment to German history."[9] Defending against what he described as "blanket condemnations" in the press and from the left-wing politicians seated before him, Rühe went on to offer that the Bundeswehr "relies on the liberal values of German military history. The Prussian reforms and the German resistance against Hitler are therefore at the center of the maintenance of tradition."[10] Besides the dangerous lack of differentiation in such a comment (which managed to gloss over approximately 120 years of German Imperial history which included Germany's colonial adventures), as Brigitte Schulte of the SPD interjected, the Bundeswehr's own internal publications betrayed a rather different historical preoccupation within its pages. *Die Truppenpraxis: Zeitschriftt für Führung, Ausbildung und Erziehung* ("Troop Preparation: Journal for Leadership, Training and Education"), Schulte pointed out, referred by instructive example to battles from the Second World

War "with remarkable frequency."[11] After a cursory promise to "take a look" at this, Rühe pivoted back to the present day, with a reminder of the momentous new role the German armed forces had increasingly played since global reorientations post-1989:

> In spite of all the justified outrage over current events, we must not forget the following: It is the same Bundeswehr, about which some are now making sweeping judgments, that has been working for peace and reconciliation in Bosnia for over two years, [and] that has put a stop to war and massacre there on our behalf.[12]

Reprehensible as it was that a neo-Nazi such as Roeder had been allowed to speak at the Bundeswehr's own training academy—for which both Lt. Gen. Olboeter and Col. Schwarzer had been dismissed by Rühe himself—the armed forces as a whole, Rühe insisted, remained a principled, democratic institution.

The Roeder scandal is emblematic of several issues which began to constellate around the Bundeswehr in the late 1990s, some of which had already been brewing since reunification. Firstly—as indicated by Rühe's response quoted above—the growing involvement, following reunification, of the German armed forces in NATO-led missions overseas became an imperative to ensure that the reputation of the Bundeswehr was kept clean both at home and abroad. From the early days of reunification onwards the executive branches of the Federal Government have been confronted with troubling reports—both in the media and in the form of requests for information filed by predominantly left-leaning politicians—concerning right-wing extremist activity within the Bundeswehr's ranks, ranging from the involvement of soldiers in violent attacks on foreigners, displays of National Socialist greetings and insignia, dangerous historical revisionism in the internal publications of the Bundeswehr (as already seen in the previous chapter), and the involvement of recruits and officers in far-right and neo-Nazi organizations. The most notable examples of the latter which will be dealt with later in this chapter are Götz Kubitschek, the famed far-right ideologue and activist who served as a reserve in Sarajevo in 1998—and whose involvement alongside Roeder in the anti-*Wehrmachtsausstellung* protests saw him discharged from the Bundeswehr—and Reinhard Günzel, former commander of the Kommando Speziälkrafte (KSK, the Bundeswehr's elite special forces) who was dismissed in 2003 following antisemitic remarks and reports of disturbing behavior within his command during their station in Afghanistan.

Second and relatedly, far from the above-mentioned examples constituting mere "isolated incidents" of fringe extremism, the Bundeswehr itself had become a target of idealization within right-wing extremist circles—from the ideologues of the Neue Rechte, some of whom have published articles in the internal publications of the Bundeswehr or elsewhere written revisionist polemics involving the Bundeswehr, to young neo-Nazis who hoped to find in army life a space to form affective bonds with like-minded comrades. Despite mounting evidence of this throughout the 1990s and 2000s, the Federal Government consistently dismissed the danger that the armed forces could be a key target for extremists who wish to recruit highly skilled new members with access to weapons.[13] Whether owing to the German defense department's quest to better incorporate the Bundeswehr into NATO throughout the 1990s and 2000s during conflicts in Kuwait, former Yugoslavia, and the war in Afghanistan, or to a general misconception of far-right terrorists as pathological lone actors, not until the late 2010s—following a series of scandals mostly concerning the KSK—did the Federal Government begin to take seriously mounting evidence that the Bundeswehr's professed commitment to "democratic tradition" (itself an arguably constructed notion) had failed, somewhere.[14] Indeed, the so-called "Day X" revelations of 2020—during which it emerged that a strong network of former veterans, police officers, and serving KSK soldiers had been "prepping," shadow army style, for an impending battle against refugees, migrants, and leftists—has revealed that not only are the armed forces an attractive proposition for extremists seeking to gain training and forge connections, but that certain divisions have themselves become spaces for radicalization.[15]

An Army of Unity Attracts Neo-Nazi Recruits

Since reunification in 1990 the Bundeswehr has been the center of political-intellectual debate over the evolving definition of what it means for Germany to incorporate a politics of historical responsibility (*Verantwortungspolitik*) into its foreign policy. While Germany came under increasing pressure from NATO nations to begin sending its armed forces abroad during the various global humanitarian crises of the early 1990s, at home this shift in diplomatic responsibilities entailed a moral dilemma at the heart of which were postwar conceptions of moral responsibility—namely, the Bundeswehr had until this point been conceived of as a solely pacifistic army, and attached to this were important notions of historical lesson-learning and democratic orientation.

Established in 1955 during the first decade of the Federal Republic, the Bundeswehr initially consisted mainly of conscripted "citizens in uniform" who were to be guided by a principle of *innere Führung* ("internal leadership")—a notion which is still central to the self-image of the Bundeswehr today and which encourages team-building as well as critical thinking in the face of receiving orders.[16] While the training of conscripts in the principles of *innere Führung* referred to a program of "leadership development and civic education" established in direct response to the Wehrmacht's "ensnarement in a war of extermination" during the Second World War,[17] the Bundeswehr's founding architects—General Hasso Eccard von Manteuffel and Federal Minister Kai-Uwe von Hassel—were themselves Wehrmacht veterans, an uncomfortable reality that necessitated a radical break be made in terms of how this new military force conceived of its heritage. In Hassel's original *Traditionserlass* of 1965—a precursor to Apel's updated 1982 edition and Ursula von der Leyen's 2018 iteration—"tradition" is defined as "the transmission of the valid legacy of the past."[18] Since neither the Reichswehr of the Weimar Republic nor Hitler's Wehrmacht could be understood as "valid" historical models for the army of a democratic nation, only the reformers of the early nineteenth century and the military resistance against Hitler seemed viable options for the transmission of historical legacy. Notably, the National Socialist regime itself is characterized, in the 1965 decree, as a historical anomaly—the only regime in German history to have "disregarded" the soldier's imperative for "self-discipline."[19] This fragmentary understanding of German history would eventually prove problematic, and not only for its avoidance of any confrontation with the continuities between German Imperialism, the First World War, and the shadow armies of the 1920s. In the 1990s, official decrees which determined the non-validity of certain branches of the German military's genealogical tree—namely, the Wehrmacht—would increasingly be labeled prescriptive and unpatriotic by veterans who aligned themselves with the Neue Rechte, as well as amongst eager new army recruits. The Bundeswehr's precariously constructed narrative surrounding its own historical lineage made it an army vulnerable to ideological subversion.

The process of reunification—which was accompanied by a Europe-wide demilitarization pact that marked the end of the Cold War, as well as the development of new global conflicts—brought new prospects and challenges for the Bundeswehr recalled thus by its own website: "The project of downsizing the Bundeswehr, disbanding the National People's Army (NVA) of the former East Germany, and building up a new kind of armed forces, an army of unity."[20]

Having originally been established only with the authorization of Allied Forces, the Bundeswehr had operated throughout the Cold War era as a distinctly pacifistic army, only to be deployed in protection of other NATO members (though it abstained even from this). Elite combat divisions such as the KSK (the special forces) were not assembled until long after unification, when deployment to global conflict zones brought with it the need for counterterrorism units that could operate abroad. As the Bundeswehr became more frequently deployed in overseas peacekeeping missions during the mid-to-late 1990s, and then in combat operations since the 2001 war in Afghanistan, it necessarily had to adapt its identity to reflect that of a military no longer confined to the limited role ascribed to it by sanctions resulting from Germany's historical crimes during the Third Reich. Being an "army of unity" meant being the army of a "normal" Western, democratic nation.

Global developments concurrent with German unification placed the Bundeswehr at the center of a domestic political-intellectual debate over the evolving definition of what it meant for Germany to incorporate a politics of responsibility informed by historical lesson-learning into its foreign policy. From 1990 to 1991, in the immediate context of the Persian Gulf conflict, UN member states increasingly insisted that Germany—now an undivided, democratic nation—should take up its full NATO responsibilities. Eager to present a reliable, democratically committed Germany to the world stage, Kohl's CDU party led an effort to amend articles of the Basic Law in order to allow the use of military force and involvement in overseas conflicts. In his speech before the Federal Government on January 30, 1991, Chancellor Kohl spoke of a "new, greater responsibility that is now accruing to us Germans,"[21] foreseeing that Germany's moral burdens were finally leading the country into an era of normality. Although the Bundeswehr was being downsized in terms of manpower and armaments as part of larger European peace treatises, Kohl announced that the armed forces would nevertheless soon come to perform duties instrumental to global peacekeeping that would in turn foster a new German patriotism:

> The United Nations is playing an increasingly important role in securing world peace. It is rightly expected that the reunited Germany will step up its commitment in this area. We want to clarify the constitutional basis for this, on which subject the Federal Government will hold the necessary talks with the parliamentary groups. Ladies and gentlemen, meeting the new responsibility requires a departure from certain comfortable ways of thinking that are now of the past. It requires courage for the future ... All of Germany now has the

chance to find its inner balance, its center. Part of this is that what is taken for granted in other nations can now also develop in Germany: lived patriotism— (*applause from members of the CDU/CSU*)—a patriotism from a European perspective, a patriotism that is committed to freedom.[22]

The shedding of the Bundeswehr's pacifistic ethos was pivotal to Kohl's project of revising the long-held truisms of what a politics of responsibility looks like in Germany. While Kohl still framed "responsibility" to mean Germany's "responsibility for peace in the world,"[23] that peace would now be kept via the new, US-led global consensus on interventionism which Germany would come to participate in.

The CDU/CSU was not alone in these sentiments. Throughout the 1990–91 Gulf War, progressive intellectuals added their pro-war voices to a public debate which unfolded in the pages of newspapers such as *Die Zeit* and *Der Spiegel* concerning whether Germany should send troops to the Persian Gulf, marking a significant ideological shift. While anti-war protestors took to the streets and were spearheaded by left-wing groups such as the Greens, public intellectuals associated with the more center-left such as Günther Grass and Hans Magnus Enzensberger argued vociferously that Germany had a moral duty to defend Kuwait against the invasion of Saddam Hussein.[24] (Though Enzensberger, as mentioned in the previous chapter, was more concerned about challenging Germany's alliance with the United States—and resorted to controversial taboo breaking in so doing. A *Spiegel* article penned by Enzensberger titled "Hitler's Revenant" triggered widespread condemnation for his comparison between Hitler and Saddam, as well as its overly hysterical tone).[25] Some center-left politicians, meanwhile, voiced strong reservations about Germany's readiness to take on the new politics of responsibility, expressing distrust in some foundational element of the German character which was often compared to that of a recovering addict or stabilized psychotic. Take, for example, former SPD party chief Oskar Lafontaine's retort in response to calls from UN leaders for the Bundeswehr to be deployed in the Persian Gulf: "Don't these foreigners understand that you can't offer brandy chocolates to a former alcoholic who has finally managed to stay on the wagon?" or the comments of SPD foreign affairs spokesperson Norbert Gansel: "My personal political philosophy, and maybe even my ambition, are based on an element of distrust in the people I represent, people whose parents and grandparents made Hitler and the persecution of Jews possible."[26] Yet some liberal critics maintained a balance between arguing in favor of German deployment abroad while also noting—as Jürgen Habermas did—that Kohl's quest for normality brought with it certain "normative deficits" concerning Germany's relationship to its past which opened the door for historical revisionism. For Habermas, Kohl's hope for "lived patriotism" revealed what the German right saw in the universalizing principles of international law and interventionist policies: "a German 'normalcy' to be re-won ... a chance of finally crossing that finish line that had always been out of their reach."[27]

Aside from these intellectual and political debates, reunification had delivered unforeseen dilemmas within the Bundeswehr which threatened not only the CDU-led narrative of normality, but the very security of the institution itself. Alongside the mandatory military service which East Germans generally were now conscripted into, a number of neo-Nazis, skinheads, and other right-wing extremists from eastern states found in the Bundeswehr prospects for forming affective bonds that would enable them to connect with a long-dreamed of proud national identity. This, in turn, highlighted the pre-existence of extremism within the West German armed forces. When journalistic investigations in October 1991 uncovered internal reports stating that twenty-four Bundeswehr soldiers and recruits had been directly involved in the Hoyerswerda riots as well as in isolated cases of xenophobic aggression, Defense Chief General Klaus Naumann issued an internal statement to the effect that the Bundeswehr was to be "no place for radicals"—who, he warned, threatened to do "damage to the good reputation of our armed forces at home and abroad."[28] However, having been filed away as "isolated incidents," it took until 1992—following agitative reporting in *Der Spiegel*—for these incidents to be addressed in parliamentary proceedings.[29] CDU defense commissioner Alfred Biehle then reluctantly presented an overview of anti-migrant and right-wing extremist behavior engaged in by Bundeswehr soldiers during the past couple of years: Some had also been involved in the arson attacks on hostels for asylum seekers in Rostock-Lichtenhagen and in Allendorf; a private from Cologne had, together with others, beaten up a German citizen of foreign origin and robbed him; a navy sailor had taken part in "right-wing riots," and in Ellwangen an infantry soldier had appeared on duty with an NSDAP badge affixed to his uniform.[30]

Despite annoyance at the army leadership's downplaying of right-wing extremist activities, the CDU, CSU, FDP, and even the SPD united in agreement that the German armed forces should not be "condemned across the board," theorizing that the problem might be generational. Adolescent conscripts in particular, argued army inspector Helge Hansen, "bring all the ideas and behaviors ... all the aberrant thoughts and actions of their peers into our barracks."[31] Yet in a representative poll conducted in 1992 by Heinz-Ulrich Kohr on behalf of the Bundeswehr's own Social Sciences Institute, it was concluded that 77 percent of participants who expressed a positive view of the German armed forces also self-identified as politically to the far-right—too large a number to be explained away as the "aberrant thoughts" of a restless youth.³²

Clearly reunification—and the subsequent conscription of former East Germans into the Bundeswehr—was provoking some kind of internal disturbance. One striking illustration of this is the amount of munitions that were stolen from army facilities throughout the following year—information which CDU PStS Bernd Wilz presented quietly and without much further comment in response to an inquiry from Ulla Jelpke of the far-left PDS party (who for their part were embarking on what would become a decades-long campaign, led by Jelpke, to draw attention to a potential rise in far-right militarism stemming from within the Bundeswehr). In 1991, PStS Wilz's report states, 96 handguns were stolen (in comparison with 13 in 1990 and 10 in 1989), 11 machine guns (4 in 1990, 2 in 1989), 1,084 hand grenades and explosive devices (540 in 1990, 123 in 1989), and 35,456 rounds of ammunition (tens of thousands less in previous years). Wilz, speaking on behalf of the Defense Ministry, put these alarming numbers down to the short-term merging of the Stasi and combat troop's inventory and expressed no particular concern.³³

Yet by 1993 defense personnel could no longer ignore that the Bundeswehr was struggling to resist an influx of neo-Nazis. As Commissioner Biehle confirmed for *Spiegel* reporters, throughout that year applicants "from the right-wing spectrum" had intensified their quest to forge careers within the Bundeswehr. These instances ranged from minor outrages such as potential recruits arriving at volunteer reception points already uniformed in combat boots, T-shirts reading "*Blut und Ehre*" ("Blood and Honor"), and inked with unmistakably right-wing extremist tattoos, to more severe incidents, as when four infantry privates in an armored vehicle shouted the infamous far-right protest chant "*Deutschland den Deutschen, Ausländer raus*" ("Germany for Germans, foreigners out") outside of a restaurant before attacking a group of alleged foreigners. Sociologists within the Bundeswehr's own research institutes began to worry that the armed forces were becoming particularly attractive to young men who, as economic casualties of the reunification process, did not feel any commitment to "democratic principles or values."³⁴

One Panzer Grenadier Captain Thomas Hahs expressed that he was beginning to see in troops a "latent right-wing radicalism" that, he feared, the "Bundeswehr cannot control."³⁵ The term "latent" is, here, carefully chosen, referring not to fears that such latency existed amongst West German recruits but that it stemmed in particular from the East, where fascist tendencies had ostensibly been repressed under the mask of socialism. As both the media and political commentators were quick to observe, many of these young skinhead and neo-Nazi recruits came from the "new states" and belonged to the various disaffected social milieu described in Chapter 1. Yet while most of these East German far-right milieu had been in development since the early 1980s, reunification seemed to be providing a new social space for recruitment: as criminal sociologist Wolfgang Brück observed, drawing upon his own research for the Leipziger Zentralinstitut für Jugendforschung, youths who became neo-Nazis *after* fulfilling their compulsory service with the Bundeswehr soon became one of several subgroups who comprised the broader neo-Nazi scene in Germany.[36] (Uwe Mundlos of the Thuringia-based NSU terror trio was, himself, such a case.)

Military Revisionism as "Contemporary History"

Yet as the previous chapter has shown, far-right activity in the Bundeswehr following unification was not limited to the recruitment of angry, disaffected youths or instances of xenophobic aggression but also involved the dissemination of Neue Rechte ideology within the various institutions of the armed forces, as revisionist and nationalistic texts began to circulate in army barracks. The year 1995 saw the appearance of a new magazine titled *Deutsche Militärzeitschrift* (German Military Magazine; *DMZ*), which was marketed toward both Wehrmacht veterans and Bundeswehr soldiers and reservists. *DMZ* was founded by Harald Thomas, the editor-in-chief of Neue Rechte magazine *Zeitenwende* ("Turning Point") and member of the Witikobund, a community of so-called ethnic Sudeten Germans classified, since 1967, as a right-wing extremist network.[37] Thomas opened the very first issue of *DMZ* with an editorial titled "May 1945: Final Battle for Berlin" that emphasized the victim status of ethnic Germans following the Second World War while glorifying the heroism of the Wehrmacht. The generation of post-'89, Thomas implored, had an opportunity and an obligation to reject "lies and slander, and to explain to our compatriots that millions of those killed in the world wars, millions of victims of flight and expulsion, and the countless Germans who died of mass murder after the war, have a permanent place in the memory of the nations."[38] Seeking to restore the gaps that had been deliberately left out of the Bundeswehr's own understanding of its military heritage, Thomas seemed also to imply (though did not cite the source of such information) that new recruits were already experiencing an orientation program that differed from the values enshrined in the *Traditionserlass*:

> The Bundeswehr does itself some good when, as part of its reorientation and deliberations, it falls back on what is now historical, draws on the painful experiences and lessons of a previous generation, and learns its tradition—which had been limited to the postwar period—through self-confessional retrospection. ... Not with national forgetting, but national consciousness; not with historical forgetting, but with the courage to confess German history as a whole.[39]

Suggesting that the memory of the Second World War and the actions of the Wehrmacht—"now historical"—no longer need be recalled in shame but, rather, used as a marker of something like personal growth, Thomas drew upon emotion to argue that this chapter of history should be incorporated into the Bundeswehr's understanding of tradition: the "painful experiences and lessons" of the generation who fought in the Second World War deserved remembrance and recognition, and the battles they fought, won, and lost contain useful instruction on military tactics. Neue Rechte voices like Thomas' would soon be joined, in the late 1990s, by increasingly mainstream figures whose agendas involved centralizing German victimhood during the Second World War—and also by far-right actors incensed by the besmirching of the Wehrmacht in popular discourse.

DMZ has played a crucial role in shaping far-right revisionist narratives well beyond veteran circles, presenting itself as a magazine not only for military personnel and veterans but—in Thomas' highly coded language—for "all citizens interested in contemporary history."[40] The mid-1990s saw the term "contemporary history" (*Zeitgeschichte*) transformed, in Neue Rechte circles, into a euphemistic buzzword that referred *not* to recent history or to the practice of unearthing the history of the present moment (as the term is most commonly used), but to revisionist counternarratives concerning the battles of the Second World War. Such revisionism also entailed a challenge to the Bundeswehr's own foundational pedagogic values regarding historical "tradition," with the broader aim of restoring the lost memory of a heroic Wehrmacht as well as a narrative of German victimhood following 1945. Since 2012, *DMZ* has published a bi-monthly spin-off magazine titled *DMZ-Zeitgeschichte*, which typically contains articles entirely unrelated to events that might actually be considered "contemporary" or recent. Most if not all articles in each issue address the battles of the Second World War, glorifying what is referred to in one recent issue as the "combat effectiveness of the Waffen-SS"[41] and, as one journalist has criticized, "present[ing] the Waffen-SS as a military elite unit … view[ing] them as victims of alleged disinformation that has a negative impact on their public reputation."[42] Not only does this deliberately confuse what is meant by "contemporary history" (*DMZ-Zeitgeschichte* appears under the "History" section at magazine kiosks), it also imparts to young right-wing extremists an historical ideal, encouraging them to study the tactics and strategies of the Nazi military elite. *DMZ-Zeitgeschichte* is effectively a survivalist prepper manual masquerading as a journal for military history hobbyists.

As soon as *DMZ* first appeared at newsstands in 1995, the PDS party—concerned by the destabilizing potential of its rhetoric circling amongst both active-duty soldiers and an older generation of veterans—pressed the Federal Government for more information on the magazine, its origins, aims, and distribution. In particular, PDS representatives wanted to know whether this publication had any professional connections to those currently serving. Besides featuring editorials that challenged the closely held democratic values of the Bundeswehr, the first issue of *DMZ* also contained articles written by notorious Neue Rechte authors such as Hans-Ulrich Kopp (himself a former II. Korps recruit tasked with defending the eastern border during the Cold War, who also edited the extremist Witikobund's official newsletter), who trivialized and at times denied entirely the crimes of the Wehrmacht and glorified the Waffen-SS.[43] *DMZ* also promoted new works of revisionist history via laudatory review articles and printed advertisements for classic denialist publications such as SS Standartenführer Rudolf Lehmann's three-volume history of the SS Panzer Division "Leibstandarte SS Adolf Hitler," as well as *Wenn alle Brüder schweigen* ("When all Brothers are Silent"), a large coffee-table book containing over 1,100 photographs of the Waffen-SS, first published in 1973 by the Hilfsgemeinschaft auf Gegenseitigkeit der Angehörigen der ehemaligen Waffen-SS (Mutual Aid Community for Members of the Former Waffen-SS), a veteran's group founded in 1951.[44]

Yet—as in 1993 with regard to *Information für die Truppe*—the Ministry of Defense, speaking on behalf of the Federal Government, was curtly dismissive in its 1995 response to the PDS, stating that it was aware of the existence of *DMZ* but that it was not within the interests of the general public to publish any data on its readership or reach.[45] Not until 2006 did PDS MPs (though by this time the party had dissolved and been reborn as Die Linke) succeed in getting *DMZ* classified as "near right-wing extremist"[46] (though never banned outright). It is not without significance that the PDS party should have received such a dismissive response from Kohl's Federal Government; as a party of almost exclusively former GDR representatives—among them Gregor Gysi—the PDS was viewed by many conservatives as a successor party to the East German SED, their frequent small inquiries treated as troublesome instigation. As a result, what should have been regarded on both sides as a blatant destabilizing threat to a West German democratic institution (and West German "norms" in general) became, instead, a deeply politicized and overly ideological skirmish, the PDS vying to prove that West German institutions were doomed to relapse into fascism if not heavily monitored for internal misconduct, and the CDU dismissing evidence of worrying trends as overblown anti-fascist provocations.

Fueling this ideological spuriousness was the bigger, rather tense dilemma the Kohl government found itself in regarding Germany's obligations to its global allies concurrent with conflicts in the Persian Gulf as well as in former Yugoslavia. In 1995 during the Bosnian War Germany, for the first time in postwar history, began to send troops abroad in the name of commitment to Western, democratic alliances. While anti-war voices on the left—which had been vociferous during the Persian Gulf crisis—now died down and ceded to a liberal discourse of humanitarian intervention, the ideologues of the Neue Rechte began to criticize Kohl for integrating Germany into the newly consolidated European Union and for allowing new influxes of refugees in spite of the immigration reforms that had taken place in 1993.[47] Though critical of Kohl's foreign policy, the writings of the Neue Rechte also lauded the newly combative Bundeswehr as an historical achievement, underscoring its significance with regard to prospects for a so-called "self-assured nation," to recall the phrasing of decorated former paratrooper Schwilk (see Chapter 2).

Yugoslavia, Historical Reckonings, and the Anti-*Wehrmachtsausstellung* Protests

Amidst the ongoing Balkans conflicts of the late 1990s came an effort, at home in Germany, for a renewed public confrontation with the worst of German military history. While tensions between the newly sovereign states of former Yugoslavia had erupted into violence during the early 1990s, even Chancellor Kohl initially expressed some queasiness over the prospect of German involvement in NATO-led intervention; as no-one had forgotten, Yugoslavia had been subject to German occupation during the Second World War. A watershed moment came, however, in July 1995, when roughly 8,000 Muslim men and boys were massacred at

Srebrenica by the Army of Republika Srpska. It was precisely due to German historical consciousness—as well as evidence of ethnic cleansing—that both the Defense Ministry and the Bundestag agreed to intervene in this instance of ethno-nationalist violence, following pressure from NATO.[48] Conscious, also, of the historical memories evoked when German Tornado warplanes flew into Bosnia during July 1995, yet eager to create the narrative of normality required in order to discard postwar pacifism, the Kohl government remained guarded against inquiries into whether so-called isolated incidents of far-right expression within the Bundeswehr were indicative of any wider issue.[49]

At the level of public engagement, the Defense Ministry's agonized decision to deploy troops to Bosnia in 1995 and to Kosovo in 1998 provided a context in which renewed reflection upon the necessity of historical consciousness provoked resentful pushback from the far-right. The mid-to-late 1990s saw a sharp acceleration of flagrantly revisionist campaigns from the Neue Rechte which, apart from viewing 1945 as a year of defeat rather than liberation from Nazi rule, also insisted upon the untarnished honor of the Wehrmacht and the right to mourn its fallen men. The previous chapter has shown how this played out in the world of far-right intellectuals. But the resonance of these ideas with a wider public was made clear during the intense protests led by neo-Nazis and military veterans against the exhibition titled *Vernichtungskrieg. Verbrechen der Wehrmacht 1941 bis 1945* ("War of Annihilation: Crimes of the Wehrmacht, 1941 to 1945"—often simply referred to as the *Wehrmachtsausstellung*), organized by the Hamburg Institute for Social Research, which toured thirty-three cities in Germany and Austria between 1995 and 1999.

Displaying previously unseen photographs of the Wehrmacht's crusade in Eastern Europe against the Soviet Union, many of which depicted German soldiers engaging in coldblooded war crimes (though some, it later turned out, in fact showed the Soviet NKVD),[50] the principal aim of the *Wehrmachtsausstellung* was to dispel the myth of the "clean" and even "patriotic" Wehrmacht which had popularly prevailed since the years of Konrad Adenauer's chancellorship.[51] Against any claim that the Wehrmacht might be separated from the Holocaust and thus spared the burden of historical guilt, the exhibit demonstrated that not only had the Wehrmacht murdered thousands of innocent civilians and allowed 3.3 million Russian POWs to perish in the name of "combating partisans," they had also taken an active role in the extermination of Jews in Eastern Europe.[52] The long-standing necessity of dispelling the "clean Wehrmacht" myth aside, perhaps the most timely aspect of the *Wehrmachtsausstellung* was a section devoted to Hitler's determination to destroy Yugoslavia, which culminated in a bombing campaign over Belgrade in April 1941. The Wehrmacht had slaughtered around 20,000 civilians during the occupation of Serbia, Jews, and partisans alike, while ethnic Germans across Yugoslavian territories were recruited into the Waffen-SS (meanwhile the Croatian Ustaše initiated its own fascist campaign of annihilation upon Jews and Roma).[53] It is in large part due to the historical memory of these events that Defense Minister Volker Rühe initially ruled out, at the start of the Balkans conflict, sending the Bundeswehr to intervene in former Yugoslavia: the optics of German soldiers combating militants in this region seemed unsettling, doubly so to anyone who later visited the *Wehrmachtsausstellung*.[54]

Protests against the exhibition seem to have begun in earnest in 1996 after the traveling exhibit had built up momentum the previous year, provoking broader debates which highlighted the ways in which revisionist historical narratives had become a shibboleth between the political right and the far-right. While the unruly street demonstrations were dominated by a neo-Nazi presence, initial objection to the exhibition and its representation of German soldiers as war criminals was in fact voiced by mainstream conservatives—most notably representatives from the Bavarian CSU party—who publicly aired their disdain for this "moral campaign of annihilation against the German people."[55] Soon, voices from across the far-right spectrum from the REP to the NPD expressed their assent and solidarity with the CSU, one representative of which—Munich MP Peter Gauweiler—provokingly described the exhibition as the "blanket condemnation of all those who took part in the war."[56] Following these widely publicized remarks, the exhibition began to attract small-scale demonstrations and acts of vandalism, the first of which were organized by convicted terrorist and neo-Nazi elder Manfred Roeder and his new-found compatriots—most notably army reserve officer and future far-right publisher/pundit Götz Kubitschek. Early on in these protests Roeder was charged a fine for property damage after graffitiing the word *"Lügen"* ("lies") across some information boards at the Erfurt installment of the exhibition. His court trial was later attended by young neo-Nazi fanatics, including Uwe Mundlos and Uwe Böhnhardt of the NSU terror cell, who waved banners reading "Our grandfathers were not criminals."[57]

With Roeder charged, the protests nevertheless continued. In Karlsruhe on January 10, 1997, thirty or so members of the REP, the NPD, and the Junge Nationaldemokraten (JN; the youth offshoot of the NPD) demonstrated under the slogan "The German soldier: Honest, decent, loyal! No more anti-German agitation!"[58] Other protests were organized on the growing online neo-Nazi network ThuleNetz, with JN representative Michael Wendland announcing further marches against the "anti-German exhibition of shame" at its other locations.⁵⁹ The protests reached a particular height in Munich on March 1, 1997, when a 10,000-strong demonstration composed of the Second World War veterans and at least 4,000 skinhead neo-Nazis marched through the city and came into violent clashes with anti-fascist counter-demonstrators as well as around 1,000 riot police. At least forty-seven participants were arrested, many of them wearing or carrying prohibited Nazi-related symbols.⁶⁰ Other demonstrations continued over the next couple of years and were increasingly met with anti-fascist resistance (which, as in Dresden, often attracted just as much of a response from police as the actions of neo-Nazis),⁶¹ and culminated in a bomb attack on the exhibition when it reached the town of Saarbrücken in March 1999.⁶²

The 1997 Munich protests provoked large debates in the Bundestag, and the "anti-*Wehrmachtsausstellung*" movement as a whole earned itself special attention in that year's BfV report, which noted the leading role of the NPD and its JN offshoot as well as right-wing extremists' escalating use of online spaces and "internet homepages"⁶³ for organizational purposes—a trend which had been growing globally since the late 1980s and which would rise sharply in the years to come.⁶⁴ The BfV also noted in its analysis of right-wing extremist online posts around this time that anti-*Wehrmachtsausstellung* sentiment and reverence for the Wehrmacht seemed to be serving as a focal point around which all sorts of other right-wing grievances could constellate. As well as continuing with the usual xenophobic agitation, right-wing extremists increasingly exploited "other problem areas and mixed them in with their standard topics: economic and socio-political issues e.g., in connection with the European Union; the introduction of the euro; unemployment; housing shortages or national debt," for the purposes of "gain[ing] attention from the wider population and gain acceptance within general political debate."⁶⁵ The intelligence bureau was seemingly at least somewhat aware, already in 1997, of the destabilizing potential of online spaces in which political debate skewed by various types of misinformation could circulate. The BfV also continued to monitor the centrality of historical revisionism to right-wing extremist discourse, as it expressed in that year's report:

> Agitation against "re-education [*Umerziehung*]" by the Allies after the end of the Second World War has also played an important role: right-wing extremists see the free democratic basic order as forced "re-education" and thus fundamentally question the legitimacy of this order. Contemporary historical revisionism [*zeitgeschichtliche Revisionismus*] has remained an overarching topic of agitation that connects the different currents of right-wing extremism.⁶⁶

As is clear from the writings of Neue Rechte agitators such as Alfred Schickel, who was discussed in the previous chapter, the term "re-education" had by this time come to denote not only the brief period of forced, Allied-led denazification during the years of occupation (1945–9), but the earnest moral enlightenment and self-criticism efforts of the later postwar period—which had taken decades to even become a significant cultural-political force. The Neue Rechte placed its dispute over the role and historical memory of the Wehrmacht at the center of broader, contemporary debates about Germany's role in new global power alignments post-1989.

With the memory culture of the Federal Republic (and thus its moral basis) under discursive attack from the political right, and the cities which hosted the *Wehrmachtsausstellung* under physical attack from neo-Nazis, the exhibition protests provoked massive debate in the Bundestag—especially at their peak in March 1997.[67] Left-wing parties such as the SPD, Alliance 90/Greens, and the PDS praised the Hamburg Institute for Social Research for contributing to a public discussion on the involvement of the Wehrmacht in war crimes during the Second World War and fought back against right-wing claims that the exhibition "generalized" unfairly ("It is an undeniable fact that the German Wehrmacht was involved in war crimes and crimes against humanity during World War II. Such a statement does not generalize, it says nothing about the individual guilt or innocence of the individual soldier," read a statement signed by Gregor Gysi).[68] Meanwhile the CDU/CSU doubled down on its defense of the Wehrmacht almost as if it were defending the present-day Bundeswehr. In a statement authored by Wolfgang Schäuble, Michael Glos, and Hermann Otto Solms, the CDU/CSU faction stated that "[t]he German Bundestag resolutely opposes any unilateral or blanket condemnation of members of the Wehrmacht."[69]

Yet the CDU/CSU's attempt to have the final word on matters concerning the German military—both historical and contemporary—its image and reputation would, by the end of 1997, be further complicated by discovery of Roeder's appearance at the Bundeswehr leadership academy two years prior. The journalistic unearthing of this event, which caused such public outcry in December 1997, prompted renewed questions about the Bundeswehr's understanding of its history and traditions at a time when far-right revisionism seemed to be gaining popular momentum. In the parliamentary assembly that followed (which was discussed at the opening of this chapter), Defense Minister Rühe even displayed his own clumsy attempt to reconcile with German history when, after assuring those present in the Bundestag that the March debates had been a sobering reminder of the Bundeswehr's professed "history and tradition," there had nevertheless been "brave, irreproachable soldiers of the Wehrmacht in the Second World War [who] can be a role model for the soldiers of the Bundeswehr today."[70] Rühe's broader point seemed to be that Bundeswehr personnel, schooled from the moment of orientation onwards in their democratic commitments and traditions, were critically minded enough that they could be trusted to distinguish between a criminal regime and average soldiers who faced tough choices. In answer to questions from the disquieted public about Roeder's 1995 lecture, Rühe issued a statement affirming that rare instances of extremism within the Bundeswehr were dealt with severely—while also taking the opportunity to defend against generalizations when he spoke before his audience in the Bundestag.[71]

Raki am Igman: Bosnia, Götz Kubitschek, and Increasing Radicalization

Despite Rühe's assurances, the neo-Nazi protests against the *Wehrmachtsausstellung* were accompanied by a steady rise in racist aggression. The year 1997 became a year of intense right-wing extremist activity, with more than eighty instances of violence perpetrated against foreigners in which the assailants were Bundeswehr soldiers, including physical assaults on individuals—such as the attack of two Turkish German residents by a soldier named in the press as Christian F., in Detmold, and an arson attack on a hostel for migrants in Dresden. By only September of that year, 110 soldiers stood accused of such actions.[72] The political left expressed increasing concern, toward the end of that year, that the Bundeswehr might itself be incubating right-wing extremism and hatred of foreigners.[73] Yet the Ministry of Defense remained on the defensive. One very typical response to a PDS small enquiry reads as follows:

> Even in view of the increase in suspected right-wing extremist cases [in 1997], it is wrong to speak of right-wing extremist tendencies in the Bundeswehr. If the report for the protection of the constitution from 1996 states that among the alleged right-wing extremist violent offenders the proportion of 16- to 20-year-olds is around 66%, and the number of violent right-wing extremists in 1996 was around 6,400, then even the Bundeswehr, as a conscript army, cannot be spared this undesirable development in society. Specific "internal armed forces" factors as the cause for the increase in the incidents concerned cannot be identified.[74]

Striking, here, is the manner in which the Ministry of Defense brushed off as merely "undesirable" (yet, implicitly, unavoidable) not only right-wing extremism within its active military but in society at large, expressing little to no sense that further investigation need take place. To the question of whether the Federal Government had any relevant information as to whether there were right-wing extremist tendencies in the officer corps of the Bundeswehr, the answer was simply a curt "*Nein*."[75]

The German media, meanwhile, had throughout 1997 been busy unearthing other disturbing cases of the "brown spots"[76] within Rühe's armed forces—the most unsettling being video footage in which soldiers at a facility in Hammelburg simulated the rape and execution of civilians while training for their peacekeeping operations in the Balkans, reported by *Die Welt* in July of that year.[77] Though Rühe had stated to the media that those responsible would be held accountable he nevertheless maintained, in his typically cavalier manner, that the Bundeswehr was an army of "decent boys."[78] The press was not convinced; *Der Spiegel* devoted countless pages throughout 1997 to exposing the prevalence of xenophobic and neo-Nazi ideas within the Bundeswehr, interviewing soldiers who solemnly traced a line of continuity and honor from the Wehrmacht to the Bundeswehr and noting that the Hammelburg case was not the first time video footage of simulated rape at a German military barracks had been leaked to the media.[79]

The Neue Rechte press, meanwhile, defended the Hammelburg soldiers. Götz Kubitschek, who would within the next ten years become one of the most prominent "activists" within Germany's far-right scene, argued in the pages of *Junge Freiheit* that the torture scenes captured on tape only simulated what recruits might realistically encounter during deployment in the Balkans and that the individuals in the video do not "represent" Bundeswehr soldiers but the "countless" mercenaries operating in former Yugoslavia. The training was therefore intended to prepare German soldiers to "behave correctly in possible crisis situations."[80] Yet Kubitschek was glossing over some of the more crucial details concerning the context of the footage—namely that these rape and execution simulations had taken place during a break in training and were not themselves part of any official training exercise; more likely, they depicted an unsavory form of roughhouse amongst soldiers at the expense of the civilians they were deployed to protect. The Defense Ministry, moreover, considered the footage a grave offense, and stated that those involved could "expect the severest and possibly also criminal consequences."[81] Kubitschek's July 1997 defense of the footage is particularly disturbing when read with the knowledge that within six months he himself would be stationed in Bosnia on a peacekeeping mission.

For three months between December 1997 and March 1998, Kubitschek volunteered as a reserve officer for the Bundeswehr during a reconnaissance mission in Bosnia, serving as platoon leader for a tactical PSYOPS unit. He documented these experiences in *Raki am Igman*, an autobiographical novel written and published in 1999 with input from Peter Felser, a former first lieutenant of the same unit as Kubitschek (and present-day AfD politician).[82] *Raki am Igman* (which refers, in its title, to Raki—a Turkish grape- and anise-based spirit that Kubitschek and his reserve drank copious amounts of while stationed at the base of the Igman mountain in Sarajevo), is nothing sensational. Composed of twenty-one short vignettes of various, often banal, incidents which occurred during the UN peacekeeping mission, Kubitschek fictionalizes his experiences by writing as his alter-ego Oberleutnant Riebach. Significant in this text, however, is what it reveals about the allure of military service to a far-right ideologue like Kubitschek, who views the Bundeswehr as direct successor to the Wehrmacht. For example, Kubitschek/Riebach recalls that a poster featuring the text of a 1933 *Panzerlied* was hanging in the camp of the German troops ("To die for Germany / Is our highest honor") and devotes several pages to quoting the work of Ernst Jünger, the news of whose death reached Kubitschek while he was stationed at the base of the Igman; he recalls reciting pages from Jünger's *Stahlgewittern* ("Storm of Steel") for his fellow soldiers, in commemoration.[83]

These paeans to the old guard of Prussian war lust strike an ill-fitting tone considering the humanitarian purpose of his detachment's station in Bosnia, as does his assertion at the outset of the text that the general political climate of his time is overrun by what he calls "Western peace-heads" (*westliches Friedensgehirn*). In Kubitschek's assessment, armistice is an unrealistic and unsatisfying aim for the people of the newly independent Bosnia-Herzegovina:

> Perhaps only a Western peace-head [*Friedensgehirn*] could come up with the idea that, after a brutal civil war, the obligation to come together, the door-to-door existence of former mortal enemies, is the right way to go. After a few weeks of on-site inspection, most of the soldiers are ready for a Realpolitikal turning point [*eine realpolitische Wende*]: a view towards what is feasible, utopias shelved.[84]

Kubitschek argues that this is not his view alone; that the nature of a peacekeeping mission transforms the values of young soldiers into conservatism. "Society, whose reflection is the Bundeswehr in the Balkans," he writes, cannot understand what it means to take on an "ethics of responsibility" (a subverted allusion, no doubt, to then-recent political discussions about the meaning of responsibility) and a "willingness to lead"—which these soldiers will bring back home with them in order, first and foremost, to stabilize their own families from which they have been absent.[85] These views are not, to be clear, merely a critique of the democratic hubris of UN interventionalist tactics. For one thing, such a view would have been out of place at the time given the overall determination, from across the German political spectrum, that a democratic "ethics of responsibility" precisely meant intervention on humanitarian grounds (not to mention shame and horror following the massacres at Srebrenica in July 1995—not simply a case of "mortal enemies" in conflict, but of nationalism and ethnic cleansing). What Kubitschek passes off as pragmatic *Realpolitik* is in fact his attempt to validate the possibility of German soldiers returning home from the Balkans with a troubling set of new values.

A section titled "Wehrmacht" serves as the denouement of Kubitschek's text and is the section which is most obviously autobiographical. Kubitschek—or "Riebach"—is asked one evening during a lively dinner discussion about the *Wehrmachtsausstellung* then "haunting"[86] Germany, against which the real-life Kubitschek alongside Roeder and other extremist cohorts had been leading their violent demonstrations.[87] *Junge Freiheit*, of which Kubitschek himself was an editor, had published a slew of anti-*Wehrmachtsausstellung* articles throughout 1997—some of them written by notable figures such as the revisionist Schickel, who referred to the exhibit as "post-fascist propaganda."[88] In this chapter of *Raki am Igman*, Riebach is asked by the mystified yet inquisitive Major Bach to explain his public opposition to the exhibit. Riebach does so by telling the parable of an unaccountably impartial historian with neither political leaning nor prior awareness of any historical debate surrounding the Wehrmacht—nevertheless, a *"wisschenschaftlicher* [sic]" ("scientific"), historian, as Kubitschek puts it—who visits the exhibition and painstakingly deduces that there is little evidence to substantiate the claims being made therein. While there do indeed seem to be photographs of civilians being shot by Wehrmacht soldiers at point-blank range, the historian can find no contextualizing explanation of the international laws of the time, nor are the circumstances of war explained to observers. "Where, the historian [*Wissenschaftler* (sic)] wonders, are the photos clearly documented according to place, time, act, people involved and previous history? Who is being shot by whom, and why?"[89]

Kubitschek's autobiographical novel—which was promoted in the pages of the REP's official newsletter—gained him enough notoriety to earn his dismissal from the Bundeswehr, in 2001.[90] In this instance, Kubitschek's high-profile involvement at *JF*, combined with his novel, was considered by the

Bundeswehr to be enough of a clear-cut case of right-wing extremism. In his official notice of dismissal, Major General von Scotti made clear that Kubitschek had "fundamentally violated" the core democratic duties of the military: "Right-wing extremist efforts represent a great danger for the free democratic basic order of the Federal Republic in general and for the order and security of the Bundeswehr in particular."[91] Nevertheless, in 2002 this dismissal was revoked following a vocal and sustained campaign by *JF*, the authors of which challenged the legitimacy of Kubitschek's dismissal and protested that their own publication should not be categorized as right-wing extremist but merely "conservative."[92] It remains unclear whether the *JF* campaign was the principal motivating force for reversing Kubitschek's dismissal, though scholars have speculated that the Bundeswehr merely wished to avoid potential legal trouble.[93] While Kubitschek remains off duty to this day, he nevertheless seems to still think of himself as a combatant: he has aphorized that "To be a soldier, you don't have to wear epaulettes; to serve the state, you don't have to be a state servant."[94]

Alongside Kubitschek's 2001 dismissal, another troubling crisis regarding German soldiers in the Balkans made its way into the media that year. On May 6, Spiegel-TV broadcast a report on the case of R. B., a German mercenary who had been arrested in Kosovo and was held accused of at least four right-extremist terrorist attacks. Amongst other charges relating to neo-fascism and extremism, it was believed that R. B. had been involved in a massacre of Serbian men, women, and children which occurred on February 16, 2001, in which ten people were killed and many others injured.[95] According to documents from the Federal Government, R. B. was a former paratrooper for the Bundeswehr who had been dishonorably discharged in 1991 before heading out to fight as a mercenary during the Yugoslavian civil war, first on the Croatian side and then on the Muslim side, later joining the Albanian Kosovo Liberation Army (KLA). UN investigators suspected that R. B. had performed various "dirty work" for the Albanians, involving planting mines and targeting Serbs with explosives.[96] When PDS MPs submitted a small enquiry to the Federal Government in late May of 2001, the Foreign Office revealed that, according to the findings of the BfV and the Federal Police, an estimated 100 German mercenaries had taken part in the conflict in former Yugoslavia—fighting "almost without exception" on the Croatian and Bosnian-Croatian sides. The Foreign Office further commented that while German mercenaries usually did have "a right-wing extremist background," it could not be determined whether these particular individuals were placed abroad as part of an organized right-wing extremist structure. However, the government conceded, various far-right journals—for example the *NS-Kampfruf* ("National Socialist Battle Cry," which is based in the United

States) and the *Nationalsozialistische Deutsche Arbeiterpartei/Auslands—und Aufbauorganisation* ("National Socialist German Workers' Party—Overseas and Development Organization")—openly advertised mercenary deployments.⁹⁷ Nonetheless, the neo-fascist international born out of the far-rightward shift that took place in Eastern Europe in the wake of 1989, which truly began to constellate transnationally during the early 2000s, would come to incorporate a network of German neo-Nazi and paramilitary groups which had themselves been steadily growing more organized and more coherent in their aims and ethos for some time.

This is a topic which, more than twenty years on, still requires attention and research: in the last few years it has come to the attention of those who monitor neo-fascism in the Balkans that German right-wing groups such as the AfD party do indeed seem to have been organizing an "outreach" program with the aim of exporting far-right ideology to the Balkans. Prior to this, in 2014 representatives of the NPD had sought out "collaborators in Serbia and Croatia." Given that the roots of German far-right activity in the Balkans reach back to the mid-90s, this would suggest a much longer timescale for the evolution of international, ethnopluralist alliances. As one commentator observed: "In the international networking of these groups, we are witnessing the creation of the right-wing pro-fascist International. And it is being created in the heart of the West."⁹⁸

"Officers of a New Generation": Shadow Armies and the KSK

The possible existence of right-wing extremist shadow armies—and fear thereof—was a major focus of contention at the turn of the new millennium. The 1998 commencement of newly appointed Chancellor Gerhard Schröder's left-wing SPD/Green coalition did not necessarily usher in a new era of government willingness to share data on far-right activity with the media. While the BfV report for that year gave a standard overview of some "essential findings" relating to extremist movements, publications, organizations, and ringleaders, the Federal Government stated that it would not make public an exhaustive overview of the details of such findings, explaining that it feared disclosure of such information might provoke a *"Warneffekt"* ("warning effect") that could interfere with the work of the BfV (a new defense which had not been tried in the CDU era, designed to present the image of a contrastingly tactful and responsive SPD government).⁹⁹

In response, an ever-growing faction of left and center-left representatives took the BfV and the Federal Government to task for omitting from official reports what they saw as the most alarming exemplification of right-wing extremism: the growth of a "complex of traditional militaristic associations of the NSWehrmacht [sic]"—a worrying sign that a Weimar-style shadow army might be forming amongst veterans and active duty servicepeople alike. As the PDS party argued, organizations such as the Angehörigen der Waffen-SS—Hilfegemeinschaft auf Gegenseitigkeit (Members of the Waffen-SS Mutual Aid Community; HIAG) were but one of the most prominent among a growing list of groups and organizations "that propagate historical revisionist and right-wing extremist ideas such as the 'war guilt lie,' 're-education' etc. in their publications."[100]

Moreover, some such groups were in fact not new phenomena but seemed to be the long arm of the Wehrmacht itself—e.g., the Verband deutscher Soldaten (Association of German Soldiers; VdS), which was originally formed during the early 1950s out of the various soldiers' associations that had existed within the Wehrmacht. By the late 1990s/early 2000s, the VdS boasted around 80,000 members and published various articles sympathizing with Hitler and revising narratives about the Wehrmacht in its publication *Soldat im Volk* ("Soldier of the People").[101] In a 1998 issue of *Soldat im Volk*, for example, Bundeswehr Major General Jürgen Schreiber penned an essay arguing that the Wehrmacht—which Hitler had ostensibly allowed to remain non-partisan—was led by conservatives who could not possibly be blamed for supporting Hitler's dismantling of the Versailles Treaty:

> Many politicians and historians from Germany and abroad have described the Versailles Treaty as a basic evil that was largely responsible for the negative developments that took place in politics and in the world. How can one blame German generals and admirals when they took pleasure at the fight against that unfortunate treaty in 1933?[102]

Shamefully, as the Alliance 90/Greens coalition pointed out in a small parliamentary enquiry, the Bundeswehr seemed to be maintaining close contact with these associations through meetings, fellowship evenings, and memorial ceremonies.[103] In addition, those monitoring the growth of militant far-right activity noted an increasing preparedness for paramilitary-style combat within certain factions. The umbrella organization Arbeitsgemeinschaft für Kameradenwerke und Traditionsverbände (Society for Comrade Workshops and Traditional Associations; AfKT), for example, conceptualized itself as a "combat- and emergency community"[104] composed of former veterans, as stated in its official magazine *Alte Kameraden* ("Old Comrades") alongside other aims, such the dissemination of "historical truth about the war generation" whose memory had been besmirched throughout the postwar era in mainstream historical discourse.[105] Taken in hindsight alongside revelations, in recent years, that have concerned the existence of paramilitary prepper groups with connections to the Bundeswehr, it appears that the memory of the Versailles Treaty still provides some ideological link between the shadow armies of the 1920s and the paranoid mistrust of federal institutions espoused by far-right prepper groups today.

Arguably such groups would not have come about, in Germany, had it not been for one crucial development which occurred as a result of the Balkans conflict and also the Salafi-Jihadist terror attacks of September 11, 2001: the establishment of a Special Forces unit within the German military for the first time in the history of the Federal Republic. The Balkans conflict—in which German reserves were for the first time sent abroad to aid in conflict resolution— had given rise to the need for German counterterrorist and special operations abroad.[106] Following this, 9/11 dramatically changed the global situation with regard to defense policy; for many Western nations, the meaning of "responsibility" shifted from the responsibility to intervene to the responsibility to deploy force as legitimized by the UN Security Council. The 9/11 terror attacks led NATO for the first time in history to invoke Article 5 of its founding treaty, which demanded that Germany participate in response to the attacks; as LtGen Hans-Werner Wiermann, Germany's NATO representative at the time, explained it, refusal to participate would mean a violation of the NATO treaty and subsequent diplomatic isolation.[107] This ultimatum challenged Germany's military culture, which until now had been extremely strategic; whereas during the conflict in Croatia, Bosnia, and Kosovo Germany had only gradually—and under intense international pressure—changed its policies, following 9/11 many of the political elite felt it was now self-evident that Germany would contribute militarily as a show of global alliance and solidarity. In the immediate wake of 9/11, Chancellor Schröder inaugurated yet another "new responsibility," one that "explicitly includes ... the participation in military operations to defend freedom and human rights and to create stability and security."[108] While Schröder would eventually refuse to allow Germany to take part in the United States' war of aggression in Iraq,[109] by the time of the 2001 US-led war in Afghanistan, the Komando Spezialkräfte (KSK)—the Bundeswehr's newly formed, 1,000-strong elite special forces division—was regularly carrying out successful raids on al-Qaeda safehouses for which it received multiple decorations from NATO.[110] The German military had, for the first time in history, integrated itself fully into Western alliances by providing ground forces to participate in NATO-led combat operations.[111]

It is also around this time that reserve soldiers and even elite commanders who today are prominent ideologues of the Neue Rechte started to emerge, via their swift dismissal, from within the Bundeswehr's ranks. While the dismissal of Kubitschek in 2001 did not receive much public attention, far more sensational was the 2003 dismissal of general officer and KSK Commander Reinhard Günzel, who had led the KSK in combat missions in Afghanistan. Günzel's dismissal came in response to his having written a letter of praise to CDU MP Martin Hohmann, who had in October 2003 given a speech to his local constituents in which he described Jews as "a race of perpetrators," comparing Jews who had taken part in the 1917 October Revolution in Russia to Nazis.[112] The leitmotif of Hohmann's speech was that, while Germany still bore the yoke of responsibility for its historical crimes, "other nations with bloody pasts [i.e. Israel] continue to play the role of 'innocent lambs,'" by now a well-worn theme amongst Neue Rechte ideologues.[113] In a letter to Hohmann—which came to light when Hohmann brandished it before the audience of public television station ZDF as justification for his refusal to issue an apology—Günzel praised the "courage, truth and clarity" of the MP's speech, continuing that "even if all those who agree with me or even clearly articulate this opinion will be referred to as right-wing extremists by the media, I can assure you that the majority of our people share your thoughts" (it was not clear to whom the words "our people" referred—possibly Günzel's personal circle within the Bundeswehr; possibly Germans as a whole).[114]

Though Günzel was swiftly axed from his position by then Defense Minister Peter Struck, who described Günzel as a "lone, confused general,"[115] the Defense Ministry stated that it had "no knowledge" of any other cases which might cause it to investigate other soldiers within the KSK.[116] Yet it would appear that, at least in Günzel's own reserve, KSK soldiers may have been inducted into a tradition that has threatened the Bundeswehr's professed understanding of its history and its aims: in 2006 he would go on to co-author a book titled *Geheime Krieger. Drei deutsche Kommandoverbände im Bild—KSK, Brandenburger, GSG 9* ("Secret Warriors: A Portrait of Three German Commandos—KSK, Brandenburgers, GSG 9"), in which he proudly placed the KSK in the tradition of the Brandenburgers, the Nazis' notorious special forces unit which perpetrated numerous war crimes, including massacres of Jews.[117] Günzel has also published a text with Kubitschek for Kubitschek's far-right publishing house Antaios, and remains a popular speaker at far-right events.[118]

The Günzel case was an early warning sign that the KSK may be incubating something ugly, and more signs would soon transpire; in 2006, for example, a KSK section stationed in Afghanistan used a version of the Wehrmacht's Afrika Korps insignia on their vehicles.[119] Also in 2006, a Turkish citizen with German residency by the name of Murat Kurnaz accused KSK soldiers of having subjected him to mistreatment during his wrongful detainment at Guantanamo Bay. Kurnaz had been arrested during a trip to Pakistan and imprisoned at Guantanamo for four years with no proof of guilt; the government of Chancellor Angela Merkel eventually was able to negotiate for his release. Upon his repatriation to Germany, Kurnaz penned a memoir titled *Five Years of My Life: An Innocent Man in Guantanamo*, in which he identified several of his interrogators at Guantanamo as KSK soldiers, and subsequently cooperated with a full parliamentary investigation into his allegations, in 2007.[120] Although the investigation was eventually dropped with no conclusive evidence proving Kurnaz's allegations concerning the KSK, the scandal stoked fears that had already been burgeoning amongst some MPs—particularly those from the Greens and Die Linke—that KSK units severely lacked government oversight. Parliamentary debates in 2004 and 2006 over the dearth of publicly available information about the KSK, its missions, and their justification tended to be unproductive despite the existence of a "constitutional requirement of parliamentary consent to foreign deployments."[121] That the operations of the KSK were by nature shrouded in mystery made for intense anxiety amongst MPs when reports of extremism within the elite unit made their way into the media.

One such case prompted Die Linke (as the PDS was now known) to express concern that the KSK—especially units which were supervised by Günzel— might be developing into a something that resembled a Weimar-era shadow army. In August 2007, KSK Captain Daniel K. emailed threats of a right-wing extremist nature to Lieutenant Colonel Jürgen Rose, who was at the time a member of Darmstädter Signal—a military watchdog group which opposes the use of weapons of mass destruction in conflict resolution. Referring to Rose as a believer in "Stone Age Marxism," Daniel K. warned him: "You are being watched, no, not by impotent, instrumentalized [state] services, but by officers of a new generation who will act when the time comes."[122] Linke MPs took news of this threat and its alarming language highly seriously. In a small enquiry to the Federal Government, a faction of MPs put forth the following argument:

According to the questioners [MP Ulla Jelpke *et al.*], the KSK fellow [Daniel K.] is thus embarking on the tradition of the Freikorps, the Schwarze Reichswehr and the SA, who took action against a so-called internal enemy during the Weimar Republic by *Fememorden*[123] among other means. In view of the tradition to which the KSK is committed, this email cannot be dismissed as simple lunacy. The former commander of the KSK, Reinhard Günzel, explicitly named the criminal Wehrmacht unit known as the "Brandenburgers" as a model [for the KSK]. And no KSK fellow objected when Reinhard Günzel compared the KSK emblem with the Knight's Cross of the Wehrmacht and invoked the "achievements" of Wehrmacht members. After his retirement, Reinhard Günzel described in detail the corps spirit of the KSK soldiers ... Therefore, the claim in this hate mail that there is a group of "officers of a new generation" who want to take action against the "enemy within" must be taken seriously.[124]

The Linke politicians went on to note that Rose's complaint about the email he had received had been followed only by a "simple disciplinary measure" from the Bundeswehr, and that there had not yet been a public statement by the Bundeswehr or the Defense Ministry. The Federal Government could not provide any details as to what exactly this disciplinary measure had entailed—only that Daniel K. had not been dismissed from duty and remained a serving captain in the KSK. To the question of whether the Federal Government had made efforts to check whether there was indeed an extremist faction brewing within the KSK—as had been the clear and threatening claim in Daniel K.'s email—the official response was that "There are no indications that within the Kommando Spezialkräfte unit there is a group of officers or other soldiers from whom right-wing extremist activities originate, or who participate in such endeavors."[125] Federal representatives went on to state that they did not consider Daniel K.'s email to be of a right-wing extremist nature.[126] Daniel K. was eventually dismissed from duty in 2019, after authoring a series of public social media posts expressing support for the far-right, conspiracy theorist Reichsbürger Movement.[127]

A slight change in the Defense Ministry and the Federal Government's willingness to acknowledge right-wing extremism in the Bundeswehr came about following the suspension of conscription in 2011, which was introduced by Chancellor Merkel as an austerity measure alongside budget and personnel cuts in response to the Eurozone debt crisis.[128] With military service now entirely voluntary, Parliamentary Commissioner for the Bundeswehr Hellmut Königshaus was pressed to admit in a 2013 report that the reorientation of the armed forces provided "an opportunity to devote even more attention to the acknowledgement of the constitution by applicants during the selection procedure"—i.e., to a more thorough process of screening for potential extremism amongst recruits.[129] Revealing that sixty-three "'serious incidents' where a right-wing extremist, antisemitic or xenophobic background was suspected" had been reported as occurring within the Bundeswehr in 2011, and a further sixty-seven in 2012 (many of them involving the display of banned Nazi propaganda, raising of Nazi salutes and shouting "*Sieg Heil*," as well as listening to neo-Nazi music on Bundeswehr premises), Königshaus seemed to thereby acknowledge the appeal of military service amongst right-wing extremists. He also indicated the possibility that other soldiers might be susceptible to such ideology, stating that "disciplinary offences of this kind must be consistently punished in every instance, also in order to counteract the danger of radicalization [within the ranks]."[130]

Yet punishment was not altogether consistent, and links between areas of the Bundeswehr and extremist groups outside of it continued to develop. In 2011, for example, Die Linke discovered that various neo-Nazis and members of the NPD had easier access to gun permits due to their membership in the Verband der Reservisten der Deutschen Bundeswehr (Association of Reservists of the German Federal Armed Forces), a federally commissioned agency. As a result of this, target practice sessions organized by known neo-Nazis and NPD members had been held at several rifle club locations.[131] Throughout 2012 and 2013 a growing number of Linke MPs became concerned about the discrepancy between right-wing extremist incidents recorded by the parliamentary commissioner for the Bundeswehr and those recorded by the Militärischer Abschirmdienst (Military Counterintelligence Service; MAD). MAD, which detects and analyzes potential anti-constitutional efforts (such as espionage and sabotage) within the Bundeswehr, recorded considerably more cases, particularly in instances which occurred outside of military service.[132] And from 2014 to 2015, MPs began to press the Federal Government for a tougher response to so-called "isolated incidents" of far-right activity within the military which were becoming increasingly less isolated.[133]

Between 2017 and 2020 a series of revelations would ultimately lead to the total disbandment of the KSK division. They begin with the case of then 28-year-old Franco Albrecht, a KSK officer who, with the aid of blackface and forged documents, posed as a Syrian refugee while carrying out small-scale terror attacks against high-profile German politicians.[134] Federal investigators discovered that Albrecht had been stockpiling military weaponry obtained from a base in the French town of Illkirch, where he had been stationed; Albrecht was also found in possession of a collection of Nazi memorabilia. Journalistic investigation would further reveal that Albrecht's ultra-nationalist ideas were known to his superiors at the military academy where he had trained; his master's thesis, titled "Political Change and Subversion Strategy," was submitted to the Bundeswehr training academy in January 2014. As reported by *Der Spiegel*, central to this thesis were the latest Identitarian and Neue Rechte/Nouvelle Droite ideas concerning population replacement, a subversive plan allegedly masterminded by liberal politicians in order to replace Europe's white population via mass immigration.[135] In one key passage, Albrecht argues that immigration is the "cause of today's genocide of the peoples of Western Europe" and that "massive immigration, as we have experienced in the past and as we are experiencing today, leads to the demise of the peoples concerned."[136] In light of the apparent acceptance of Albrecht's extremist views within the Bundeswehr's academy, as well as growing evidence that he was part of a small right-wing extremist group operating within the military, Ursula von der Leyen—who had been serving as Defense Minister since 2013—broke with the traditional stance of earlier ministers such as Rühe, stating publicly and cuttingly that "the German army has an attitude problem, and it appears to have weak leadership at various levels."[137]

This extreme shift in stance from the Defense Ministry—as well as the massive enquiry launched by the Federal Government in light of the Albrecht case—led investigators to Uniter, an association for military veterans and security-related personnel (taking its name from the Latin *uniter*, "together in one") which communicated using the encrypted messaging app Telegram, and which was harboring a sub-group of far-right, survivalist "preppers" known as Nordkreuz; Albrecht himself had been an active member. Nordkreuz closely resembled a cell-based terrorist structure, composed as a network of various regional divisions modeled on the Bundeswehr's own *Wehrbereichskommandos* (military district commands). The group's views on immigration were paranoid, and their aims beyond extreme: in the doomsday scenario referred to as "Day X," which would eventually acquire grim notoriety in the press, Nordkreuz recruits planned to "round up political enemies and those defending migrants and refugees, put them on trucks and drive them to a secret location" where they would be killed, their bodies disposed of with the aid of quicklime.[138] Part of Nordkreuz's preparations involved stockpiling weapons, ammunition, and body bags, partly by stealing from the Bundeswehr's inventory, which several of the group's recruits had authorized access to. They met and trained for several years at various safe locations including a rifle club in Güstrow, Mecklenburg-Vorpommern, where they held regular shooting competitions and conducted

Nazi-themed ceremonies.¹³⁹ And, as it turned out, Nordkreuz operated from inside the KSK itself.

Pieces of the story began to assemble via journalistic reporting throughout 2018 and 2019, culminating in the July 2020 revelations—triggered by a police raid on the property of a KSK soldier—which reached international audiences to much sensation.¹⁴⁰ Alarmingly resonant with the spread of far-right paramilitary and fringe conspiracist groups in the United States, news that members of Germany's special forces had been "prepping" for an impending battle against refugees, migrants, and leftists who were ostensibly plotting to bring about the destruction of German society—the scenario referred to by preppers as "Day X"—emphasized the increasingly global nature of right-wing extremist networks in the age of encrypted messaging services and online forums. Through Uniter's Telegram group, former KSK officer André Schmitt (who used the online alias "Hannibal") had organized a network of chats in which former servicemen, police officers, and civilians anticipated and planned for the collapse of the German government. In 2018, Schmitt had organized civilian combat training on former army grounds; in high-definition drone footage broadcast on ARD's *Monitor* program in 2019, half a dozen civilian men in military-style gear can be seen engaging in combat training led by Schmitt at a former army barracks in the town of Mosbach, Baden-Württemberg.¹⁴¹ The exercises, according to *Monitor* and *The Guardian*, "were part of 'Kommando Pipeline' training designed to produce in its last phase 'combat-ready' fighters trained in handling rifles and handguns, as well as close combat and urban warfare."¹⁴²

Here, finally, was devastating proof of the shadow army that left-wing politicians had feared existed—and had tried for years, in vain, to uncover. Yet the reality was almost worse than anything that had been imagined. Utilizing the digital technology that had rapidly advanced over the past decade culminating in sophisticated, encrypted messaging services, as well as the elite training and weaponry acquired in counter-insurgency missions abroad, the KSK soldiers and others who comprised Nordkreuz had prepared for an apocalyptic final battle with tactics and an organizational structure that resembled part paramilitary organization, part terrorist network. In September 2020, hundreds more incidents which took place in the armed forces, the police, and even the BfV itself were publicly revealed in the BfV's first ever special report into right-wing extremism in the German security services—an unprecedented undertaking which had sadly become necessary.¹⁴³

This report was long overdue. The German public, especially its migrant population and those from families of non-German origin, were still at the time calling for a fuller parliamentary investigation into another neo-Nazi terror cell—the NSU—a trio of terrorists with strong ties to the NPD who, in 2011, had been revealed as the perpetrators of a spate of racially motivated killings after a decade of failed police investigations. For many spectators, the KSK scandal of 2020 occurred on a continuum with the NSU scandal—which, with its ongoing court trials and parliamentary reviews, had hardly receded from public consciousness since 2011. Moreover, as both the BfV report and journalistic reporting emphasized, Nordkreuz and the NSU shared many of the same organizational tactics—covert online communication, cell-based structures, sympathizers within the security services—and aims, such as the eradication of Germany's migrant population. As the next chapter will demonstrate, lessons learned from the NSU revelations should have prompted German lawmakers and parliamentarians to investigate the Bundeswehr (and, for that matter, the police and security services) for signs that cell-based, right-wing terror and its sympathizers reached into every avenue of democratic life in Germany. Desperation to present an active German military to the world, cementing Germany's place in the global power shifts that occurred post-1989, had caused consecutive governments to prioritize reputation and image over true commitment to implementing policies based in historical lesson-learning—a sign that the painful memory of postwar defeat exerted more control over German political life than an earnest politics of responsibility.

4

LEADERLESS RESISTANCE

Failings in Counterterrorism from the NPD to the NSU

The 2000s and 2010s saw a surge in the growth of far-right and ultranationalist parties across Europe, from the British National Party to the French Front National, the Golden Dawn in Greece and the radically antisemitic Jobbik in Hungary.[1] Typically characterized by strong opposition to immigration, in this time period these parties saw their highest electoral results since their inception—a trend which, in the case of some parties, has continued in an upward tick following the 2015 refugee crisis. Still others have merged with or into one of the many Euro-skeptical parties of the mid-to-late 2010s, as Chapter 5 will address.[2] In Germany during the 2000s the far-right party experiencing its biggest regional and national successes since unification was the Nationaldemokratische Partei Deutschlands (NPD), which in September 2004 succeeded—for the first time since 1967—in entering a state parliament, in Saxony, with a remarkable 9.4 percent of the vote.[3] Though this success was followed over the next few years by a period of decline, the NPD has been since its inception in the 1960s an important vehicle for the growth and mobilization of right-wing extremist networks in Germany, presenting itself as the voice of a silenced and marginalized hard right in a nation with a political spectrum that, supposedly, ran only from left to center (one of the party's early campaign slogans ran "Now one can choose again").[4] The NPD's electoral successes in the 2000s overlapped with a notable surge in neo-Nazi activity and racist violence, the most notorious case being that of the National Socialist Underground (NSU) murders which were perpetrated between 2000 and 2007, though were only discovered in 2011.

Since the 2011 revelations surrounding the NSU's existence many commentators have highlighted the connections between the NSU and the NPD, several key representatives of which were found to have aided the neo-Nazi terrorists in their survival underground. Biographers Christian Fuchs and John Goetz have detailed extensively the social network surrounding the NSU and the accomplices who provided weapons, funding, and housing for the core terror trio Uwe Mundlos, Uwe Böhnhardt, and Beate Zschäpe, who first met one another in the neo-Nazi scene of their hometown of Jena, in Thuringia.[5] One such accomplice was Ralf Wohlleben, who at the time was NPD state chairman for Thuringia as well as chairman of the district association of the NPD in the city of Jena, and was found guilty during the extensive NSU court trials which began in 2013 in Munich of aiding a terrorist organization along with accomplices Andrè Eminger, Holger Gerlach, and Carsten Schultze. The NPD has therefore been a vital branch of the broader NSU network, providing a space for "socialising new recruits to its far-right agenda" and "radicalizing some of its adherents to deepen their involvement within the extreme right scene and form groups that engage in politically motivated acts of confrontation and violence."[6] As Fuchs and Goetz— as well as countless investigative journalists—have shown, Wohlleben and his accomplices were at the nexus of both political agenda and social movement. They provided spaces for socialization by establishing neo-Nazi youth clubs and *Kameradschaften* (fellowships) such as the Thüringer Heimatschutz and its smaller counterpart Kameradschaft Jena, promoted international neo-Nazi music groups, and even held benefit concerts to raise funds for the NSU trio.

The NSU itself can therefore be situated within the wider European phenomenon of ultra-nationalism as a resurgent electoral force. Even before the NSU revelations, some scholars of the European far-right were already urging for neo-Nazi social scenes to be taken as seriously as any other organized terrorist network. Bert Klandermans and Nonna Mayer observed as early as 2006 that, despite a notable upsurge in far-right and ultranationalist parties since the 1980s, much of the existing literature still treated violent right-wing extremist groups as "irrational and eruptive," ignoring the ways in which these groups behaved like any other social movement: sourcing funding, recruiting radicals, and mobilizing popular support.[7] In the wake of the NSU's discovery, the failure of the BfV to act upon its extensive knowledge of this intricate and transnational network of right-wing extremist radicals (not to mention the especially vehement scene in Thuringia) became a subject of intense criticism amongst the German public at large.[8] Many activists have since pointed out the deficits in Germany's willingness to take seriously right-wing extremist threats, with the German government accused of being blind in the right eye. Moreover, as terrorism expert Daniel Koehler has repeatedly pointed out, counterterrorism departments throughout the Western world tended, during the 2000s and 2010s—a period marked by widespread global fear of Jihadi terror—to treat Islamist and far-left terror as organized, sustained, and mission-led, while instances of neo-Nazi and white supremacist violence were typically viewed as "lone wolf" attacks committed for pathological reasons.[9] To these arguments can be added the observation that the full timeline of the NSU and its activities illustrates the existence of an established, well-connected global network of far-right terror groups who have shared with each other tactical approaches to the spread of terror practiced within neo-Nazi and white supremacist scenes since the mid 1980s.

There is much about the NSU case which now needs to be revisited in light of an ever strengthening far-right, not only in Germany but globally. As this chapter will show, many features of neo-Nazi and white supremacist extremism that still tend to be thought of as new and confounding were already present in Germany from the early 1990s onwards. The tactics, tendencies, and ideological underpinnings of right-wing extremism evolved steadily from the 1990s into the 2000s and 2010s, and were to a large extent imported or adopted from US-based militia and white supremacist groups, most significantly Hammerskin Nation and the KKK.[10] International communication between right-wing extremist groups and networks may currently be at its strongest and most technically proficient, with the use of encrypted messaging apps adding new practical and legal dilemmas to counterterrorism efforts, as was seen already in the previous chapter.[11] However, as early as the 1990s international think tanks, as well as scholars and reporters who monitor trends in terrorism, warned that neo-Nazi extremists (and also radical Islamists) were using then relatively new and largely unregulated internet communication technologies to organize, recruit, and disseminate tactical manuals without interference.[12]

For example, in the United States, influential Ku Klux Klan (KKK) leader Louis L. Beam proposed as early as 1984 the networking of white supremacist groups, terror cells, and individuals on the nascent internet. Beam's encrypted message forum LibertyNet, which he launched in 1984, was by the mid-1990s known globally amongst far-right circles who used the now commercially available World Wide Web to access recruitment materials.[13] In this manner Beam's enduring legacy was to bring to fruition a vast, decentralized organizational structure which he termed "Leaderless Resistance"—his 1992 tract of the same title was later discovered on the hard drives of the NSU trio.[14] A tactic not so dissimilar to the cell-based terror structures of radical leftist terror groups like the RAF, or anti-colonial guerrilla groups such as the Algerian FLN, Leaderless Resistance facilitated the misleading perception that far-right attacks occurred according to no centralized, organizational structure or long-term political goal.

The seemingly isolated nature of neo-Nazi acts of violence was frequently taken at face value by politicians, security services, and the media alike throughout the 1990s and 2000s, encouraging the widespread notion that far-right terror is most often perpetrated by "lone wolf" actors for largely pathological reasons, ostensibly in contrast to the deeply political, ideological, and sustained tactics of far-left, anti-colonial, or Islamist terror.[15]

This is a notion which persisted throughout the 1990s and continued into the 2000s and 2010s due to several high-profile instances of right-wing extremist terror such as the Oklahoma City Bombing perpetrated by Timothy McVeigh and Terry Nichols in 1995, the London nail bombings committed by David Copeland in 1999, the massacre committed by Anders Breivik in Norway in July 2011, and the murder of nine African American worshipers at an Episcopal church in Charleston, South Carolina, by then-teenager Dylann Storm Roof in June 2015. All of these were cases in which the perpetrators acted as presumed "lone wolves," often leaving behind dense manifestos which, while infused with familiar far-right ideas and conspiracy theories, were also deeply personal. As well as lending the authorities a sense that there was no organized network to which these "lone wolves" belonged, such instances—and the popular mythologizing that accumulated around them—tended to play into public fascination with criminally disturbed minds, rather than confronting a broader political movement.[16]

Evidence regarding the widespread dissemination and adaptation of Leaderless Resistance suggests, however, that there is—and never has there been—any such thing as a true lone wolf terrorist, at least within the spectrum of right-wing extremism. Moreover, in Germany right-wing extremism did not begin to be taken seriously as a determined political movement until the NSU case brought about intrinsic revelations concerning the heavy involvement of the NPD in facilitating far-right militia groups, neo-Nazi music concerts, and in aiding the NSU trio themselves. Yet subsequent and successive failures to ban the NPD throughout the 2000s and 2010s—even after the discovery of the NSU provoked such intense public reckoning—raise serious questions about the efficacy of state structures in putting an ostensible commitment to suppressing right-wing extremist elements into practice. This chapter will address those questions as they came to light through journalistic and parliamentary investigation, beginning with the ways in which the media handled the NSU revelations of 2011 and then working backwards to excavate the layers of malfeasance which occurred at the hands of the security services. The assumptions, misjudgments, and blind spots of the media and the security and intelligence services alike betray a Germany which still, despite a culture of historical consciousness—and despite growing evidence of a thriving far-right scene—could not make sense of the reality of Nazi terror when it occurred in the present.

The *NSU Komplex*: The Terror Trio and the Media

In early November 2011, following a double suicide, an RV fire, and an exploded apartment, the identities of three neo-Nazi terrorists responsible for the murder of nine men of Turkish, Kurdish, and Greek origin and one German police officer finally became known to the authorities and to the public.[17] The NSU—which in essence consisted of Uwe Mundlos, Uwe Böhnhardt, and Beate Zschäpe, though investigations suggest hundreds of potential accomplices and allies—had evaded detection since their disappearance underground in 1998, which was triggered by a police raid on a garage in which the three were storing supplies for homemade explosives.[18] Between then and 2011, the NSU had perpetrated not only the ten murders, nine of which were committed using the same weapon—a silenced Česká 83 with a highly distinctive 7.65 millimeter caliber, a pistol of Czech manufacture uncommon on the streets of Germany. The neo-Nazi terrorists were also responsible for fourteen bank robberies as well as several nail bombings and letter bombings, though police had failed to connect any of these crimes to the perpetrators, whose whereabouts they had lost sight of in 1998.[19] The NSU murder series has been referred to by former prosecutor general Harald Range as "Germany's 9/11," not only due to the intense reflection upon the domestic presence of neo-Nazi terrorism which it provoked, but also because it initiated a crisis within the German security services, whose misconduct was exposed throughout prolonged journalistic investigations and parliamentary enquiries which followed the events of November 2011.[20]

On November 4 in the town of Eisenach, Thuringia, the two male assailants Mundlos and Böhnhardt were chased down by police in connection to their latest bank heist. Finding themselves cornered, the two men set fire to the RV in which they had traveled to each crime location—and which contained a vast stockpile of weapons, ammunition, and stolen money—before turning their guns on themselves.[21] Later that day, Zschäpe—obeying a detailed plan the three had previously agreed upon in the event of their capture—set fire to the apartment in which the trio had been living undercover for the past few years in Zwickau, Saxony. Though the fire caused an unexpected explosion which destroyed much of the building, a significant number of materials and personal belongings comprising evidence of the trio's activities survived.²² In the days that followed, media outlets received copies of a DVD which Zschäpe had mailed out shortly after setting the apartment fire, before turning herself in to the police.

Made up of scenes from the cartoon TV show *The Pink Panther* spliced together with news coverage and macabre images of the murders, the confession film tells the story of a jobless and disaffected Pink Panther committing racially motivated executions and placing bombs in the name of the NSU, whose logo appears throughout.²³ Evading the authorities at every turn, the Pink Panther carries out these attacks to the familiar, plodding theme music of the original cartoon. This was the first that the media or the German public had ever heard of the NSU, which presented itself in the film as a potentially sizable and well-organized underground network of right-wing terrorists. "The National Socialist Underground is a network of comrades with the principle: Actions over words," the opening frame declared. "Stand with your *Volk*. Stand with your country. Support the NSU."²⁴ The events of November 2011 were immediately shocking to the public, who were not accustomed to thinking of neo-Nazis as a strategic or well-organized terror threat. The discovery of the NSU was therefore also revelatory and clarifying, as it retrospectively revealed dramatic dynamics that had been ongoing for years.

In the wake of Mundlos and Böhnhardt's suicides inside the burning RV (in the rubble of which police recovered the Česká pistol),²⁵ and following Zschäpe's arrest, the next scandal to unfold concerned the culpability of the BfV as well as the federal police (the Bundeskriminalamt; BKA) and state police (Landeskriminalämter; LKA). While the police had, throughout the previous decade, led a nationwide manhunt for the perpetrator of the nine murders, their investigation had been seriously compromised by underlying racial bias. Not only had state police aggressively subjected the *victims'* families to intense interrogation in their mistaken pursuit of a non-German perpetrator, scoffing at advice from the US Federal Bureau of Investigation (FBI) that all evidence suggested the murders were racially motivated.²⁶ In addition, the BfV had known all along the strength, size, and fervor of the neo-Nazi scene to which Mundlos, Böhnhardt, and Zschäpe had belonged in the eastern state of Thuringia— and the trio in particular had made themselves conspicuous. In September 1996, Mundlos and Böhnhardt—along with Ralf Wohlleben of the NPD and his compadre André Kapke—had appeared at the trial of infamous neo-Nazi terrorist Manfred Roeder, who was appearing in court for acts of vandalism relating to the anti-*Wehrmachtsausstellung* protests; the group heckled the courtroom and rolled out a large banner which read "Our grandfathers were not criminals." Two months later the same group were escorted from the Buchenwald concentration camp memorial site having arrived there in full SA uniforms. Local police in the city of Jena had even briefly held all three members of the terror trio in custody; in September 1997 Mundlos, Böhnhardt, and Zschäpe were interrogated for placing a dummy explosive inside a large suitcase with a swastika painted on it in front of a Jena theater. Despite this interrogation, no arrest followed—though in January 1998 police discovered four operational pipe bombs and a notable quantity of TNT stored in a garage in the Lobeda neighborhood of Jena and again suspected the trio, who evaded an attempt at arrest and fled underground. As Koehler points out, these early events demonstrate the existence of a wider network that surrounded the cell: the far-right scene in Germany was already, from 1998, tracking the journey of the trio and funding their life underground.[27] Kapke, Wohlleben, and Holger Gerlach, a loyal NSU supporter and neo-Nazi music enthusiast, organized benefit concerts in order to raise money for the cell; neo-Nazi band Eichenlaub even dedicated a song to the trio titled "5. Februar"—the presumed date of their disappearance.[28] This organized and well-funded network would enable the trio to outrun the police after a five-year-long manhunt, which was eventually considered a cold case and closed in 2003.

Despite the clarifying light shone by journalistic investigation onto the NSU and its wider network following the 2011 revelations, the mainstream media exhibited an overall confoundment that remains indicative of the difficulties liberal institutions face in explaining right-wing terror. One aspect of the media's difficulty in coming to terms with the revelation of an organized neo-Nazi terror network existing in Germany was the reach for a psychological or sociological explanation—rather than a political one—via extensive examination of the trio's biographies. It is worth restating some of that biographic material here, not only because it demonstrates that the trio belonged to a growing, coherent network of neo-Nazis from reunification onwards (a topic of huge political significance that few in 2011 seemed to have a meaningful response to). The framing of these biographical narratives also reveals much about the pathologizing devices utilized to explain the motivations of the terror trio.

Uwe Mundlos, Uwe Böhnhardt, and Beate Zschäpe were all born in Jena in the mid-1970s and came of age during the turbulent period of the GDR's collapse and subsequent reunification with the Federal Republic. Within this atmosphere of collapse and economic upheaval, like others their age the trio fell in with a local skinhead and neo-Nazi group called Kameradschaft Jena. Although Kameradschaft Jena—which was a subsection of a larger, state-wide group called the Thüringer Heimatschutz—was founded in 1995, the trio's radicalization had begun much earlier.[29] They attended concerts organized by British neo-Nazi record label and militia group Blood & Honor, as well as NPD events and the annual Rudolf Hess memorial rally in Jena.[30] They also forged connections with the US-based white supremacist network Hammerskin Nation, which first formed in Texas in 1986 and whose high levels of recruitment from within the US prison system made them an extremely violent and criminal element, proficient at obtaining weapons and explosives.[31] From the Hammerskins and from the growing, pan-German network of neo-Nazi "*Freie Kameradschaften*," ("free fellowships") the trio learned and adopted many of the tactical approaches they would later put into practice while committing bank robberies, racially motivated murders, and other acts of terror such as sending mail bombs and planting dummy explosives, carefully evading capture while doing so. The NSU is therefore a case study in how vast, organized, and prepared the far-right was becoming throughout the 1990s, and how internationally connected. Yet while anti-fascist publications such as *Antifaschistisches Infoblatt* had been diligently monitoring this growing network and its constituent cells, groups, music acts, etc., since 1987, more mainstream news outlets were slow to situate the NSU within this milieu, opting instead for cartoonish and salacious characterization of their individual personality traits.

Uwe Böhnhardt (b. 1977) was said by his peers to have been an aggressive and antisocial person with a "fetish for weapons"—a fact seized upon and repeated often in early reportage.[32] In 1993, at the height of nationwide violence against foreigners in Germany, Böhnhardt joined the Winzerclub—a youth club which had opened just after reunification and quickly became a stronghold of the neo-Nazi scene in Jena—where he met Mundlos and Zschäpe. Media outlets such as *Spiegel* tended to frame Böhnhardt as the "weapons nut" of the trio, as if he were the meathead aggressor in a small group of burned-out youths.[33] Uwe Mundlos (b. 1973), by contrast, was treated with some fascination for having apparently been the intellectual of the group—a notion confirmed by his peers as well as by investigators.[34] Mundlos' biographers tend to treat him as an outlier amongst his working-class neo-Nazi peers in Jena; his good education and his family's economic security were said to have contributed to his self-assured and affable character in apparent defiance of what many expected from the stereotypical skinhead.[35] He is said to have often engaged in amicable debates with those who did not share his far-right worldview, accepting their counterarguments while himself remaining "consistent" and "liv[ing] by his beliefs."[36] While his peers clung to groundless adages such as "The foreigners are taking our jobs,"[37]

Mundlos, it was said, sought never to appear as foolish and preferred to present his radical views as grounded in knowledge and fact.[38] Journalistic surprise at these accounts from Mundlos' peers illustrates a tendency to compartmentalize violent skinhead neo-Nazis and the intellectual Neue Rechte, as if there is no relationship between the ideological branch of the German far-right and the street-level racist violence it inspires.

Media reportage—and, indeed, subsequent biographies and scholarly studies—has puzzled over what could possibly have prompted a middle-class, intelligent young person such as Mundlos to join the neo-Nazi scene, as if these attributes are mutually exclusive. Former acquaintances attest that as early as 1988 Mundlos began styling himself as a skinhead and spending time with local neo-Nazi and skinhead groups in Jena, where a scene had been for some time acquiring a certain dark glamor that attracted many young people who felt stifled by stagnant life in the GDR and repulsed by anything remotely socialist. While few commentators, if any, have taken seriously the possibility that Mundlos found the far-right scene an ideologically stimulating channel, this idea does seem to have occurred to the Militärischer Abschirm Dienst. When Mundlos earned himself a reputation, while fulfilling his compulsory military service between 1994 and 1995, as an outspoken and charismatic neo-Nazi, MAD offered him a position as a paid informant—the revelation of which would scandalize the German public when it came to light during the NSU trials in 2013. Mundlos, however, turned down the offer owing to an unswerving commitment to his peers.[39] Media focus on Mundlos' "intellectualism" tended to sensationalize while drawing few conclusions or offering any updated, nuanced understanding of the dynamics of East German neo-Nazi groups. Seldom did the German media ask where Mundlos acquired his ideological position—i.e., whether it originated from a wider intellectual far-right movement—preferring instead to treat him as unique amongst typically thuggish neo-Nazis and to pathologize the trio's individual motives.

However, perhaps neither of the boys in the NSU trio was pathologized as heavily as their sole female accomplice, Beate Zschäpe (b. 1975). As the only surviving member of the trio, Zschäpe became the perpetrator at the center of the NSU trials in 2013, and from 2011 onwards her character and biography were the subject of heavy media attention and speculation. According to Zschäpe's own court testimony, her life of deviance began around 1991 once her mother became unemployed due to the events of the *Wende*; no longer receiving any money from her mother, she got herself involved in minor thefts along with her circle of friends.[40] Shortly after this she met Mundlos, with whom she began a brief romantic relationship (she would later end up with Böhnhardt), and became a prominent member of the neo-Nazi scene in Jena, participating in and organizing rallies.[41] She continued to demonstrate organizational skills in her capacity within the NSU, overseeing the money brought in through their bank robberies, renting a garage in which the trio assembled bombs, and facilitating amicable relationships with their local neighborhood in order to avoid suspicion. Local police reports from the years prior to the trio's disappearance underground describe Zschäpe as "devious and cunning" as well as "very self-assured and condescending."[42]

Media depictions of Zschäpe, both in the run-up to her 2013 trial and throughout, tended to oscillate between portrayals of her as sly and devious, on the one hand, and submissive and dependent, on the other—the latter being an image that Zschäpe herself would eventually adopt as part of her court defense.[43] Portraits of Zschäpe throughout various media from tabloids, to television coverage of her trial, to respected publications such as *Spiegel* and *Welt* frequently employed gendered language which either demonized or sexualized her (or both simultaneously), while clambering to make sense of the trio's internal dynamics. Zschäpe's initial silence during the 2013 court trials, which she finally broke with a written statement read aloud in court in 2015, led various news outlets to fill in the gaps with speculation and sensationalism, as demonstrated by this 2011 example from the tabloid newspaper *Bild*:

> Did Beate Zschäpe also murder? Zschäpe refuses to testify. So far, however, there are many indications that the two men in the trio are responsible for the murders ... However, the Nazi bride is said to have often driven the mobile home in which the trio traveled to their deeds.[44]

Generally speaking, in much of the media's reportage Zschäpe was rarely held accountable for the trio's murders and was frequently described as an "accomplice," a "roommate," or a "Nazi bride"—a phrase which, besides being inaccurate (she was married neither to Mundlos nor Böhnhardt), aims to evoke a kind of horror movie subservience.[45]

Bild also obtained and published a collection of private photos taken during the early 1990s of the trio together in their abode in which, according to the ostensibly more highbrow *Die Zeit*, Zschäpe appears as "Almost a child, a little tousled, cute" in her Minnie Mouse pajamas.[46] These infantilized depictions, which so often framed media speculation about Zschäpe's role within the NSU and her romantic involvements with both Mundlos and Böhnhardt, reinscribed long-standing assumptions about how and why women become involved in right-wing extremism—which has broader implications for how the severity of far-right violence is understood in general.[47] As both the media and the German government made clear throughout the extensive, years-long trials that followed Zschäpe's arrest, German authorities and the public at large have struggled to acknowledge or even visualize the reality of right-wing extremist networks in Germany. At the level of media discourse, one highly convenient means through which to try and understand the gender dynamics, the impressive evasion of capture, and the organizational cohesion of the NSU was that of comparisons to the infamous RAF, the far-left urban guerilla movement which had terrorized West Germany throughout the 1970s and 1980s. A special edition of *Spiegel International* emblazoned with the headline "The Brown Army Faction" and featuring an image of a gun as well as a triptych of passport-style photographs of the trio—Zschäpe, wearing sinister dark sunglasses, placed front and center—promised to reveal "the uncanny confessions of a radical right-wing terrorist group."[48] Under the subheading "Echoes of the RAF," *Spiegel* asked:

> Were [the trio] a miniature underground army, a sort of Brown Army Faction like the far-left Red Army Faction which terrorized Germany in the 1970s, consisting of two men and one woman, equipped with 19 weapons and the ability that all terrorists share, namely to deactivate their conscience?[49]

Seizing upon the vaguely similar sexual dynamics of both the NSU and the RAF,[50] *Spiegel* demonstrated that German media discourse was ill-equipped to take the NSU seriously on their own terms. Claiming that there is "no precedent" in postwar German history for such a highly organized, active, and well-funded far-right combat group, *Spiegel International* noted with some astonishment that "this sort of terrorism has until now only been associated with a group operating on the other side of the political spectrum."[51] Moreover, the possibility of widespread social and institutional racism in Germany was hardly ever raised in the media—nor was it discussed in the NSU trials or in the parliamentary investigation into the malfeasance of the authorities, except when brought up by Die Linke (as discussed below). Instead, the trio were framed as "three young people who broke away from society and submerged themselves [underground]."[52]

The attribution of pathological—rather than political—motives to the NSU trio fits into an ongoing trend, seen in the previous chapters of this book, for framing acts of racist aggression and the adopting of Nazi insignia and language as "isolated incidents" rather than situating them within a broader culture of structural racism and resurgent ethnonationalism. In addition, the revelation that a neo-Nazi terror cell was responsible for a series of killings which had been ongoing since the year 2000 caused some retroactive soul-searching over how those murders had been reported on at the time. Although the German public learned about the NSU for the first time in 2011, the murders of nine men of Turkish, Kurdish, and Greek origin had been widely followed in the news, where they earned the racially insensitive epithet "Döner Murders."[53] As Friedrich Burschel of the Rosa Luxemburg Stiftung has pointed out, the media, which in many ways constitutes "a democratic society's fourth estate responsible for holding the government to account," shaped a stereotype-laden narrative which would come to characterize public discourse surrounding the murders. Moreover, this narrative uncritically parroted the same racially driven assumptions made by police throughout their misguided investigation.[54] In this manner, neither the media nor the police seem to have been able to entertain the possibility of a right-wing extremist terror cell existing in Germany, nor were these institutions capable of recognizing their own racial biases.

Errors in Forensic Psychology: Failings of the Police and Intelligence Services

On September 9, 2000, Enver Şimşek, a 38-year-old florist of Turkish origin, was shot while working at his flower stand in Nuremberg, Bavaria; two days later, he died of his wounds in hospital. At a tailor shop in the same city almost a year later on June 1, 2001, Abdurrahim Özüdoğru was killed by two shots to the head using the same weapon—the Česká pistol—that had killed Enver Şimşek.[55] Despite the similarities between these two killings—the location, the execution-style shooting at close range using the same silenced weapon, and the migrant backgrounds of the victims—the victims themselves were not connected in any way. Neither would police discover any apparent connection between seven more racially motivated executions committed with the Česká over the next five years: Süleyman Taşköprü, who was shot three times in the head on June 27, 2001, in Hamburg; Habil Kılıç, murdered on August 29, 2001, in Munich; Mehmet Turgut, murdered in Rostock on February 25, 2004;[56] İsmail Yaşar, shot five times and found dead on June 9, 2005, in Nuremberg; Theodoros Boulgarides, killed in Munich on June 15, 2005; Mehmet Kubaşık, shot dead on April 4, 2006, in Dortmund; and Halit Yozgat, shot dead at the internet café he owned on April 6, 2006, in Kassel.[57] This last case became of particular focus in a scandal which has never been sufficiently resolved or explained, when it transpired that an undercover BfV agent by the name of Thomas Richter (code name "Corelli"), who was also a prominent member of the European White Knights of the Ku Klux Klan (EWK KKK), had been present in a back room of the internet café as Yozgat was murdered.[58]

Each of these victims was executed in the open at their place of work, though several were only at the scene by chance as they were covering a shift, a detail which made it harder for detectives to determine a motive. Seemingly unrelated, at the time, were three nail bomb attacks which took place in Nuremberg, in 1999, and Cologne, in 2001 and 2004, in areas of business popular with the Turkish communities of those cities. Though these attacks resulted in no fatalities, many individuals were severely injured—more than twenty in the 2004 Cologne attack alone.[59] One additional, final victim in the NSU murder series was 22-year-old police officer Michèle Kiesewetter, who was shot in her patrol car on April 25, 2007, in Heilbronn, although this case was not initially connected to the other murders and remained unsolved until 2012.[60] During this attack Kiesewetter's duty partner was also shot and injured, though survived, and both had their service weapons stolen from them.[61] It would later emerge that the killers, Mundlos and Böhnhardt, were looking for a weapon to replace the Česká, which kept jamming—this was the sole reason for Kiesewetter's murder.[62]

After the events of November 2011 which revealed, finally, the culprits behind these murders, an additional layer to the story came to light which made the trio's evasion of the police even more confounding. The domestic intelligence services—the BfV—had between 1996 and 2003 led a highly classified investigation in Thuringia by the name of "Operation Rennsteig" for which they had recruited dozens of high-profile neo-Nazis as *Vertrauensmänner* (*V-Männer*)—inside informants—who were paid generously in exchange for information on the far-right scene and its planned activities.[63] Journalistic investigations in early 2012 revealed that, on November 11, 2011, amidst the media swirl surrounding the newly discovered NSU, a BfV employee had shredded several files pertaining to Operation Rennsteig, news of which prompted the resignation of then-BfV president Heinz Fromm.[64] Due to the malfeasance of federal and state police as well as the intelligence services, an extensive parliamentary enquiry was launched alongside the 2013 NSU court trials in Munich, in which a committee formed of representatives from each mainstream political party found that "sweeping incompetence by the investigative agencies" was to blame for failing to link the murders, small-scale explosions, and bank robberies that had persisted for years.[65] However, as expressed by members of the Turkish community as well as representatives from Die Linke, who submitted a dissenting contribution to the 2013 final report, the enquiry did not provide any meaningful answers as to the cause of the authorities' incompetence, nor did it address the institutional racism which had led police down a confected line of investigation.[66] A subsequent enquiry which concluded in 2017 did not, in all 1,800 pages, offer any new insight in this regard.[67]

What therefore requires consideration are the modes of thought which led both federal and state police to completely rule out a far-right suspect (or suspects) while the Českà murders were taking place. This includes the "ethnicizing perspectives,"[68] as Linke MP Petra Pau put it, which led police to treat the victims' grieving family members as suspects. The Českà murders—officially referred to, in police proceedings, as "Sonderkommission [SoKo] Bosporus," ("special commission Bosporus," referring to the Bosporus strait near Istanbul, Turkey)—had ostensibly been confounding investigators at all levels, from the LKA to the BKA, who for years pursued the assumption that an unspecified Turkish mafia group was responsible. By the late 2000s both state and federal police across Germany expressed themselves bewildered by this case. The crime scenes provided no trace of DNA fiber, no fingerprints, no useful witness testimonies, and no apparent motive—nothing, in the view of the police, which linked the murders together apart from the Českà weapon. Police had even gone public with SoKo Bosporus, appearing in news segments in which they showed images of a Českà pistol, soliciting vigilance and information from the German populace.[69] Yet a crucial oversight was that the non-white identities of the victims were not considered a possible link beyond the suspected involvement of foreign crime groups.

By 2008 hundreds of officers had "investigated 3500 leads, checked 11,000 people, saved 32 million pieces of data and filled 1200 files" to no avail.[70] Many if not all of these leads were falsely directed by theories that the victims all shared a connection with foreign organized crime units; at various stages both the Turkish mafia and the PKK (Kurdistan Workers' Party, an armed guerrilla movement) were suspected, in addition to gambling, tax dodging, and even marital jealousy as possible motives. Adile Şimşek, wife of the first victim Enver Şimşek, was subjected to particular mistreatment by the police, who attempted to compel her to admit to having murdered her husband in a jealous rage. Adile was shown a photograph of a "blonde German woman" who, the police insisted, had been having an affair with her husband; not until much later did the Şimşek family learn that this was entirely false.[71] In fact, from the start of these investigations the families of the victims were placed at the center of police enquiries which were marked by racist ascriptions. According to the findings of

Die Linke, which was represented by Petra Pau during the 2013 parliamentary enquiry:

> The relatives of the murder victims ... were placed in a thoroughly ethnically ascribed milieu of so-called "Turkish crime," "organized crime," "drug trafficking," "illegal gambling," "human trafficking." "Döner-Mafia," and "Flower Mafia." The police and the state prosecutors used the aforementioned and other attributions in their search for the motives and the masterminds of the Česká murder series. The investigators also used these terms for their filing system of hundreds of "leads."[72]

As Pau went on to point out, in hindsight it seems inexplicable that the victims' migrant backgrounds were not considered a possible motive.[73]

Yet federal police, and some state police, refused to entertain the idea of a far-right assailant. According to the findings of the 2013 parliamentary enquiry, in the summer of 2006 the LKA Baden-Württemberg commissioned an Operative Case Analysis (Operative Fallanalyse, OFA) of SoKo Bosporus for which they recruited expert criminal profilers from the LKA Bavaria, who reached the conclusion that the killers were right-wing extremists who acted out of "hatred against Turks."[74] Not impressed with this analysis, the BKA along with special police commissions from several *Länder* embarked on a campaign to discredit this OFA, pressuring the LKA Baden-Württemberg to produce a counter-analysis, which was presented in January 2007. This second OFA heavily asserted the alleged migrant status of the perpetrator, stating: "Given that the killing of human beings is highly taboo within our cultural space [i.e., Germany], we can safely assume that the perpetrator is, in terms of his behavioral system, located far outside our local system of values and norms."[75] It is unclear on what basis the killing of people can be considered any more "taboo" in Germany than anywhere else (and, moreover, it could be countered that every violent or antisocial personality locates themselves outside of their "local system of values and norms"). The case study relies on emphasizing narratives that ascribe violence and immorality to non-Western migrants, concluding that, in light of evidence which points to the planned, deliberate nature of these killings, the perpetrator's motive could be explained by a "Code of Honor" pointing to "a group in the East and/or South-East European region (not a West European background)."[76]

In the summer of 2007, the Bavarian LKA invited agents from the American FBI to aid in another OFA. During this exchange the FBI expressed with confidence that these were racially motivated killings. Yet while the Bavarian

LKA were moved to reach the same conclusion, the BKA were decidedly unimpressed with the outcome of this analysis. Having reviewed case reports and evidence from the crime scenes, in a letter dated August 7, 2007, the FBI offered its assessment that:

> The offender is a disciplined, mature individual who is shooting the victims because they are of Turkish ethnic origin or appear to be Turkish ... The offender has a personal, deep rooted animosity towards people of Turkish origin.[77]

In addition, the FBI profile concluded that the perpetrator's "motivation was a mixture of personal instigation and thrill" and that "he is also prepared to take a high risk, with his acts committed in broad daylight."[78] These were perceptive interpretations of the accumulated evidence. On the topic of the weapons used, the FBI noted that in addition to the Česká the killers had also used an unspecified, antiquated pistol of 6.35 millimeter caliber both in their first murder in Nuremberg and their third murder in Hamburg. The FBI profilers concluded that this was likely an "old weapon" that "the attacker could be very proud of,"[79] implying a weapon with some historical significance attached to it. This second weapon in fact turned out to be an Italian Bruni Mod. 315—a blank-firing pistol which had been adapted to take live ammunition.[80] Nevertheless, the suggestion that the killers might be "proud" to own an antiquated weapon—i.e., that they held reverence for historical paraphernalia—emphasizes that the FBI profile strongly hinted at a potential neo-Nazi or white supremacist.

The FBI recommended that investigators conduct a search for someone with a "grudge against Turks" who could have been at each crime scene at the date and time in question. However, German federal authorities dismissed this advice. Jürgen Maurer of the BKA, who in 1990 had in fact served as an exchange officer with the FBI in Washington, DC, noted in the margins of his copy of the FBI analysis: "Not very helpful!"[81] It is disputed what Maurer meant by this; one member of the parliamentary committee claims that the BKA had in fact come to the same conclusions as the FBI, and that their analysis was "unhelpful" in that it added nothing new. Another parliamentary representative, however, contended that the problem comes down to different approaches in profiling. While the FBI process involves considering multiple expert opinions and differing points of view, the BKA process relies on data patterns alone, with the result that "that which has not previously occurred"—in this case, a racially motivated murder series taking place in Germany—is considered improbable and thus ruled out.[82]

State police in Hamburg, Mecklenburg-Vorpommern, North Rhine-Westphalia, and Hesse therefore continued to take SoKo Bosporus down false lines of enquiry, subjecting the families of the murder victims to suspicion and interrogation. Relatives were suspected of having in some way carried out or caused the murders themselves, and in some cases siblings of the murder victims acted as translators during the interrogations of their parents.[83] Federal investigators, too, believed that the murders could have been committed either by a lone perpetrator who chose their victims at random, or else that there was some kind of connection with a Turkish organized crime unit to which the victims owed some sort of debt—but definitely not to right-wing extremist groups, which the authorities were "convinced that they had under control."[84] Despite LKA Thuringia having on file leads suggesting that Böhnhardt, Mundlos, and Zschäpe—still wanted for interrogation following the 1998 garage raid—were living in the city of Chemnitz and later in Zwickau (both in the state of Saxony), and that they were being supported by well-known neo-Nazis from the UK Blood & Honour network as well as the US Hammerskin Nation, no attempt was ever made to act upon this knowledge or to link the trio to the murder series or to the nail bomb attacks.[85]

Meanwhile in the clubhouses of neo-Nazi *Kameradschaften* throughout the states of Thuringia, Saxony, and Mecklenburg-Vorpommern, a new Nazi punk anthem was making the rounds on contraband CDs. On the album *Adolf Hitler Lebt!* by Gigi und die braunen Stadtmusikanten, which was released in 2010 long before the NSU outed themselves to the public, the track "Döner-Killer" hinted that the identities of the murderers were widely known in neo-Nazi circles, their confounding of police investigations a source of entertainment: "He's already done it nine times / SoKo Bosporus, it sounds the alarm / The investigators are electrified / A bloody trail and nobody can stop the phantom."[86] The song exemplified a reverent lore that had long surrounded the fugitive NSU trio within the vast underground scene presided over by representatives of the NPD. The neo-Nazi music scene existed as a nexus point for several notorious neo-Nazi and white supremacist groups including Blood & Honour, which primarily promoted neo-Nazi music but also engaged in militarism; the US-based Hammerskins, which now had ten chapters in its "German Division"; the UK-based Combat 18, who were behind the 2019 assassination of Walter Lübcke;[87] and thousands of individuals from smaller, local cells throughout Germany and the West. United around the concept of "Leaderless Resistance," this international terror network was growing in ideological cohesion, political-mindedness, and tactical preparedness for a prophesized "race war."

"Leaderless Resistance" Part I: The NSU and the Global Far-Right

In the January 1998 raid on the NSU's Jena storage garage, one of the items seized—besides all the requisite materials with which to make pipe bombs—was a stack of neo-Nazi magazines, amongst them several copies of Blood & Honour's *Division Deutschland*. In issue no. 2 from the year 1996 an article titled "Politics" made the following call to arms:

> You do not have to sit in your own four walls and wait for the insurrection by candlelight ... If we succeed—with imagination and humor, but also with the necessary determination and seriousness—to become an unassailable, well-networked movement of independently acting groups, fate will not deny us victory. But we mustn't wait for a guide to show up at some point, for someone to always come and say what needs to be done. No! Everyone is called to do something! LEADERLESS RESISTANCE is the motto![88]

Leaderless Resistance—a non-hierarchical, cell-oriented approach to conducting militant action—had been popularized in a 1992 article written by Louis L. Beam of the American KKK, though Beam first formulated the idea in 1984 and had borrowed from much earlier sources.[89] Beam's doctrine initially found appeal amongst US-based militia groups such as the KKK, Aryan Nations, and the Aryan Brotherhood prison gang—which, though disparate in their historical and political origins, had by the early 1980s integrated into a nationwide White Power movement united around conspiracy theory-fueled opposition toward the federal government.[90] By the mid-1990s it had also spread via the encrypted online messaging forums of the white supremacist underworld such as LibertyNet, Stormfront, and the Germany-based ThuleNetz, and was earnestly discussed as a political tactic in the pages of neo-Nazi magazines and "field manuals" throughout the United States and Europe.

Beam had identified the nascent internet early on as the perfect vehicle for diffusion of command and control across a vast network of white supremacist gangs and organizations, and also as a means to recruit disparate individuals to the movement. Having taken LibertyNet nationwide in 1985, Beam waxed futurist in an essay titled "Computers and the American Patriot":

> Finally, we are all going to be linked together at one point in time. Imagine, if you will, all the great minds of the patriotic Christian movement linked together and joined to one computer. Imagine any patriot in the country being able to call up and access these minds ... You are online with the Aryan Nations brain trust. It is here to serve the folk [*sic*].[91]

Beam's internet compendium of recruitment materials, including an "index on traitors" and an assassination "point system," as well as a pen-pal match program to put white supremacists in touch with one another, had by the end of the decade inspired other networks which used newer technologies.[92] One important example still highly active up until 2017 is Stormfront, which began in 1990 as a bulletin board system (BBS) and was transformed into a full website in 1996 by KKK leader Donald Black. By the late 1990s the World Wide Web had become commercially available throughout Europe, including in Germany, and right-wing extremists were amongst the first to dial up. As terrorism and intelligence expert James Adams acknowledged already in 1997:

> The arrival of the Internet has provided the first forum in history for all the disaffected to gather in one place to exchange views and reinforce prejudices. It is hardly surprising, for example, that the right-wing militias' favourite method of communication is e-mail and that forums on the Internet are the source of many wild conspiracy theories that drive the media.[93]

In Germany, Karl-Heinz Sendbuhler of the NPD identified email and other forms of internet communication technology as advantageous to telephone and radio communication, writing on ThuleNetz that "the advantage of electronic mailboxes is that they are free of censorship and bug-proof." In this manner the NPD had been able to use this new form of covert communication and anonymity to plan neo-Nazi actions as early as 1993.[94]

Above all, the internet worked to further the project of Leaderless Resistance. "It is time … for a voice unhindered by loyalty to a single Klan or leader," Beam had written in 1985.[95] As with the US White Power movement, the concept of Leaderless Resistance served as a unifying force between formerly oppositional neo-Nazi groups in Europe; by the 2000s, Blood & Honour, Combat 18, and the German branches of the Hammerskins had set aside earlier rivalries and become an organized, pan-European network with connections to their US counterparts. These three groups in particular established divisions throughout Germany, with the NPD party serving as an important facilitator of events, funding, and communications—as well as operating as the political arm of the neo-Nazi militia movement. Crucial to the functioning of this global terror network was a shared ethos of racial hatred and white supremacy—a guiding *idea* rather than a guiding leader, ideologue, or group. As the 2013 parliamentary enquiry into the NSU iterates, the source of this idea—beyond Beam's doctrine or the rhetoric circulating on internet bulletin boards—was the notorious *Turner Diaries*, written in 1978 by American right-wing extremist William Luther Pierce. While the *Turner Diaries* predated Beam's adoption of the concept of Leaderless

Resistance, it intricately and in violent, graphic detail fictionalized a future dystopia in which disparate cells of white supremacists take up armed resistance against the US federal government in a race war which eventually turns global.[96] The text circulated at gun shows in the United States throughout the 1980s and was available by mail order from National Alliance, the West Virginia neo-Nazi militia founded by Pierce, and has long been considered the most widely distributed and read book in the global right-wing extremist scene. By the 1990s, PDF and raw text copies of the *Turner Diaries* had spread amongst the neo-Nazi scene in Germany; one such file was found on Mundlos and Böhnhardt's shared hard drive.[97] Advocating attacks on the government as well as symbolic civilian targets, *The Turner Diaries* served as the shared ideological basis on which to act, with Leaderless Resistance as a tactical guide.[98]

Several tactics central to the idea of Leaderless Resistance which appear in various publications known to the German intelligence services long before 2011 describe accurately the strategies employed by the core NSU trio and their wider network of accomplices and allies. The first and most important of these is targeted actions carried out either alone or in small cells, in order to give the deliberate impression that the attacks are being carried out by "lone wolf" perpetrators. One of the reasons for organizing in this manner is so that neo-Nazi factions striving for political legitimacy—far-right fringe parties, for example—do not lose their credibility by association with terrorism. As Scandinavian right-wing extremist Erik Nilsen (alias "Max Hammer") put it in the Blood & Honour *Field Manual*, a copy of which was found amongst the NSU trio's belongings:

> In Scandinavia—especially in Sweden and Denmark—there are currently well-organized Nazi movements that know what is important. They are willing to work legally if "democracy" will let them. But they are also willing to change their *modus operandi* when there is no other option. Unity means strength, and a movement of strong lone warriors, provided it is well organized, multiplies that strength by the number of its members. On the other hand, some comrades work best on their own. Their actions are designed to require absolute anonymity. No organization could take responsibility for this without losing its legal status forever.[99]

Nilsen went on to instruct that in the event of an apparent attack perpetrated by a neo-Nazi comrade, although distance is required for strategic reasons, honor within the community is to be granted: "These lone white wolves must be respected and left alone to bring down our race's worst enemies."[100] The manifesto of UK terror group Combat 18, also closely connected with the network surrounding the NSU, stressed the strategic superiority of "lone wolf" actions, though allowed for the formation of small cells of highly reliable individuals.[101] In addition, in 2002 Combat 18 proposed a shift away from attempted assassinations of high-profile figures such as politicians, judges, and public prosecutors—targets which represented the so-called "Zionist Occupation Government" (ZOG) believed to be in control of global liberal democracies—due to the slim chances of success. Instead, the new targets were to be "antifas, drug dealers, foreign pimps and criminals, as well as one or the other small business owner who mainly employs cheap foreign labour." The advantage to this, according to Combat 18, was that "nobody would cry" over these victims and that "The search pressure from ZOG would not be very great either"[102]—a chillingly accurate assessment, considering the missteps taken by the German security services throughout SoKo Bosporus.

The 2013 parliamentary enquiry reveals that publications such as the ones quoted above were long known to German domestic intelligence agencies as well as the Federal Government, yet do not seem to have been taken seriously as earnest tactical manuals for armed political resistance.[103] In 2002 the *Field Manual* of Blood & Honour, as well as another of the group's brochures titled *The Way Forward*, was used by the German Federal Ministry of the Interior in order to justify the banning of Blood & Honour on German soil. The BfV nevertheless considered, at the time, the *Field Manual* to be only the "private opinion" of Nilsen, who lived in Sweden, and concluded that its impact or potential implementation within the German division of Blood & Honour was "not a given."[104] In 2012—with grave hindsight—the BfV acknowledged its mistake, finding parallels between the instructions published in these publications and the actions of the NSU trio, including "assassination attempts on people with a migration background—without having had a personal connection to these people; bank robberies for self-financing; escape by bike; living with false identities" and a planned escape abroad, which was never followed through.[105] In addition, the NSU revelations of 2011 prompted the BfV to renew its assessment of the threat posed by the NPD party and its deep entanglements with international neo-Nazi militia groups.

"Leaderless Resistance" Part II: The NPD and the Far-Right Community

While the NSU trio received direct backing—including weapons—from members of Blood & Honour as well as Combat 18, the German state of Thuringia was home to the terror cell's most involved support network.[106]

Founded by prominent neo-Nazi and NPD state chairman Ralf Wohlleben and fellow NPD members André Kapke and Holger Gerlach in 1995, the Thüringer Heimatschutz—and its smaller, local branch Kameradschaft Jena—grew out of the milieu that had formed in the very early 1990s around a youth club in Jena known as the Winzerclub, where Mundlos, Böhnhardt, and Zschäpe first met. Though Wohlleben, Kapke, and Gerlach were all born in Jena around the same time as the terror trio, they were of a distinctly more political mindset than many of their neo-Nazi peers, having immediately integrated themselves into the NPD as it opened its first East German branches during 1990. The Winzerclub was initially formed as a right-wing radical alternative to the left-wing youth clubs which still populated the eastern states in the years of the GDR's collapse and integration into the FRG.

In these early years, the culture of the Winzerclub largely concerned opposition to left-wing politics; apart from the relatively small number of foreigners who inhabited Jena, left-wing punks were a primary target of angry skinhead youths, who picked fights, organized "anti-antifa" riots, and formed music groups of a genre known as "Rock Against Communism." In 1995, however, Wohlleben, Kapke, and Gerlach's Thüringer Heimatschutz had consolidated the most devoted of this neo-Nazi milieu and aimed their sights higher, targeting state institutions in their propaganda. The eventual goal of the Heimatschutz—which it shared with the NPD—was to instigate broad political change at a national scale in the direction of the far-right. While the Heimatschutz operated mostly as an underground subculture, it also sought integration with the NPD. By 1999 the Heimatschutz had established considerable influence within both the state and district associations of the NPD, with seven out of twelve members of the party's state board belonging to the Heimatschutz, as well as four out of twelve district chairmen.[107]

Wohlleben, Gerlach, and accomplices André Eminger and Carsten Schultze are the only four figures to be prosecuted along with Zschäpe in the NSU trials (Kapke was summoned as a witness), for their undeniable involvement in facilitating the trio's terrorist acts and helping them to immerse themselves in hiding.[108] When the trio went underground in 1998, these men organized solidarity concerts in order to raise money for the purchase of false identity papers; they made discrete wire transfers to the trio and found temporary places for them to live; and they provided the famed Česká weapon. However, in the duration of the court trials authorities estimated there to be as many as 129 people assumed part of the close inner circle of the NSU, many of them belonging to the Heimatschutz, the NPD, Blood & Honor, Combat 18, or the Hammerskins.[109] It is almost impossible to disentangle the German branches of these groups from one-another; as terrorism expert Koehler has noted, in contrast to previous assumptions that neo-Nazi groups exist in a tense rivalry between one another, "multiple group affiliations" are in fact a distinguishing feature of modern right-wing extremist organizations, and this networking "serves a distinct strategic purpose."[110] Kapke, Wohlleben, and Gerlach—the latter of whom was a well-connected neo-Nazi music promoter—were pivotal figures in the organization of a vast social and political network around the core three members of the NSU.[111]

Kameradschaft Jena/the Thüringer Heimatschutz had provided a central space in which young Thuringians became socialized into the neo-Nazi scene. Tom T., who sang in the neo-Nazi band Vergeltung ("Retribution") and, along with Mundlos, Böhnhardt, and Zschäpe, was a founding member of Kameradschaft Jena, recalled during his 2015 witness statement that socialization was key to his immersion into the neo-Nazi scene, rather than any prior political commitment. "I got into the group and it took on a momentum of its own. I didn't fall from the sky as a right-wing radical, it went step by step; hair cut shorter, bomber jacket bought. It was just a youth movement and I disappeared [from it] a few years later."[112] When asked by leading judge Manfred Götzl to describe the political activities of Kameradschaft Jena, T. recalled vaguely: "It was about the foreigner problem [*Ausländerproblematik*], unemployment, young people hanging out on the street, being left hanging in the air, that's how you felt back then and so you did something."[113] Thousands of youths such as T. were drawn to a thriving new subculture of neo-Nazi music, dress code, and hatred of non-white races—a scene which had grown significantly in capacity and organizational sophistication since the early 1990s. By the 2000s, large-scale music festivals were held in Jena, organized by Wohlleben and NPD Thuringia. "Thuringia National Youth Day" in 2002, "Rock für Deutschland" in 2003, and "Festival of Nations: For a Europe of Fatherlands," ongoing since 2005, not only provided important spaces for socialization and affective solidarity but were also political events in the eyes of NPD organizers, the purpose of which was to assemble and radicalize.

In the early 2000s the NPD embarked on a propaganda campaign dubbed "Project Schoolyard" which targeted high school pupils in particular, manually distributing 50,000 neo-Nazi music CDs in 2004 alone within the vicinity of schools throughout Germany. The CDs featured songs of a nationalistic, antisemitic, and racist attitude, and sometimes even aimed directly at hijacking elections; during the 2004 state elections in Saxony, for example, the NPD burned its own compilation CD of skinhead music titled "Fed Up? Election Day is Payday!"[114] The BfV noted a steady increase in skinhead bands, magazines, and concerts throughout 2002, 2003, and 2004. Via the propagated concept of a "German People's Front," the NPD played an increasing role in the consolidation of disparate right-wing extremist youth groups who were violent in nature and in rhetoric, integrating leading neo-Nazis into its party structure.[115] The Hammerskins and Blood & Honour—both of which were record labels as well as militant organizations—also organized neo-Nazi concerts in Germany during the 2000s, bringing together acts such as Bound for Glory, who were from the United States; Brutal Attack (UK); Frakass (France); Jungsturm, from southwestern Germany, and Division Germania, from the north-east.[116]

The fusing of these two organizations and their respective subcultures with the NPD formed a neo-Nazi "superstructure" skilled at conspiratorial practices.[117] In order to get around German prohibitions on media deemed "harmful to young persons," for example, music promoters used clandestine online file sharing systems and forums such as Thiazi.net (since defunct) to distribute music, and left trails of misinformation concerning the date, location, and the nature of neo-Nazi concerts.[118] The website for Wohlleben's 2002, 2003, and 2005 festivals would display the lineup of music acts as well as a program of political speakers long in advance, but ticketholders had to wait to be contacted by email or SMS just a few days before the festival in order to find out the location.[119] Yet despite the BfV's growing awareness of the neo-Nazi music scene's organizational sophistication, as well as the importance of the scene for forging affective bonds of solidarity, stoking violent energies, and intoxicating youths with a sense of power and purpose, very little could occur at the legislative level apart from the occasional ban on particular bands.[120] The scene as a whole had begun to thrive with a determined political energy.

The NPD in the eastern states of Thuringia, Saxony, and Mecklenburg-Vorpommern were by no means covert about the party's association with the neo-Nazi music scene. An illustrative example of this is the notorious "Thinghaus" (a medieval term which roughly translates as "community house") in the tiny village of Jamel, near Grevesmühlen, Mecklenburg-Vorpommern, which—besides being a popular neo-Nazi music venue—has also served as an office space for NPD parliamentary chairman Udo Pastörs and regional head Stefan Körster until at least 2014.[121] The Thinghaus is not glamorous, consisting of a moderate-sized barn, its name fixed over the entrance in medieval German typeface, located behind a shoddy picket fence in an overgrown patch of grass at the center of the "neo-Nazi village" of Jamel. A newer-build "office" extension to the back of the original barn is decorated on one exterior wall with a mural depicting an Aryan peasant family swaddled by the protective wings of a bronze eagle—an image taken directly from a 1930s Nazi Party propaganda poster.[122] An Imperial-era flag flies out front, accompanied by a flag emblazoned with the NPD logo. Though Jamel is small, the BfV has classified the Thinghaus as an "example of networking between the NPD, neo-Nazis and a structural right-wing extremist scene."[123] The Thinghaus is also the seat of several smaller groups associated with the NPD, including the Jungen Nationaldemokraten Mecklenburg und Pommern (Young National Democrats of Mecklenburg and Pomerania; JN MuP), the Rings Nationaler Frauen (National Women's Ring; RNF), and the Gemeinschaft Deutscher Frauen (Community of German Women; GdF)—all youth and women's offshoots of the main party—as well as the online news portal MUPinfo, and holds events ranging from music shows to internal meetings and "lecture" events.[124]

The formation of these subgroups within the NPD constellation indicates the new directions the far-right scene was moving in, by the end of the 1990s. Having directed effort toward the recruitment of disaffected, angry youths in the eastern states during the *Wende* years, the NPD presided over a well-organized far-right society that held space for women and included them in important organizational roles, and also renewed its focus on a youth wing modeled on the Hitler Youth. The aim was to raise a generation of disciplined young soldiers who could be counted upon to operate independently toward the shared will of the party (i.e., Leaderless Resistance). As the NPD's Wolfgang Bendel put it in 1991, "the Jungen Nationaldemokraten must become an activist, highly mobile, completely de-bureaucratized, autonomous group of political militants."[125] While the JN has existed since 1969, the addition in 1991 of the Junge Landsmannschaft Ostpreußen (Young Fraternity of East Prussia; JLO), which focused on the paramilitary training of its recruits, signaled that the NPD was now explicitly aiming its sights toward militant action. Following the federal government's ban of the militant Wiking-Jugend (Viking Youth) in 1994—to which no other neo-Nazi group compared, in terms of emphasis on paramilitary training—the NPD began to train the JLO as its "front line" cadre, with intensive theoretical lectures and military-style instruction a central element of its program. By 1999 there were branches of the JLO established throughout most of the federal states.[126]

Women's right-wing extremist groups, meanwhile, had undergone their own evolution. The GdF was one of the first such groups to emerge out of the small, self-organized skingirl scene of the early 1990s. Skingirls tended to stick close to the neo-Nazi music scene, forming connections with members of Blood &

Honour. Since the official establishment of the GdF in 2001, more than forty other women's organizations have modeled themselves on this group. The RNF, for example, was established in 2006 as a sub-organization of the NPD. Founded by Saxony MP Gitta Schüßler, Lower Saxony NPD member Katharina Becker, and Judith Rothefrom of NPD Saxony-Anhalt, the RNF not only served a "mouthpiece for women of the NPD" but also sought to recruit "national-minded, non-partisan women" as members.[127] The underestimated significance of women's autonomous involvement in far-right politics and violent actions aside,[128] the broader picture that this evolving network of organizations illustrates is that into the 2000s the far-right was finding it more and more possible to establish itself as an ethnically defined community. The NPD's white supremacist ideology in this sense forecast the racist *Familienpolitik* (family policies) of the AfD party to come, with an ethnopluralist framework increasingly used to conceptualize the far-right vision for a Europe of sovereign ethno-states.

The use of ethnopluralist language within the NPD's events programs indicates a nexus point between the intellectual Neue Rechte and the militant neo-Nazi fringe, as encapsulated in Wohlleben's 2005 "Festival of Nations: For a Europe of Fatherlands." The festival brought together as many as 1,500[129] nationalists from all over Europe in a shared crusade against globalization, understood as the "disenfranchisement" of sovereign states "disguised as an EU constitution." The now-defunct webpage for "Festival of Nations" displayed a call to arms translated into more than a dozen European languages, arguing for the legitimacy of ethnopluralism as a form of foreign policy. "We nationalists are not xenophobes as the press likes to claim," the page reasoned; "we respect every culture and every person, but we believe that every person and every culture has its traditional place in this world, which must also be respected by everyone."[130] This deceitful reworking of *völkisch* ideology emphasized the international nature that right-wing extremism had taken on since the early 1990s. Although the ethnopluralist movement was still, in the early 2000s, confined to the fringes, it's call for an anti-EU alliance across cultural and geographical divides ("We are the youth of Europe, a different Europe than the EU aristocrats in Maastricht and their culture-destroying vassals"[131]) would in the 2010s become widely adopted by a growing pan-European Identitarian movement.[132]

Thus did a racist opposition toward so-called *multi-kulti* society, once confined to neo-Nazi circles, find broad popular appeal via the avenues of mainstream politics. Even the Thüringer Heimatschutz, on a webpage which disappeared shortly after the NSU revelations of 2011, had by then begun to parrot this language: "The establishment of a multicultural society is one of the greatest crimes that has been committed against humanity. It equals the systematic extermination of cultural identities and thus entire peoples."[133] If it was difficult for the intelligence services to envisage the mainstream growth of this worldview in just a few short years, it should at least have been aware that the far-right scene surrounding the NPD, Blood & Honour, and Combat 18 would produce from its decentralized midst a fatal terror attack. As the 2013 parliamentary enquiry notes in several places, the BfV had knowledge of the import of Leaderless Resistance, the *Turner Diaries*, and the presence of foreign neo-Nazi groups on German soil. In fact, the BfV had been gathering this kind of intelligence through its inside informant program since 1992, when the incidents in Rostock-Lichtenhagen provoked new awareness of the breadth of the neo-Nazi scene, particularly in the eastern states. The mishandling of this informant program not only underpinned the failure of federal and state detectives to link the Česká murder series to the NSU trio—it also resulted, for complex bureaucratic reasons, in successive legislative failure to ban the NPD.

The *V-Mann* Affairs, "Operation Rennsteig," and the BfV

There is essentially no equivalent to the BfV anywhere else in the world. That an intelligence agency should, each year, compile and make openly available to the public a detailed report on domestic threats to the constitution, in particular threats from neo-Nazi and white supremacist groups, is an unparalleled mark of progress and democratic transparency. Because of this, however, it is especially confounding and disturbing that the BfV acted with such little transparency regarding its program of inside informants (*V-Männer*). The *V-Mann* program had since the 1960s provided the BfV with crucial information on the activities of militant fringe parties like the NPD, as well as the network surrounding Michael Kühnen in the 1970s, '80s, and early '90s, and the Thüringer Heimatschutz and its international allies throughout the '90s and 2000s. It had also, however, walked a thin line between constitutionality and implication in right-wing extremist crime, as the courts and the public would discover when shocking information came to light regarding the failings of the informant program at the cost of taxpayer money. This scandal first arose in the course of a legislative attempt to ban the NPD between 2001 and 2003 and was revisited ten years later when the NSU case prompted renewed banning attempts in 2011 and 2012.

The use of informants is ethically fraught and strategically risky. By their nature as double agents, informants tend to be unreliable—as was the case with Operation Rennsteig, in which informants from within the Thüringer Heimatschutz employed by the BfV from 1996 to 2003 used their inside knowledge of ongoing intelligence cases in order to report back to their friends and enable them to plan their activities accordingly. Moreover, the closer an informant is to the criminal group being monitored—and the better access they have to information about this group—the more likely they are to have a hand in the criminal activities of the group. Such was the case with Tino Brandt, a leading member of the Thüringer Heimatschutz and the BfV's most prized informant during Operation Rennsteig, who used his double agent status to warn friends and to ensure that his own crimes stayed clandestine enough to avoid prosecution. One of the reasons why informant programs are so sensitive is that intelligence officers who handle informants must continuously make decisions about whether to let transgressions slide or whether—and when—to intervene. Ultimately, the BfV's fear of losing informants seems to have prevailed over the bureau's good conscience.

The first "V-Mann affair" lasted from 2001 to 2003, long before the German public knew of the NSU, who at the time had only just begun their spate of racially motivated killings. German prosecutors and the public at large first became aware of the BfV's morally fraught informant program during a legislative initiative to ban the NPD led by Bavarian interior minister Günther Beckstein, when Wolfgang Frenz, vice chairman of the NPD's North Rhine-Westphalia branch, was invited to give testimony at the Federal Constitutional Court in Karlsruhe.[134] During the court hearing Frenz revealed that for thirty-six years up until 1995 he had provided information about the inner workings of the NPD in his role as a first-class double agent for the BfV, for which he was paid around 1.6 million Deutsch Marks by his own estimation.[135] The BfV had initiated *V-Mann* contracts with far-right actors as early as 1961—three years before various neo-Nazi and far-right groups would consolidate to found the NPD—an intelligence tactic by no means unusual in itself, but one that many members of the German public were not aware of.[136] In the wake of Frenz's testimony, evidence sourced from within the government showed that since 1995 approximately 30 of the NPD's 200 officials had been informants for the BfV.[137]

Udo Holtmann, the editor-in-chief of NPD party newspaper *Deutsche Stimme* ("German Voice"), was soon revealed to have been another well-paid informant for the BfV from 1978 until the time of the court hearing in 2002.[138] Holtmann had been involved in anti-*Wehrmachtsausstellung* protests in Bielefed—actions which, the press speculated, could well have been carried out on behalf of the state, as neo-Nazi demonstrations are fertile ground to observe and inform on anyone committing acts which violate the constitution.¹³⁹ Such schemes became an embarrassment for the BfV throughout this affair owing to their ultimate fruitlessness. In his statements to the press, Holtmann—who was not invited to give testimony in court—implied that informants are by nature unreliable, profiting at the expense of the BfV and also German taxpayers. Hearing that Frenz had pocketed an estimated 300,000 marks in tax money, Holtmann expressed amusement and remarked: "The Verfassungsschutz could have saved that money. Frenz would have told them irrelevant stories for free."¹⁴⁰ This was the first indication that the *V-Mann* program may have been subverted and misled by its informants.

The fact that so many party members had been on the payroll of the BfV proved an insurmountable bureaucratic hurdle toward proving the constitutional illegitimacy of this openly far-right party. The 2003 legislative attempt to ban the NPD was almost successful, having been approved by both houses of parliament. However, the initiative was ultimately rejected by German courts on the grounds that "The presence of the state at the leadership level makes influence on its aims and activities unavoidable" the use of which created "lack of clarity that can no longer be overcome,"¹⁴¹ according to presiding judge Winifred Hassemer. While only three of seven judges voted to reject the attempt at banning the party, this did not total the two-thirds majority required to proceed. The NPD was, moreover, able to defend itself against the ban by arguing that the reasoning for the party's unconstitutionality was based not only on information handed over by informants, but on reports concerning actions engaged in and instigated—in essence, created—by the informants themselves, at the behest of the BfV.¹⁴² In one sense this was transparently disingenuous and manipulative; as *Der Spiegel* observed of the NPD's tactics, the party "likes to portray itself as persecuted innocence—allegedly radicalized by *agents provocateurs* paid for by the secret services." Voigt himself audaciously claimed that "The circles that pull the NPD into the neo-Nazi corner are informers of the Verfassungsschutz."¹⁴³ On the other hand, NPD leaders could draw on concrete examples of times when the BfV had in fact engineered neo-Nazi gatherings for the purpose of making arrests—such as in 1996 when Thuringian state intelligence had facilitated a neo-Nazi concert in Ebersdorf featuring the bands Chaoskrieger and Midgards Söner. Some of the 1,000 attendees were arrested and interrogated, while BfV informant Tino Brandt pocketed a profit from ticket and CD sales.¹⁴⁴

Brandt became a focal point for scandal and outrage during the NSU trials for his prominent role in aiding the NSU and misleading the BfV during its efforts to monitor the Thüringer Heimatschutz. In spite of the eventual ostracism of

Brandt from his own circle of allies—a sure downside to being marked as a government informant—he nevertheless profited immensely from his protected status. According to a 2012 response by the federal government to questions submitted by MP Martina Renner of Die Linke, between 1994 and 2011 Brandt was investigated thirty-four times for suspected crimes such as sedition, disturbing of the peace, destruction of property, fraud, and formation of a criminal organization—investigative proceedings which were all mysteriously discontinued.[145] Brandt also profited financially from the bungled schemes of the intelligence services. Following the garage raid of January 1998, Thuringian state intelligence used Brandt in an attempt to channel 2,000 DM to Mundlos, Böhnhardt, and Zschäpe—the idea being that they would use the money to purchase fake identification and lead intelligence agents to their whereabouts. The plan failed, and Brandt later claimed, gloatingly, that he had pocketed the money himself and used it to fund neo-Nazi activities. Brandt was not the only informant close to the NSU cell who would profit from this ill-conceived kind of plot; between 1994 and 2000, Thuringian state intelligence alone spent the equivalent of €1.5 million in wages for neo-Nazi informants.[146]

The information provided by *V-Männer* did sometimes lead somewhere. Following a tip, in October 1997 the BfV conducted a raid at a restaurant in Heilsberg, Thuringia, which was being used by the Heimatschutz as a logistics center. Agents confiscated 4 modified alarm guns (like the Italian Bruni used by the NSU), 52 batons, 9 knives, 8 axes, and 70 improvised stabbing weapons. Fifty-six right-wing extremists were arrested on the suspicion—due to the alarming evidence—that they were building an army.[147] However, it remains mystifying why this did not lead to further comprehension regarding the organized structure and tactical preparedness of the neo-Nazi scene as a whole.

A similar lack of insight transpired regarding the case of informant Carsten Szczepanski, a member of the German KKK who joined the NPD at the request of the authorities. Szczepanski was recruited as an informant in 1995 while still in custody for the 1992 attempted murder of a Nigerian school teacher, who barely survived the brutal attack he was subjected to by Szczepanski and ten other neo-Nazis. Szczepanski received a reduced sentence in exchange for his informant work, and by 1998 had fallen in with Mundlos, Böhnhardt, and Zschäpe.[148] Szczepanski did, in fact, provide the BfV with meaningful information on the trio, though the agency underestimated its importance. In 1998 Szczepanski informed Gordian Meyer-Plath, then an agent for the Saxon domestic intelligence, that the trio—who at the time were wanted for interrogation following the garage raid—were plotting to buy weapons with which to conduct bank raids. At the time, Meyer-Plath simply did not anticipate that the trio might also be plotting something worse.[149]

These multiple scandals which came to light during journalistic coverage of the NSU revelations became the second "*V-Mann* affair," which, as last time, devastated a renewed attempt at banning the NPD prompted by evidence of their tangible connection to far-right terrorism. One of the main preconditions for the ban was the claim that the NPD proved a threat to the democratic order.[150] However, despite NPD's publicly avowed anti-democratic stance, Constitutional Court judges warned in 2012 that "public statements made by NPD politicians who are also informers have 'very limited value' and should not be included as part of a legal case,"[151] which severely restricted the case against the NPD due to how many of its most outspoken members had been working as lackadaisical informants. Public blame for the *V-Mann* fiasco was widely apportioned to interior minister Otto Schily, who was responsible for the BfV's activities at the federal and state level. Schily argued against the judges' warning on the grounds that "the agents were not employees of the state and had been recruited rather than infiltrated as *agents provocateurs*,"[152] that is, that the NPD is not controlled by the BfV. In the end, however, these revelations made it impossible for the case to proceed and all future hearing dates were overturned. Though the party posed an aggressive threat to democracy, many ministers worried that a ban attempt might serve to revive the party, which had in fact been dwindling in membership.[153] A renewed attempt in 2016 also failed.

One final scandal broke out when it emerged in the course of the NSU trials that documents pertaining to Operation Rennsteig had been shredded by a low-level BfV employee—who, the agency maintains, shredded the documents by mistake. Many of the details of Operation Rennsteig were recovered from other files after this was discovered; however, the entire case could not be reconstructed. What does seem to be overwhelmingly clear from the files that remain is that the *V-Mann* operation was largely unsuccessful, as little useful information was gathered.[154] As a result, the BfV and later the Thuringian state government pledged future transparency and granted the parliamentary committee in charge of the federal inquiry full access to files relating to their years-long neo-Nazi probe.[155]

Following the subsequent 2012 resignation of BfV president Heinz Fromm, some news outlets strove to assess the increasingly diverse, militant, and underestimated far-right scene more openly than the BfV apparently had done.[156] As *Deutsche Welle* pointed out, revelations about the NSU and its wider network demonstrated that "the risks of the far-right were widely underestimated" previously.¹⁵⁷ Certainly, before the NSU revelations neither state nor federal intelligence had made the connection between classic cell-based terror structures and right-wing extremism. While in early 2011 the BfV had stated publicly that it "had not noticed any terrorist structures in the far-right scene,"¹⁵⁸ the BfV's annual report for that year—released in early 2012 amidst the scandal and public outrage that surrounded the agency—described a process beginning in the 1990s by which "far-right extremism has become younger, more active, and more militant."¹⁵⁹ The 2011 BfV report began with a somewhat flimsy *mea culpa* from then Interior Minister Hans-Peter Friedrich, who acknowledged that many in both the public and political spheres were questioning the BfV's role and capabilities in the aftermath of the NSU revelations. "There is nothing to gloss over in this respect," he admitted:

> In addition to a number of successes to which the Office for the Protection of the Constitution can refer, it is a painful failure that it was not possible to identify the right-wing extremist motivation of the violent perpetrators [of the Česká murders] at an early stage in order to provide the investigating authorities with the right search approach.¹⁶⁰

Friedrich went on to voice his agreement that the BfV required restructuring at the federal and state levels. He nevertheless took the opportunity to congratulate the BfV on having recently thwarted an Islamist cell, and expressed his particular concern that left-wing radicalism was up 20 percent compared with the previous year, while right-wing extremism had remained the same.¹⁶¹ Altogether the language of the 2011 report itself is quite paradoxical: while the BfV long had knowledge of the far-right scene, its structures, and its overlap with reactionary and anti-democratic political parties like the NPD, the agency still somehow underestimated the dangers this posed, tending to reserve the term "terrorism" for the NSU in particular, when not referring to Islamist terror, and never in connection to other far-right groups.¹⁶²

Coda: Confronting the Present

In February 2012, three months after the RV explosion and apartment fire which would lead to the trio's murders being uncovered, a memorial service for the ten victims was held at Berlin's Konzerthaus.¹⁶³ The victims' relatives were present along with 1,200 attendees, and Chancellor Angela Merkel gave a speech in which she asked forgiveness from the families of those murdered. Much of this speech was as mawkish as the candle-lit ceremony itself, extoling the virtues of Germany's own Basic Law in which human dignity is enshrined as "inviolable" and which, Merkel reminded her audience, was ratified in response to the experience of twelve years of National Socialism. "Whenever people in our country are marginalized, threatened or persecuted," she stressed, "the values of our Basic Law are attacked. The murders committed by the terrorist cell from Thuringia were therefore also an attack on our country. They are a disgrace for our country."[164] This was by now the typical response of German diplomats and politicians in the wake of racially motivated or right-wing extremist attacks, that is, lip service paid to the ostensible legacy of lesson-learning in Germany and commitment to human rights and freedoms as well as diversity and inclusivity, while treating the far-right as either anomalous within this culture, or as an attack from outside of it. Although Merkel did reflect upon the "creeping and invidious" effects of indifference to racially motivated violence and announced the establishment of a Federal-to-State commission to examine the social causes of right-wing extremism (which at this stage was localized to Thuringia alone), she did not mention any plans to investigate the security services, which she herself acknowledged had wrongly pursued the victims' relatives as suspects.[165]

One of the only two relatives to give a speech at the February 2012 memorial service was Semiya Şimşek, who was fourteen years old when her father, Enver Şimşek, was executed by the NSU in 2000. Şimşek offered a powerful corrective to Merkel's lengthy, platitude-driven speech in the four minutes she was allotted on stage, addressing head-on the racism that her family and others were subjected to by the authorities. "The families I am speaking for here today know what I am talking about," she said. "For eleven years we weren't even allowed to be victims with a clear conscience. Always, there lay the burden over our lives that maybe someone in our family might be responsible for my father's death." Her father had been suspected of drug dealing, and her mother was treated as a murder suspect throughout the investigation—allegations that, Şimşek reminded those present, were made "out of thin air."

> My father was murdered by neo-Nazis. Should this knowledge reassure me now? The opposite is the case: Born, raised, and firmly rooted in this country, I never thought about integration. Today I stand here, not only mourning my father, but also tormenting myself with the question: Am I at home in Germany?
>
> Yes, of course I am. But how can I be sure of that when there are people who don't want me here and who become murderers just because my parents come from a foreign country? Should I go? No, that can't be a solution. Or should I console myself with the fact that probably only individuals are willing to do such deeds? That too cannot be a solution.[166]

Evoking the same tenets of equality and human dignity that Merkel's speech had leant on, Şimşek urged those listening not to "pretend we have already achieved this goal."[167] Certainly, the following decade would see ongoing attempts to subvert this goal by increasingly political and ideologically complex far-right elements, indicating that the German present, rather than its past, was in need of confrontation.

5

VOLK

PEGIDA, the AfD, and the Disruptive Tactics of the New-New Right

The past decade has witnessed a new era of right-wing extremism: stylized, tech-savvy, skilled at self-promotion, and increasingly mainstream. For Germany, the defining outcome of this new wave of activity is the success of the Alternative für Deutschland (AfD) party—the first far-right party to enter the German Parliament in the history of the Federal Republic. Like other right-wing populist parties of its kind—UKIP/the Brexit Party, the Italian Lega, the Rassemblement National in France, and the US Republican Party under Donald Trump—the AfD has brought the anti-Immigration, pro-traditional family policy language of organizations like PEGIDA (Patriotische Europäer gegen die Islamisierung des Abendlandes), and the pan-European Identitarian movement into the mainstream. Much of the AfD's platform overlaps with, and thus strengthens, those of these far-right street protest groups. The success of the AfD represents a disquieting shift amongst German voters and demonstrates the potency of what might be called the crusade of a Neue-Neue Rechte—a New-New Right. Until the AfD's stunning victory in the federal elections of 2017, far-right parties generally were unable to establish themselves in German politics or to overcome the 5 percent threshold necessary to win parliamentary representation in federal elections; the small feats of parties like the NPD or the REP had been sporadic and localized.[1] The AfD's recent victory in Thuringia, where it has won its first ever district council election (with 52.8 percent of the vote), demonstrates the party's sustained appeal—particularly in eastern states.[2]

Left-liberal scholars, politicians, and journalists alike have scrambled to find a straightforward explanation for the unanticipated success of the AfD. For one thing, when the party first made its entrance into German politics on an economics-based, anti-EU platform in 2013, political and social scientists debated where to place the AfD on the political spectrum.³ Since the party's internal split in 2015 and subsequent radicalization, however, the AfD has been easier to characterize as a far-right populist party. One particular narrative which has emerged from analysis of polling data has been the familiar insistence that, once again, the problem lies in the eastern states, which remains a stronghold of anti-migrant sentiment and neo-Nazi activity.⁴ There is considerable salience to this: on top of the fact that the street protest group PEGIDA was established in Dresden and has been most active throughout eastern German cities, voting data illustrates that the bulk of support for the AfD party also comes from the eastern states.⁵ While academic scholarship on the former GDR has shifted, in recent years, to strongly critique the Federal Republic's founding myth of having twice overcome totalitarianism, as well as narratives that regard the eastern states as liminal spaces "forever trapped in the incomplete moment of democratic awakening,"⁶ as Anselma Gallinat has put it, political analysis of the past decade has tended to lean into precisely this as the explanation for AfD's success.

What this analysis has often missed, or failed to engage with closely, is that the politics exemplified by the AfD, PEGIDA, and the Europe-wide Identitarian movement does not so much represent a *failure* of democratic enlightenment as it does a deliberate, ecstatic *rejection* of liberal democracy. As Adam Serwer shrewdly observed in the context of Trumpism in the United States and its attachment to a long national history of white supremacist violence, the politics of racial exclusion which has so motivated the right-wing populisms of the late 2010s and beyond finds its expression in the jubilant lampooning of perceived racial and political enemies. Both Trump's supporters in the United States and those who march at PEGIDA rallies in Germany "find community by rejoicing in the suffering of those they hate and fear."⁷ This is not because they simply know no better, as tireless "barbarians at the gate" political takes have implied.⁸ Rather, for populations neglected by the swift developments of the market-driven economy of the 1990s and 2000s, who have watched a technocratic elite champion a globalizing politics of humanitarianism while disenfranchising ever more obsolete forms of industry, the ostensible promises of liberal democracy have come to seem more like condescending sermons.⁹

Marcus Böick's recent sociological research into East German memories of the *Treuhandanstalt*—a federal commission tasked with the liquidation of the GDR's industries, following reunification—demonstrates that former GDR citizens recall the process of entering democracy as one of deep economic trauma.¹⁰ It is in large part for this reason that the AfD and PEGIDA have been able to orchestrate a successful campaign in memory politics with 1989 at its heart; PEGIDA even referred to their early demonstrations, in 2014 and 2015, as *Montagsdemonstrationen*—protest marches that, referring back to the social-democratic Monday demonstrations of 1989–90, demanded a democracy for "real" Germans which had been denied to them during reunification. On top of this, as Michael Wildt has observed, these groups and their followers relish the resurrection of an ethnically defined idea of national identity and belonging—i.e., a *Volksgemeinschaft*.[11] This specifically German taboo, at once a politics of racial exclusion and a revival of traditional family values, is also an exhilarating and deliberate slap in the face to left-liberals who champion a culture of historical consciousness, diversity, and progressiveness. Together the resentments of 1989 and the thrill of breaking cultural taboos relating to the Nazi past form the basis of today's Neue Rechte politics of memory. While liberal observers have fretted over an apparent crisis of democracy and climate of hostility toward asylum seekers and migrants, the rhetorical power of breaking taboos—the delight in transgressing a perceived culture of moral conformity—is fundamentally what motivates AfD, PEGIDA, and their followers; as Serwer puts it, the cruelty is the point.

Misdirection, disinformation, and chaos are also the point—deliberate political tactics which give rise to a sense of whiplash amongst left-liberals who take for granted neat, binary political distinctions and reliable notions of truth. This earnestness has become a particular target for mockery amongst the Neue Rechte, which has embarked on a campaign against the stability of truth itself. A program of so-called "lateral" or diagonal politics first seen in the 1990s, when numerous left-wing public figures defected to the intellectual milieu of the Neue Rechte (as seen in Chapter 2 of this book), has by now reached an epistemologically chaotic culmination in the social media age, as exemplified by the updated "media guerrilla" tactics of an extremely online ultra-right, as well as movements such as *Querdenken* ("lateral thinking") and the US-based Q-Anon.[12] The instability of truth, confusion regarding what is knowable, i.e., the notion of "fake news" as a salient vehicle for anxiety and paranoia, and a challenge to the "tyranny of experts"[13] indicate that right-wing postmodernism has reached its dizzying zenith.

The prospect of epistemic collapse even seems to excite a new generation of ideologically nebulous intellectuals; German-Iranian sociologist Armin Nassehi proclaimed in his 2015 work *Die letzte Stunde der Wahrheit* ("The Last Hour of Truth") that, while it might often seem that we are living in times of deep polarization, in fact left and right are no longer alternatives to one another at all. It is time, he says, to describe society completely differently: "The fact that something is right or left, conservative or progressive contains less and less information."[14] Nassehi, who has formed close contact with Götz Kubitschek (he claims that their correspondence is a sociological experiment), argues that the apparent effect of polarization is produced by the sense that one is living in a world that is becoming ever more complex, the lines of conflict ever blurrier, with the result that the masses cling to the only visible fragments of an obscure whole. Nassehi calls this "social digitization"—the erosion of meaning, especially the meaning of left-right distinctions.[15] The mistake here might be to take such an idea at face value rather than to recognize disruption and "lateral politics" for the strategies that they are. While a trend that began with those left-wing apostates to the Neue Rechte during the 1990s might seem to have become our political reality, this hopefully does not necessarily mean that politics are devolving irretrievably into chaos—nor, certainly, is it a welcome form of progress, as Nassehi claims. Nevertheless, it characterizes the latest stage in the evolution of the Neue Rechte.

The Neue-Neue Rechte: Political Disruption and a New *Volkskörper*

In the rural East German village of Steigra, Saxony-Anhalt, right-wing extremist organizer Götz Kubitschek—now a leading figure of the Neue Rechte—has since 2014 regularly held court for audiences comprising the next generation of Germany's far-right. The name of his estate, Schnellroda Manor, has become synonymous with a new wave of young, fired-up activists who, rather than considering themselves analogous to the combat boot-wearing skinheads of the 1990s and early 2000s, attend Kubitschek's lectures in the hope of enlightening themselves to a conservative intellectual tradition.[16] A far cry from the NPD Thinghaus at Jamel with its Nazi mural walls, Schnellroda cuts as quaint and bucolic an appearance as any other of Steigra's historical buildings, painted in that very particular shade of Hohenzollern yellow still ubiquitous throughout Central Europe. The Schnellroda estate serves not only as the headquarters of Kubitschek's publishing house Antaios, which in addition to publishing the polemics of Neue Rechte and Nouvelle Droite figureheads is also home to Kubitschek's bi-monthly magazine *Sezession*—a name that Kubitschek borrowed from a sentence in Botho Strauß' 1992 "Anschwellender Bocksgesang."[17] It also reminds one faintly of the radical anti-authoritarian *Kommunen* of the 1960s, functioning as a sustainable farmhouse home to Kubitschek and his wife Ellen

Kositza, who keep goats and chickens as well as growing their own produce. Kubitschek situates the ethical treatment of animals and nature at the heart of his deeply conservative values, chiming with the *Blut und Boden* (blood and soil) romanticization of peasant life that the Nazis once established as one of the key elements of their racially defined understanding of the German *Volkskörper* (ethnic body politic).[18]

Kubitschek's Schnellroda seminars are largely attended by the millennial generation of the Neue Rechte, a composite of separate though interrelated groups like PEGIDA, which Kubitschek helped establish alongside official leader Lutz Bachmann in 2014, and the German branch of the pan-European Identitarian movement, which emerged in France in 2012 as an offshoot of the white supremacist Bloc Identitaire. With their deft usage of online media, ability to distort public perception, and stylized clean-cut image, the Identitarians have been dubbed by the global media as "Nazi hipsters."[19] This is one facet of the new tactics employed by the far-right since the NSU revelations tarnished forever the old, hostile aesthetic of skinhead neo-Nazism; the Identitarians by contrast "want to look conservative rather than fascist, insisting that theirs is a healthy patriotism, not worn racism in new clothing."[20] And yet, like Kubitschek, the Identitarian movement's Austrian figurehead Martin Sellner is himself a sanitized neo-Nazi, espousing an aggressively anti-immigrant platform to a younger generation of extremists who prefer to think of themselves as activists. This self-styling as "activism" is another tactic of the Neue-Neue Rechte; both the Identitarians and PEGIDA have, since 2014, taken to the streets of European cities in protest against what they and countless other right-wing extremists across the Western world refer to as "The Great Replacement"—the supposed gradual extinction of the white race and "Islamization" of Europe and the West through increased immigration.[21] One 2018 demonstration took place in the French Alps, with 100 members of various Identitarian branches throughout Europe linking arms to create a human chain, each wearing the movement's official merch (down jackets emblazoned on the back with a logo incorporating a mountain range and the words—in English—"Defend Europe," attire that looked more like skiwear than Nazi regalia), forming a "symbolic border" meant to deter migrants making their way from North Africa.[22]

And yet this tactical approach—framed as the political activism of a clean-cut youth and replete with slickly produced YouTube videos espousing Great Replacement theory and all manner of anti-progressive propaganda—is supplemented with militarized vocabulary and engagement in paramilitary training in camps across Europe.[23] A manual written by Sellner titled "The Art of Redpilling"—referring, in another nod to right-wing postmodernism, to 1999 sci-fi film *The Matrix*—gives instructions on how to radicalize new recruits into the far-right fold.[24] As Julia Ebner of the Institute for Strategic Dialogue has pointed out, while the Identitarian movement "does not publicly endorse violence[…] its members prepare for combat and their training materials read like a call to arms."[25] Many of the retired and serving Bundeswehr soldiers who took part in the paramilitary training groups and encrypted far-right forums covered in Chapter 3 will have first encountered ideas such as the "Great Replacement" via an Identitarian YouTube video or other such online media. PEGIDA's approach is similar; although spokesmen such as Kubitschek profess to eschew extremism, PEGIDA's marches against the supposed "Islamization of the West" often escalate when confronted by antifa counterdemonstrations. Moreover, PEGIDA's messaging is plainly racist. Although it will often drum up mass support by capitalizing on instances of Islamist terror—such as the Charlie Hebdo attacks of January 2015, which prompted some 25,000 people to join a rally organized by PEGIDA in Dresden—its anti-Islam ideology rests upon ethnonationalist assertions about German culture and German identity.

Around the start of the 2010s the European far-right began to radically reorient its political programs, seizing the opportunity to profit from the anxieties of life under a globalized neoliberalism and increased migration.[26] In a sharp change of direction which has produced a sense of disorientation amongst progressives, a new far-rightism has emerged which strategically disavows the overt racism and glorification of Nazi aesthetics practiced by older fringe parties like the NPD. PEGIDA, for example, facetiously adopted a logo which depicts a swastika being thrown into a trashcan, misleadingly aligning its aesthetic with anti-fascism rather than fascism. The ideology espoused by the Identitarian movement, meanwhile, borrows from the intellectualized language of the French Nouvelle Droite to posit that problems concerning the failed integration of non-Western migrants into European society does not lie with a xenophobic or racist West but, rather, with the fundamental incompatibility of Islam and Western Culture.[27] While progressives have decried this argument as classic fascism stemming from an emboldened far-right, ethnopluralist ideas have not always been espoused by the far-right alone. The 2010s saw early on respected public intellectuals and politicians stumbling into controversy by questioning whether Islam is compatible with Western culture, exemplified by SPD politician Thilo Sarrazin's 2010 *Deutschland schafft sich ab* ("Germany Abolishes Itself"). Sarrazin claimed that Muslim immigrants, more than any other migrant group, refuse to "integrate" into German society and willfully emphasize their difference in public, in particular through the enforcement of hijab-wearing for women.²⁸ As with the incendiary writings of Botho Srauß and other left-wing apostates in the 1990s, the outrage over Sarrazin's work was tinged with the feeling that the former Berlin finance senator had betrayed his own political party (he was subsequently expelled from the SPD).

More than this, however, Sarrazin had hit upon an ingenious rhetorical tactic: if part of the problem with Islam could be framed around the narrative that it is an illiberal religion oppressive to women and therefore threatening to progressive sensibilities, leftists and liberals might have a harder time claiming that anti-Islamic political platforms fit squarely into the rubric of fascism. In this manner what is invariably revealed to be a classic continuation of colonial racism gets re-framed as an urgent matter of cultural and civilizational decline.²⁹ A case in point is the Islamophobic campaign posters run by the AfD party in 2017, which belie the ostensible sophistication of their political message by reducing this supposed cultural clash to a battle of burqas versus bikinis while dabbling in shameless sexploitation in the process. Across an image of three slim, white women in bikinis walking along a beach toward the waves, the text of the poster quipped "'Burqas?' We prefer bikinis."³⁰ By painting the burqa as a threat to German women, the AfD here disguises itself as a movement that seeks to defend sexual progressivism. Such tactics have compounded the sense of whiplash amongst progressives as well as scholars earnestly attempting to demonstrate the genuine threat posed by PEGIDA, the Identitarian movement, and the AfD party, all three of which relish in various ways a satirical collapsing of traditional political distinctions.

PEGIDA is, perhaps, the pioneering movement of this tactic. Kubitschek himself had long dabbled in satire; as seen in Chapter 3, he had been honing his sardonic rhetorical style since the writing of his autobiographical novel *Raki am Igman*.³¹ In 2007 Kubitschek attempted to translate satirical rhetoric into praxis, establishing a group called "Konservativ-Subversive Aktion" which mimicked the tactics of the 1960s far-left group Subversive Aktion (which was affiliated with the avant-garde Situationist International) in an attempt to spread far-right positions via offensive and spectacular happenings.³² PEGIDA's ersatz antifa logo could well have been the idea of Kubitschek, who has been a regular speaker at PEGIDA rallies since 2015, and the movement's founding nineteen theses embrace a similar mimicking of left-wing attitudes that ultimately prove disingenuous. For example, while "PEGIDA is FOR taking in war refugees and those who are politically or religiously persecuted" and adds that this is "a human duty!" the movement is also "AGAINST allowing parallel societies/

parallel courts in our midst, such as Sharia courts, Sharia police, Justices of the Peace, etc."—a specter that has haunted the Islamophobic right in many global political campaigns since the early 2010s. Furthermore, "PEGIDA is FOR the resistance against a misogynistic, violent political ideology but not against Muslims living here who are integrating!" and also "AGAINST this insane 'gender mainstreaming,' also often called 'genderization' the almost compulsive, politically correct gender neutralization of our language!"[33] In this manner, PEGIDA claims to align itself with select democratic norms, especially those that protect women from violence, while characterizing Muslim immigrants as a domestic threat from without. A tactic which has also shaped the family and immigration policies of the AfD, PEGIDA here muddles together liberal trends toward gender theory and generous asylum laws, two very separate issues, implying that lack of Muslim integration and "gender mainstreaming" are part of the same concern.

While PEGIDA took its disruptive platform to the streets, the AfD rode the ensuing wave of anti-establishment fervor into the Bundestag. As the first party to enter the German parliament in the history of the Federal Republic with a platform based on anti-immigration policies, ethnic definitions of German identity, and even antisemitism,[34] the AfD party represents the most major political development in the history of the far-right in postwar Germany. With party leaders frequently espousing familiar Neue Rechte rhetoric in eschewal of Germany's culture of remembrance—pejoratively referred to as a "cult of guilt" (*Schuldkult*)—and with party leader Alexander Gauland referring to PEGIDA as the AfD's "natural ally,"[35] the AfD shares a direct lineage with the intellectual Neue Rechte and is clearly the most recent culmination of long-standing far-right political and intellectual trends. However, a facet of today's Neue Rechte and its manifestations in the AfD which has sown confusion amongst liberal commentators and scholars is the tendency to engage in transverse politics—i.e., the scrambling of traditional left-right political distinctions in a manner that also skews in the direction of racist nationalism. As with the Neue Rechte of the 1990s, the AfD's attack on liberal democratic structures is also an attack on uniquely German taboos concerning the national past; by agitating these long-standing resentments the AfD encourages its followers to rally around an exciting new nationalism which feels, to those who engage in it, like liberation from the yoke of a perceived culture of guilt and shame.

Part of the initial confusion over where to place the AfD on the political spectrum stems from the dramatic transformation the party has undergone since its inception in 2013. The AfD's original platform of fiscal conservatism—devised in response to the Eurozone financial crisis by its 2013 leadership, which was made up of economists and intellectuals—framed the party's Euro-skeptic stance as one rooted in a politics of economic sovereignty. While the early AfD did at times capitalize upon political issues of importance to conservatives which had been abandoned by Chancellor Angela Merkel's CDU/CSU coalition (such as support for military conscription), the party's chief concern in the early years of its existence was Chancellor Merkel's agreement that Germany would aid in the Greek and Italian bailout crises.[36] This initially characterized the party as merely one of dissatisfied, anti-EU conservatives, the likes of which was nothing especially new in Germany; since the early 1990s there have existed a number of Euro-skeptical parties with economics-based platforms which together form an intellectual and political precedent for the emergence of a more successful party like the AfD.[37] However, following the party's internal fracture in 2015, the AfD shifted its emphasis from anti-EU to anti-immigration policies, swapping a platform based on economics to one rooted in ethnonationalism and gaining tremendous success as a result.

The 2015 split within the AfD saw the party radically shift to a platform which elevates an ethnicized understanding of German national identity, with immigration reform and traditional family policies at the heart of its new agenda. On the eve of the Greek bailout referendum on July 4, protracted disagreements came to a head between Bernd Lucke, one of the economists who originally founded the party, and Frauke Petry, who was at the time leader of the party's Saxony branch. Lucke chose to exit the AfD and form his own party, the ultimately unsuccessful Liberal-Konservative Reformer (LKR), leaving Petry to assume the role of AfD party chairperson and co-founder Alexander Gauland to become party leader. By the fall of 2015 a fifth of the AfD's then 21,000 members who represented the more liberal wing of the party that had encompassed Lucke would leave in protest at his perceived ousting. Following this, a significant number of representatives from the REP as well as Die Freiheit defected to the AfD, which was enjoying more success than these failing fringe parties.[38] Subsequently Björn Höcke, who maintains connections with the dwindling NPD as well as a close friendship with Kubitschek, and who many of Lucke's allies had wanted expelled from the AfD prior to 2015, became a leading figure. The party now began to resemble a true right-wing extremist party. In the 2017 Federal Elections the AfD gained 12.6 percent of the vote, making it the third largest party in the Bundestag and placing a radical right-wing opposition in parliament for the first time in postwar history.[39]

In the wake of these developments—their monumental significance widely recognized and met with considerable horror by politicians, the media, and the general public alike—the 2015 refugee crisis has come to be seen as the tipping point for the mainstreaming of racist ethno-nationalism in German politics. Many have attributed the AfD's 2017 success to Chancellor Merkel's dramatic decision, in 2015, to suspend EU Dublin Regulations (a law established in 2003 in order to determine which EU member state is responsible for receiving applicants for asylum), thus opening the gates to a considerable wave of refugees who crossed the Mediterranean Sea in the wake of the unsuccessful Arab Springs across North Africa and the Middle East and the resulting war in Syria. However, this narrative ignored the strains of populist thought which already existed within earlier versions of the party's manifesto—demonstrating, also, some amnesia surrounding Germany's entrance into the Eurozone in the early 1990s. Chancellor Kohl's agreement to adopt the common currency of the EU was, at the time, a major concession made in exchange for acceptance of German reunification abroad (designed to appease French President François Mitterrand). As discussed in Chapter 2, this formed a significant point of contention amongst the intellectual right in Germany. The 2008 Eurozone crisis was therefore always already a prerequisite for the emergence of a populist movement, as Frank Decker has argued:

> It opened the window of opportunity for a new euroskeptic [sic] party whose primary policy demands—a controlled dissolution of the monetary union and the rejection of a further deepening of the European integration process—lent themselves to the attachment of a broader right-wing populist platform to it.[40]

Moreover, anti-immigrant views were already on the rise in Germany long before the founding of the AfD—as this book has so far shown, they had been ever present since reunification, even as there was clear escalation in the second decade of the twenty-first century. The publication in 2010 of Sarrazin's *Deutschland schafft sich ab*, the increasing presence of predatory far-right pundits in online social media spaces since the early 2010s whose influence would spill over into various forms of street protest, the branching out of the Identitarians in 2012, and founding of PEGIDA in 2014—all of these illustrate that anti-immigration sentiment was percolating in Germany long before the 2015 refugee crisis, which merely galvanized, but did not create, the mainstreaming of a racist nationalism in German politics.

East German Populism? The Memory Politics of the AfD and PEGIDA

As with earlier examples of mounting racist aggression, discourse surrounding the AfD and PEGIDA has tended to home in on the movement's particular appeal amongst Germans in the eastern states. Responding to a strong public sense of urgency as the AfD made an inordinately rapid shift from its beginnings as a fringe party to becoming the main opposition party in the Bundestag, journalists and political scientists have framed their explanations for the strength of East German support for organizations like PEGIDA and the AfD in various ways that range from the cultural to the economic. One approach has been to examine voter leakage from across the political spectrum, challenging earlier assumptions that the AfD's electorate consisted mostly of former center-right voters who have drifted further to the right. Observing the AfD's rise to political prominence alongside public disavowal from German conservatives of Angela Merkel's *Wilkommenspolitik* ("open-door policy") during the 2015 refugee crisis, mainstream media outlets tended, especially following the 2017 Federal Elections, to push a narrative that the party's voter base consisted largely of former CDU/CSU voters who wished to see tight reform of German immigration policies. However, as political scientist Matthias Dilling has shown, while voter shift toward the AfD in the 2017 elections consisted of a 26 percent gain from the CDU/CSU, the party also gained 18 percent of their new votes from minor fringe parties, 12 percent from the SPD, 11 percent from Die Linke, and a significant 31 percent from former non-voters—electoral outcasts who felt represented, some for the first time ever, by a party whose platform deliberately appeals to a "heterogenous electoral basis."[41]

Despite the obvious transverse appeal of the AfD, the above figures briefly gave rise to a counter-narrative that Die Linke, rather than the CDU/CSU, had proportionately lost more votes to the AfD—an interpretation of statistical facts that, nevertheless, relies on framing the citizens of the eastern states as hapless instruments of populism from both the far-left and far-right, that is, if one defines Die Linke as "populist," as Jonathan Olsen has done.[42] This narrative became especially dominant following the AfD's 12.6 percent voter share in 2017. By comparison, the center-right SPD gained only 20.5 percent of the vote, an historical low for this party, whereas in the eastern states the vote seemed to be split in a starkly polarized way between the AfD and Die Linke.[43] One explanation for recent voter leakage from the far-left to the far-right concerns Die Linke's own shift in identity; once *the* protest-vote party for Germans in the eastern states while it was still known as the PDS, the party now has broader, more mainstream appeal across both the eastern and western states. Seen from this angle, the AfD has taken Die Linke's place as the populist party for East Germans—which is to say that its arguments and policies resonate better with contemporary East German resentments and that the AfD lays claim to the same culture of memory as East Germans. Yet this argument rests upon an incredibly broad understanding of what populism is; Die Linke and the AfD are said to share "pessimism about the state of democracy in Germany and advocacy for the use of referenda as a way to exercise control over political elites and return power to the 'people.'"[44] What this argument does not explain is why former far-leftists would suddenly be comfortable defining "the people" in ethnic terms, that is, why do they support the AfD's rehabilitation of race-based *völkisch* nationalism. This "polar flip" explanation for the AfD's popularity haphazardly swaps one form of discontentment with democracy for quite another.[45]

Lazy parallelisms between left and right ignore the various reasons why electorates may be discontented with status quo, mainstream, and pro-corporate forms of democratic governance. Arguably, the 31 percent gain from former non-voters is much more revealing of the AfD's populist appeal than the 11 percent from Die Linke. Non-voters, by their nature, are the most dissatisfied electoral demographic, making them easy prey for populist parties who claim to speak to "real Germans" who may be economically disenfranchised and who feel their basic needs have been neglected by established and ruling parties.[46] As Cas Mudde has identified, an important characteristic of right-wing populism is to appeal directly to those who are dissatisfied with democracy. While many far-right or neo-fascist political parties (especially in Eastern Europe) seek to abolish democracy entirely and replace it with authoritarian rule, populist movements tend to arise out of dissatisfaction with the current state of democracy, demanding reforms and constitutional amendments.[47] Within the AfD's concerted appeal to former East Germans—especially its deliberate *Ossi*-fied poster campaigns in the eastern states (discussed below)—fits the populist tactic of promising to "fix" or finally establish "true" democracy in Germany, a democracy promised, but not delivered, in 1989. However, these campaigns do not necessarily speak to every East German who participated in the pro-democratic marches that began in November 1989.

PEGIDA were in fact the first to capitalize upon the memory of 1989 by organizing marches referred to as *Montagsdemonstrationen* (Monday demonstrations), in reference to the peaceful marches against the East German SED state which first took place in Leipzig and soon spread to other eastern cities throughout 1989 and 1990. By mobilizing a specific East German set of signifiers PEGIDA thereby achieved "an intergenerational and more mainstream appeal by occupying the position of the persecuted,"[48] tapping into long-standing resentments over the unfulfilled promises of reunification. From its inception in 2014 PEGIDA demonstrators in eastern cities like Dresden and Leipzig reappropriated the pro-democratic slogan *"Wir sind das Volk"* ("We are the people"), chanting this while waving German flags and calling for "Revolution."[49] For many activists who wielded this slogan in protest of the SED state in '89 and '90, the term *Volk* harkened back to the left-wing spirit of proletarianism and social equality to which it was originally, in the interwar era, connected, before it was entirely co-opted by the National Socialist party. East German intellectuals and activists initially marched in the hopes of achieving social democracy, declaring themselves united as a *Volk* in the civic sense of the word and reclaiming it from the ethnonationalist Nazi context. Yet as Gideon Botsch has pointed out, the *Montagsdemonstrationen* did not remain the entirely liberal affair that they are often remembered to be in popular recollections; the spirit of these protests in fact shifted as they became overshadowed by the prospect of reunification and a wave of nationalistic fervor. As the number of demonstrators skyrocketed, their character changed—as did their demands and slogans:

> Nationalistic chants, hitherto strictly confined to skinheads and Faschos, became general, and by 20 November [1989] the crowds were calling for a "united German fatherland." It was not long before Neo-Nazis and skinheads began to show themselves openly. They profited from the unification dynamic itself, since it fostered their radical nationalistic aims; but they also joined the many elements who were actively contributing to that dynamic. Speakers who adhered to the civic agenda, or spoke against reunification, were howled down.[50]

PEGIDA's appropriated *Montagsdemonstrationen* therefore attracted a very particular eastern demographic: those who wished to recapture the undercurrent of nationalism that, during the *Wende*, gave rise to a wave of neo-Nazi destruction, racism, and anti-foreigner aggression.[51] This time, the far-right hoped to finally break through into German politics.

As early as 2015, the AfD has also claimed *"Wir sind das Volk!"* as its party slogan, to the fury of those who had been civil rights activists in the former GDR and during the *Wende*.[52] The AfD's summer 2019 campaign posters, displayed throughout eastern states, tapped into the frustrations and resentments of those for whom the prospect of reunification had promised a renewed nationalism, not to mention elevation to the economic plenitude of West Germans. One poster displayed in the state of Brandenburg proclaimed: "Then as Today: We are the People!" The poster also called for a "*Wende 2.0*," capitalizing upon the thirty-year anniversary of the end of the GDR: "1989 / 2019, Complete the *Wende!*" The claim that the *Wende* still needs "completing" lay ostensibly in the dissatisfaction, amongst the party and its electorate, with the current state of German democracy. While it is true that there remains great economic disparity between east and west, much of this dissatisfaction is tied up in the perception that Chancellor Merkel's CDU/CSU devoted more in social welfare resources toward immigrants and asylum seekers—a continuation of the same grievances expressed via the throwing of Molotov cocktails in 1991 and 1992. Since those early years, these grievances have been wound ever tighter by the condescending rhetoric of West Germans. As Gallinat has observed, there persists a trend amongst politicians in which "legitimate eastern suspicions about socioeconomic institutions become, in the estimation of official memory groups, perceived sites of *Ostalgie* born of a perceived lack of political education."[53] Anger and frustration with this condescension and with the dominant culture of memory also underpin the success of the AfD's eastern campaigns.

Many who were civil rights activists in the former GDR are furious at the misuse of their old slogans, and some argue that, while the AfD capitalizes on the frustrations of former East Germans who have been failed by the democratic process, the appeal of the AfD and its far-right agenda is in and of itself a result of the shortcomings of reunification and the illusions of democracy. In an interview with *Der Spiegel* Ehrhart Neubert, a theologian and civil rights activist during the civic protests of '89, observes that this appeal to East German memory through the reversal of old slogans is due to a failure of German reunification, observing that "the legacy and the symbols of the peaceful revolution lie idle on the street ... The AfD picks up what's lying there."[54] Neubert has found that, in his experience, the Federal Republic has not included enough of the peaceful revolution and its symbols into its post-reunification narrative.

In picking up these mnemonic fragments still metaphorically littering the ground once trod by civil rights demonstrators, the AfD is able to play around with certain malleable terms and phrases unique to German discourse. In particular, the party's use of the term *Volk* is entirely duplicitous: it at once evokes a specific moment in GDR history, one tinged with emotion over subsequent disappointments, while also winking at those who, in alignment with the AfD and PEGIDA's ethnically defined understanding of German identity, wish to belong to a *Volk* in the Nazi sense of the word.

Memory and Cruelty: The *Völkisch* Nationalism of AfD and PEGIDA

In a strategic appeal to the base emotions of their followings, the AfD and PEGIDA pair the politics of racial exclusion with a longing for agency and redemption that finds its expression in the rehabilitation of language made taboo by its association with National Socialism.[55] Referring to the electorate as *"das Volk"* is one such tactic; another is the use of terms such as *"Vaterland"* ("fatherland") which both evokes the romantic nationalism of the Imperial era and causes liberals to blanche, fearful of a genuine resurgence of the shameful outcome of colonial conquest, racial science, and *völkisch* nationalism that was the Nazi era. The AfD well understands both the divisive and affective potential of such language, having instructed in its 2016 strategy paper to "focus on being politically incorrect," to "engage in targeted provocations," and to become a "collection reservoir for protest."[56] The German far-right was not the only right-wing populist movement to tap into the carnivalesque in aid of its nativist agenda from 2016 onwards. As Cristina Beltrán has written in the context of Trumpism in the United States,

> For nativists who yearn for the freedom to police, punish, and exclude, targeting migrants makes them feel stronger, freer, and more agentic, transforming acts of racialized violence—whether people are committing, witnessing, or merely describing such acts—into feats of heroism, democratic redemption, civic engagement, and virtuous sovereignty.[57]

The language used by the AfD in their party program, as well as that of leaders Alexander Gauland and Björn Höcke—e.g., their insistent resurrection of *völkisch* terminology to describe German national identity—has evoked much outrage and soul-searching amongst German leftists and liberals as well as a posture of bewilderment from the center-right CDU/CSU. Yet the rhetoric of Gauland and Höcke is nothing new; anyone who has paid attention to the pages of *FAZ* since the 1990s should be familiar with the increasingly mainstream right-wing exhortations against German memory culture and commitment to lesson-learning. (However, in a twist which might be read as another right-wing effort to keep the left on its toes, *FAZ* has recently become a prominent critic of the usurpation of Holocaust memory, admonishing against academics who purportedly politicize the Holocaust or seek to integrate it into the history of colonialism. Doing so does, indeed, make the Imperial era an unusable past, out of which the right seeks to manufacture a "restorative nostalgia" for Imperialism, to borrow a phrase from Svetlana Boym.⁵⁸) Gauland, moreover, had been a respected member of the CDU for over forty years before helping to establish the AfD. Like the more fringe far-right campaigns of the 1990s, the AfD claims to be defending the Federal Republic against a number of familiar threats—from without, the threat of immigration and the supposed death (*Volkstod*) of a racially homogenous Germany, and from within a left-totalitarian politics that holds Germany "hostage" to the past—placing this party squarely within the constellation of Neue Rechte intellectuals and movements.

In accompaniment to the provocative use of *völkisch* terminologies, the new far-right also employs language and symbolism that, while not explicitly Nazi, flirt with certain Nazi-adjacent taboos—pushing the boundaries of what can be said or displayed according to German social conventions. As the handbook for Identitarian Movement describes:

> We don't want to exclusively address the mainstream and reflect its ideas. [Rather] we want to enforce, sharpen and polarize their opinions. Our political communication must therefore stay close to the limit and expand the "Overton Window" i.e., the framework of what can be said in the mainstream.⁵⁹

In this manner the Identitarians share their strategic goal with Kubitschek and with PEGIDA: to gradually shift Germany's political culture toward ultra-conservative, nationalist values.⁶⁰ Demonstrators at PEGIDA's rallies against the alleged "Islamization" of Germany have often proudly carried versions of the nineteenth-century Imperial War Flag and the Wirmer flag, displaying a proud nationalism which at once glosses over and makes conspicuous the ghost of National Socialism and its roots in German Imperialism.⁶¹ The use of the Wirmer flag is particularly derisive: a symbol of conservative anti-Hitler resistance in the 1930s, the adoption of this flag is an attempt to situate PEGIDA within the legitimizing framework of German mainstream conservatism—though ultimately revealing its shared genealogy with the Conservative Revolution and, by extension, the postwar Neue Rechte.

The effect amongst protest-goers and attendees at party rallies is one of overwhelming release. At an AfD rally in January 2017, prominent party member Höcke—who regularly gives lectures at Kubitschek's Schnellroda compound and refers to Germany as "*unser Vaterland*"—complained that "German history is handled as rotten and made to look ridiculous," in response to which the assembled crowd chanted "*Deutschland, Deutschland!*"⁶² Höcke then appealed to his audience's deep distain for what they perceived to be Germany's hallowed culture of guilt—a disdain which, as seen in Chapter 2, has become the lynchpin of the Neue Rechte's anti-memorial movement: Germans are "the only people in the world to plant a monument of shame in the heart of its capital," he said, referring to Berlin's Memorial to the Murdered Jews of Europe, adding that Germans have the "mentality of a totally vanquished people."[63] Skewed though this broad view of the average German mentality might be, Höcke nevertheless connected with his particular audience's desire for agency. Party leader Gauland was then able to capitalize on the intensity and fervor swept up by party pundits like Höcke, vowing, on election night in 2017, to "take back our country and our *Volk!*"[64]

Fearful that the world might be witnessing a second Weimar, liberal commentators and academics have largely taken this Nazi roleplaying at face value. Samuel Salzborn and Michael Wildt have both urged that, more than simply attempting to throw off the burden of historical guilt, breaching these rhetorical taboos threatens to take the normalization of the Nazi past to its extreme conclusion. As Salzborn argues, "if one can make the Nazi heritage seem harmless, then it becomes possible to take its associated concepts like the *Volksgemeinschaft* (ethnonational community) and resurrect it in public speech, before then striving to make it a reality."[65] And, as Wildt points out, the Neue Rechte's re-framing of racist sentiments as ethnopluralism is ultimately a vehicle for the same kind of racialized family policies—proposed in the AfD's party manifesto—which underpin the National Socialist notion of the *Volksgemeinschaft*.[66] Yet it is not at all apparent that the AfD, PEGIDA, or even the Identitarians really do seek to "make the Nazi heritage seem harmless"—if this were to happen, the taboo thrill of evoking Nazi terms would be lost, as would the entire *raison d'être* of the Neue Rechte.

This is not to say that the Neue Rechte is not sincere in its racist worldview. However, the rhetorical power of forbidden and exclusionary language is precisely in its cruelty and its ability to infuriate the liberal left. It also serves self-aggrandizing purposes; Kubitschek, for one, rarely speaks of the Nazi era and does not waste time justifying or relativizing its crimes. Rather, he prefers to fantasize of a Germany before Nazism, a country that hasn't yet been "refuted by history." Identitarian leader Sellner (who Kubitschek, with noted irreverence, likens to a young Rudi Dutschke)[67] meanwhile poses for photographs with a copy of Heidegger in hand; both Sellner and Kubitschek style themselves as intellectuals of a dark enlightenment.[68] Botho Strauß, meanwhile, believes himself to be "the last German," the direct and final literary descendent of Ernst Jünger, Stefan George, and Friedrich Nietzsche. He considers hatred against racial minorities to be merely a "superficial" expression of frustration at those politically responsible for broader cultural collapse and moral conformity.[69]

There are some notable ways in which the Neue Rechte's language in recent years has become more calculated—both a continuation of the anti-migrant sentiments of the 1990s and, now, deliberately designed to provoke the left, which is just as much an enemy of the far-right as are racial minorities. Whereas once the German far right's racism was directed toward Turkish, Vietnamese, and North African guest workers, since 9/11 it has been aimed more specifically at Islam as an "anti-German" influence, capitalizing on global trends toward the racialization of terror in order to heighten the perceived cultural and existential threat brought about by increased immigration. For example, following the Berlin lorry attack of December 19, 2016, when an Islamist extremist deliberately swerved his vehicle into the crowds of a busy Christmas market, AfD MP Marcus Pretzell tweeted in supposed solidarity with the victims, "They are Merkel's dead!"[70] Laying the blame for terrorism at the feet of Merkel's immigration policy was transparently provocative, and yet Merkel—struggling to preserve a receding political middle ground—responded with a penitent concession to this accusation: "It would be particularly hard to bear for all of us," she said, "if it was confirmed that a person had committed this crime who had asked for protection and asylum in Germany."[71] In making this concession Merkel unwittingly invigorated further delight in the sly cruelty of the AfD and PEGIDA; underpinning the movement's Islamophobia is the pleasure of catching progressives in their own seeming contradictions, i.e., the tension between anti-racism and the right to asylum on the one hand and discomfort with theocratic fundamentalism on the other, while also being pro-gender equality, pro-sexual freedom and also, necessarily, against the suppression of women's rights.

As is clear from the AfD's campaign posters and manifestos, the party's family policies and their calls for strict immigration reform are explicitly tied together in a manner that combines gender theory and racial equality within one and the same worldview of ethnopluralist struggle against the tides of multiculturalism. In their bluntly Islamophobic 2017 campaign posters—such as "'Islam?' Doesn't fit with our cuisine" alongside, confusingly, a picture of a cute fuzzy piglet—an ethnic identity for Germans is being defined against a perceived threat or enemy; as Salzborn has observed of PEGIDA, fear of the "Islamization" of Germany is used as "a pretext for inserting racist and *völkisch* positions back into the public sphere."[72] A gendered discourse is also central to such tactics, with German women represented as the object in need of protection against Islam. Posters such as the burqas vs. bikinis example and, even more absurdly, "'Burqa?' I prefer Burgundy!" as three women in traditional dirndl dresses raise their wine glasses—while defining two very different, yet both attractive, images of German women—at once raise fears of a threat to German culture and a threat to German women specifically. The sexual politics of this approach are thrown most sharply into relief by a poster that was issued in direct response to Merkel's comments that Middle Eastern refugees should be welcomed to Germany as "New Germans." Under an image of a pregnant, white, blonde-haired woman, the poster read: "New Germans? We'll make them ourselves."[73]

Yet manipulation is also an overt tactic in the AfD's campaign posters. In 2016 the party had even featured a gay couple presented as spokesmen against oppressive Islamic orthodoxy: "My partner and I place no value on acquaintance with Muslim immigrants," reads the text, over an image of two men looking very solemn indeed, "for whom our love is a mortal sin." The party's posters have also on occasion featured migrants—though, like the gay couple, these are used as strawmen to defend German culture, either against Islam or against leftist critique. Another 2016 poster features what looks to be a Middle Eastern woman—smiling, with long, flowing hair—who hopes for her son to become more fluent in German so that he can find a decent job. "The AfD takes the school system seriously and that's why I vote for it," she tells the viewer.[74] While these posters paved the way for the presentation, in 2017, of straightforwardly anti-migrant views, such sentiments were barely masked in 2016—merely obscured by a subverted parody of perceived liberal values which produced, amongst liberals, the grotesque sense of being mocked.

The grotesqueness of these campaign posters was precisely the point of them; they were offensive enough to be *enjoyable* to those who either agreed with their underlying policies or who were democratically ambivalent enough to appreciate the resulting political discord. The posters also worked by elevating Germans—white, attractive, and sometimes even wearing *Tracht*— above Muslim immigrants, a self-aggrandizement framed by the enjoyment of subjugating a chosen minority. The ends of this campaign are most starkly illustrated by the "New Germans" poster—a family policy based on ethnically defined notions of national identity. In 2016 the AfD drew an explicit connection between family policies and immigration, calling for "larger families instead of mass immigration."[75] Here they sketch an apocalyptic worldview of a supposed decline in birth rate among so-called "native" Germans, writing that:

> Germany's negative demographic trend must be counteracted. Mass immigration has a high potential for conflict and is not a viable economic solution. The only mid- and long-term solution is to attain a higher birth rate by the native population by stimulating family policies.[76]

Yet the "threat" does not merely stem from a projected ethnographic shift amongst Germans, but also from liberal or progressive attitudes toward gender equality and sexual freedoms which are presented as undermining the traditional family structure. This was the sense of whiplash that many left-liberal observers felt: first the AfD, as well as PEGIDA and the Identitarians put liberals on the back foot by attacking "neo-fundamentalist" Islam for its homophobia and repressive gender views—hiring, in 2017, Alice Weidel as a tokenistic queer party leader. Next, the AfD switched to a platform of traditional family values and an attack on the cultural influence of gender theory.

The AfD's 2017 party program referred to "gender ideology" as "*verfassungsfeindlich*"—more than being simply *un*constitutional (*verfassungswidrig*), it is decried here as *anti*constitutional. This is deliberate language which should not be brushed aside as mere semantics; while "unconstitutional" merely refers to what is or should be prohibited, "anti" (*feindlich*) implies that gender equality and sexual freedoms are an attack on the very Basic Law of Germany. "Gender ideology," they wrote, "wants to abolish the family as a life-model and role-model" and stands "in clear contradiction of the Basic Law, of (classically understood) marriage, and of the family as a state-supporting institute" as well as contradicting "both the scientific knowledge of biology and developmental psychology as well as the practical life experience of many generations."[77] This sudden switch to the language of science, of the law, and of the constitution is a further affective strategy designed to lend the party and its following a sense of righteous authority. (The party also outright enjoys poking fun at "gender ideology," as is shown in its satirical advertisement from 2020: "Dear voters: AfD election program now available in gender-neutral language!")[78]

As Beltrán points out, discourses which frame migration, or for that matter non-traditional family structures, as criminal, with rhetorical recourse to the language of law, are also "about overt enactments of racial domination: the violent freedom to both wield and exceed the law."[79] In the run-up to the 2017 federal elections, the AfD employed a populist language that was both anti-establishment *and* pro-constitutional—a language of disappointment with the state of democracy in Germany which would emphasize respect for the rule of law as the lynchpin of its anti-immigration policies. An article published on the AfD's website titled "We Are the Basic Law!" claimed that Germany's Basic Law needs protecting and only "we Germans"—i.e., "real" Germans—can perform such a duty.[80] The subsequent wave of euphoria following the AfD's election victory also brought with it new waves of violence, illustrating Beltrán's observation about both wielding and exceeding the law. In the name of a Germany for Germans, in August 2018 PEGIDA demonstrators and neo-Nazis in the city of Chemnitz rioted with an intensity unseen since the early 1990s. Fueled by rumors that two refugees from Iraq and Syria had committed a knife attack earlier in the week, 8,000 rioters rampaged through the streets of Chemnitz for two solid days, with further marches occurring over subsequent weeks.[81] A new-found sense of legitimacy following the AfD's success gave an increasingly mainstream far-right permission to violently police the boundaries of the *Volk*.

As well as wielding the law, the AfD also wields tradition and its importance, again in distinctly manipulative ways. Since the blatantly racist campaigns of 2017 the AfD has upped the anti of its manipulative tactics, commissioning further posters ostensibly aimed at migrants. An attempted stopgap against dwindling popular appeal, this campaign pretended to welcome migrants into the fold of the *Volksgemeinschaft*, depicting them as hard-working young people with a respect for German culture and democratic values of tolerance, plurality, and secularism.[82] A poster for the 2021 federal elections featuring an image of a young, Brown woman wearing what appears to be workers' overalls reads "Why did my father come to Germany back then? For German *Leitkultur*" above the inclusive-sounding slogan "Our country. Our values."[83] Like the 2016 posters, this fictionalization of a migrant worker turns the issue of immigration on its head—in this case, presenting the *right* kind of migrant, one who holds Germany aloft as the pinnacle of Western values.

Yet these kinds of rhetorical tactics also epitomize a trend for disorientation, manipulation, and mockery which, while begun by AfD and PEGIDA, has continued elsewhere to the effect of deep epistemic confusion. As Stefan Scharf and Clemens Pleul have argued, PEGIDA was one of the first far-right organizations to utilize social media platforms such as Facebook and Twitter in order to establish a "parallel public sphere" unattached to/at odds with regular mass media. Kubitschek et al. were thus able to mobilize followers both online and on the streets of Dresden and Leipzig—but the movement has since been joined by an amorphous array of other, more obscure groups that exist within this alternate public sphere, resulting in an increasingly unstable political landscape.[84]

Fake News and "Lateral Thinking": The Instability of Truth in the Age of Social Media

The use of digital communication platforms by right-wing extremists in recent years has evolved considerably from the forms of online organization during the 1990s and early 2000s that were discussed in the previous chapter, which primarily saw neo-Nazis and white supremacists forging international alliances based on distinctly right-wing extremist ideas. In the age of social media, online right-wing extremism blurs boundaries between traditional political distinctions and, through the proliferation of misinformation, disinformation, and conspiracy theories, attracts some unwitting and at times unlikely participants.[85] The popularity and ubiquity of platforms such as Twitter, Facebook, and YouTube have narrowed the gap between social media and sociality in general. Online spaces today therefore do not only make possible a far-right network that is truly global, but one that has been able to infiltrate mainstream discourse like a virus. The entrepreneurial owners and programmers of these platforms have also, as many concerned commentators stress, splintered the shared reality of their users through irresponsibly allowing the spread of divisive content.[86] It has, however, taken the spillage of hatred and conspiracy theories into everyday politics for most liberal commentators to take seriously the crass and puerile rhetoric of online extremists. Since 2020—the year that a global pandemic was seized upon by conspiracy theorists and politicized by radicals, a mob of neo-Nazis and a curious mixture of politically eclectic fellow travelers stormed the Reichstag in Berlin, and former US President Donald Trump claimed widespread election fraud, provoking an attempted insurrection at the US Capitol in January 2021—the perils of ignoring a threat that had been burgeoning for the last half of the previous decade have become clear.

The social media era has greatly enabled the far-right's ability to attract new participants. One initial such wave consisted of a handful of short-lived far-right groups who each followed a strategic *Aktionsmodell* of, first, organizing online, then protesting in relatively small numbers, and finally disseminating coverage of the protest to YouTube, where it gained further viewership. While these groups and flash mobs had short lifespans, the basic *Aktionsmodell* has nevertheless proved successful and adaptable. Originated by Marcel Forstmeier of the Spreelichter, a protest group which formed in the state of Brandenburg, in 2009, out of members from the JN (the youth division of the NPD, discussed in the previous chapter), this organizational strategy is powerful because it manages to form an intersection between the older, established far-right elite and a younger demographic who socialize online. For example, the neo-Nazi flash mob known as Die Unsterblichen (The Immortals), active in 2012, combined torch-bearing, mask-wearing theatrics with Identitarian politics and characterized itself as "young Germans who assemble in public places throughout the country in order to call attention to the deception of democrats."[87] As Patricia Anne Simpson observed in 2016, "self-credentializing internet publicists whose rhetoric and web presence aligns the privileged far-right with grassroots extremism" are incredibly savvy at maintaining both broad and local appeal through their "fluent use of digital media."[88] Simpson notes that like PEGIDA, murkier groups such as the Querdenker movement (discussed below) utilize the rhetorical ability to "produce new meanings within historical discourses about old threats."[89] This tactic is not so new: the Neue Rechte has, since its inception in the 1950s, found ways to revitalize again and again its old themes and grievances (the honor of the Wehrmacht, for example), incorporating these into contemporary discourses about perceived new threats. Similarly, the online far-right today recycles age-old conspiracy theories—with the added advantage of new technologies through which these falsehoods and paranoias can be rendered ever more convincing and reach a far wider audience. Weaponization of the instability of meaning and truth has therefore become the latest tactic of the far-right, far more effective and catastrophic than the earlier flash mobs. Given the global capacity for recruitment and the viral diffusion of misinformation, online extremists use social media as a new platform for leaderless resistance.

In January 2018 an online manual for the waging of "media guerrilla warfare" surfaced in various locations online and was soon endorsed by Identitarian leader Sellner, who posted it to his personal webpage.[90] The "Handbuch für Medienguerillas" had originally been posted to a gab.ai forum by an anonymous group calling itself "D Generation," before circulating on a channel of the popular social networking app Discord called "Reconquista Germanica." Media reporting on the manual tended to lambast its immaturity; Belltower news, a German online journal that monitors right-wing extremism, observed that "the budding 'media guerrillas' take themselves very seriously and seem to have only a vague understanding of public relations or the lasting influence of opinion."[91] This initial response was understandable enough; the first section of the manual, titled "Shitposting," refers to "meme warfare" and trolling online users in the comments sections of news stories, in YouTube posts, or in the "housewife forums" of Facebook. Yet, unsophisticated as a guerrilla warfare manual centered around memes and childish provocation might seem, the anonymous writers of the manual had taken their lead from other prominent far-right leaders who recognize how pernicious and indeed long-lasting the spread of disinformation and discord can be. In the same year that the "Handbuch für Medienguerillas" appeared, Steve Bannon, the former adviser to Donald Trump, was quoted in an interview as saying that the best way to deal with the media is to "flood the zone with shit."[92] Bannon was describing a tactic he had likely learned from observing Vladimir Putin's "firehose of falsehood" propaganda model, which takes advantage of the contemporary information environment in order to cause obfuscation at a scale the Soviets could only have dreamed of.[93]

Indeed, two years later in 2020 Belltower ate its own words, devoting an article in association with the Amadeu Antonio Foundation to the examination of how far-right narratives influence public debates and "lead to distorted perceptions of reality"[94] through subverting the basic features and algorithms of social media platforms. A closer look at the "Handbuch für Medienguerillas" reveals a set of carefully chosen targets—not bored housewives but, instead, "the Greens, well-known feminists, government lackeys ... and all propaganda government press like ARD, ZDF, Spiegel and the rest of the fake news mishmash. And, of course, the desk censors Correctiv and the Amadeu Antonio Foundation."[95] By relentlessly tagging the online posts of these legitimate groups and individuals as #fakenews, as well as engaging liberals in tiresome contrarian discussion (referred to in the handbook as "Eristic Dialectics," a tactic adopted from Schopenhauer's 1831 *The Art of Being Right*),[96] the "media guerrillas" not only create an alternative version of what counts as truth but stir up enough confusion to influence the naive and the uninformed into questioning their own common sense assumptions about complicated political issues.[97] Well-meaning professional and amateur media outlets have unwittingly played into the hands of online trolls by allowing themselves to be deceived by the outwardly puerile nature of what is, in fact, a highly effective PSYOP.

What had initially been brushed aside as the trifling antics of a few anonymous—and therefore seemingly immaterial—online users soon turned out to be having a significant effect on German politics. As *Deutsche Welle* reported later in 2018, the "highly organized approach and hierarchical structure" of far-right trolls on social media may have influenced the 2017 general election, skewing enough votes in favor of the AfD party to yield its success.[98] A study led by the London-based Institute for Strategic Dialogue (ISD) in collaboration with the *Süddeutsche Zeitung* described how Reconquista Germanica—which, it turned out, held at least 5,000 authentic members—had launched daily attacks on Merkel's CDU/CSU, the SPD, and the Greens in the days before the election, following "strict instructions to bad-mouth the main political parties and candidates, talk up the far-right Alternative for Germany, and to spread negative remarks about Germany and its refugee policy."[99] In one instance, the online guerrillas were able to get #notmychancellor trending on Facebook and Twitter—a tactic which strategically weaponized social media hashtags, referred to in the "Handbuch für Medienguerillas"[100] as an effective way of creating the illusion of an organic groundswell of opinion. Through generating at least two or three Twitter accounts each and then using these to disseminate anti-democratic opinion and disinformation, these "Electronic Shock Troops," as the handbook describes them, mounted not only an attack on the election but a campaign of obfuscation against public perception. These methods have been described by ISD researchers as a military-style PSYOP campaign replete with a hierarchical chain of command.[101]

The "Handbuch für Medienguerillas" was not so dissimilar in concept to a "style guide" that had been leaked from US-based neo-Nazi blog *The Daily Stormer* just month before, in December 2017. As well as fastidiously advising prospective writers for the blog on formatting standards, the style guide, written by site owner Andrew Anglin, emphasized house tactics that aimed toward convincingly challenging the truth claims of mainstream media sources. Anglin's guide oscillates between open admissions of the blog's disingenuity ("We should always claim we are winning, and should celebrate any wins with extreme exaggeration") and straight-faced claims that established media outlets are the real source of disinformation, with the *Stormer*'s discursive tactics proposed as a necessary corrective. One such tactic involves block-quoting at length from the mainstream sources under scrutiny in order to frame said text as spurious, and, as noted by Huffington Post journalist Ashley Feinberg (to whom the style guide was directly leaked), "to borrow some of mainstream media's air of scrupulousness and good hygiene."[102] The guide advises:

- Being able to see the mainstream source quoted allows us to co-opt the perceived authority of the mainstream media, and not look like *one of those sites we are all probably familiar with where you are never certain if what they are saying has been confirmed.*
- By simply commenting on existing news items, rather than rewriting the facts of the story, *we can never be accused of "fake news"*—or delisted by Facebook as such—as it is clear that all we are doing is commenting on existing news.[103]

The emphasized text in the above quote points to yet another component to this tactic which has produced a mixture of frustration and confusion amongst liberal commentators: if Anglin and other writers for sites like the *Daily Stormer* are aware that they are engaging in the proliferation of epistemic chaos, then how seriously do they believe their own claims that the mainstream media is the real "fake news"? And what could concretely be done to stop the influence of these blogs and their vast army of anonymous online instigators, who harassed and threatened Jewish and left-leaning journalists?[104]

The latter question may only begin to be answered with some kind of globally recognized legislation that determines what, exactly, a social media space is (private company or public forum?) and how to define the rights and responsibilities of its users and administrators.[105] Regarding the former, researchers who have closely studied the befuddling tactics of the so-called "alt-right"[106] note the significance of the weaponization of humor in the overall epistemic destabilization process. As Lukas Jäger and Mitro Dittrich of de:hate, a project run by the Amadeu Antonio Foundation, put it: "One of the main goals of alt-right actors is to influence social discourse in terms of their misanthropic ideology. In order to achieve this, strategies of provocation, insinuations, derogatory humor and the reevaluation of terms are used."[107] Or, as Anglin himself put it, "The unindoctrinated should not be able to tell if we are joking or not."[108] This does not however mean that the alt-right does not have an earnestly felt complaint against liberal democracy at the heart of its agenda. A Volker Weiß notes, "right-wing movements like Pegida [sic] have a keen sense that perceived reality differs from explanations. This difference can only be perceived as a conspiracy. This is shown by their slogans about the 'lying press' and the 'traitors of the people.'"[109] Making visible the difference between perceived reality and the explanations of liberal politicians and journalists is both a source of discordian enjoyment for the far-right/alt-right *as well as* its earnest mission. Moreover, while radical mistrust of liberal democratic institutions has been at the heart of Neue Rechte ideology at least since reunification, paranoid trends are by no means endemic to the far-right alone. As recent developments demonstrate, there is a broad audience for the poking into of contradictions, imperfections, and hypocrisies that are inevitably present within Western corporate democracies.

Since the start of the Covid-19 pandemic in early 2020 the destabilizing potential of dis- and misinformation spread via social media platforms has intensified, spilling out into the streets of major cities across the global West as demonstrators with a diverse range of political leanings, lifestyles, and class demography protested against governmental efforts to flatten the rate of infection.[110] In Germany, these demonstrations have seen neo-Nazis marching alongside former '68ers who harbor a distrust of authoritarianism, as well as self-styled non-conformists who take a New Age approach to medicine (i.e., "anti-vaxxers"). The "anti-covid" marches of August 2020—first, the "Tag der Freiheit" ("Day of Freedom") march in Berlin on August 1, which attracted some 20,000 participants, followed by a 38,000-strong protest on August 29 which culminated with the far-right faction of the demonstration rushing the doors of the Reichstag—saw constitutional loyalists side-by-side with the anti-state

Reichsbürger movement; hippies and anti-war activists together with libertarians and *Selbstverwalter* (sovereign citizens); neo-Nazis alongside holistic medicine practitioners and anti-vaxxers. While this "diagonalism" (i.e., the apparent traversal of the vast gulf between far-left and far-right politics and everything in between) has confounded onlookers, as this chapter has shown, parties like the AfD and groups like PEGIDA have long employed populist tactics capable of winning over disgruntled former Linke voters as well as a considerable (arguably apolitical) demographic of first-time voters. Moreover, the political apostasy of former leftists to the Neue Rechte during the 1990s demonstrates that the fluidity of boundaries between political extremes has long been the case, and that the taboo thrill of defecting to the enemy has not lost its appeal.

The organization at the heart of the Covid-19 protests is at once a result of long-percolating political shifts and ultimately far stranger than the AfD or PEGIDA. Like Sarrazin and the other "left-wing defectors" who came before him, adherents of the Querdenker ("lateral thinker") movement vocally contest the traditional binary scale of left- and right-wing politics and express cynicism toward the parliamentary system (though the movement skews heavily to the far-right in the anti-democratic ideas that it espouses). The discourse on individual liberties championed by this group and others like it attracts a demographic of unwitting and, in a sense, vulnerable new adherents who have fallen prey to the epistemic chaos produced by news feed-style social media platforms like Facebook and Twitter. In fact, as sociologists from Universität Basel discovered in their early empirical study of the Covid-19 protests in Germany and Switzerland, despite the recognizably right-wing extremist rhetoric of the leaders of the Querdenker movement, right-wing extremists by no means dominated the Querdenker-led protests of 2020, with only 15 percent of participants being AfD voters and very few expressing anti-immigrant or Islamophobic sentiment.[111]

The Querdenker movement has earlier origins than casual observers and commentators tend to address. While journalistic reporting commonly attributes the emergence of Querdenker to the start of the Covid-19 pandemic, framing this as a movement that exists adjacent to the US-based Q-Anon conspiracy network albeit with much more emphasis on protesting pandemic lockdown measures, the movement's ethos is far broader than this single-issue concern and its history stretches back to the early 2010s. The concept of *Quer-denken* ("lateral thinking") as a key expression within far-right thought became popularized in the early 2010s by Michael Vogt, a former Media Studies professor at the University of Leipzig. It also recalls the interwar Querfront—an attempt by the Weimar Republic's Conservative Revolutionaries to forge a transverse (or "diagonal") cooperation between the opposing camps of fascism and socialism in order to gain political power. Along with this link to the interwar Conservative Revolution (and, by genealogical extension, the postwar Neue Rechte) Querdenker also incorporates a strong element of the New Age esotericism propagated by Vogt, whose online platform Quer-denken.tv—a "free platform for free spirits" and "non-conforming, transverse minds"—has promoted a cocktail of conspiracist thought, revisionist history, and anti-Federal Republic rhetoric disguised as inquisitive individualism.[112] As journalists William Callison and Quinn Slobodian recall, from early on Quer-denken.tv (which now re-directs to "M-V.tv") collated videos and articles produced by members of the so-called "truther" community on topics ranging from chemtrails to pandemics and vaccines, even promoting a piece in 2014 titled "Is the Ebola pandemic a lie?"[113]—topics which have long been the focus of paranoid conspiracy peddlers who claim to offer "holistic" approaches to health care and wellness over the practices of modern medicine.[114] Mixed in with this kind of content—which, accounting for the diffuse nature of online content circulation, often draws an audience comprising all manner of esotericists and anti-establishment libertarians—are examples of far-right rhetoric. For instance, the annual Querdenken Kongreß has gathered a diverse in-person audience together with appearances by right-wing entrepreneurs such as UKIP's Nigel Farage, anti-feminist author and TV personality Eva Herman, and doomsday preacher Andreas Popp.[115]

Vogt is, himself, a right-wing extremist thinker whose worldview came into focus during his graduate studies in Munich in the late 1970s, during which time he took on a prominent role in ultra-right *Burschenschaften* (fraternities) and clandestine neo-Nazi student associations (such as the *völkisch* Danubia Munich fraternity, which is monitored by the Bavarian BfV).[116] His decade-long career as a lecturer in Communication & Media Studies came to an end in 2007 when he was dismissed for having made a revisionist documentary film with right-wing extremist and NPD politician Olaf Rose, titled *Geheimakte Heß* ("Secret File Hess"), which engaged in still popular far-right conspiracy theories surrounding Rudolf Hess—the former Deputy Führer around whom a reverent mythology has accrued, in neo-Nazi circles—and his flight to Scotland in 1941.[117] Turning to freelance journalism since his academic dismissal, Vogt has appeared in online broadcasts with several notable conspiracy theorists who engage in revisionism, antisemitism, and *völkisch* esotericism before establishing his own platform.[118] His 2012 manifesto, "Weg in die Freiheit—Deutschlands Aufbruch 2012" ("Way to Freedom—Germany's Awakening 2012") was published in the

Burschenschaftliche Blätter, the magazine for German fraternity members, and proposes the abolishment of the party state in favor of "real popular rule" as well as an exit from NATO and the EU.[119] Pseudo-scientific esotericism and far-right extremism intersect, online (in terms of place), and also through a "recoding" of racist impulses "by interpreting through the lens of revisionist German histories."[120] Vogt, for example, uses the *Burschenschaften* not only as a forum for his views but also as a vehicle for re-situating Nazi youth movements within an imagined history of resistance to the ostensibly oppressive power structure of the modern democratic state.[121]

Since the start of the pandemic, Querdenker has been co-opted by tech entrepreneur Michael Ballweg, who copyrighted the term "*Querdenken*" and then spun the movement into an off-shoot of the US-based QAnon. Speaking at the August 2020 "Tag der Freiheit" demonstration from the large stage that was constructed on Berlin's Strasse des 17. Juni, Ballweg explicated his own etymology of the concept: "Querdenken comes from the English letter Q for question," as in, "second-guess the source." Now the head organizer of the Querdenker movement, Ballweg is just one of numerous predatory entrepreneurial contrarians who have been able to take advantage of the anxieties induced not only by the pandemic, but as the result of the mistrust in democratic governmental structures that AfD has been touting for years already. Some have remarked that the Covid iteration of the Querdenker movement is "only concerned with their individual freedom and have no further socio-political demands." The findings of the Universität Basel study offered some evidence to support this; nearly half of those interviewed had never taken part in a political demonstration before the covid protests.

However, movements like Querdenker—much like sovereign citizen/Reichsbürger movements in Germany, the United States, and elsewhere—rest on the belief that all power is conspiracy, trading in fantasies about elite power and control that link together allegedly "totalitarian" authorities and corporate entities from the state to the banks, "Big Pharma," and "Big Tech" with ostensible regimes of knowledge such as political correctness, historical consciousness, climate science, and mainstream journalism. In this manner they construct their own victim narrative, as exemplified by a particularly dismaying instance of ironic cruelty in the Covid demonstrators' appropriation of the yellow Star of David as their own symbol of oppression. A show of stunning ignorance of the nature of real fascism and its exterminatory practices, German protestors who marched against Covid restrictions and mandatory vaccinations in 2020 and 2021 bore a yellow Star of David emblazoned with the word "*Ungeimpft*" (unvaccinated).[122] Mixing anti-vaccination esotericism, lack of historical awareness, and implicit antisemitism, this example is the latest iteration of a decade of cruel humor, rhetorical subversion, and diagonal politics combined. Querdenker therefore comprises the Neue Rechte's long-standing challenge to German democratic norms, constellating far-right views alongside New Age spiritualisms and enabling the chaotic infiltration of right-wing extremist ideas into seemingly disparate movements. The anti-lockdown protests of 2020 were a prime example of this intersection bearing socially disruptive fruit.

Epilogue: Confronting the Present

One of the dangers of writing a history of the present is that the present is changing every second. At the risk of stating what is surely by now a truism amongst historians: what seems urgent at this very moment may soon turn out to have been a flash in the pan, and what strikes the historian as an important archival discovery can later come to seem trivial. I began the research presented in this book in 2019, which was the thirtieth anniversary of German reunification, at a time when the world seemed to be experiencing a wave of right-wing populisms—from the Brexit vote in the UK and the election of Donald Trump in the United States to the victory of the AfD party in Germany. Academic historians were, at that time, taking the opportunity to revisit 1989 by way of challenging its victorious narrative in light of the manifest instability of liberal democracy.[1] Meanwhile public discourse in the United States and in Europe, at least amongst liberals, pulled apart much older national myths rooted in colonialism in an effort to push back against potentially encroaching nationalisms.[2] For my part it seemed an important task to get to the root of the AfD, which had launched its own attack on founding national myths by challenging the German culture of remembrance, hurling accusatory phrases such as "*Schuldkult*" (cult of guilt) and relishing the use of words like "*Volk*" and "*Vaterland*."

As I embarked on this research new things kept occurring: the KSK scandal of 2020 prompted me to shift my archival gaze toward the Bundeswehr, and the growing prominence of the Querdenker movement brought with it a whole set of new and confusing problems concerning the apparent relativity of traditional left-right distinctions. With far-right paramilitary groups training on former army grounds and celebrity vegan chefs protesting Covid-19 restrictions alongside neo-Nazis on the streets of Berlin,[3] many prior assumptions made by historians, journalists, and politicians concerning the origins of far-right ideology began to feel ever flimsier for understanding the present moment.

Since the onset of the growth of right-wing populism beginning around 2016, I had been deeply suspicious of a few things in particular, and these suspicions had some effect on the shaping of this book. First, prior to 2020 in both Germany and the United States there took place a considerable amount of public discourse in which nobody could resist making direct comparisons between the present day and the early twentieth century, namely the fragility of democracy during the Weimar Republic and the resulting rise of National Socialism. Whether trying to make sense of Trump by comparing him to the totalitarian "strongmen" of yore[4] or highlighting the anti-democratic nature of the AfD party by closely comparing its rise (and its rhetoric) with that of National Socialism, everywhere the discourse ignored almost an entire century's worth of historical developments known as the postwar era.[5] In some ways this indicated that the myth of 1989 was still holding strong: interpreting the emergence of right-wing populisms in the West as a plunge straight back into a pre-War, pre-Civil Rights world implies that there is no direct continuity between yesterday and today, or, to be precise, between the 1980s and the 1990s; the 1990s and the 2000s; etc. It also implies a certain generational naïveté, as if the movement of '68 had solved everything—as well as some amnesia, as if the world that was forged after the collapse of the Soviet Union wasn't a world still rooted in the deep fiscal and social conservatism of the 1980s. The 1980s, after all, produced Trump the celebrity tycoon; it also produced Kohl the Deutschmark Nationalist and a slew of early fringe parties that opposed European integration. Equally significant is that the 1980s gave us the personal computer and the internet, technologies embraced from the start by right-wing extremists who recognized their subversive potential, as well as by entrepreneurs who were almost entirely unimpeded by any regulations on the rapidly growing tech industry.[6] All of this is to say that solutions to present-day problems will not be found by making far-reaching historical analogies. This book comprises an attempt at resisting such oversimplification. What motivated people in the 1920s and '30s is not what motivates them today, and the means of social disruption have become ever more sophisticated.

For these reasons it made a lot of sense to begin the narrative of this book in that moment of transition from the 1980s into the "new world" of post-'89—as much to provide a history of the far-right in recent decades as to challenge an outdated narrative of liberal democracy's triumph. Yet while the idea of an epochal cut-off date has long been regarded as ridiculous by historians who know full well that history tends to keep on going even after momentous events like the fall of the Berlin Wall, my own postmodernist leanings inhibit me to discount the symbolic importance of "1989" in the political rhetoric and the maneuverings of power that have shaped the world since. There are, moreover, a lot of other "posts" which describe the era covered in this book: post-war, post-fascist, post-communist, post-industrial, post-modern, post-truth—all of which, in that prefix "post," imply the powerful "sense of living in interstitial time" identified long ago by American sociologist Daniel Bell in his analysis of post-industrial society.[7] This might explain the temporal lacuna that persists in public discourse between our present decade and the early twentieth century— an instinctive reach back toward the collective memory of a more tangible era. As François Hartog has noted, there has persisted a peculiar feeling of temporal flatness since 1989, owing partly to the effects of globalization and partly to the manufactured sense of living "post-history"[8]—the end of totalitarianism having discredited the teleological view of history.

While the persistent unfolding of the present moment will inevitably continue to determine and redetermine which earlier moments in time German historians, politicians, and citizens come to view as foundational to the nation's identity and values, there are nevertheless some solid (and dismaying) conclusions to be drawn from the research presented in this book. There are numerous examples throughout the previous five chapters of moments in which new developments emerged out of the fresh dilemmas of the post-1989 period, yet the response amongst German politicians was one of either denial or befuddlement. Perhaps most pernicious were the responses to growing right-wing extremism that outright cast blame anywhere but at the present moment in Germany: at the ruined GDR state, or, in the case of the NSU scandal, at imagined "foreign" crime rings. In the first two chapters of this book, a political narrative which claimed the eastern states to be the root of all neo-Nazism proved distracting enough to allow for the infiltration of revisionist ideas into mainstream conservative discourse. In Chapter 3, the pressure and responsibility of becoming an active NATO participant left Germany's Defense Ministry willfully blind to the reality that the Bundeswehr was becoming a target of idealization by right-wing extremists. The consequences of this have been disastrous, culminating in the emergence of a highly trained and heavily armed paramilitary faction from out of the Bundeswehr itself—but it was also incredibly frustrating to read the persistent and stubborn refusal of government representatives to take these developments seriously.

In the same vein, the racial bias of the German police and the mishandling of neo-Nazi informants by the BfV, covered in Chapter 4, demonstrate severe malfeasance which has yet to be properly addressed. Even following the NSU revelations of 2011, little was done at the legislative level to counter the reality of right-wing extremist terror networks in Germany. As journalists and activists alike point out, a package of measures against right-wing extremism in Germany that was first proposed in 2013 during extensive parliamentary investigations into the NSU has been perennially stalled, with meetings adjourned, BfV documents remaining classified, and conversations about structural racism avoided time and again by the Federal Government.[9] In part, these oversights mirror parallel trends in counter-terrorism in the United States and beyond that have for too long relied upon the trope of the "lone wolf" perpetrator to characterize acts of white supremacist and neo-Nazi terror. In both cases, there has long persisted an assumption that right-wing extremist violence is perpetrated for pathological rather than political reasons, ignoring the ways in which right-wing extremists organize like any other political terror movement: sharing a distinct ideology with an intellectual tradition of its own, compiling enemy lists, and sourcing weapons as well as funding for their strategically planned attacks.[10] Yet in the German case, these errors are deepened by a pervasive blind-spot produced by the deeply entrenched belief that the German culture of historical memory, remembrance, and lesson-learning is robust enough that instances of neo-Nazi violence can be considered isolated and anomalous.[11]

As I came to the end of writing this book yet another right-wing extremist coup attempt occurred—this time involving the monarchist Reichsbürger movement, a conspiracy theory-fueled network which has historically been mocked even amongst neo-Nazis.[12] The news that a small faction of Reichsbürger adherents—who reject the constitutional legitimacy of the Federal Republic and wish to reinstate the pre-First World War German Empire—had been planning an armed insurrection at the Bundestag gripped international media as much for its eccentricity as for the insurgency that had, apparently, been thwarted.[13] At the center of the highly publicized police raids which took place at dawn on December 7, 2022, was one Prince Heinrich XIII of Reuss, aged seventy-one, whose aristocratic idiosyncrasy was met with both revulsion and mirth by the international press; the idea that this tweed-clad Imperial fantasist was the ringleader of a "ragtag bunch of wannabe revolutionaries" from various respectable walks of life became a momentary sensation.[14] Given the scope of everything that has been covered in this book, the Reichsbürger plot could be an obscure flash in the pan compared to the full scope of the right-wing extremist movement which has been building in scale and complexity for at least several decades, not to mention the related scandals concerning persistent government malfeasance and failures of intelligence, as well as the AfD party's continued electoral success. However, the Reichsbürger plot is inextricable from the wider story of the German far-right's decades-long evolution as told in this book. For example, one of the 27 individuals who recently stood trial over their involvement in the coup plot—Rüdiger von Pescatore—is a former paratroop commander of the Bundeswehr who has served jail time for embezzling left over weapons stock from the East German National People's Army during the *Wende* years.[15] This latest diversion, moreover, touches upon some themes which deserve much closer attention: the connection between historical revisionism, cultivated by the Neue Rechte since the mid-1980s, the worrying spread of conspiracy theories, and challenges not only to commonly accepted truths but to the social value of truth itself.[16]

There is at this time a growing discourse about the relationship between digital media and the erosion of truth.[17] From RAND's observation that a significant segment of the public can no longer distinguish between opinion, editorial, and fact, to the polarization spiral into which social media has pulled Western political life by centripetal force, there is a belated yet urgent awareness that the disruptive potential of digital media makes us all more vulnerable to sedition and subversion.[18] Yet these dilemmas have potent antecedents in the foundational years of the post-'89 period. As early as the 1990s the Neue Rechte postmodernists claimed themselves the victims of "discourse apartheid"—a phrase not so dissimilar to the term "cancel culture" in use today, loathsome for its empty ability to signify whatever it needs to signify depending on who is wielding it in any given argument. At the same time, nascent electronic shock troops were downloading infinitely reproducible copies of founding far-right texts and tactical guides to their personal computers, forging transnational alliances in the realms of the virtual. Historical revisionism, Holocaust denial, and ever more strange iterations of age-old conspiracy theories have gained currency throughout the past few decades as chaotic political tactics amongst a hard right that no longer skulks on the fringes. And, in Germany, the concept of "confronting the past" underwent a brutal loss of signification, though continued to be held aloft as a panacea to every new instance of racist aggression in the present.

Notes

Introduction

1. Dirk Laabs, *Staatsfeinde in Uniform: Wie militante Rechte unsere Institutionen unterwandern* (Bonn: Econ Verlag, 2021). See also Katrin Bennhold, "Body Bags and Enemy Lists: How Far-Right Police Officers and Ex-Soldiers Planned for 'Day X'" in *The New York Times* (August 1, 2020).
2. Laabs, *Staatsfeinde in Uniform*; Bennhold, "Body Bags … " see also Bennhold, "As Neo-Nazis Seed Military Ranks, Germany Confronts 'an Enemy Within'" in *The New York Times* (July 3, 2020).
3. This question had earlier been raised in response to displays of racist aggression from far-right protest groups such as PEGIDA, which is discussed in Chapter 5 of this book, especially following the success of the Alternative für Deutschland party in the 2017 federal elections; see, for example, Paul Hockenos, "Has Germany Forgotten the Lessons of the Nazis?" in *The New York Times* (April 15, 2019). However, as this book aims to demonstrate, far-right political parties, protest groups, and intellectual circles had opposed Germany's culture of remembrance since its very beginnings.
4. See recent reflections, in the US context, on what Kathleen Belew has referred to as the "crunchy-hippy-to-alt-right pipeline" and the populist right's "skeptical, pessimistic, paranoid," attitude toward state institutions: Ross Douthat, "How the Right Became the Left and the Left Became the Right" in *The New York Times* (November 2, 2022); Kathleen Belew, "The Crunchy-to-Alt-Right Pipeline" in *The Atlantic* (December 14, 2022); see also Ross Douthat, "How Michel Foucault Lost the Left and Won the Right" in *The New York Times* (May 15, 2021).
5. Kathleen Belew, *Bring the War Home: The White Power Movement and Paramilitary America* (Cambridge, MA: Harvard University Press, 2018).
6. Often summed up, in the German-speaking world, with the phrase *Vergangenheitsbewältigung*, or "coming to terms with the past." The term has seen various differing translations in English; while "coming to terms with the past" is the most common variation, with "coming to terms" implying something like a therapeutic "working through," the political sentiment of the term is something closer to "reckoning with the past" or "confronting the past." For a fantastic account of how the concept of "working through the past" developed in West Germany throughout the postwar period, see Jeffrey K. Olick, *The Politics of Regret: On*

Collective Memory and Historical Responsibility (New York: Routledge, 2007); *The Sins of the Fathers: Germany, Memory, Method* (Chicago: University of Chicago Press, 2016). See also Theodor W. Adorno, "Was bedeutet: Aufarbeitung der Vergangenheit" in *Gesammelte Schriften 10.2. Kulturkritik und Gesellschaft II: Eingriffe. Stichworte. Anhang* (Suhrkamp: Frankfurt am Main, 1977), pp. 555–72; *Aspekte des neuen Rechtsradikalismus* (Berlin: Suhrkamp, 2019).

7 "Authorities had planned to probe the scale of ethnic profiling after a lawmaker claimed that 'latent racism' exists in German police ranks. The proposal followed a wave of protests in the US against police brutality." *Deutsche Welle*, "Germany: Study halted into racial profiling by police" (July 5, 2020).

8 As Chapters 2 and 3 discuss, Die Linke party—known until 2007 as the Partei des Demokratischen Sozialismus (Party of Democratic Socialism)—had diligently attempted to inform the federal government of the potential for neo-Nazi terror and paramilitarism since the early days of the new Federal Republic, only to be rebuked time and again by a government that was intensely, and myopically, focused on Germany's new national image of normality.

9 The KSK scandal became the latest installment in what was dubbed the "NSU 2.0" affair, after investigations into the presence of far-right actors in the German police were abruptly stopped earlier in 2020. See Jorg Luyken, "Frankfurt Police Officers Suspected of Complicity in Neo-Nazi Death Threat Campaign" in *The Independent* (July 19, 2020); *Deutsche Welle*, "Calls for Police Racism Investigation in Germany Despite Seehofer's Disapproval" (July 10, 2020).

10 See Tamir Bar-On, "Fascism to the Nouvelle Droite: The Dream of Pan-European Empire" in *Journal of Contemporary European Studies,* vol. 16, no. 3 (2008), pp. 327–45; Bar-On, *Rethinking the French New Right: Alternatives to Modernity* (London: Routledge, 2013).

11 For the creation of this right-wing reactionary culture during the 1970s, see Anna von der Goltz, *Inventing the Silent Majority in Western Europe and the United States: Conservatism in the 1960s and 1970s* (Cambridge: Cambridge University Press, 2017).

12 Walter Laqueur, "Postmodern Terrorism" in *Foreign Affairs,* vol. 75, no. 5 (September/October 1996), p. 24.

13 Louis L. Beam, "Leaderless Resistance" in *The Seditionist,* no. 12 (February 1992).

14 For a recent and lucid revisitation of these events, see Jeffrey Toobin, *Homegrown: Timothy McVeigh and the Rise of Right-Wing Extremism* (New York: Simon & Schuster, 2023).

15 Terrorist groups, as well as state-sponsored terrorism, were also increasingly likely to turn to cyberterrorism as the world's industries, societies, and government entities became increasingly reliant on digital communications for the storage of data and the powering of infrastructure—a reality which is now very much on top of us.

16. For an analysis of how this has played out in the United States, see former CIA analyst Martin Gurri, *The Revolt of the Public and the Crisis of Authority in the New Millennium* (San Francisco: Stripe Press, 2018). See also Ben Buchanan, *The Hacker and the State: Cyber Attacks and the New Normal of Geopolitics* (Cambridge, MA: Harvard University Press, 2020); Philip N. Howard, *Lie Machines: How to Save Democracy from Troll Armies, Deceitful Robots, Junk News Operations, and Political Operatives* (New Haven: Yale University Press, 2020).

17. See above note. For a history of disinformation campaigns throughout the twentieth century, see Thomas Rid, *Active Measures: The Secret History of Disinformation and Political Warfare* (New York: Farrar, Straus and Giroux, 2020). See also Rid's earlier work, *War 2.0: Irregular Warfare in the Information Age* (London: Praeger, 2009) and David Omand, *How Spies Think: Ten Lessons in Intelligence* (London: Penguin, 2020), especially chapter 10: "Subversion and Sedition Are Now Digital," pp. 233–72.

18. Peter Gill and Mark Pythian, *Intelligence in an Insecure World*—Third Edition (Cambridge, UK: Polity Press, 2018), p. 30.

19. The instability of information systems and truth's vulnerability to subversion in an increasingly complex digital world has long been a concern of intelligence analysts, especially following the terror attacks of 9/11 in the United States. As political scientist Thomas Rid argues in his 2013 work *Cyber War Will Not Take Place* (the title itself referring to Baudrillard's 1991 essay "The Gulf War Did Not Take Place," a comment on the nature of warfare in the postmodern era), one of the challenges of cyberspace has been a resultant emphasis on non-violent means of warfare which have, in some arenas, replaced violent forms of warfare. Rid, *Cyber War Will Not Take Place* (Oxford: Oxford University Press, 2013).

20. Ernst Jünger, *Sämtliche Werke in 18 Bänden, Band 9, Essays III: Das Abenteuerliche Herz* (Stuttgart: Klett-Cotta, 2020) p. 153. For more on Kubitschek's usage of this quotation, see Volker Weiß, "Ab wann ist konservativ zu rechts?" in *Die Zeit* (February 19, 2016).

21. As discussed at length in Chapter 2. See also Ernst Nolte, "Vergangenheit, die nicht vergehen will" reprinted in Rudolf Augstein, Karl Dietrich Bracher, Martin Broszat, Jürgen Habermas, and Joachim C. Fest eds., *Historikerstreit: Die Dokumentation der Kontroverse um die Einzigartigkeit der nationalsozialistischen Judenvernichtung* (Munich: Piper Verlag, 1987), pp. 39–61.

22. Examples of Nolte's Holocaust denial are discussed in Chapter 2. See also Nolte, *Streitpunkte: Heutige und künftige Kontroversen um den Nationalsozialismus* (Berlin: Ullstein Verlag, 1993).

23. Heimo Schwilk and Ulrich Schacht, *Die selbstbewusste Nation. "Anschwellender Bocksgesang" und weitere Beiträge zu einer deutschen Debatte* (Berlin: Ullstein, 1994).

24 "RAND defines 'Truth Decay' as the diminishing role of facts and analysis in American public life. This phenomenon has taken hold over the last two decades, eroding civil discourse, causing political paralysis, and leading to general uncertainty around what's true and what isn't." Jennifer Kavanagh and Michael D. Rich, *Truth Decay: An Initial Exploration of the Diminishing Role of Facts and Analysis in American Public Life* (Santa Monica, CA: RAND Corporation, 2018).
25 To quote Martin Walser, a left-wing apostate who famously attacked Germany's culture of commemoration in his acceptance speech for receiving (ironically) the Peace Prize at the Frankfurt Book Fair in 1998.
26 Botho Strauß, "Anschwellender Bocksgesang" in *Der Spiegel* (February 7, 1993).
27 See Chapter 4 of this book. See also Belew, *Bring the War Home*.
28 See the following strong examples: Daniel Koehler, "Right-Wing Extremism and Terrorism in Europe … "; Koehler, *Right-Wing Terrorism in the 21st Century: The "National Socialist Underground" and the History of Terror from the Far-Right in Germany* (London: Routledge, 2018); Julia Ebner, Johannes Baldauf, and Jakob Guhl eds., "Hassrede und Radikalisierung im Netz" in *Der OCCI-Forschungsbericht* (London: Institute for Strategic Dialogue, 2018); Philip Kreißel, Julia Ebner, Alexander Urban, and Jakob Guhl, *Hass auf Knopfdruck: Rechtsextreme Trollfabriken und das Ökosystem koordinierter Hasskampagnen im Netz* (London: Institute for Strategic Dialogue, July 2018).
29 With the notable exception of Patricia Ann Simpson and Helga Druxes eds., *Digital Media Strategies of the Far Right in Europe and the United States* (Lanham, MA: Lexington Books, 2015); Simpson, "Mobilizing Meanings: Translocal Identities of the Far Right Web" in *German Politics and Society*, vol. 34, no. 4 (Winter 2016), pp. 34–53.
30 See Shoshana Zuboff, "The Coup We Are Not Talking About" in *The New York Times* (January 29, 2021). See also Zuboff, *The Age of Surveillance Capitalism: The Fight for a Human Future at the New Frontier of Power* (New York: Hachette Book Group, 2019).

Chapter 1

1 The film debuted for German audiences in January of 2015, though it was first screened at the International Rome Film Fest in October 2014.
2 Burhan Qurbani dir., *Wir sind jung, wir sind stark* (film, 2015).
3 Ibid.
4 For the author's previous writing on this topic, see Esther Adaire, "Destroying German History: The Work of Heiner Müller as a Challenge to Public Memory" in *Communications of the International Brecht Society* (April 2016), https://e-cibs.org/issue-2020-1/#adaire.

5   Rico Grimm, "20 Jahre Rostock-Lichtenhagen: Das große Verdrängen" in *Der Spiegel* (August 21, 2012). Emphasis added. All translations are the author's own unless stated otherwise.
6   For further writing on the evolution of, and interplay between, the two distinct cultures of memory in East and West Germany, see Jeffrey Herf, *Divided Memory: The Nazi Past in the Two Germanys* (Cambridge, MA: Harvard University Press, 1997); Christoph Kleßman, *Zwei Staaten, eine Nation: deutsche Geschichte 1955–1970* (1988); Kleßmann ed., *The Divided Past: Rewriting Post-War German History* (New York: Berg Publishers, 2001).
7   See select examples of contributions to this discussion, in the 1990s, which drew explanatory links between the GDR's "anti-fascism" and contemporary right-wing extremism: Peter Ködderitzsch and Leo A. Müller, *Rechtsextremismus in der DDR* (Göttingen: Lamuv Verlag, 1990); Frank Schumann, *Glatzen am Alex: Rechtsextremismus in der DDR* (Berlin: Edition Fischerinsel, 1990); Christoph Butterwegge and Horst Isola eds., *Rechtsextremismus im vereinten Deutschland: Randerscheinung oder Gefahr für die Demokratie?* (Bremen: Steintor, 1991); Bernd Siegler, *Auferstanden aus Ruinen … Rechtsextremismus in der DDR* (Berlin: Bitterman Verlag, 1991); Klaus Florin and Eberhard Seidel-Pielen, *Rechtsruck: Rassismus im Neuen Deutschland* (Hamburg: Rotbuch, 1992); Thomas Assheuer and Hans Sarkowicz, *Rechtsradikale in Deutschland: Die alte und die neue Rechte* (Munich: C. H. Beck, 1992); Robert Harnischmacher ed., *Angriff von rechts: Rechtsextremismus und Neonazismus unter Jugendlichen Ostberlins. Beiträge zur Analyse und Vorschlage zu Gegenmassnahmen* (Rostock: Hanseatischer Fachverlag für Wirtschaft, 1993); Heinz Lynen von Berg, "Rechtsextremismus in Ostdeutschland seit der Wende" in Wolfgang Kowalsky and Wolfgang Schroeder eds., *Rechtsextremismus: Einführung und Forschungsbilanz* (Opladen: Westdeutscher Verlag, 1994), pp. 103–26.
8   In the phrasing of psychologist Hans-Joachim Maaz, referred to later in this chapter.
9   As subsequent chapters—especially Chapter 3—will discuss, organizations such as the PDS, which was the legal successor to the East German Sozialistische Einheitspartei Deutschlands (SED), were largely treated as extreme left agitators by mainstream German politicians—especially the center-right—following reunification. For how the PDS was formed out of the vestiges of the SED in 1990, see Eric Weitz, *Creating German Communism, 1890–1990: From Popular Protests to Socialist State* (Princeton, NJ: Princeton University Press, 1997), pp. 387–94.
10 There are also, it must be noted, vast differences between right-wing extremism in the west and in Eastern Europe regarding how these political phenomena have developed. While in Western Europe, Britain, and the United States mainstream political parties—including conservative ones—almost unanimously refused to

co-operate with fringe far-right movements and actors, in Eastern Europe the spectrum of right-wing extremism from ultra nationalism to neo-fascism was, itself, becoming the political mainstream during the early 1990s and in some cases has remained so.

11   Kathleen Belew, *Bring the War Home: The White Power Movement and Paramilitary America* (Cambridge, MA: Harvard University Press, 2018), p. 192.

12   Cas Mudde, *Populist Radical Right Parties in Europe* (Cambridge: Cambridge University Press, 2007); Andrea Mammone, Emmanuel Godin, and Brian Jenkins eds., *Mapping the Extreme Right in Contemporary Europe: From Local to Transnational* (London: Routledge, 2012); Ruth Wodak, Majid Khosravinik, and Brigitte Mral, *Right-Wing Populism in Europe: Politics and Discourse* (London: Bloomsbury, 2013).

13   For an overview on this subject, see Cas Mudde ed., *Racist Extremism in Central and Eastern Europe* (New York: Routledge, 2005); Sabrina P. Ramet ed., *The Radical Right in Central and Eastern Europe since 1989* (University Park, PA: Penn State University Press, 1999).

14   See the following select examples: Klaus von Beyme, "Rechtsextremismus in Osteuropa" in Jiirgen W. Falter, Hans-Gerd Jaschke, and Jiirgen R. Winkler eds., *Rechtsextremismus: Ergebnisse und Perspektiven* (Opladen: Westdeutscher Verlag, 1996), pp. 423–42; Cas Mudde, "Extreme-Right Parties in Eastern Europe" in *Patterns of Prejudice*, vol. 34 (2000), pp. 5–27; Mudde, "Central and Eastern Europe" in Mudde ed., *Racist Extremism*, pp. 267–85; Jozsef Bayer, "Rechtspopulismus und Rechtsextremismus in Ostmitteleuropa" in *Österreichische Zeitschrift für Politikwissenschaft*, vol. 31 (2002), pp. 265–80; Timm Beichelt and Michael Minkenberg, "Rechtsradikalismus in Transformationsgesellschaften: Entstehungsbedingungen und Erklärungsmodell" in *Osteuropa*, vol. 52 (2002), pp. 247–62; Michael Minkenberg, "The Radical Right in Postsocialist Central and Eastern Europe: Comparative Observations and Interpretations" in *East European Politics and Societies*, vol. 16 (2002), pp. 335–62.

15   See a wide body of literature that encompasses both sides of this debate, many of these works serving as examples of attempts to analyze East German neo-Nazi activity during the 1990s into the 2000s: Frank Neubacher, *Jugend und Rechtsextremismus in Ostdeutschland vor und nach der Wende. Umwelt, Kriminalität, Recht* (Godesberg: Forum Verlag, 1994); Harry Waibel, *Rechtsextremismus in der DDR bis 1989* (Cologne: Papyrossa Verlag, 1996); Siegler, "Rechtsextremismus in der DDR und den neuen Ländern" in Jens Mecklenburg ed., *Handbuch deutscher Rechtsextremismus* (Berlin: Elefanten Press, 1996), pp. 616–38; Bernd Wagner, "Rechtsradikale Entwicklungen in Ostdeutschland: Historische und aktuelle Aspekte" in *Osteuropa*, vol. 52 (2002), pp. 305–19; Norbert Madloch, "Rechtsextremismus in Deutschland nach dem Ende des Hitlerfaschismus" in

Klaus Kinner and Rolf Richter eds., *Rechtsextremismus und Antifaschismus: Historische und aktuelle Dimensionen* (Berlin: Dietz, 2000), pp. 57–214; Britta Bugiel, *Rechtsextremismus Jugendlicher in der DDR und in den neuen Bundesländern von 1982 bis 1998* (Munster: Lit Verlag, 2002); Jan C. Behrends, Thomas Lindenberger, and Patrice Poutrus eds., *Fremde und Fremdsein in der DDR: Zu historischen Ursachen der Fremdenfeindlichkeit in Ostdeutschland* (Berlin: Metropol, 2003); Klaus Schroeder, *Rechtsextremismus und Jugendgewalt in Deutschland: Ein Ost—West-Vergleich* (Paderborn: Ferdinand Schöningh Verlag, 2003); Christoph Kopke, "Die 'nationale Bewegung' in Brandenburg: Rechtsextreme Parteien, Wahlvereine, Verbände und Vereinigungen seit 1990" in Julius H. Schoeps, Gideon Botsch, Christoph Kopke, and Lars Rensmann eds., *Rechtsextremismus in Brandenburg: Handbuch für Analyse, Prävention und Intervention* (Berlin: Verlag für Berlin-Brandenburg, 2007), pp. 69–89.

16 Hajo Funke, *Brandstifter: Deutschland zwischen Demokratie und völkischen Nationalismus* (Göttingen: Lamuv, 1993); Claus Leggewie, *Druck von Rechts: Wohin treibt die Bundesrepublik?* (Munich: Beck, 1993); Armin Pfahl-Traughber, *Rechtsextremismus: Eine kritische Bestandsaufnahme nach der Wiedervereinigung* (Bonn: Bouvier, 1993); Richard Stöss, "Rechtsextremismus in einer geteilten politischen Kultur" in Oskar Niedermayer and Klaus von Beyme eds., *Politische Kultur in Ost—und Westdeutschland* (Berlin: VS Verlag für Sozialwissenschaften, 1994), pp. 105–39; Stöss, *Rechtsextremismus im vereinten Deutschland* (Berlin: Friedrich-Ebert-Stiftung, 2000).

17 Gideon Botsch, "From Skinhead-Subculture to Radical Right Movement: The Development of a 'National Opposition' in East Germany" in *Contemporary European History*, vol. 21, no. 4 (November 2012), pp. 553–73.

18 For instance, the argument that state-mandated anti-fascism under the GDR led to a suppression—and then an outburst—of nationalistic fervor tended to diagnose the problem of xenophobic violence in the new states as a social ill localized to those states and curable through proper Holocaust education. For an example of such an argument, see Karl-Heinz Heinemann and Wilfried Schubarth eds., *Der antifaschistische Staat entlässt seine Kinder. Jugend und Rechtsextremismus in Ostdeutschland* (Cologne: Papyrossa, 1992).

19 As discussed later in this chapter and explored more thoroughly in Chapter 4.

20 See, for example, Gábor T. Rittersporn, "Fremde in einer Gesellschaft der Fremden: Das sowjetische Beispiel" in Behrends, Lindenberger, and Poutros eds., *Fremde und Fremd-Sein*, pp. 43–56.

21 Behrends, Lindenberger, and Poutros, "Fremde und Fremd-Sein in der DDR: Zur Einführung" in Behrends, Lindenberger, and Poutros eds., *Fremde und Fremd-Sein*, pp. 9–22.

22 Paul Hockenos, *Free to Hate: The Rise of the Right in Post-Communist Europe* (New York: Routledge, 1993), p. 4.

23 Despite scholars' claims during the early 1990s that a kind of Socialist *Volksgemeinschaft* must have *de facto* excluded the GDR's Vietnamese, Angolan, and Cuban contract workers, aggression toward these groups—who were in fact considered to be from "fraternal socialist states"—was treated as decidedly antisocial behavior by the SED for much of the GDR's existence. See Botsch, "Skinhead-Subculture," p. 557. See also Thomas Lindenberger ed., *Herrschaft und Eigen-Sinn in der Diktatur. Studien zur Gesellschaftsgeschichte der DDR* (Cologne: Böhlau, 1999).

24 The East German National-Demokratische Partei Deutschlands (NDPD), established in 1948 by the SED as an "attempt to integrate 'nationalist' politico-social forces," was not, according to scholars, a full-fledged opposition party but an anti-fascist initiative aimed at inducting the middle classes into socialism. As Botch clarifies, the party "may have included people with national or even nationalistic sentiments, but no autonomous nationalistic agenda existed prior to the opening of the border between the two Germanys on November 9, 1989." Botsch, "Skinhead-Subculture," p. 557. See also Norbert Podewin, "Blockpolitik" in Andreas Herbst, Gerd Rüdiger, Stephan and Jürgen Winkler eds., *Die SED. Geschichte—Organisation—Politik: Ein Handbuch* (Berlin: Dietz, 1997), pp. 332–44.

25 Wolfgang Brück, "Skinheads als Vorboten der Systemkrise: Die Entwicklung des Skinhead-Phänomens bis zum Untergang der DDR" in Heinemann and Schubarth eds., *Der antifaschistische Staat*, pp. 37–46; Brück, "Studie über Erkenntnisse der Kriminalpolizei zu neofaschistischen Aktivitäten in der DDR" in Kinner and Richter, *Rechtsextremismus*, pp. 273–93.

26 See Ködderitzsch and Müller, *Rechtsextremismus*.

27 Though several notable punk acts notoriously used swastikas in their promotional material (or wore swastika-embellished clothing, in the cases of Sid Vicious of the Sex Pistols and Siouxsie Sioux of Siouxsie and the Banshees), to read this as pro-Nazi is to gloss over the underlying cultural history of postwar generational antagonisms. The original intent behind punks' usage of the swastika in the West (especially in Britain) was to incense the generation of their parents—who, while bragging of moral victory over Germany during the Second World War, maintained institutions which, in the eyes of punk youths, were inherently authoritarian. The subtlety of this was, alas, lost on the fringes of the skinhead movement, who simply enjoyed embodying violence and violent ideas. See Karen Fournier, "Nazi Signifiers and the Narrative of Class Warfare in British Punk" in Cyrus M. Shahan, Seth Howes, and Mirko M. Hall eds, *Beyond No Future: Cultures of German Punk* (New York: Bloomsbury Academic, 2016), pp. 91–108.

28 Peter Brandes, "The Politics of Lyrics in German Punk" in Shahan, Howes, and Hall eds., *Beyond No Future*, pp. 55–70.

29 For histories the relationship between ultra conservative trends and the far-right in the West, see for example Belew, *Bring the War Home*; Nigel Copsey and John E. Richardson eds., *Cultures of Post-War British Fascism* (New York: Routledge, 2015).

30 The band recorded this track in response to a spate of ugly skirmishes between punks and neo-Nazi skins which had occurred at various punk shows across the United States. Reminding their listeners of punk's true anti-authoritarian roots, the Dead Kennedys mocked any gormless neo-Nazis who might appear at their shows: "You still think swastikas look cool / The real Nazis run your schools / They're coaches, businessmen and cops / In a real Fourth Reich you'll be the first to go." The Dead Kennedys, *In God We Trust, Inc.*, Track 6: "Nazi Punks Fuck Off" (Alternative Tentacles, 1981). For a wonderful account of this saga, see Steve Knopper, "Nazi Punks F**k Off: How Black Flag, Bad Brains, and More Took Back Their Scene from White Supremacists" in *GQ Magazine* (January 16, 2018).
31 See the memoirs of former neo-Nazi Ingo Hasselbach, *Die Abrechnung: ein Neonazi steigt aus* (Berlin: Aufbau Taschenbuch Verlag, 2001).
32 For a highly engaging account of the East German punk scene and its opposition to neo-Nazi/Skinhead culture (as well as attempts by the SED to smear the punk scene with the brush of neo-Nazism), see Tim Mohr, *Stirb nicht im Warteraum der Zukunft: Die ostdeutschen Punks und der Fall der Mauer* (Munich: Wilhelm Heyne Verlag, 2017).
33 Harry Waibel, *Die braune Saat. Antisemitismus und Neonazismus in der DDR* (Stuttgart: Schmetterling Verlag, 2017). See also Christoph Butterwegge, *Rechtsextremismus* (Freiburg: Herder Verlag, 2002), p. 88.
34 Morh, *Stirb nicht*. See also Botsch, "Skinhead-Subculture," p. 560.
35 Botsch, "Skinhead-Subculture," p. 559.
36 Mohr cites a 1985 book published in the GDR by "a government-approved journalist," which "described David Bowie calling Adolf Hitler 'the first superstar' and reported on Eric Clapton and Rod Stewart's support for xenophobic British politician Enoch Powell" in an attempt to link racism and ostensible neo-fascism with capitalist popular culture. Mohr, *Stirb nicht*, p. 262.
37 See Mohr, *Stirb nicht*, pp. 262–9; Ködderitzsch and Müller, *Rechtsextremismus*, pp. 15–6; Waibel, *Rechtsextremismus*, p. 56.
38 This incident by no means led to the threat of neo-Nazism being taken seriously by the SED. Moreover, while the East German media reported on the event, it claimed that it had been "engineered by forces from the West." Mohr, *Stirb nicht*, pp. 264–7.
39 Ibid., p. 266.
40 Hockenos, *Free to Hate*, p. 2.
41 Many East Germans, especially those who marched for democratic reform in the weeks leading up to November 9, 1989, hoped that the GDR could remain an autonomous state with political and economic independence as well as its own distinct identity, one founded in democratic socialism. See Andreas Rödder, *Deutschland einig Vaterland. Die Geschichte der Wiedervereinigung* (Munich: Beck, 2009). For a great primary example of these hopes being expressed, see "Protest

Demonstration at Berlin-Alexanderplatz: Texts of recorded speeches by Stefan Heym, Christoph Hein, and Christa Wolf, November 4, 1989" in Harold James and Marla Stone eds., *When the Wall Came Down: Reactions to German Unification* (New York: Routledge, 1992), pp. 125–9.

42 Michael Schomers, *Deutschland ganz rechts: Sieben Monate als Republikaner in BRD und DDR* (Cologne: Kiepenheuer & Witsch, 1990); Peter Ködderitzsch, "Republikaner in der ehemaligen DDR" in Butterwegge and Isola, *Rechtsextremismus*, pp. 82–7.

43 As one REP leaflet from early 1990 reported: "Leipzig has had its own district association of Republikaner since January 29. More than two hundred members from all over the GDR gathered to take part in the founding meeting … [Bavarian state chairman Franz] Glasauer's demand for immediate reunification of the two constituent states, the FRG and GDR, was enthusiastically received by the predominantly young women and men." Facsimile in Ködderitzsch and Müller, *Rechtsextremismus*, p. 54.

44 Journalist Michael Schomers quoted in Ködderitzsch and Müller, *Rechtsextremismus*, p. 35.

45 The founding of the GdNF followed the 1983 banning of Kühnen's previous group, the Aktionsfront Nationaler Sozialisten/Nationale Aktivisten (ANS/NA), which at the time was the leading neo-Nazi group in West Germany. For further reading, see Michelle Lynn Kahn, "The American Influence on German Neo-Nazism: An Entangled History of Hate, 1970s–1990s" in *The Journal of Holocaust Research*, vol. 35, no. 2 (2021), pp. 91–105.

46 Siegler, *Auferstanden*, p. 46; Bugiel, *Rechtsextremismus Jugendlicher*, p. 265; Hasselbach, *Die Abrechnung*, p. 19.

47 Lauck also produced a handy order form which could be used to place orders of Nazi insignia stickers, LPs of Nazi marching songs, and military paraphernalia. The authenticity of some of these last items is questionable, given the size of the US market for forged Nazi weapons, swastika armbands, uniforms, and other paraphernalia.

48 Hasselbach, *Die Abrechnung*, pp. 165–76.

49 Madloch, "Rechtsextremismus in Deutschland," p. 90.

50 See Madloch, "Rechtsextremismus in Deutschland …," p. 141. The scope of women's involvement in the neo-Nazi/right-wing extremist scene, particularly within the NPD, will be explored further in Chapter 4.

51 Kühnen, who died in 1991 of AIDS-related diseases, started to be open about his sexuality in 1986 while in prison on charges relating to neo-Nazism. Notably, Kühnen modelled his conception of organized far-right terror on the Sturmabteilung (SA) before it was purged in 1934. A major part of his ethos involved moving away from the neo-Nazi culture of Hitler adoration as well as

denouncing the assassination of SA leader Ernst Röhm, a known homosexual, to whom he increasingly referred for inspiration. See Hasselbach, *Die Abrechnung*.
52 Ibid.
53 Hannes Bahrmann and Christoph Links, *Chronik der Wende. Die Ereignisse in der DDR zwischen 7. Oktober 1989 und 18. März 1990* (Berlin: Ch. Links Verlag, 1999), p. 177.
54 Botsch, "Skinhead-Subculture," p. 570.
55 Ibid. These demonstrations were largely an attempt, by Kühnen's movement, to gain popular recognition as the new voice of German nationalism. Yet, as Botsch points out, this was a wholesale failure as most nationalists simply placed their vote with the CDU party.
56 Florin and Seidel-Pielen, *Rechtsruck*, pp. 60–6.
57 Bernd Wagner, "Extreme in Rechts: Die DDR als Stufe zum Heute" in Harnischmacher ed., *Angriff von rechts*, pp. 117–24 (p. 122).
58 Bundesamt für Verfassungsschutz, *Verfassungsschutzbericht, 1990* (Bonn: Bundesministerium des Innern, 1991), pp. 79–80; Bundesamt für Verfassungsschutz, *Verfassungsschutzbericht, 1991* (Bonn: Bundesministerium des Innern, 1992), p. 75.
59 Ködderitzch and Müller, *Rechtsextremismus*. Also see the recollections of American foreign correspondent Jane Kramer, *The Politics of Memory: Looking for Germany in the New Germany* (New York: Random House, 1996), ch. "Skins" pp. 215–53.
60 Clemens Höges, "Wie ein verirrter Hund" in *Der Spiegel* (October 6, 1991).
61 Ibid.
62 These statistics had also been printed in *Der Spiegel* the previous day. See *Der Spiegel*, "Lieber sterben als nach Sachsen" (September 30, 1991). The *Times* article continued: "Given Germany's 20th-century history, political leaders do not want to be seen as acting against foreigners. But many citizens say it is time to halt or curb the flow of refugees." Stephen Kinzer for *The New York Times*, "A Wave of Attacks on Foreigners Stirs Shock in Germany" (October 1, 1991).
63 *Antifa Infoblatt* no. 95, "25 Jahre Mythos 'Rudolf Heß'" (July 13, 2012).
64 Angelic Upstarts, *We Gotta Get Out of This Place*, Track 3, "Lonely Man of Spandau" (Warner Bros., 1980).
65 *Antifa Infoblatt*, "25 Jahre Mythos … " For more on the conspiracy theories surrounding Hess, see Richard J. Evans, *The Hitler Conspiracies: The Third Reich and the Paranoid Imagination* (London: Penguin, 2021).
66 Fabian Virchov, "Creating a European (neo-Nazi) Movement by Joint Political Action?" in Andrea Mammone, Emmanuel Godin, and Brian Jenkins eds., *Varieties of Right-Wing Extremism in Europe* (Oxford: Routledge, 2013), pp. 197–214 (p. 205).
67 *Antifa Infoblatt* no. 20, "Rudolstadt—Rudolf Hess March 1992" (February 1, 1993). For further mention of Pamyat and its aims/relationship with the German far-right, see Chapter 2.

68 *Antifa Infoblatt* no. 19, "Rudolf Heß Marsch—Kristallisationspunkt der militanten Rechten" (September 29, 1992). For more recent writing on the marches and the mythology surrounding Hess, see Julia Jüttner, "Lernen mit Rudolf Heß" in *Der Spiegel* (November 11, 2011).
69 Hockenos, *Free to Hate*, p. 23.
70 Ibid., p. 24.
71 *Süddeutsche Zeitung*, "Die Krawalle in Hoyerswerda" (September 24, 1991); *Die Zeit*, "Hoyerswerda in den Köpfen" (September 26, 1991).
72 Complaints to local law enforcement concerning racial harassment had been met with indifference long before these events. In July 1991 the leader of Hoyerswerda's local council had written to the Saxon Minister-President, informing him that the safety of the asylum hostel could not be guaranteed due to "lack of police resources." *Stern*, "Die deutsche Schande: Jagd auf Ausländer" (October 2, 1991).
73 *Spiegel* reported that the bus caravan was cursed at and pelted with stones along its journey. *Der Spiegel*, "Jagdzeit in Sachsen" (September 30, 1991).
74 Ibid. See also this retrospective from ten years later in *Die Welt*, "Die Generation Hoyerswerda radikalisiert sich" (November 21, 2001).
75 *Der Spiegel*, "Lieber sterben … "
76 The tabloid *Stern* opted for the headline "Germany's Disgrace: Hunting for Foreigners" and an almost whimsical photomontage of a young skinhead with the branches of a foam swastika imposed around his head like a mohawk. *Der Spiegel*, "Lieber sterben … "; *Stern Magazin* (October 2, 1991).
77 *Der Spiegel*, "Lieber sterben … "
78 See Rödder, *Deutschland einig Vaterland*, p. 158; Werner Weidenfeld, Peter Wagner, and Elke Bruck, *Außenpolitik für die deutsche Einheit: Die Entscheidungsjahre 1989/1090, Geschichte der deutschen Einheit 4* (Stuttgart: dtv, 1989), pp. 131–2.
79 These attacks included physical violence against individual persons, vandalism and defacement of property, and a total of 701 small-scale arson attacks mostly on the homes of foreign residents. Bundesamt für Verfassungsschutz, *Verfassungsschutzbericht 1992* (Bonn: Bundesministerium des Innern, 1993), pp. 69–71.
80 *Der Spiegel*, "20 Jahre Rostock-Lichtenhagen: Das große Verdrängen" (August 21, 2012).
81 See archival video footage at *Spiegel Online*, "20 Jahre Rostock-Lichtenhagen: Das große Verdrängen" (September 21, 2012).
82 Leggewie, *Druck von Rechts*, p. 15.
83 Funke, *Brandstifter*, pp. 106–7.
84 Hockenos, *Free to Hate*, p. 29.
85 Helsinki Watch report, "'Foreigners Out'—Xenophobia and Right-Wing Violence in Germany" (New York: Human Rights Watch, 1992) downloaded from www.hrw.org, p. 12.

86 As one news reporter told the organization: "After [I had conducted] the interviews [with the residents of the asylum], at approximately 9:30 p.m., I looked out the window of the [seventh floor] and saw to my shock that the police had withdrawn from the area and were stationed on the hill, at some distance from the building. I could see their blue flashing lights, but they did not come closer. The house was surrounded by right-wing skinheads and others who were throwing molotov [sic] cocktails and trying to storm the building."

87 Helsinki Watch, "'Foreigners Out' …, " p. 91.

88 Helsinki Watch reported that, for instance, in the state of Saxony-Anhalt the number of foreigners had declined from 9,200 in 1990 to a mere 1,400 in 1992. Ibid., p. 7.

89 Hockenos, *Free to Hate*, p. 30.

90 *Süddeutsche Zeitung*, "Einsatzleitern drohen disziplinarische Folgen" (November 12, 1993); *Deutschland Nachrichten*, "Rostocks Bürgermeister zurückgetreten" (November 19, 1993).

91 Hockenos, *Free to Hate*, p. 30.

92 Recollection of the German writer Peter Schneider, *Berlin Now* (New York: Farrar, Straus and Giroux, 2014), p. 207.

93 Chancellor Kohl quoted in *Der Spiegel*, "Ernstes Zeichen an der Wand" (September 30, 1992).

94 Kramer, *Politics of Memory*, p. 222.

95 Kohl pointed out that violence against foreigners commonly occurred "also in other countries in Europe and the world." Helmut Kohl, "Jedem einzelnen Schicksal schulden wir Achtung" in *Frankfurter Allgemeine Zeitung* (May 6, 1995).

96 For more of this rhetoric after Hoyerswerda, see *Der Spiegel* "Ausländerfeindlichkeit nimmt zu" (September 30, 1991); after Rostock, see Robert Leicht for *Die Zeit*, "Anschlag auf die Republik" (August 28, 1992); *Der Spiegel* "Rechtsradikalismus: Linke Strategien gescheitert" (August 21, 1992).

97 Owing to the influence of Hannah Arendt's *Origins of Totalitarianism*, for much of the postwar era Nazism and Soviet-style communism were often framed as being two sides of the same coin, like mirror-images of the same fundamentally authoritarian power structure. This framework, however, neglects to comprehend fascism on its own terms—for example, it avoids comparisons between German Nazism and Italian Fascism.

98 Olaf Groehler, "Der Umgang mit dem Holocaust in der DDR" in Rolf Steininger ed., *Der Umgang mit dem Holocaust: Europa—USA—Israel* (Köln: Böhlau Verlag, 1994), pp. 233–45.

99 In fact, while the GDR placed responsibility for National Socialism solely on the shoulders of the Federal Republic, the show trials of the early GDR years were arbitrary and served to cover up what amounted to an ultimately ineffectual

pursuit of Nazi criminals. As Henry Leide's important, recent research into the Stasi archives has shown, in later years the prominent narrative that punishment of Nazi crimes within the GDR's borders was "done and dusted" even motivated state security to protect former Nazis, as any unmasked perpetrator might lead to loss of state credibility. See Leide, *Auschwitz and the State Security: Prosecution, Propaganda and Secrecy in the GDR* (Berlin: Stasi-Unterlagen-Archiv, 2022).

100 For example, historians Olaf Groehler and Annette Leo, themselves from East Germany, each attributed the emergence of a neo-Nazi scene in the former East to the discursive uses of "anti-fascism" in the GDR and its function in impeding knowledge of the Nazi past or the destruction of European Jewry during the Holocaust, the result being that the GDR did not experience the same process of "working through the past" at either the political, social, or individual level. Groehler, "Der Umgang … "; Annette Leo, "Als antifaschistischer Staat nicht betroffen? Die DDR und der Holocaust" in Bernd Faulenbach and Helmuth Schütte eds., *Deutschland, Israel und der Holocaust* (Essen: Klartext Verlag, 1998), pp. 89–10.

101 *Der Spiegel*, "Ernstes Zeichen … "

102 Hans-Joachim Maaz, "Zur psychischen Verarbeitung des Holocaust in der DDR" in Bernhard Moltmann et al, *Erinnerung: Zur Gegenwart des Holocaust in Deutschland-West und Deutschland-Ost* (Frankfurt am Main: Haag & Herchen Verlag, 1993), pp. 163–8.

103 Ibid., p. 164.

104 Christoph Classen, "Fremdheit gegenüber der eigenen Geschichte. Zum öffentlichen Umgang mit dem Nationalsozialismus in beiden deutschen Staaten" in Behrends, Lindenberger and Poutros eds., *Fremde und Fremd-Sein*, pp. 101–26 (p. 126).

105 Ibid. This framework for comprehending GDR society—especially in light of the continued broad appeal of far-right politics in the eastern states—is still being explored today by figures such as Patrice G. Poutros and Anetta Kahane (founder of the the Amadeu Antonio Foundation against right-wing extremism). The most recent study on this topic, a volume edited by Enrico Heitzer and Kahane, argues for a linguistic analysis of words such as "fascism" and "anti-fascism" and their usage in the GDR as propagandistic terms which stifled any provocative or free discourse, thereby circumscribing objective debate about the legacy of National Socialism. Enrico Heitzer, Martin Jander, Anetta Kahane, and Patrice G. Poutrus eds., *Nach Auschwitz: Schwieriges Erbe DDR. Plädoyer für einen Paradigmenwechsel in der DDR-Zeitgeschichtsforschung* (Frankfurt am Main: Wochenschau, 2018).

106 Botsch also argues that much of the 1990s/2000s commentary on GDR anti-fascism conveniently edited out oppositional movements. Botsch, "Skinhead-Subculture," p. 562. See also Siegler, *Auferstanden*, p. 74.

107 See Sabine Moller, *Vielfache Vergangenheit: öffentliche Erinnerungskulturen und Familienerinnerungen an die NS-Zeit in Ostdeutschland* (Tübingen: edition diskord, 2003).
108 Johannes Gerster (Mainz) (CDU/CSU), *Deutscher Bundestag Stenographischer Bericht, 43. Sitzung* (Bonn: Wednesday, September 25, 1991), p. 3566.
109 Dr. Dietmar Matterne (SPD), *Deutscher Bundestag Stenographischer Bericht, 43. Sitzung* (Bonn: Wednesday, September 25, 1991), pp. 3571–2. See also *Der Spiegel* "Gewalt gegen Fremde Hass" (September 30, 1991).
110 Klaus Rainer Röhl, "Lebenslüge Antifaschismus" in *Frankfurter Allgemeine Zeitung* (October 9, 1993).
111 Ibid.
112 Ottmar Schreiner (SPD), *Deutscher Bundestag Stenographischer Bericht, 43. Sitzung* (Bonn: Deutscher Bundestag, Wednesday, September 25, 1991), p. 3567.
113 *Der Spiegel*, "Anklang an Weimar" (October 5, 1992).
114 Ibid.
115 *Der Spiegel*, "Nach Mölln ein Volk im Schock" (December 6, 1992).
116 Bundesamt für Verfassungsschutz, *Verfassungsschutzbericht 1992* (Bonn: Bundesministerium des Innern, 1993).
117 *Los Angeles Times*, "Anti-Foreigner Attack Kills 3 in Germany" (November 24, 1992).
118 Human Rights Watch, "'Germany for Germans'—Xenophobia and Racist Violence in Germany" (April 1995); Thomas Ohlemacher, "Public Opinion and Violence against Foreigners in the Reunified Germany" in *Zeitschrift für Soziologie*, vol. 23, no. 3 (June 1994), pp. 222–36.
119 Stephen Kinzer, "Germany Outlaws a Neo-Nazi Group" in *The New York Times* (November 28, 1992).
120 By this stage Kühnen was dead, having succumbed to AIDS the previous year, although his movement—which, up until this sage had been the largest neo-Nazi network in West Germany (and had since spread to the eastern states)—was still going strong. *Verfassungsschutzbericht 1992*, pp. 99–101.
121 *Verfassungsschutzbericht 1993* (Bonn: Bundesministerium des Innern, 1994), pp. 82–4.
122 Kay Hailbronner, "Asylum Law Reform in the German Constitution" in *American University International Law Review*, vol. 9, no. 4 (1994).
123 Ibid., pp. 159–79.
124 Ohlemacher, "'Germany for Germans …,'" p. 222.
125 Hailbronner, "Asylum Law Reform …," p. 161.
126 *The New York Times*, "Thousands of Germans Rally for the Slain Turks" (June 4, 1993).
127 The unreliability of BfV informants—a topic which gained significant attention during the trials which followed the NSU terror killings—will be discussed

further in Chapter 4. Although there is to this day little information on what precise role Schmitt played for the BfV, he is said to have proved an unreliable informant. Like many others, he likely used his position in order to siphon crucial information from the BfV in order that he and his comrades could stay one step ahead of intelligence officers. *TAZ*, "15 Jahre nach dem Solingen-Anschlag: Die Lücke in der Stadt" (May 28, 2008); *Der Spiegel*, "Affären: 'Das wäre eine Bombe'" (May 29, 2005). See also *WDR*, "Brandanschlag in Solingen: Innenministerium reagiert auf Vorwürfe" (April 22, 2022).

128 *The New York Times*, "Thousands of Germans Rally … "; *The Washington Post*, "Turks Riot; Set Fires in Germany" (June 1, 1993).
129 Turkish Minister of Human Rights, Mehmet Kahraman, quoted in *The New York Times*, "Thousands of Germans Rally … "
130 Photograph by Jochen Eckel for *Süddeutsche Zeitung*. Solingen, North Rhine-Westphalia (May 30, 1993).
131 *Die Tageszeitung*, "Zwölf Gründe, diese Regierung abzuwählen" (September 30, 1994), pp. 22–3.
132 Bundespräsident Richard von Weizsäcker quoted in *The Washington Post*, "German President Links Deaths to Far-Right 'Climate'" (June 4, 1993). Emphasis added.

Chapter 2

1 Ernst Nolte quoted by Jacob Heilbrunn, "Germany's New Right" in *Foreign Affairs* (November/December 1996), pp. 80–98 (p. 85).
2 Nolte's 1963 work *Der Faschismus in seiner Epoche* was in its time credited for moving scholarship on National Socialism away from the totalitarian model, which posited that Nazi Germany and the Soviet Union shared important similarities, to a model that instead compared National Socialism with Italian Fascism and *Action Française*, moving toward a theory of generic fascism. However, some reviewers did note the exculpatory treatment Nolte gave to the German people in this work, for example his claim that "after the Führer's death, the core of the leadership of the National Socialist state snapped back, like a steel spring wound up too long, to its original position and became a body of well-meaning and cultured Central Europeans." Furthermore, Nolte would in the 1970s appear to retract many of his claims about "generic fascism," returning to the totalitarian model and claiming that Nazi Germany and the Soviet Union were a "mirror image" of one another. See Ernst Nolte, *Der Faschismus in seiner Epoche. Action française, Italienischer Faschismus, Nationalsozialismus* (Munich: Piper Verlag, 1963); *Deutschland und der kalte Krieg* (Munich: Piper Verlag, 1974). For contemporary critique, see Zeev Sternhell, "Fascist Ideology" in Walter Laqueur ed., *Fascism: A Reader's Guide* (Berkeley: University of California Press, 1976), pp. 315–71.

3 Nolte, "Vergangenheit, die nicht vergehen will" reprinted in Rudolf Augstein, Karl Dietrich Bracher, Martin Broszat, Jürgen Habermas, and Joachim C. Fest eds., *Historikerstreit: Die Dokumentation der Kontroverse um die Einzigartigkeit der nationalsozialistischen Judenvernichtung* (Munich: Piper Verlag 1987), pp. 39–61.

4 A phrase popularized by Heimo Schwilk and Ulrich Schacht's edited anthology of the same title, which will be discussed throughout this chapter. *Die selbstbewusste Nation. "Anschwellender Bocksgesang" und weitere Beiträge zu einer deutschen Debatte* (Berlin: Ullstein, 1994).

5 Here I am taking my definition of discursive power from the French philosopher Michel Foucault, who observed that discourse is a social system that produces knowledge and meaning, eventually shaping material reality. Michel Foucault, *Archaeology of Knowledge and the Discourse on Language* (London: Tavistock, 1972), pp. 135–40.

6 As went the main argument of Botho Strauß' highly controversial and influential essay "Anschwellender Bocksgesang," which first appeared in the pages of *Der Spiegel* in February 1993 and which will be discussed later in this chapter. Botho Strauß, "Anschwellender Bocksgesang" in *Der Spiegel* (February 7, 1993).

7 Nolte's 1987 work *Der europäische Bürgerkrieg* challenged mainstream historical periodization, positing that the years 1917–45 (the Russian Revolution through to the end of the Second World war) should be thought of as a European "civil war" characterized by a life-or-death struggle against Communism. Nolte would later re-work this periodization, considering the civil war to stretch from 1914 through to the collapse of the Soviet Union in 1991. Following that, his 1993 *Streitpunkte: Heutige und künftige Kontroversen um den Nationalsozialismus*, discussed later in this chapter, engaged in blatant Holocaust denial. Nolte, *Der europäische Bürgerkrieg 1917–1945. Nationalsozialismus und Bolschewismus* (Frankfurt am Main: Propylaen Verlag, 1987); Nolte, *Streitpunkte: Heutige und künftige Kontroversen um den Nationalsozialismus* (Berlin: Ullstein Verlag, 1993).

8 In the phrasing of Ulrich Schacht. Ulrich Schacht, "Gefährliche Erbschaft: Die PDS und ihre klandestinen Verehrer" in Heimo Schwilk and Ulrich Schacht eds., *Für eine Berliner Republik: Streitschriften, Reden und Essays nach 1989* (Munich: Langen Müller, 1997), pp. 181–5 (p. 184). See also Steffen Heitmann, "Revolution und Wende: Über den schwierigen Aufbau des vereinten Deutschlands" in Schwilk and Schacht eds, *Die selbstbewusste Nation*, pp. 447–56, and Wolfgang Templin, "Selbstwebußtsein und Verantwortung: Über Unheilsgeschichte und neue Deutsche Identität" in the same, pp. 457–63.

9 Aleida Assmann, "Transformations between History and Memory" in *Social Research*, vol. 75, no. 1: "Collective Memory and Collective Identity" (Spring 2008), pp. 49–72 (p. 61). For continued discussion of the fragmentation of memory in the post-'89 era, see also the articles in Assmann ed., *Memory in a Global Age: Discourses, Practices and Trajectories* (Basingstoke: Palgrave Macmillan, 2010).

10 Ibid.
11 See for example Hayden White's seminal analysis of the deep structure of historical imagination, *Metahistory: The Historical Imagination in Nineteenth-Century Europe* (Baltimore: Johns Hopkins University Press, 1975).
12 Beyond the scope of this chapter is the broader intellectual crisis that reunification caused on the political and scholarly left. See Jan-Werner Müller, *Another Country: German Intellectuals, Unification, and National Identity* (New Haven, CT: Yale University Press, 2000).
13 This was, in part, an attempt to confound the police, who from 1994 onwards had been closely monitoring the rallies and their organizers. The Wunsiedel Committee hoped that by holding an entire "Month of Memory" the authorities would not be able to determine when the main event might be planned to occur. Virchov, "Creating a European (neo-Nazi) movement," p. 205.
14 Svetlana Boym, "Nostalgia and Post-Communist Memory" in *The Future of Nostalgia* (New York: Perseus, 2001), pp. 57–73 (p. 61). Not to be confused with Memorial, a human rights group which brings awareness to the crimes of Stalin and other Soviet leaders in Russia.
15 Ibid., p. 63.
16 See the exchange of letters between Broszat and Saul Friedländer in Martin Broszat and Saul Friedländer, "Um die 'Historisierung des Nationalsozialismus': Ein Briefwechsel" in *Vierteljahreshefte für Zeit—geschichte*, vol. 36 (April 1988), pp. 339–72. The exchange was sparked by Friedländer's response to Broszat's "Plädoyer für eine Historisierung des Nationalsozialismus" in *Merkur* vol. 39 (May 1985), pp. 373–85, in which he suggests that in their aesthetic references to the fascist era, monuments risk burying events beneath layers of national myth and rationalization, rather than remembering.
17 James E. Young, "The Countermonument: Memory against Itself in Germany" in Young, *The Texture of Memory: Holocaust Memorials and Meaning* (New Haven: Yale University Press, 1993), pp. 27–49.
18 Jochen and Esther Gerz's "Monument against Fascism," a 12-meter-tall lead column which slowly, between 1983 and 1986, sank into the ground of the Hamburg shopping district where it was prominently installed, was grounded in cynicism about the efficacy of memorials (which the artists described as "impotent") and the impermanence of memory. The Aschrott Fountain in Kassel, designed by Horst Hoheisel in 1985, also played with subterranean space. A replica of the original fountain, which was commissioned in 1908 by Jewish entrepreneur Sigmund Aschrott and torn down under the Nazi regime in 1939, was flipped upside down and sunk into the ground where the original once stood. Visitors to the monument outside Kassel's City Hall can stand on a metal grate and hear the rush of the fountain's water echoing underground. And Norbert Radermacher's film slide projections in Neukölln—which were triggered by the movement of

passers-by—engaged the unwitting visitor in the projection of memory into an urban space. Each of these innovations led the way for the famous *Stolpersteine* first devised by Gunter Demnig in 1992, which commemorate individuals at their precise place or residence, work, or hiding before falling victim to the Nazi regime.

19 The Topographie des Terrors project began in 1987 as a temporary arrangement but became a permanent documentation and visitor center in 1990 due to its popularity and widely agreed-upon importance. See www.topographie.de.

20 Dirk Moses, "The German Catechism" in *Geschichte der Gegenwart* (May 23, 2021).

21 Frank Biess, "Confessions of an Ex-Believer," a response to Dirk Moses' controversial essay "The German Catechism" in *Geschichte der Gegenwart* (May 23, 2021). Posted online at *www.newfascismsyllabus.com* (June 1, 2021).

22 As American foreign correspondent Jane Kramer bravely reported in 1995, the years-long competition to design a Holocaust memorial on the former site of the Berlin Wall's death strip cascaded into "ghoulish public entertainment" with a 12 million dollar budget, presided over by television personality Lea Rosh (whose own tenuous Jewish identity is disputed, although she is read by the German public as Jewish and therefore as authoritative on the topic of Holocaust memory). As well as the ludicrousness of many of the 528 designs which were entered into the competition, the fact of the competition itself implied that there could be an "aesthetic 'solution' to the memory of mass death." The site of Buchenwald concentration camp in Weimar, in the former East, meanwhile underwent a significant political transformation following reunification. Between 1945 and 1950 the Soviet NKVD had used the site as a *Speziallager* for the imprisonment of former Nazis and anti-communist dissidents, after which period it was closed and transformed by the GDR government into a memorial to anti-fascist struggle. Following reunification, a commission of West German historians headed by Eberhard Jäckel transformed the Buchenwald site from anti-fascist monument to Holocaust memorial, rightly adding in 1993 and 1995 sections that commemorated Jews and Roma and Sinti, respectively, but also removing memorials to communist leaders who had been murdered by the Nazi regime. While the camp's use as a *Speziallager* during the Stalinist years could finally begin to be talked about in the public realm after the GDR's demise, many questioned the ethics of erasing entirely the history of communist persecution under National Socialism. See Jane Kramer, "The Politics of Memory" in *The New Yorker* (August 1995), pp. 48–65; Peter Monteath, "Buchenwald Revisited: Rewriting the History of a Concentration Camp" in *International History Review*, vol. 16, no. 2 (1994); Klaus Neumann, ch. 8: "Weimar and 'the Great Intellectual Designs of the Past'" in *Shifting Memories: The Nazi Past in the New Germany* (Ann Arbor: University of Michigan Press, 2000), pp. 178–98.

23 According to Kramer, "Stölzl ignored anyone who tried to remind him ... that Germany never had a successful revolution, or even, until Weimar, a democratic

parliamentary system." To make up for this deficit, one of the earliest items Stölzl purchased for the exhibit was a German translation of the American Declaration of Independence—an original transcript from 1776 which cost three-quarters of a million dollars. The exhibit also further compartmentalized the Nazi era by placing the histories of the two Germanys side-by-side, like two sides of a totalitarian coin, with Nazi uniforms next to Communist uniforms—and, shockingly, equivocated very different kinds of victimhood by commemorating Wehrmacht soldiers alongside Jews. Kramer, "The Politics of Memory," pp. 57–8.

24 Vastly extrapolated and ultimately different from, say, Arendtian notions of totalitarianism. See Michael Stürmer, *Dissonanzen des Fortschritts: Essays über Geschichte und Politik in Deutschland* (Munich: Piper Verlag, 1986); Andreas Hillgruber, *Deutschlands Rolle in der Vorgeschichte der beiden Weltkriege* (Göttingen: Vandenhoeck & Ruprecht, 1967); Klaus Hildebrand, *Das Deutsche Reich und die Sowjetunion im internationalen System 1918–1932: Legitimität oder Revolution?* (Wiesbaden: Steiner Verlag, 1977).

25 For contemporaneous appraisals of this theory, see Hans-Ulrich Wehler, *The German Empire, 1871–1918* (Leamington Spa: Berg Publishers, 1985); Geoff Eley and David Blackbourn, *The Peculiarities of German History: Bourgeois Society and Politics in Nineteenth-Century Germany* (Oxford: Oxford University Press, 1984).

26 Stürmer, *Das ruhelose Reich 1866–1918* (Berlin: Siedler Verlag, 1983); Hildebrand, "Deutscher Sonderweg und 'Drittes Reich': Betrachtungen über ein Grundproblem der deutschen und europäischen Geschicte im 19. und 20. Jahrhundert" in Wolfgang Michalka ed., *Die nationalsozialistische Machtergreifung* (Münster: Schöningh, 1984), pp. 392–4. See also Geoff Eley, "Nazism, Politics and the Image of the Past: Thoughts on the West German Historikerstreit 1986–1987" in *Past & Present*, no. 121 (November 1988), pp. 171–208.

27 While the "encirclement" narrative undoubtedly explains the German nationalist mindset at the turn of the twentieth century (a significant contributing factor to the outbreak of the First World War), the nefariousness of Stürmer's comparison was that it stoked similar fears in the context of the postwar European Economic Community, which would later become the European Union.

28 The Heidelberg manifesto of 1981, an anti-immigration screed signed by fifteen college professors and published in the pages of *FAZ*, was widely condemned by the public and yet circulated broadly on college campuses and reprinted in several far-right publications. The manifesto was preceded, in 1980, by two of its main instigators—astronomer Theodor Schmidt-Kaler, from Ruhr-Universität Bochum, and mineralogist Helmut Schröcke of Ludwig-Maximilians-Universität München—publishing in *FAZ* their *völkisch* thesis, which would become central to the subsequent manifesto. Borrowing from eugenicist theories of race, the authors defined "*Völker*" as "living systems of a higher order" and went on to express

concern for the "over-foreignization" (*Überfremdung*) of the German language and national character. Theodor Schmidt-Kaler and Helmut Schröcke, "Letter to the Editors" in *Frankfurter Allgemeine Zeitung* (January 22, 1980). See also "Heidelberger Manifest" in *Deutsche Wochenzeitung*, no. 6 (November 1981).

29 Schmidt's comments were made in response to Israel's anger over the sale of West German Leopard II tanks to the Saudi government.

30 For assessments of the Bitburg affair itself and its political and moral implications, see Geoffrey Hartman ed., *Bitburg in Moral and Political Perspective* (Bloomington: Indiana University Press, 1986).

31 On the contrary, Kohl's 1990 campaign had made an emotional appeal to frustrated desires for a German national identity which could be celebrated.

32 Stefan Berger, *The Search for Normality: National Identity and Historical Consciousness in Germany Since 1800* (New York: Berghahn Books, 2003).

33 For more on museum culture in the *Wende* period, see Andreas Huyssen, "Escape from Amnesia: The Museum as Mass Medium" in Huyssen, *Twilight Memories: Marking Time in a Culture of Amnesia* (New York: Routledge, 1995), pp. 13-36.

34 *Der Spiegel*, "Einmal Heil Hitler" (June 19, 1994).

35 Clemens Range, "Unabhängig und defensiv—Ungarns neue Wehrpolitik" in *Information für die Truppe: Zeitschrift für Innere Führung*, no. 6 (June 1992), pp. 4-9. See also Range, *Die geduldete Armee. 50 Jahre Bundeswehr* (Müllheim: Translimes Media Verlag, 2005) and *Tapferer Adel: eine Dokumentation des Opfergangs in zwei Weltkriegen* (Müllheim: Translimes Media Verlag, 2010).

36 Alfred Schickel, "Nationen vereint im Kampf gegen Deutschland, Italien und Japan" in *Information für die Truppe: Zeitschrift für Innere Führung*, no. 2 (February 1992), pp. 58-64. Throughout the article Schickel describes the allied nations as "the 'United Nations,'" in scare quotes, seemingly to draw some line of continuity between nations which were allied against Germany during the Second World War and those which would go on to form the official United Nations in 1945—and who now played such a pivotal role in global intervention during humanitarian crises. Schickel's hostility toward what he pointedly refers to as "the victors" —i.e., the global Western order—seems to extend to his present day. In particular, he expresses dissatisfaction with a victors of history narrative that frames the entirety of German history as a story of authoritarianism, violence, and ultimately defeat.

37 While Schickel only referenced Hillgruber's 1982 text *Der Zweite Weltkrieg, 1939-1945: Kriegsziele und Strategie der grossen Mächte*, he will undoubtedly have been aware of the more controversial *Zweierlei Untergang: Die Zerschlagung des Deutschen Reiches und das Ende des europäischen Judentums*, published in 1986, in which Hillgruber drew a moral equivalency between the Holocaust and the collapse of the German Reich.

38 Schickel, "Nationen vereint ... " p. 64. The implications of something like colonialism continue: according to Schickel, Roosevelt's demand for "unconditional

surrender" had been directly modeled on the collapse of the confederacy in 1865—the outcome of which was the adoption of an "internal political order of the victors."

39 This use of the Morgenthau Plan had become a well-known trope of Neue Rechte thought; Klaus Rainer Röhl linked it to his own claims that the Greens are a "fundamentalist" movement, as well as the apparent taboo on discussing Allied war crimes. See Klaus Rainer Röhl, "Morgenthau und Antifa: Über den Selbsthaß der deutschen" in Heimo Schwilk and Ulrich Schacht eds., *Die selbstbewusste Nation*, pp. 85–100 (p. 92).

40 Ibid., p. 64.

41 Clemens Range, "Perspektiven einer neuen Völkerwanderung" in *Information für die Truppe: Zeitschrift für Innere Führung*, no. 3 (March 1992), pp. 28–37 (p. 29). See also Jan Werner, *Die Invasion der Armen: Asylanten und illegale Einwanderer* (Mainz: Hase & Koehler, 1991).

42 The MDF party identified itself as a champion for democracy in the context of Soviet downfall, though the party ran on a distinctly nationalistic campaign which promised to restore Hungary's pre-First World War borders. The MDF would eventually be dissolved, in 2011, by the Fidesz party, with which it had effectively merged in the years prior.

43 Heimo Schwilk, *Was man uns verschwieg: Der Golfkrieg in der Zensur* (Frankfurt am Main: Ullstein Sachbuch, 1991), p. 33.

44 Deutscher Bundestag, Drucksache 12/4202, "Antwort der Bundesregierung auf die Kleine Anfrage der Abgeordneten Ulla Jelpke und der Gruppe der PDS/Linke Liste – Drucksache 12/3925" (January 27, 1993).

45 Cord Pagenstecher, "'Das Boot ist voll.' Schreckensvision des vereinten Deutschland" in Gerhard Paul ed., *Das Jahrhundert der Bilder: 1949 bis heute* (Göttingen: Vandenhoeck & Ruprecht, 2008), p. 123.

46 The full scope of which is explored at length in Christian Wicke, *Helmut Kohl's Quest for Normality: His Representation of the German Nation and Himself* (New York: Berghahn, 2015). See also Berger, *The Search for Normality*.

47 See two contemporary essays on this subject: Wolfgang Gessenharter, "Die 'Neue Rechte' als Scharnier zwischen Konservatismus und Rechtsextremismus in der Bundesrepublik" in Rainer Eisfeld and Ingo Müller eds., *Gegen Barbarei: Essays Robert M. W. Kempner zu Ehren* (Frankfurt am Main: Athenäum, 1989); Armin Pfahl-Traughber, "Brücken zwischen Rechtsextremismus und Konservatismus: Zur Erosion der Abgrenzung auf publizistischer Ebene in den achtziger und neunziger Jahren" in Wolfgang Kowalsky and Wolfgang Schroeder eds., *Rechtsextremismus: Einführung und Forschungsbilanz* (Opladen: Westdeutscher Verlag, 1994), pp. 160–82.

48 The full, almost comically bureaucratic name of the memorial is the Central Memorial of the Federal Republic of Germany for the Victims of War and Tyranny (*Zentrale Gedenkstätte der Bundesrepublik Deutschland für die Opfer von Krieg

und Gewaltherrschaft). For a history of the Neue Wache building, see https://www.protokoll-inland.de/Webs/PI/DE/staatliche-symbole/neue-wache/neue-wache-node.html
49 Kramer, "The Politics of Memory," p. 52.
50 Peter Handke, *Eine winterliche Reise zu den Flüssen Donau, Save, Morawa und Drina oder Gerechtigkeit für Serbien* (Frankfurt am Main: Suhrkamp, 1996); Martin Walser, *Vormittag eines Schriftstellers* (Frankfurt am Main: Suhrkamp, 1994).
51 Botho Strauß, "Anschwellender Bocksgesang" in *Der Spiegel* (February 7, 1993); Walser, *Ansichten, Einsichten. Aufsätze zur Zeitgeschichte*, vol. XI of XII (Frankfurt Frankfurt am Main: Suhrkamp, 1997); Wolfgang Templin, "Selbstbewußtsein und Verantwortung: Über Unheilsgeschichte und neue deutsche Identität" in Schwilk and Schacht eds., *Die selbstbewusste Nation*, pp. 457–63; Templin, "Das schlechte Vorbild der Anpassung: Hindernisse für die innere Einigung" in Werner Weidenfeld ed., *Deutschland. Eine Nation—doppelte Geschichte. Materialien zum deutschen Selbstverständnis* (Cologne: Wissenschaft und Politik, 1993), pp. 113–16; Hans Magnus Enzensberger, *Aussichten auf den Bürgerkrieg* (Frankfurt am Main: Suhrkamp, 1993); Brigitte Seebacher-Brandt, *Die Linke und die Einheit* (Berlin: Siedler Verlag, 1991); Seebacher-Brandt, "Norm und Normalität: Über die Liebe zum eigenen Land" in Schwilk and Schacht eds., *Die selbstbewusste Nation*, pp. 43–56.
52 Rumblings of a schism began in the late 1960s when notable figures such as philosopher Hermann Lübbe voiced concern over the influence of left-wing, extra-parliamentary opposition, contextualizing the broader student movement alongside terrorist organizations such as the RAF. Lübbe went on to become one of the leading representatives of German neoconservatism in the 1970s and 1980s. See Jürgen Habermas, "Neoconservative Culture Criticism in the United States and West Germany: An Intellectual Movement in Two Political Cultures" in *Télos*, vol. 56 (1983), pp. 75–89; Jerry Z. Muller, "German Neo-Conservatism, ca. 1968–1985: Hermann Lübbe and Others" in Jan-Werner Müller ed., *German Ideologies since 1945: Studies in the Political Thought and Culture of the Bonn Republic* (New York: Palgrave Macmillan, 2003), pp. 161–84.
53 Jay Julian Rosellini, *Literary Skinheads? Writing from the Right in Reunified Germany* (West Lafayette, IN: Purdue University Press, 2000).
54 "Negative, querulous, pathetic" was British historian Richard Evans' assessment. "In a word, the book amounts to little more in the end than one long whinge." Richard J. Evans, "Prisoners of the German Past" in *Patterns of Prejudice*, vol. 30, no. 1 (1996), pp. 73–81 (p. 78).
55 Armin Mohler, *Die konservative Revolution in Deutschland 1918–1932* (Stuttgart: F. Vorwerk, 1950).
56 Nolte, "Links und rechts: Über Geschichte und Aktualität einer politischen Alternative" in Schwilk and Schacht eds., *Die selbstbewusste Nation*, pp. 145–62

(p. 153); Rainer Zitelmann, "Position und Begriff: Über den Kampf gegen die linke Meinungsdominanz" in Schwilk and Schacht, *Die selbstbewusste Nation*, pp. 163–81 (p. 172).

57 Zitelmann, "Wiedervereinigung und deutscher Selbsthaß: Probleme mit dem eigenen Volk" in Weidenfeld ed., *Deutschland, eine Nation*, pp. 235–48 (p. 248).
58 Rosellini has astutely translated "Anschwellender Bocksgesang" as "Impending Tragedy," which very much captures Strauß' intended idiomatic meaning.
59 Hans Magnus Enzensberger, "Ausblicke auf den Bürgerkrieg" in *Der Spiegel* (June 20, 1993).
60 Martin Walser, "Deutsche Sorgen" in *Der Spiegel* (June 27, 1993).
61 Each of the five sections of *Die selbstbewusste Nation* begins with their own epigraph quotation from "Bocksgesang" and most of the contributing essays are written as direct responses to it.
62 Strauß, "Anschwellender Bocksgesang."
63 Strauß goes on to quote Girard directly.
64 All quotes extracted from the extremely lengthy and meandering doctrine that is "Anschwellender Bocksgesang."
65 Ulrich Schacht, "Stigma und Sorge: Über deutsche Identität nach Auschwitz" in Schacht and Schwilk eds., *Die Selbstbewusste* Nation, pp. 57–68 (pp. 57, 60).
66 Rosellini, *Literary Skinheads?*, p. 47. See also Schwilk, "Schmerz und Moral: Über das Ethos des Widerstehens" in Schacht and Schwilk eds., *Die Selbstbewusste* Nation, pp. 393–403.
67 John Ely, "The 'Frankfurter Allgemeine Zeitung' and Contemporary National-Conservatism" in *German Politics and Society*, vol. 13, no. 2 (1995), pp. 81–121. The Neue Rechte's misuse of postmodernist claims has also recently been explored by Carolin Amlinger, "Rechts dekonstruieren. Die Neue Rechte und ihr widersprüchliches Verhältnis zur Postmoderne" in *Leviathan*, vol. 48, no. 2 (2020), pp. 318–37.
68 This is not dissimilar to the "post-truth" nature of political discourse in the Trump era, in which what counts as truth has been undermined by a replacement of objectivity with even-handedness, and by the construction of notions such as "alternative facts," which could be described as relativism *ad absurdum*.
69 Schwilk refers to the television as a "machine that destroys meaning [*Sinnzertrümmerungsmaschine*]" through reduction of all topics (his main example is talk shows), which has the general public in hypnotic thrall to their own "unconscious longing for self-extinction." Schwilk, "Mittelmaß und Kulinarik: Rückblick auf die bundesdeutsche Idylle" in Schwilk ed., *Wendezeit – Zeitenwende: Beiträge zur Literatur der achtziger Jahre* (Berlin: Bouvier Verlag, 1991), pp. 15–26 (p. 21).
70 Ibid., p. 23.
71 Seebacher-Brandt, "Norm und Normalität," p. 45.

72 Röhl, "Morgenthau und Antifa."
73 Templin, "Selbstbewußtsein und Verantwortung … "; Steffen Heitmann, "Revolution und Wende … "
74 See Schacht and Schwilk, "Einleitung" in *Die Selbstbewusste* Nation, pp. 11–18, as well as Schacht and Schwilk, *Für eine Berliner Republik: Streitschriften, Reden und Essays nach 1989* (Munich: Langen Müller, 1997).
75 Peter Glotz, "Freunde, es wird ernst" in *Der Wochenpost* (February 25, 1993). For an idea of the public outcry at large, see the following select headlines: Thomas Assheuer, "Was ist rechts?" in *Frankfurter Rundschau* (February 10, 1993); Willi Winkler, "Ist Botho Strauß ein Faschist?" in *taz* (February 13, 1993); Tillman Spengler, "Der Ekelpegel sinkt: Die stumme Rechte wird laut. Ihr neue Rufer heißt Botho Strauß" in *Die Woche* (February 18, 1993); Hilmar Hoffmann, "Sprachverwirrungen eines Unpolitischen: Zu Botho Strauß's Bocksgesang und seinen Schwellungen" in *Die Welt* (March 29, 1993); Eckhard Nordhofen, "Vor der Bundeslade des Bosen" in *Die Zeit* (April 9, 1993).
76 *Spiegel* editors, "Hausmitteilung: Intellektuelle" (June 27, 1993).
77 See Adaire, "Destroying German History … " See also Brian Ladd, *The Ghosts of Berlin: Confronting German History in the Urban Landscape* (Chicago: University of Chicago Press, 1997); Jon Berndt Olsen, *Tailoring Truth: Politicizing the Past and Negotiating Memory in East Germany, 1945–1990* (New York: Berghahn Books, 2015).
78 Rosellini, *Literary Skinheads?*, p. 63.
79 Snippets of Templin's interview reported by Uwe Rada for *taz*, "Bürgerrechtler in der rechten Ecke" (March 5, 1994).
80 Birthler and Volmer's views expressed in the above.
81 *Antifaschistische Initiative Moabit*, "Anmerkungen zum derzeitigen Handeln von Wolfgang Templin" (March 20, 1995).
82 *Die Zeit*, "Die Akte Verräter: Auszüge aus den 'Maßnahmeplänen' der Stasi gegen Wolfgang Templin" (March 6, 1992).
83 *Die Zeit*, "Vorgang auf!" (March 6, 1992).
84 Ibid.
85 See Templin, "Selbstbewußtsein und Verantwortung: Über Unheilsgeschichte und neue deutsche Identität" in Schwilk and Schacht eds., *Die selbstbewusste Nation*, pp. 457–63 and Templin, "Das schlechte Vorbild der Anpassung: Hindernisse für die innere Einigung", pp. 113–16.
86 Thilo Sarrazin, *Deutschland schafft sich ab: Wie wir unser Land aufs Spiel setzen* (Munich: Deutsche-Verlags Anstalt, 2010).
87 Ethnopluralism, contrary to ethnocentrism (the belief that all cultures and ethnicities are essentially the same and can find common ground), rests on the idea that different peoples are wholly incompatible.

88 Henning Eichberg, *Nationale Identität: Entfremdung und nationale Frage in der Industrie Gesellschaft* (Munich: Langen Muller, 1978).
89 Benno Hafeneger, "Rechtsextreme Europabilder" in Wolfgang Kowalsky and Wolfgang Schroeder, *Rechtsextremismus: Einführung und Forschungsbilanz* (Wiesbaden: Springer Fachmedien, 1994), pp. 212–27 (p. 223).
90 BfV, "VIII. Intellektualisierungsbemühungen im Rechtsextremismus" in *Verfassungsschutzbericht 1996* (Bonn: Bundesministerium des Innern, May 1997), pp. 155–7.
91 BfV, "Annex: Intellektualisierung des Rechtsextremismus ('Neue Rechte')" in *Verfassungsschutzbericht 1995* (Bonn: Bundesministerium des Innern, May 1996), p. 163.
92 Ibid.
93 BfV, "Internationale Aspekte des deutschen Rechtsextremismus" in *Verfassungsschutzbericht 1995*, pp. 164–74.
94 BfV, *Verfassungsschutzbericht 1996*, p. 156.
95 See for example Ulrich Greiner, "Der Seher auf dem Markt: Botho Strauß, Ernst Nolte, die FAZ und der Rechtsintellektualismus: Auf der Suche nach dem richtigen Rechten" in *Die Zeit* (April 22, 1994); Ely, "The 'Frankfurter Allgemeine Zeitung … '"
96 Deborah E. Lipstadt, *Denying the Holocaust: The Growing Assault on Truth and Memory* (London: Penguin Random House, 1993).
97 See Richard J. Evans, *Telling Lies about Hitler: The Holocaust, History and the David Irving Trial* (London: Verso, 2002).
98 Mark Weber, "A Prominent German Historian Tackles Taboos of Third Reich History: Prof. Nolte's Controversial New Book" in *The Journal of Historical Review*, vol. 14, no. 1 (January 1994), pp. 37–41.
99 Nolte, *Streitpunkte*, pp. 308–9.
100 Eckhard Jesse, "Innensicht der Extreme: Ernst Nolte und die Totalitarismustheorie" in *FAZ* (January 1993); *FAZ* editors, "Ende eines Kampfes: Zum siebzigsten Geburtstag des Historikers Ernst Nolte" (January 1993).
101 See Jens Jessen, "Siebzig verweht III: Ernst Jüngers Tagebücher als Vorabdruck in der F.A.Z." in *FAZ*, (July 12, 1993).
102 See "Briefe an die Herausgeber" in *FAZ* (July 13, 1992); Johann Georg Reifimuller, "Irrtumer und Perversionen" in *FAZ* (June 30, 1992); see also "Asylanten auch für Düsseldorf eine Last," cartoon in *FAZ* (August 7, 1992); Walter Hanel's Noah's Ark depictions in *FAZ* (August 7, 1991, and July 29, 1992); Fritz Behrendt's racist portraits of refugees as terrorists in *FAZ* (July 14, 1992, and June 20, 1994).
103 Wolfgang Schäuble, "Der Platz in der Mitte: Sonderwege und Staatsräson" in *FAZ* (March 3, 1994).
104 Friedbert Pflüger, *Deutschland driftet. Die Konservative Revolution entdeckt ihre Kinder* (Düsseldorf: Econ, 1994). In addition, Heiner Geissler's 1995 text

Der Irrweg des Nationalismus ("The Fallacy of Nationalism") warned against a potential resurgence of right-wing nationalism which would threaten the laudable democratic progress made in the Federal Republic throughout its history. For Geissler, the German Federal Republic had "achieved its great successes in economic, social, and foreign policy not as a classical nation state, but rather as a democratic, cosmopolitan, and European-oriented country." Heiner Geissler, *Der Irrweg des Nationalismus* (Weinheim: Beltz Athenäum Verlag, 1995), p. 9. Despite his CDU origins, Geissler has since shifted considerably over to the left.

105 Hans-Peter Schwarz, *Die Zentralmacht Europas. Deutschlands Rückkehr auf die Weltbühne* (Berlin: Siedler, 1994).

106 Eckhard Fuhr, "Westen, was sonst?" in *FAZ* (June 8, 1994).

107 Heilbrunn, "Germany's New Right," p. 96.

108 *Finis Germania* was published posthumously by Neue Rechte publishing house Antaios following Sieferle's suicide. Siefele's tone was too morbid even for *FAZ*, which before his death had described him as "embittered, humorless, and increasingly isolated" in response to his writings on the refugee crisis—which, like Thilo Sarazzin, he viewed as an existential threat. See Christopher Caldwell, "Germany's Newest Intellectual Antihero" in *The New York Times* (July 18, 2017). See also Rolf Peter Sieferle, *Finis Germania* (Schnellroda: Antaios, 2017).

109 Rainer Zitelmann, "Wiedervereinigung … " in Weidenfeld ed., pp. 235–48.

110 See "Debatten ums deutsche Selbstverständnis" in *FAZ* (June 1993). See also "Mißgeburt der Moderne: Neue Studien zur nationalsozialistischen Herrschaft" in *FAZ* (April 1993) and Zitelmann, *Hitler: Selbstverständnis eines Revolutionärs* (Hamburg: Berg, 1987).

111 Interestingly, Zitelmann has in recent years ceased to publish historical writings and has since become a kind of neo-capitalist self-help guru, promoting the idea that there is a unique psychology, or mindset, to becoming wealthy. Zitelmann often claims that the academic institution is prejudiced against the rich, who he characterizes as an unfairly maligned minority group.

112 Bundespräsident Richard von Wieszäcker, "Gedenkveranstaltung im Plenarsaal des Deutschen Bundestages zum 40. Jahrestag des Endes des Zweiten Weltkrieges in Europa" (Bonn, May 8, 1985), available at www.bundespraesident.de.

113 See Gideon Botsch, Christoph Kopke, and Karsten Wilke, *Rechtsextrem: Biografien nach 1945* (Berlin: De Gruyter, 2023). As a result of this acknowledgment, Israel invited Weizsäcker on a diplomatic visit—the first ever visit of a German head of state to Israel.

114 Full text of "Appell 8. Mai 1945—gegen das Vergessen" reprinted in the autobiography of Rainer Zitelmann, *Wenn du nicht mehr brennst, starte neu: Mein Leben als Historiker, Journalist und Investor* (Munich: FinanzBuch, 2017), p. 120. Originally printed in *FAZ* (April 7, 1995).

115 For a shrewd critique of "Appel 8. Mai 1945", see *taz*, "Strategen der Retourkutsche" (April 15, 1995).
116 *Der Spiegel*, "Kriegsende: Volle Wahrheit" (April 16, 1995).
117 BfV, *Verfassungsschutzbericht 1996*, p. 151.
118 Meanwhile left-wing apostate provocateurs such as Strauß, Enzensberger, and Walser continued only to dig themselves into pariahdom. Walser infamously sabotaged his career for good with a speech he gave upon receiving the 1998 Frankfurt Book Fair Peace Prize, in which he condemned the "Holocaust industry" and the exploitation of Auschwitz as a "ceaseless presentation of our shame." Much has been written on the topic of Walser's speech. For a sense of the widespread furor that Walser inspired, see Thomas Kovach, *The Burden of the Past: Martin Walser on Modern German Identity: Texts, Contexts, Commentary* (Rochester: Camden House, 2008).

Chapter 3

1 Alexander Szandar, "Bundeswehr: Neonazi Eingeladen" in *Der Spiegel* (December 7, 1997); Deutsche Bundestag Drucksache 13/11005, "Beschlußempfehlung und Bericht des Verteidigungsausschusses als 1. Untersuchungsausschuß gemäß Artikel 45a Abs. 2 des Grundgesetzes" (June 18, 1998), p. 11.
2 *Spiegel* reporters, "Hitlerjunge mit Tränensäcken" (April 26, 1998); Frank Keil, "Anschlag auf Flüchtlinge: Der blanke Hass" in *Die Zeit* (February 23, 2012).
3 The "Gemeinschaftswerk" was founded by Roeder in 1993, the same year in which he was invited to Moscow for a congress of the ultra-nationalist, right-wing extremist Liberal Democratic Party of Russia. See Stefan Rehder, Gisbert Mrozek, and Rüdiger Kreissel, "Schirinowskij: Die Braunen locken" in *Focus*, no. 51 (December 20, 1993); BfV, *Verfassungsschutzbericht 1993* (Bonn: Bundesministerium des Innern, 1994), p. 118.
4 The materials had originally been requested by Roeder in a formal letter dated December 21, 1993, as confirmed in Drucksache 13/11005, subsection 2: "Unterabschnitt Materiallieferungen des Bundesministeriums der Verteidigung an das Deutsch-Russische Gemeinschaftswerk," pp. 66–79 (p. 66). See also "Bundeswehr rüstete Neonazis aus" in *TAZ* (December 9, 1997).
5 The Hamburg-based magazine *Stern* published an article about the right-wing extremist activities of Bundeswehr soldiers at an air landing school in Altenstadt and air transport school Schongau; *Bild am Sonntag* printed an apparent affidavit concerning a conscript who alleged there were regular right-wing extremist incidents in the 5th company of a paratrooper battalion in Varel, Lower Saxony; and PRO 7 broadcast recordings of a video produced in the offices of the air transport school showing Bundeswehr soldiers performing

Nazi "*sieg heil*" greetings. Drucksache 13/11005, part 1: "Einsetzung des Untersuchungsausschusses und Verlauf des Untersuchungsverfahrens sowie Parallelverfahren," pp. 11–20 (p. 11).

6   *Spiegel* reporters, "Chronik: Die Wehrmachtsausstellung zwischen Krawallen und Kritik" (November 27, 2001).

7   Andreas Baumann, "Ein notorisch Rechtsextremer will nach Bonn" in *Die Welt* (September 18, 1998).

8   Volker Rühe, "Vereinbarte Debatte über den Bericht des Bundesministers der Verteidigung zum Vortrag des Rechtsextremisten Manfred Roeder an der Führungsakademie der Bundeswehr im Jahre 1995" in *Deutscher Bundestag Plenarprotokoll*, vol. 13, no. 209 (December 10, 1997), pp. 19070–90 (p. 19072).

9   Deutscher Bundeswehr, Zielsetzung no. 17, "Richtlinien zum Traditionsverständnis und zur Traditionspflege in der Bundeswehr" (September 20, 1982), p. 2.

10 Rühe, Deutscher Bundestag Plenarprotokoll 13/209, p. 19072.

11 Brigitte Schulte (SPD), ibid., p. 19073.

12 Rühe, ibid.

13 This dismissiveness also occurred in spite of a wave of revelatory academic research from the 2000s onwards, some of it government-backed, into the presence of former Nazis in state institutions, e.g., the Foreign Office and the Interior Ministry, and major private concerns such as journalism and industrial family dynasties. See for example Norbert Frei, Tobias Freimüller, Marc von Miquel, Tim Schanetzky, Jens Scholten, and Matthias Weiß, *Karrieren im Zwielicht: Hitlers Eliten nach 1945. Das Buch zur Fernsehserie Herausgegeben* (Frankfurt am Main: Campus Verlag, 2001); Lutz Hachmeister and Friedemann Siering, *Die Herren Journalisten. Die Elite der deutschen Presse nach 1945* (Munich: C. H. Beck Verlag, 2002).

14 See Kate Connolly, "Far Right Military Scandals Put German Defence Minister under Pressure" in *The Guardian* (May 3, 2017). See also Philip Oltermann, "German Far-Right Group 'Used Police Data to Compile Death List'" in *The Guardian* (June 28, 2019); *Der Spiegel*, "Militärgeheimdienst versagt im Kampf gegen Rechtsextremisten" (November 24, 2020); *The Guardian*, "Ex-soldier faces gun ban and fine over illegal 'prepper' training in Germany" (October 13, 2020).

15 Katrin Bennhold, "Body Bags and Enemy Lists: How Far-Right Police Officers and Ex-Soldiers Planned for 'Day X'" in *The New York Times* (August 1, 2020); Bennhold, "As Neo-Nazis Seed Military Ranks, Germany Confronts 'an Enemy Within'" in *The New York Times* (July 3, 2020).

16 For a full history of the development of the Bundeswehr's internal policy leadership during the Cold War era, see Tom Dyson, ch. 2 "The Bundeswehr in its Historical and Structural Context: The Scope for Policy Leadership" in *The Politics of German Defence and Security: Policy Leadership and Military Reform in the post-Cold War Era* (New York: Berghahn, 2008), pp. 18–49.

17 See Uwe Hartmann, "Was ist los mit der Inneren Führung?" in *Ethik und Militär: Kontroversen in Militärethik & Sicherheitspolitik* (2016) http://www.ethikundmilitaer.de/de/themenueberblick/2016-innere-fuehrung/hartmann-was-ist-los-mit-der-inneren-fuehrung/.
18 Bundesarchiv, BArch BH 7–1/565 file no. 35–08–02, "Traditionserlass 1965 'Bundeswehr und Tradition'" (Freiburg: I. Korps, 1956–1995), p. 1.
19 Ibid., Article 14, p. 3.
20 See "History," https://www.bundeswehr.de/en/about-bundeswehr/history. The downsizing of the Bundeswehr occurred as part of Germany's contribution to the Treaty on Conventional Armed Forces in Europe, which was negotiated during the final years of the Cold War in anticipation of limiting military equipment and abolishing excess weaponry in peacetime.
21 Federal President Dr. Kohl, "Erklärung vom 30. Januar, 1991" in *Plenarprotokoll der 5. Sitzung* (Bonn: Deutscher Bundestag, January 30, 1991), pp. 3–90 (p. 89).
22 Ibid., p. 90.
23 Ibid.
24 See, for example, the essays, poetry, and prose collected in the following titles, which feature amongst its contributors Günther Grass, Christa Wolf, Christoph Hein, and Hans-Magnus Enzensberger. Klaus Bitterman ed., *Liebesgrüße aus Bagdad* (Berlin: Tiamat, 1991); Luchterhand Flugschrift, "*Ich will reden von der Angst meines Herzens.*" *Autorinnen und Autoren zum Golfkrieg* (Frankfurt am Main: Luchterhand, 1991). See also Sommer, "Jetzt ein Krieg? Auf keinen Fall!" in *Die Zeit* (January 11, 1991); Lothar Baier, "Kostümprobe" in *Die Zeit* (July 19, 1991).
25 Enzensberger touched upon an especially raw nerve when he drew comparisons between the paranoid rhetoric of Saddam and Hitler in particular relation to Hitler's anti-Semitism and Saddam's tirades against Israel, which the dictator attempted to provoke into war in the hopes that it would motivate other Arab nations to join forces with Iraq. Enzensberger chose to view these provocations not through the lens of geopolitics but rather characterizing Saddam's antisemitism as the self-same paranoid antisemitism of the Nazi era: "[Saddam's] project advances not through ideas but through obsessions. Of the ideas he exploits, the closer they come to craziness, the more powerful they become. This paranoia, which can explain real events only through terms of conspiracy and betrayal, is therefore not an individual sickness of the Führer, but both the necessary precondition of his agitation and its echo. For this, hatred of Jews is the ideal vehicle, an emotion that consumed Hitler and his followers as it does their modern-day counterparts." What made this comparison so taboo for German readers was that, in its muddying of distinctions and motivations, it violated the notion of the Holocaust as a singularly unique event. Hans Magnus Enzensberger, "Hitlers Wiedergänger" in *Der Spiegel* (February 14, 1991). See also the highly critical response of Detlev Claussen,

"War of Words: An Intellectual Damage Assessment after the Gulf War" in *New German Critique*, no. 57 (Autumn 1992), pp. 67–85, as well as an overview by Anson Rabinbach, "German Intellectuals and the Gulf War" in *Dissent* (Fall 1991), pp. 459–63.

26 Oskar Lafontaine and Norbert Gansel quoted in Ian Buruma, "The Pax Axis" in *The New York Review of Books* (April 25, 1991).

27 Jürgen Habermas, *Vergangenheit als Zukunft: Das alte Deutschland in neuen Europa?* (Zürich: Pendo Verlag, 1991), pp. 24–5.

28 Deutscher Bundestag, Drucksache 12/3925, "Kleine Anfrage der Abgeordneten Ulla Jelpke und der Gruppe der PDS/Linke Liste—Die Bundeswehr und der Rechtsextremismus" (December 1, 1992). See also *Der Spiegel*, "Bundeswehr: Sieg Heil" (November 16, 1992).

29 Deutscher Bundestag, Drucksache 12/4202, "Antwort der Bundesregierung auf die Kleine Anfrage der Abgeordneten Ulla Jelpke und der Gruppe der PDS/Linke Liste—Drucksache 12/3925" (January 27, 1993).

30 *Der Spiegel*, "Sieg Heil."

31 Ibid. This is a reality which has been corroborated by counterterrorism experts; as mandatory military service for all male German citizens over the age of eighteen continued until 2011, people from various different social and economic backgrounds with views ranging from across the political spectrum—even, at times, to its extreme far reaches—have regularly and unavoidably been brought into service. Yet, as Daniel Koehler has pointed out, "the question is not whether or not right-wing extremists are able to enter the military but rather if they are identified in time and if the military reacts adequately to the case (e.g., disciplinary or removal from service)." In this regard, Hansen's response at such a critical moment seems somewhat *laissez-faire*. See Daniel Koehler, "A Threat from Within? Exploring the Link between the Extreme Right and the Military" ICCT—International Center for Counter-Terrorism Policy Brief (September 2019), p. 3.

32 In this particular segment of the study participants were asked: "If you now think of the Bundeswehr as the German armed forces [as opposed to the East German NVA], what is your personal attitude towards the Bundeswehr?" Possible answers ranged from *sehr negativ* to *sehr positiv*. Heinz-Ulrich Kohr, *SOWI Arbeitspapier 77: Rechts zur Bundeswehr, Links zum Zivildienst? Orientierungsmuster von Heranwachsenden in den alten und neuen Bundesländern Ende 1992* (Strausberg: Sozialwissenschaftliches Institut der Bundeswehr, 1993), p. 8. Similar results were corroborated by a subsequent study almost ten years later in 2001 and again in 2007. See Sven Bernhard Gareis, Peter Michael Kozielski, and Michael Kratschmar, *SOWI Arbeitspapier 129: Rechtsextreme Orientierung in Deutschland und ihre Folgen für die Bundeswehr* (Strausberg: Sozialwissenschaftliches Institut der Bundeswehr, 2001); Thomas Bulmahn, *Ergebnisse der Studentenbefragung an*

den Universitäten der Bundeswehr Hamburg und München, in *Forschungsbericht* (Strausberg: Sozialwissenschaftliches Institut der Bundeswehr, 2007).

33 Drucksache 12/4202, p. 9.
34 *Der Spiegel*, "Einmal Heil Hitler" (June 19, 1994).
35 Ibid.
36 Wolfgang Brück, "Skinheads als Vorboten der Systemkrise: Die Entwicklung des Skinhead-Phänomens bis zum Untergang der DDR" in Karl-Heinz Heinemann and Wilfried Schubarth eds., *Der antifaschistische Statt entlässt seine Kinder: Jugend und Rechtsextremismus in Ostdeutschland* (Cologne: PapyRossa Verlag, 1992), pp. 37–46 (pp. 44–5).
37 Andreas Hedwig, "NS-Vergangenheit ehemaliger hessischer Landtagsabgeordneter. Dokumentation der Fachtagung 14. und 15. März 2013 im Hessischen Landtag." Hessische Landtag (2014), p. 187.
38 Harald Thomas for *DMZ*, quoted by Ulla Jelpke in "Kleine Anfrage der Abgeordneten Ulla Jelpke und der Gruppe der PDS—Die 'Deutsche Militärzeitschrift' (DMZ), der DMZ-Verlag und der Rechtsextremismus." Deutscher Bundestag, Drucksache 13/1226 (April 27, 1995).
39 Ibid.
40 As cited by Katja Thorwarth in her article on far-right communities of so-called ethnic Germans, "Heimattreue Netzwerke im tiefbraunen Sumpf" in *Frankfurter Rundschau* (September 24, 2019).
41 *DMZ* reporters, "Ursachenforschung: Eine weitere Studie sucht nach Gründen für die Kampfkraft der Waffen-SS" in *DMZ-Zeitgeschichte*, no. 56 (March/April, 2022).
42 Elmar Vieregge, "Das Magazin 'DMZ Zeitgeschichte' und die Verherrlichung der Waffen-SS am Zeitschriftenkiosk" for *Endstation Rechts* (May 18, 2013).
43 Kopp has also been an editor for *Junge Freiheit*, one of the longest-running neo-Nazi magazines in Germany. See Drucksache 13/1226.
44 The photographs contained in *Wenn alle Brüder schweigen* neither shy away from depictions of battle nor face up to the criminality of the Waffen-SS. The book's main goal is to highlight the hardships of war via images of fatigue, hunger, and steadfast comradeship, culminating in the sly portrayal of an honorable Waffen-SS fit for historical rehabilitation. Hilfsgemeinschaft auf Gegenseitigkeit der Angehörigen der ehemaligen Waffen-SS, *Wenn alle Brüder schweigen: Grosser Bildband über die Waffen-SS* (Osnabruck: Munin Verlag, 1973).
45 Deutscher Bundestag, Drucksache 13/1460, "Antwort der Bundesregierung auf die Kleine Anfrage der Abgeordneten Ulla Jelpke und der Gruppe der PDS—Drucksache 13/1226" (May 19, 1995).
46 Deutscher Bundestag, Drucksache 16/1282, "Antwort der Bundesregierung auf die Kleine Anfrage der Abgeordneten Ulla Jelpke, Sevim Dagdelen, Kersten Naumann, weiterer Abgeordneter und der Fraktion Die Linke—Drucksache 16/1083—

Traditionsverbände, Kameradschaftsvereine und der Rechtsextremismus" (April 25, 2006); Deutscher Bundestag, Drucksache 16/9550, "Antwort der Bundesregierung auf die Kleine Anfrage der Abgeordneten Ulla Jelpke, Inge Höger, Petra Pau, Paul Schäfer (Köln) und der Fraktion Die Linke—Drucksache 16/9292—Kontakte zwischen Bundeswehr und Anzeigenkunden der im rechtsextremistischen Spektrum angesiedelten Deutschen Militärzeitschrift" (June 12, 2008).

47 Rosellini, *Literary Skinheads?*
48 *Deutsche Welle*, "The Balkan Dilemma: Germany returns to military action" (December 28, 2010). *Inter Press Service News Agency*, "Conflict-Europe: German Involvement in Yugoslavia Criticised" (March 28, 1999); *Deutsche Welle*, "Germany's struggle with military power in a changing world" (December 28, 2010).
49 As evidenced above in the government's response to inquiries about *DMZ*. See Drucksache 13/1460.
50 The mistaken display of images of the Soviet NKVD would, in 1999, see the exhibition temporarily closed amid much public and political criticism—which in turn contributed to feelings of justification amongst those on both the mainstream right and the far-right who had railed against the exhibition from its inception. The emotionally laden nature of the *Wehrmachtsausstellung* debate provided an unfortunate climate in which the discovery of falsely labelled photographs quickly became sensationalized. Though the content of the exhibition was revised by a transnational panel of historians—and a new version (which toured from 2001) was praised for including more historical analysis and for centering the victims in its narrative—this new exhibit still drew small-scale protests from far-right groups. The original curator of the exhibit, Hannes Heer, vocally distanced himself from the second *Wehrmachtsausstellung*, complaining that too few historical exhibitions focus on identifying the perpetrators, resulting in a continued amnesia regarding the participation of ordinary Germans in a war of extermination. See Hannes Heer, *Vom Verschwinden der Täter: Der Vernichtungskrieg fand statt, aber keiner war dabei* (Berlin: Aufbau Verlag, 2004). See also Hans Monath, "Falsche Bilder, echte Gefühle—die Wehrmachtsausstellung muss nun überprüfen, was sie zeigt und erzeugt" in *Der Tagesspiegel* (October 21, 1999); *Die Welt*, "Die zweifelhafte Macht der Bilder" (October 21, 1999); Omer Bartov, "The Wehrmacht Exhibition Controversy: The Politics of Evidence" in Omer Bartov, Atina Grossmann, and Mary Nolan eds., *Crimes of War: Guilt and Denial in the Twentieth Century* (New York: The New Press, 2002), pp. 41–60; Bill Niven, ch. 6 "The Crimes of the *Wehrmacht*" in *Facing the Nazi Past: United Germany and the Legacy of the Third Reich* (New York: Routledge, 2002), pp. 143–74.
51 For the role of this founding myth in the shaping of the Federal Republic under Adenauer, see Norbert Frei, *Vergangenheitspolitik: Die Anfänge der Bundesrepublik und die NS-Vergangenheit* (Munich: DTV Verlag, 1999); Mary Fulbrook,

Reckonings: Legacies of Nazi Persecution and the Quest for Justice (Oxford: Oxford University Press, 2018).

52 Augstein for *Der Spiegel*.
53 Michael Frucht Levy, "'The Last Bullet for the Last Serb': The Ustaša Genocide against the Serbs, 1941–1945" in *Nationalities* Papers, vol. 37, no. 6 (December 2009), pp. 807–37; Jozo Tomasevich, *War and Revolution in Yugoslavia, 1941–1945: Occupation and Collaboration* (Stanford, CA: Stanford University Press, 2001); Holm Sundhaussen, "Jugoslawien" in Wolfgang Benz ed., *Dimension des Völkermords: Die Zahl der jüdischen Opfer des Nationalsozialismus* (Munich: R. Oldenbourg, 1991), pp. 311–30; Gerhard Grimm, "Albanien" in Wolfgang Benz ed., *Dimension des Völkermords: Die Zahl der jüdischen Opfer des Nationalsozialismus* (Munich: R. Oldenbourg, 1991), pp. 229–39.
54 Other German politicians from across the political spectrum argued that there was no reason for Germany to abstain from involvement in UN-sanctioned actions. Most, however, argued that Germany was still prohibited under the Basic Law from deploying forces unless in defense of itself or of a NATO ally. Since the Gulf War, Chancellor Kohl had campaigned for an amendment to this article of the Basic Law. See Glatz, Hansen, Kaim, and Vorrath. See also "The Bosnia Crisis: Germany rules out Balkans war role" in *The Independent* (August 7, 1992).
55 The words of Florian Sturmfall for *Der Bayernkurier*, "Wie Deutsche diffamiert werden" (February 22, 1997). The snowballing of right-wing critique against this exhibit was initiated by CSU MP Peter Gauweiler, who at the first annual dinner of the CSU at the Hofbräuhaus in Munich, on February 14, 1996, described the director of the Hamburg Institute for Social Research, Jan Philipp Reemtsma, as the "tobacco millionaire Reemtsma" and argued "[Reemtsma] should put on an exhibition about the dead and injured from the billions of cigarettes he sold and to whom he owes his fortune." Other CSU members present expressed their assent with enthusiastic applause. See Deutsche Bundestag, Drucksache 13/7311, "Kleine Anfrage der Abgeordneten Ulla Jelpke und der Gruppe der PDS: Die bundesweite Kampagne der Neonazi-Szene gegen die Ausstellung 'Vernichtungskrieg. Verbrechen der Wehrmacht 1941 bis 1944'" (March 17, 1997).
56 *TAZ*, "Schwarzbraune Allianz: Neonazis und CSU kämpfen für die Ehre der Wehrmacht" (February 2, 1997).
57 Ibid.; see also *MDR*, "Die Debatte der 90er-Jahre: Die Wehrmachtausstellung und das weit verzweigte Netz der Neonazis" (April 12, 2021).
58 Anton Maegerle for *Blick Nach Rechts* (today known as *Endstation Rechts*), "'Anti-deutsche Hetze'—Rechtsextremisten machen bundesweit mobil gegen eine Ausstellung, die die Verbrechen der Wehrmacht dokumentiert" (February 4, 1997).

59 Fabian Virchow, *Gegen den Zivilismus: Internationale Beziehungen und Militär in den politischen Konzeptionen der extremen Rechten* (Wiesbaden: VS Verlag für Sozialwissenschaften, 2008), p. 430.

60 BfV, *Verfassungsschutzbericht 1997* (Bonn: Bundesministerium des Innern, 1998), pp. 71–2. See also *Associated Press*, "Rightists demonstrate in Munich, leftists stage counter protest" (March 1, 1997); *TAZ*, "Münchner Wehr gegen rechte Macht: Bayerische Landeshauptstadt verbietet Großdemo von Rechtsextremisten zur neuen Wehrmachtsausstellung" (October 11, 2002).

61 *The New York Times*, "Neo-Nazis Battle German Leftists Over Anti-Nazi Exhibit" (January 25, 1998).

62 *Die Welt*, "Sprengstoffanschlag auf Wehrmacht-Ausstellung" (March 10, 1999); *The Independent*, "Neo-Nazi bomb blast wrecks army war crimes exhibition" (March 10, 1999).

63 BfV, *Verfassungsschutzbericht 1997*, p. 72.

64 The far right's decades-long reliance on digital communication forums will be explored further in Chapter 3.

65 BfV, *Verfassungsschutzbericht 1997*, p. 72.

66 Ibid., p. 72.

67 For a journalistic take on these debates see Rudolf Augstein, "Anschlag auf die ‚Ehre' des deutschen Soldaten?" in *Der Spiegel* (March 10, 1997).

68 Deutscher Bundestag, Drucksache 13/7188, "Antrag der Abgeordneten Gerhard Zwerenz, Heinrich Graf von Einsiedel, Dr. Gregor Gysi und der Gruppe der PDS Ausstellung 'Vernichtungskrieg. Verbrechen der Wehrmacht 1941–1944'" (March 12, 1997). See also Deutscher Bundestag, Drucksache 13/7175 "Antrag der Abgeordneten Otto Schily [et al.] … und der Fraktion der SPD. Ausstellung 'Vernichtungskrieg. Verbrechen der Wehrmacht 1941–1944'" (March 12, 1997).

69 Schäuble, Glos, and Solms also voiced sympathy for the "deep pangs of conscience" experienced by innocent soldiers who had been embroiled in a war of aggression by a totalitarian regime: "The tragedy of many soldiers is characterized by the fact that subjectively honorable and brave service was objectively done in unison with commitment to a criminal regime." Deutscher Bundestag, Drucksache 13/7162 "Antrag der Fraktionen der CDU/CSU und F. D. P. Ausstellung 'Vernichtungskrieg. Verbrechen der Wehrmacht 1941–1944'" (March 11, 1997).

70 Rühe, *Deutscher Bundestag Plenarprotokoll*, 13/209, p. 19072.

71 *Der Spiegel*, "Neonazi eingeladen" (December 8, 1997); *The New York Times*, "Convicted Neo-Nazi's Lecture at Army School Shocks Germans" (December 10, 1997).

72 Deutscher Bundestag, Drucksache 13/9077, "Kleine Anfrage der Abgeordneten Ulla Jelpke, Eva-Maria Bulling-Schröter, Heinrich Graf von Einsiedel, Gerhard Zwerenz, Dr. Gregor Gysi und der Gruppe der PDS—Zunahme von rechtsextremen Vorfällen in der Bundeswehr" (October 28, 1997).

73 These concerns were in direct response to in response to both Roeder's appearance at the Hamburg Leadership Academy and the ongoing anti-*Wehrmachtsausstellung* demonstrations. See Deutscher Bundestag, Drucksache 13/8929, "Kleine Anfrage der Abgeordneten Ulla Jelpke und der Gruppe der PDS—Die Hochschulen der Bundeswehr und national-konservatives Denken" (November 3, 1997) as well as Drucksache 13/7311.

74 Deutscher Bundestag, Drucksache 13/9456, "Antwort der Bundesregierung auf die Kleine Anfrage der Abgeordneten Ulla Jelpke, Eva-Maria Bulling-Schröter, Heinrich Graf von Einsiedel, weiterer Abgeordneter und der Gruppe der PDS—Drucksache 13/9077" (December 12, 1997).

75 Ibid.

76 *Der Spiegel*, "Die schwarze Serie" (December 15, 1997).

77 The footage had originally been filmed in April 1996. *Die Welt*, "Skandal erschüttert Bundeswehr" (July 7, 1997).

78 *Der Spiegel*, "Schwarze Serie."

79 See the afore mentioned *Spiegel* articles as well as "Höchst problematisch" (May 23, 1997) and "Militär: Greise Popstars mit Ritterkreuz" (October 27, 1997).

80 Götz Kubitschek, "Soldaten sind Schauspieler" in *Junge Freiheit* (July 11, 1997).

81 *Die Welt*, "Skandal …"

82 Felser, today an MP for the Alternative für Deutschland party who characterizes himself as part of their so-called "moderate" wing, studied from 1992 to 1996 at the Universität der Bundeswehr Hamburg, where he was accepted into a "*völkisch* and nationalist" student association which required its members to pledge their lifelong devotion. He later became the spokesperson for a Munich branch of the Deutsche Gildenschaft ("Heinrich der Löwe"), a network of elite guilds with historical roots in the Wandervogel movement as well as in *völkisch*-nationalist ideology. Though Felser today denies, where possible, all connection to his former comrade Kubitschek, in 1998 the two co-founded, along with Bernd Widmer, the far-right film production company WK&F (which stands for Widmer, Kubitschek and Felser—though Felser claims the "K" stands for "Kommunikation"), a distributor of extremist DVDs, CDs, and literature—including, in 2001 and 2003, antisemitic election materials for the REP party. Kubitschek himself seems to have agreed at some stage to go along with denying his and Felser's association; copies of the now out-of-print *Raki am Igman* are almost impossible to find. When I contacted Antaios—Kubitschek's highly successful far-right publishing house, who once issued a second edition of *Raki am Igman*—they assured me I would not find a single copy in the world today. I found a copy, however, at the New York Public Library. Sebastian Lipp, "Die rechten Seilschaften des AfD-Vizes" in *Die Zeit* (May 18, 2018); Etienne la Marie, "Unternehmen des Allgäuer Bundestagsabgeordneten Peter Felser (AfD): Propaganda-Material für Rechtsextremisten" in *Allgäuer Zeitung* (December 15, 2017).

83 Kubitschek and Peter Felser, *Raki am Igman: Texte und Reportagen aus dem Bosnien-Einsatz der Bundeswehr* (Schnellroda: Edition Antaios, 2001 [1999]), p. 87. The first printing of *Raki am Igman* was issued by an unknown publisher referred to as Edition die Lanze, which provided only a PO Box in Steinheim, Bavaria and seems to have published no other texts. It features, in its endpapers, poetry by interwar *Blut- und Boden* writers such as Hermann Löns and Agnes Meidel, as well as several advertisements for CDs filled with *Bündisch* folk songs. These are absent from the second edition.

84 Kubitschek, p. 8.

85 Kubitschek, pp. 8–9.

86 Kubitschek, *Raki am Igman*, p. 121.

87 Tobias Rapp, "Der dunkle Ritter Götz" in *Der Spiegel* (December 2016). The first *Wehrmachtsausstellung* would be followed by a second installment which toured from 2001 to 2004, titled *Verbrechen der Wehrmacht. Dimensionen des Vernichtungskrieges 1941–1944*.

88 Alfred Schickel, "Wanderausstellung: Neuauflage propagandistischer Schauprozesse" in *Junge Freiheit* (April 25, 1997). See also Ellen Kositza, "Anti-Wehrmachtsausstellung: Die Nachdenklichkeit nimmt zu" in *Junge Freiheit* (April 18, 1997); Frank Liebermann, "Liberaler Totalitarismus" in *Junge Freiheit* (August 29, 1997).

89 Kubitschek, *Raki am Igman*, p. 124. Unfortunately, these criticisms closely mimic the issues that many historians eventually agreed upon in their assessment of the exhibit in 1999, after it was confirmed that some of the photographs showed NKVD soldiers. See again Monath, "Falsche Bilder"; *Die Welt*, "Die zweifelhafte"; and Bartov, "The Wehrmacht Exhibition Controversy."

90 It seems to be this dismissal which prompted him to reissue *Raki am Igman* with some amendments and a second foreword.

91 Major General von Scotti quoted in the pages of *Junge Freiheit*, in which the notice was re-printed in full as part of the magazine's campaign against Kubitschek's dismissal. *Junge Freiheit*, "Appell an die Bundeswehr: Gegen die Entlassung konservativer Soldaten. Der 'Fall Götz Kubitschek'" (September 28, 2001).

92 Ibid.

93 Helmut Kellershohn, "Provokationselite von rechts: Die Konservativ-subversive Aktion" in Regina Wamper, Helmut Kellershohn, and Martin Dietzsch eds., *Rechte Diskurspiraterien. Strategien der Aneignung linker Codes, Symbole und Aktionsformen* (Münster: Unrast, 2010), pp. 224–40.

94 Kubitschek quoted in Kellershohn, "Provokationselite von rechts ... " p. 228.

95 Deutscher Bundestag, Drucksache 14/6205, "Kleine Anfrage der Abgeordneten Carsten Hübner, Ulla Jelpke, Heidi Lippmann, Roland Claus und der Fraktion der PDS—Deutsche Söldner in bewaffneten Konflikten" (May 30, 2001).

96 "Antwort der Bundesregierung auf die Kleine Anfrage der Abgeordneten Carsten Hübner, Ulla Jelpke, Heidi Lippmann, Roland Claus und der Fraktion der PDS—Deutsche Söldner in bewaffneten Konflikten." Deutscher Bundestag, Drucksache 14/6413 (June 21, 2001).
97 Ibid.
98 Nenad Radicevic, "'We Are Their Voice': German Far-Right Builds Balkan Alliances" in *Balkan Insight* (October 24, 2019).
99 Deutscher Bundestag, Drucksache 14/859, "Kleine Anfrage der Abgeordneten Ulla Jelpke, Petra Pau und der Fraktion der PDS—Der Verfassungsschutzbericht des Bundes für das Jahr 1998" (April 23, 1999).
100 Deutscher Bundestag, Drucksache 14/1485, "Antwort der Bundesregierung auf die Kleine Anfrage der Abgeordneten Ulla Jelpke, Heidi Lippmann-Kasten, Petra Pau und der Fraktion der PDS—Drucksache 14/1376" (August 13, 1999).
101 Ibid.
102 Major General Dr. Jürgen Schreiber, *Soldat im Volk,* no. 3 (1998), p. 64.
103 "Antwort der Bundesregierung auf die Kleine Anfrage der Abgeordneten Winfried Nachtwei, Angelika Beer, Christian Sterzing, Annelie Buntenbach und der Fraktion Bündnis 90/Die Grünen—Drucksache 13/10273—Soldatische Traditionsverbände und ihre Beziehungen zur Bundeswehr." Deutscher Bundestag, Drucksache 13/10593 (May 5, 1998).
104 *Alte Kameraden* no. 44 (December 1996), p. 8.
105 Ibid.
106 *Inter Press Service News Agency*, "Conflict-Europe: German Involvement in Yugoslavia Criticised" (March 28, 1999). *Deutsche Welle*, "The Balkan Dilemma: Germany returns to military action" (December 28, 2010).
107 Carolin Hilpert, *Strategic Cultural Change and the Challenge for Security Policy: Germany and the Bundeswehr's Deployment to Afghanistan* (New York: Palgrave, 2014), p. 41. See also Ralf Beste et al., "Ein deutscher Krieg" in Der Spiegel (September 5, 2011).
108 Chancellor Gerhard Schröder, Plenarprotokoll 14/192 (October 11, 2001), p. 18682. See also. Dyson, *Politics of German Defence and Security*, pp. 87–147.
109 Anja Dalgaard-Nielsen, "The Gulf War: The German Resistance" in *Survival—Global Politics and Strategy* vol. 45, no. 1 (Spring 2003), pp. 99–116.
110 Defense Chief General Harald Kujat had initially presented a number of military capabilities with which Germany could contribute to the United States' response to 9/11 "on the basis of what could be needed, what Germany could offer, and what would be acceptable in the eyes of the public." This is how the KSK were deployed in the first instance—100 men to Afghanistan, to the Arabian Peninsula, and to north-eastern Africa and bordering sea areas. These were the first German

ground forces to participate in combat operations outside of Europe since the Second World War. Hilpert, p. 42.
111 *Deutsche Welle*, "Germany's struggle with military power in a changing world" (December 28, 2010).
112 Hohmann was subsequently expelled from the CDU in 2004 and has, since 2017, returned to the Bundestag as an MP for AfD.
113 *Deutsche Welle* (*DW*) reporters, "Top General Sacked as Anti-Semitism Scandal Spreads" (November 5, 2003).
114 Richard Bernstein, "German General Fired for Backing Slur on Jews" in *The New York Times* (November 5, 2003).
115 *DW*, "Top General Sacked."
116 Response of State Parliamentary Secretary for the Federal Ministry of Defense Walter Kolbow to the written question of Martin Hohmann himself (by this time no longer representing the CDU party). Hohmann's motivations for asking about this are unclear in the document. See Abgeordneter Martin Hohmann (fraktionslos), Deutscher Bundestag, Drucksache 15/3253, "Schriftliche Fragen mit den in der Woche vom 24. Mai 2004 eingegangenen Antworten der Bundesregierung" (May 28, 2004), pp. 22–4 (p. 24).
117 The GSG 9 is a counterterrorist tactical unit of the federal police in Germany, founded and given its initial methodological doctrine by Ulrich K. Wegener, who co-authored this volume. Note that *Geheime Krieger* was published and distributed by an independent publishing imprint that called itself "Pour le Mérite"—the name of an order of merit established by King Frederick II of Prussia. The imprint almost exclusively publishes volumes devoted to the history of the Waffen-SS. Reinhard Günzel, Wilhelm Walther and Ulrich K. Wegener, *Geheime Krieger. Drei deutsche Kommandoverbände im Bild—KSK, Brandenburger, GSG 9* (Martensrade: Pour le Mérite, 2006).
118 Kubitschek and Reinhard Günzel, *Und plötzlich ist alles politisch. Im Gespräch mit Brigadegeneral Reinhard Günzel* (Schnellroda: Edition Antaios, 2004).
119 *Der Spiegel*, "KSK-Soldaten sprühten Wehrmachtssymbol auf Wagen" (November 11, 2006).
120 *Deutsche Welle*, "German Soldiers Accused of Abusing Terror Suspect" (January 8, 2007); John Goetz and Holger Stark, "New Testimony May Back Kurnaz Torture Claims" in *Spiegel International* (September 3, 2007).
121 Hilpert, p. 71. See also the following parliamentary debates: Deutscher Bundestag, Plenarprotokoll 15/139, Tagesordnungspunkt 19: "Beschlussempfehlung und Bericht des Auswärtigen Ausschusses zu dem Antrag der Bundesregierung: Fortsetzung des Einsatzes bewaffneter deutscher Streitkräfte bei der Unterstützung der gemeinsamen Reaktion auf terroristische Angriffe gegen die USA … " (November 12, 2004), pp. 12783–96; Deutscher Bundestag, Plenarprotokoll 16/2, Tagesordnungspunkt 4: "Abgabe einer Erklärung durch die

Bundesregierung: Weißbuch 2006 zur Sicherheitspolitik Deutschlands und zur Zukunft der Bundeswehr" (October 26, 2006), pp. 5782–803.

122 Original phrasing and syntax of Daniel K. in his email, quoted in Deutscher Bundestag, Drucksache 16/8821, "Kleine Anfrage der Abgeordneten Ulla Jelpke, Sevim Dağdelen, Inge Höger, Petra Pau, Paul Schäfer (Köln) und der Fraktion Die Linke—Rechtsextrem motivierte Gewaltdrohungen eines KSK-Hauptmanns gegen einen Angehörigen des 'Darmstädter Signals'" (April 10, 2008).

123 *Fememorden* were politically motivated killings perpetrated by conspiratorial right-wing groups during the Weimar Republic. The term, adopted by the far-right of the 1920s itself, comes from *feme*, or *veime* in Middle Low German, meaning "punishment"—in the Middle Ages, *Femegerichten* served as a form of criminal justice.

124 Drucksache 16/8821.

125 See Deutscher Bundestag, Drucksache 16/9017, "Antwort der Bundesregierung. auf die Kleine Anfrage der Abgeordneten Ulla Jelpke, Sevim Dağdelen, Inge Höger, weiterer Abgeordneter und der Fraktion Die Linke—Drucksache 16/8821" (April 30, 2008).

126 Ibid.

127 *Süddeutsche Zeitung*, "Bundeswehr suspendiert Offizier wegen Reichsbürger-Verdachts" (February 8, 2019).

128 Adam Tooze, *Crashed: How a Decade of Financial Crises Changed the World* (New York, NY: Viking Press, 2018), p. 345.

129 Deutscher Bundestag, Drucksache 17/12050, "Unterrichtung durch den Wehrbeauftragten. Jahresbericht 2012" (January 29, 2013), p. 12.

130 Ibid.

131 Deutscher Bundestag, Drucksache 17/8061, "Kleine Anfrage der Fraktion Die Linke—Schusswaffentraining für Nazis bei Reservisten—und Schützenvereinen und möglicher Änderungsbedarf beim Waffengesetz" (November 30, 2011).

132 Deutscher Bundestag, Drucksache 17/8334, "Kleine Anfrage der Fraktion Die Linke—Erfassung rechtsextremer Aktivitäten von Bundeswehrsoldaten" (January 17, 2012); Deutscher Bundestag, Drucksache 17/10831, "Kleine Anfrage der Faktion Die Linke—Hinweise auf rechtsterroristische Strukturen" (September 25, 2012); Deutscher Bundestag, Drucksache 17/14532, "Kleine Anfrage der Faktion Die Linke—Rechtsextreme Vorfälle in der Bundeswehr" (August 8, 2013); Deutscher Bundestag, Drucksache 17/12666, "Kleine Anfrage der Faktion Die Linke—Rechtsextreme in privaten Wachschutzunternehmen" (March 11, 2013).

133 Deutscher Bundestag, Drucksache 18/2113, "Kleine Anfrage der Faktion Die Linke—Rechtsextreme Vorfälle in der Bundeswehr und die Reaktion der Militärführung" (July 10, 2014); Deutscher Bundestag, Drucksache 18/4677, "Kleine Anfrage der Faktion Die Linke—Umgang der Bundeswehr mit Rechtsextremisten in ihren Reihen" (April 21, 2015).

134 *The Guardian*, "Far Right Military Scandals Put German Defence Minister under Pressure" (May 3, 2017).
135 These concepts, which became widely popularized throughout Europe during the years of the refugee crisis, are discussed in greater depth in Chapter 5.
136 Severin Weiland, "Der rechte Kosmos des Franco A." in *Der Spiegel* (May 20, 2017).
137 *The Guardian*, "Far Right Military Scandals …" Von der Leyen's remarks made her extremely unpopular amongst Bundeswehr soldiers, who felt that their patriotism and service had been insulted. See *Bild*, "Warum stellen Sie alle Bundeswehr-Soldaten in den Senkel?" (May 5, 2017).
138 Bennhold, "Body Bags and Enemy Lists."
139 Bennhold, "Body Bags and Enemy Lists" and "Neo-Nazis Seed Military Ranks."
140 *Der Spiegel*, "Militärgeheimdienst versagt im Kampf gegen Rechtsextremisten" (November 24, 2020); *The Guardian*, "Ex-soldier Faces Gun Ban and Fine over Illegal 'Prepper' Training in Germany" (October 13, 2020).
141 *Monitor*, "Uniter: Paramilitärisches Training für Zivilisten?" (Uploaded to YouTube December 19, 2019) https://www.youtube.com/watch?v=bDEe_R9W1Q0.
142 *The Guardian*, "German Group with Far-Right 'Prepper' Links Trains Civilians for Combat" (December 7, 2019).
143 BfV, *Rechtsextremisten in Sicherheitsbehörden. Lagebericht* (Köln: Bundesamt für Verfassungsschutz September 2020).

Chapter 4

1 Notable works on this topic include Cas Mudde, *Populist Radical Right Parties in Europe* (Cambridge: Cambridge University Press, 2007); Andrea Mammone, Emmanuel Godin, and Brian Jenkins eds., *Mapping the Extreme Right in Contemporary Europe: From Local to Transnational* (London: Routledge, 2012); Ruth Wodak, Majid Khosravinik, and Brigitte Mral, *Right-Wing Populism in Europe: Politics and Discourse* (London: Bloomsbury, 2013).
2 The BNP in Britain has been in steady decline since 2014 as many of its former followers and adherents have migrated over to the much more successful British Independent Party/Brexit Party. Meanwhile the Hungarian Jobbik has in many ways conceded to the ultra-conservative Fidesz party.
3 The NPD also won 4 percent of the vote in the Saarland region and, earlier that year in June, had been able for the first time to take up city council seats in Mecklenburg-Vorpommern, benefitting from the landmark abolition of the 5 percent threshold rule. Uwe Backes, "The Electoral Victory of the NPD in Saxony and the Prospects for Future Extreme-Right Success in German Elections" in *Patterns of Prejudice*, vol. 40, no. 2 (2006), pp. 129–41 (p. 131).

4   Adorno, *Aspekte des neuen Rechtsradikalismus*, p. 15.
5   Christian Fuchs and John Goetz, *Die Zelle. Rechter Terror in Deutschland* (Reinbek bei Hamburg: Rowohlt, 2012).
6   Lee McGowan, "Right-Wing Violence in Germany: Assessing the Objectives, Personalities and Terror Trail of the National Socialist Underground and the State's Response to It" in *German Politics*, vol. 23, no. 3 (2014), pp. 196–212 (p. 197).
7   Bert Klandermans and Nonna Mayer eds., *Extreme Right Activists in Europe: Through the Magnifying Glass* (New York: Routledge, 2006).
8   Most notable here is NSU-Watch, an independent watchdog maintained and funded by volunteers and donations from a variety of anti-fascist organizations and research groups, which has been archiving documents and providing background information since before the NSU trials began in Munich, 2013. www.NSU-watch.info.
9   Daniel Koehler, *Right-Wing Terrorism in the 21st Century: The "National Socialist Underground" and the History of Terror from the Far-Right in Germany* (London: Routledge, 2018); Koehler, "Right-Wing Extremism and Terrorism in Europe: Current Developments and Issues for the Future" in *PRISM*, vol. 6, no. 2, Institute for National Strategic Security (2016).
10 Caspar Bildner, "Tatort Netzwerk: Wie weit reichen die Kreise des rechten Terrors? Eine Bestandsaufnahme" in *Das Dossier: Portal für kritischen Journalismus* (January 7, 2012); Eike Sanders, Kevin Stützel, and Klara Tymanova, "Taten und Worte—Neonazistische 'Blaupausen' des NSU" in Bodo Ramelow ed., *Schreddern, Spitzeln, Staatsversagen. Wie rechter Terror, Behördenkumpanei und Rassismus aus der Mitte zusammengehen* (Hamburg: VSA Verlag, 2013); Dirk Laabs, "Der NSU, 'The Order' und die neue Art des Kampfes" in *Antifaschistisches Infoblatt* (February 11, 2015); Michael Weiss, "The NSU in the Network of Blood & Honor and Combat 18" for *NSU-Watch.info* (August 6, 2015); Ulli Jentsch, "Im 'Rassenkrieg'—Von der Nationalsozialistischen Bewegung zum NS-Untergrund" in Heike Kleffner and Anna Spangenberg eds., *Generation Hoyerswerda. Das Netzwerk militanter Neonazis in Brandenburg* (Berlin: be.bra Verlag 2016).
11 See Martin Gurri, *The Revolt of the Public and the Crisis of Authority in the New Millennium* (San Francisco: Stripe Press, 2018).
12 See *Communication on Criminal Use of the Internet*, European Commission/Europol (April 9, 1997); Les Back, Mitchell Keith, and John Solomos, "Nation and Race: The Developing Euro-American Racist Subculture" in Jeffrey Kaplan and Bjorgo Tore eds., *Racism on the Internet: Mapping Neo-Fascist Subcultures in Cyberspace* (Boston: Northeastern University Press, 1998); Michael Whine of theUK's Community Security Trust, "Cyberspace—A New Medium for Communication, Command, and Control by Extremists" in *Studies in Conflict & Terrorism*, vol. 22, no. 3 (1999), pp. 231–45.
13 Kathleen Belew, *Bring the War Home: The White Power Movement and Paramilitary America* (Cambridge, MA: Harvard University Press, 2018), p. 120.

14 Louis L. Beam, "Leaderless Resistance" in *The Seditionist*, no. 12 (February 1992).
15 As argued compellingly by Koehler, "Right-Wing Extremism and Terrorism in Europe."
16 In addition, from 2001 onwards this oversight had been compounded by intense focus on Islamist terror following the attack on the World Trade Center on September 11, 2001. In Germany, where several Al Qaeda members had lived for years undetected—aka the "Hamburg Cell"—the BfV received increased funding in order to better monitor potential Islamist extremism. Marking a shift away from a focus on domestic terrorism which had peaked throughout the 1970s and 1980s due to the prolific activities of the Red Army Faction, post-9/11 threats to domestic security were viewed as stemming from outside of Germany's borders. See Francis T. Miko and Christian Froehlich, Congressional Research Service Report for Congress, "Germany's Role in Fighting Terrorism: Implications for U.S. Policy." Library of Congress (December 27, 2004).
17 Jacob Kushner, "10 Murders, 3 Nazis, and Germany's Moment of Reckoning" in *Foreign Policy* (March 16, 2017).
18 Koehler, *Right-Wing Terrorism*, p. 129.
19 See Fuchs and Goetz.
20 *FAZ*, "Generalbundesanwalt Harald Range: 'Die NSU-Morde sind unser 11. September'" (March 25, 2012).
21 Kushner, "10 Murders … "; *Spiegel*, "Brown Army Faction"; Koehler, p. 131.
22 *Die Welt*, "Dokumentation. Die Aussage der Beate Zschäpe" (December 9, 2015).
23 Antifaschistisches Pressearchiv und Bildungszentrum (APABIZ), "Transkript Bekennervideo NSU" (Berlin: November 2011).
24 Ibid.
25 Koehler, *Right-Wing Terrorism*, p. 131.
26 *Spiegel*, "FBI vermutete Ausländerhass als Tatmotiv" (April 23, 2012).
27 Koehler, *Right-Wing Terrorism*, pp. 128–9.
28 "I guess you had no other choice / You probably can't go back now / The camaraderie remains / The fight goes on for our German Fatherland." Eichnlaub lyrics quoted in Simone Rafael, "Nazi-Bands singen seit Jahren über die NSU" for *Belltower News—Netz für Digitale Zivilgesellschaft* (November 17, 2011).
29 Koehler, *Right-Wing Terrorism*, p. 128.
30 Ibid., p. 133.
31 Deutscher Bundestag Drucksache 17/14600, "Rechtsextremismus in Deutschland seit den 90er Jahren und Rolle der Sicherheitsbehörden in Bezug auf Rechtsextremismus" in *Beschlussempfehlung und Bericht des 2. Untersuchungsausschusses nach Artikel 44 des Grundgesetzes* (August 22, 2013), pp. 137–256 (p. 175). See also *Antifaschistisches Infoblatt*, "Das Netzwerk der Hammerskins"—a compendium of *Infoblatt* reportage on the Hammerskins since 1998. https://www.antifainfoblatt.de/dossier/das-netzwerk-der-hammerskins.

32 Böhnhardt's troubles began after he was made to transfer schools during the nation-wide education reforms which followed unification in 1991. By 1992, his parents had contacted the Thuringian social services due to his ever more worrying behavior; he had become involved with a local skinhead gang, with whom he committed acts of violence and petty crimes. After a brief stint at a school for troubled youths, Böhnhardt left without a degree and drifted deeper into a life of crime and violence. Following a sixteen-week sentence at a juvenile detention facility in 1993, Böhnhardt seemed to adopt a new approach. He went back to school to obtain his certificates and to train as a craftsman. He also briefly stopped committing crimes, yet became even closer to Mundlos and Zschäpe, who were practically the only two people he was ever seen with in public during this time. It could be surmised that Böhnhardt's short-lived period of reform is attributable to advice received from Mundlos and Zschäpe in the interests of avoiding drawing too much attention to both himself and his cohorts. Fuchs and Goetz, pp. 88–100; Koehler, *Right-Wing Terrorism*, pp. 133–4; *Der Spiegel International*, "The Brown Army Faction: A Disturbing New Dimension of Far-Right Terror" (November 14, 2011).
33 In addition, Kameradschaft Jena were considered to be a group of "no more than eight people." *Der Spiegel*, "Brown Army Faction."
34 See the conclusions drawn by the Thuringian Interior Ministry. Gerhard Schäfer, Volkhard Wache, and Gerhard Meiborg, "Gutachten zum Verhalten der Thüringer Behörden und Staatsanwaltschaften bei der Verfolgung des 'Zwickauer Trios'" (Thüringen Innenministerium, 2012), p. 57.
35 The son of a computer science professor, Mundlos was raised in a six-story prefabricated home in which his parents gave him his own apartment on the second floor, over the garage. *TAZ*, "Irgendwann trug er Bomberjacke" (November 15, 2011).
36 Ibid.
37 *Der Spiegel*, "Brown Army Faction."
38 Fellow students who attended Abitur with Mundlos recalled that he was particularly adept at physics and mathematics, well read on the subject of the Second World War, and that he wore "black, uniform-like clothing." Ibid.
39 Koehler, *Right-Wing Terrorism*, p. 133.
40 Though Zschäpe finished school in 1991 with a degree and went on to train as a gardener, she failed to find long-term work. *Welt*, "Aussage der Beate Zschäpe." See also *Spiegel*, "Brown Army Faction"; Koehler, *Right-Wing Terrorism*, p. 134.
41 Koehler, *Right-Wing Terrorism*, p. 134.
42 Schäfer, Wache, and Meiborg, p. 57.
43 Zschäpe heavily framed her involvement in the trio's crimes as that of a woman financially dependent on Mundlos and her lover Böhnhardt, and afraid of facing police conviction if she were to leave her underground life with them. In

a follow-up statement given in March 2016, Zschäpe recalled that an argument between herself and Böhnhardt over the fact that a gun had been left laying out on a table "ended with beatings." See *Die Welt*, "Dokumentation. Die Aussage der Beate Zschäpe" (December 9, 2015); *Die Zeit*, "NSU-Prozess: Zschäpe berichtet über Prügel von Böhnhardt" (March 16, 2016).

44 *Bild*, "Killer-Nazis: Die 5 größten Rätsel der Todes-Serie" (November 15, 2011). Two years later during Zschäpe's first 2013 court appearance *Bild* took a different tone, running a front-page image of Zschäpe in blazer and button-down shirt accompanied by the headline "The devil has dressed herself up. The Nazi terrorist wears a business look in court—she smiles and is silent." While this headline appears to attribute complicity to Zschäpe by affirming her status as "Nazi terrorist" —something that no-one denied, including the courts, which judged her complicit in all of the NSU's crimes and sentenced her to life imprisonment—Zschäpe as a smiling, silent "devil" not only sexualizes her crimes for the sake of sensationalism, but also depoliticizes their significance. Front cover of *Bild* (May 7, 2013). See also Michaela Köttig, "Gender Stereotypes Constructed by the Media: The Case of the National Socialist Underground (NSU) in Germany" in Michaela Köttig, Renate Bitzan, and Andrea Pető eds., *Gender and Far Right Politics in Europe* (New York: Palgrave Macmillan, 2017).

45 Anna Oelhaf points out that Zschäpe's role as a "bride" or romantic partner to Mundlos and/or Böhnhardt is above all simply not relevant to her actions within the NSU: "The term 'Nazi bride' thus reproduces the predominant discursive classification of women in right-wing structures as (sexual) partners of right-wing men." See Oelhaf, "Zwischen Nazi-Braut und Nazi-Killer. Der Diskurs um Frauen im Rechtsextremismus am Beispiel des NSU" in *Duisburger Institut für Sprach—und Sozialforschung Journal*, no. 23 (2012), pp. 6–10; Charlie Kaufhold, *In guter Gesellschaft? Geschlecht, Schuld & Abwehr in der Berichterstattung über Beate Zschäpe* (Münster: Assemblage, 2015).

46 *Die Zeit*, "Niedlich, kindlich: Aus dem Fotoalbum der Neonazis" (November 18, 2011).

47 As a 2011 petition by the research network Frauen und Rechtsextremismus pointed out, "unreflective reproduction of the 'usual cliché[s] of the apolitical woman,' according to which women are not considered right-wing extremist perpetrators but are only conceivable as sexualized appendages" risks a "trivializing of the racist and anti-Semitic acts themselves." Quotation from Oelhaf. Original petition by Michaela Köttig and Rena Kenzo, "'Und warum ist das Interessanteste an einer militanten Rechtsextremistin ihr Liebesleben?' Offener Brief des Forschungsnetzwerks Frauen und Rechtsextremismus zur Berichterstattung über die Rechtsextremistin Beate Zschäpe" for Frauen und Rechtsextremismus (2011).

48 Front cover of *Der Spiegel* no. 46 (November 14, 2011).

49 *Spiegel*, "Brown Army Faction."

50 One such similarity is that the two ringleaders of the RAF, Andreas Baader and Gudrun Ensslin, had been romantically involved—the kind of detail that was rife for sensationalism in both the case of the RAF and the NSU. However, more troubling is the media's apparent inability to comprehend the involvement of women in both these terror movements. For further critique of this theme, see Patricia Meltzer, *Death in the Shape of a Young Girl: Women's Political Violence in the Red Army Faction* (New York: New York University Press, 2015).

51 Ibid.

52 *Bild*, "Der kranke Hass der Nazi-Killer" (November 14, 2011).

53 This epithet initially came about because one of the victims worked in a kebab shop.

54 Friedrich Burschel, "The NSU Complex: Racist Murder, Neo-Nazi Terror and State Collusion in the Federal Republic" for *NSU-Watch* (July 29, 2016).

55 Ibid., p. 129.

56 In many of the NSU case files and early journalistic reporting, Turgut is falsely identified using the first name of his brother Yunus, as their passports had been mixed up.

57 Claus Peter Müller, Axel Wermelskirchen, and David Klaubert, "Verbrechensserie vor Aufklärung. Heillbronn, Eisenach, Dönermorde" in *Frankfurter Allgemeine Zeitung* (November 11, 2011); *Spiegel*, "Brown Army Faction"; *SpiegelOnline*, "Graphic: Trail of Hate" (February 23, 2012).

58 *Tagesschau*, "Fall 'Corelli'—Verfassungsschutz unter Druck" (May 31, 2016); Deutscher Bundestag, Drucksache 18/6545 "Bericht gemäß § 7 Absatz 2 des Gesetzes über die parlamentarische Kontrolle nachrichtendienstlicher Tätigkeit des Bundes zu den Untersuchungen des Sachverständigen Rechtsanwalt Jerzy Montag zum V-Mann Corelli" (November 4, 2015); Landtag Nordrhein-Westfalen / Deutscher Bundestag, Drucksache 16/14400 "Bericht des Parlamentarischen Untersuchungsausschusses III (NSU). 27. März 2017, Kapitel D: Thomas Richter alias VP 'Corelli' in NRW" (March 27, 2017).

59 Koehler, *Right-Wing Terrorism*, p. 130.

60 *Spiegel International*, "DNA Tests Solidify Suspicions in Police Killing Case" (August 13, 2012).

61 *Hamburger Abendblatt*, "Medien: NSU-Terrorist an Kiesewetter-Mord beteiligt" (August 13, 2012).

62 According to the courtroom testimony of Beate Zschäpe. *Welt*, "Aussage der Beate Zschäpe."

63 Deutscher Bundestag, Drucksache 18/12950, *Beschlussempfehlung und Bericht des 3. Untersuchungsausschusses gemäß Artikel 44 des Grundgesetzes* (June 23, 2017).

64 *Der Spiegel*, "Endstation Rennsteig: Rücktritt von Verfassungsschutzpräsident Fromm" (July 2, 2012); *FAZ*, "Fromm: Meine Mitarbeiter haben mich getäuscht" (July 5, 2012). This was not the first time that a scandal concerning neo-Nazi

V-Männer had embarrassed the BfV. In 2002, an attempt to ban the NPD was foiled due to the presence of informants in its upper ranks, as discussed later in this chapter.

65 *Deutsche Welle*, "NSU inquiry report released" (August 22, 2013); Deutscher Bundestag, Drucksache 17/14600.

66 "Zusammenfassung der Ergebnisse und Schlussfolge-rungen zur Stellungnahme der Fraktion Die Linke" in Deutscher Bundestag, Drucksache 17/14600, pp. 983–1028.

67 One of the main conclusions of the 2013 parliamentary enquiry into the mishandling of investigations into the Českà murder series was that the failure of the police and the intelligence services to detect a far-right motive behind the Českà murder series can be partly explained by the structural separation of these agencies. There is some truth to this: Owing to strict German data and privacy laws that are a consequence of the overreaching powers of the Sicherheitsdienst during the Nazi era, the federal crime and intelligence offices—the BKA and the BfV—are barred from sharing too much information with the LKA and vice versa. In the case of the Českà murders this made for considerable disjuncture between state police, who felt they were pursuing a foreign assailant with organized crime connections, and federal crime and intelligence agencies, whose own investigation into the neo-Nazi scene was compromised by the use of unreliable paid informants. Both of these factors have provoked considerable outrage in the wake of the NSU revelations, prompting members of the Turkish community as well as Die Linke to call for the total dissolution of the BfV. However, not all parties represented in the 2013 parliamentary enquiry could agree upon the meaning of the disjuncture between state and federal police; most framed it as a mere miscommunication, while Die Linke pointed out that in most cases state and federal departments in fact worked very well together. In any case, the misconduct of the police and the security and intelligence services raises questions about the efficacy of the Federal Republic's state structures with regard to the practical application of its ideological commitment to suppressing right wing extremist activity. See Deutscher Bundestag, Drucksache 18/12950, and " … Fraktion Die Linke" in Deutscher Bundestag, Drucksache 17/14600, pp. 983–1028. See also Koehler, *Right-Wing Terrorism in the 21st Century*, p. 157.

68 " … Fraktion Die Linke" in Deutscher Bundestag, Drucksache 17/14600, p. 991.

69 As chronicled in *Der NSU-Komplex*, a documentary film directed by Stefan Aust and Dirk Laabs (Germany: 2016).

70 *Spiegel*, "Neun Leichen, eine Pistole, kein Motiv" (July 10, 2008).

71 Burschel, "The NSU-Complex."

72 Deutscher Bundestag, Drucksache 17/14600, " … Stellungnahme der Fraktion Die Linke," p. 989.

73 Ibid.

74 Ibid., p. 990.

75 Ibid., p. 878.
76 Ibid., p. 991. In conjecture that followed bafflingly simplistic logic, the Baden-Württemberg LKA also posited that since "most" of the victims spoke Turkish it could "not be ruled out" that the perpetrator also spoke Turkish.
77 Original FBI report quoted in Deutscher Bundestag, Drucksache 17/14600, p. 578.
78 These remarks quoted in *Der Spiegel*, "FBI vermutete Ausländerhass als Tatmotiv" (April 23, 2012).
79 *Spiegel*, "Neun Leichen … "
80 Deutscher Bundestag, Drucksache 17/14600, p. 921.
81 Ibid., p. 578.
82 Deutscher Bundestag, Drucksache 17/14600, compare subsection "Profiling" on p. 827 and footnote no. 7410 on p. 990.
83 *Spiegel*, "Brown Army Faction."
84 Ibid.
85 On May 27, 1999, an individual named Jürgen H. was questioned by police officers from the special investigations unit of LKA Thuringia regarding the whereabouts of the trio, at his post in the army barracks of Mellrichstadt. H. admitted to having helped the trio in the early stages of their disappearance and said that he had followed the instructions of Ralf Wohlleben to pass on money, identity papers, and weapons to a neo-Nazi in Zwickau. See Deutscher Bundestag, Drucksache 17/14600, p. 1003.
86 Gigi und die braunen Stadtmusikanten, "Döner-Killer," quoted by Andrea Röpke in *Antifaschistisches Infoblatt* no. 93, "'Hammerskins'—Elitäre Neonazistruktur im Hintergrund" (December 5, 2011).
87 Of all these groups, Combat 18 (1 and 8 being the numerical equivalent of A and H—the initials of Adolf Hitler) has perhaps the strongest connection to politically motivated terror, including to Ulster loyalists. The group began in 1992 as a protection service for British National Party leaders Charlie Sargent and Harold Covington, but by 1993 it had grown into its own violently racist and anti-immigrant terror group. Combat 18 regularly publishes internal "hit lists" of politicians and has been linked to several assassinations in the UK, Germany, and Canada. See Bundesministerium des Innern für Bau und Heimat, "Bekanntmachung eines Vereinsverbots gegen 'Combat 18 Deutschland'" (January 13, 2020).
88 *Blood & Honour Division Deutschland* no. 2 (1996) quoted in Deutscher Bundestag, Drucksache 17/14600, "Rolle der Sicherheits—und Ermittlungsbehörden bei der Beobachtung der rechtsextremistischen Szene bis zum 4. November 2011," pp. 190–224 (p. 206). Uppercase emphasis in original.
89 Beam originally wrote his "Leaderless Resistance" tract in 1984, though he cites one Colonel Ulius Louis Amoss as the originator of the concept. Amoss, a US Intelligence officer during the 1950s and 1960s, proposed the idea of non-hierarchical resistance cells who do not maintain contact with US Intelligence

agents, which would thwart infiltration efforts led by the Soviet Union. Amoss argued that leading *ideas*, rather than leaders *per se*, were of utmost importance in said fight. With communism no longer perceived as a threat after 1990, Beam now identified "federal tyranny" as the number one threat against US citizens—a notion sympathized with and adapted by white supremacists and neo-Nazis from other liberal democracies throughout the western world. See Beam, "Leaderless Resistance"; Ulius Louis Amoss, "Leaderless Resistance: New Tactics for an Old War" in *Inform*, no. 6205 (April 16, 1962).

90 Kathleen Belew maps the evolution of a coherent White Power movement from the anti-communism of Vietnam war veterans during the 1970s through to the Ruby Ridge siege and Oklahoma City bombing in the mid-1990s. See Belew, *Bring the War Home*.

91 Beam had first set up LibertyNet in 1984 as a local area network that could be reached using telephone numbers in Idaho, Texas, and North Carolina. Beam, "Computers and the American Patriot," first published in *Inter-Klan Newsletter and Survival Alert*, ca. 1983–1984; quoted here from Belew, *Bring the War Home*, p. 120.

92 Wayne King, "Computer Network Links Rightist Groups and Offers 'Enemy' List" in *The New York Times* (February 15, 1985).

93 James Adams, "Clinton's Dreams Die a Dirty Death" in *The Sunday Times* (London: July 27, 1997).

94 *The Guardian*, "Neo-Nazis Go Hi-Tech with Electronic Mailboxes" (November 19, 1993).

95 Beam, "Computers and the American Patriot."

96 The book also stokes paranoid fears that the Civil Rights movement will lead to the subjugation of whites. In one chapter, the titular protagonist Turner, who is a member of a white revolutionary movement known as "the Organization," watches an anti-racism rally on television and witnesses whites being pulled aside and beaten by non-white marchers. Kathleen Belew has also linked the book to the January 6, 2021, attack on the US Capitol, noting similarities with a section of the book that refers to "the day of the rope," in which a white supremacist-led insurrection on the Capitol leads to the public execution of liberal democratic officials and members of non-white races. The *Turner Diaries* has inspired several high-profile right-wing extremist attacks throughout the decades including the Oklahoma City Bombings and David Copeland's bomb attacks in London and has become known as the "Nazi Bible" to counterterrorism experts. Known to the BfV as early as 2001, by 2006 it had been indexed as right-wing extremist material and banned throughout Germany. See Belew, pp. 117–20; *Verfassungsschutzbericht der Landesregierung von Schleswig-Holstein* 2001 (Schleswig-Holstein: Innenministerium des Landes Schleswig-Holstein, 2002), pp. 20–1.

97 See "Der NSU im Netzwerk von 'Blood & Honour'" in Deutscher Bundestag, Drucksache 17/14600, pp. 924–34 (p. 931).

98   Ibid.
99   Erik Nilsen, *Blood & Honour Field Manual*, published in 2000, quoted in Deutscher Bundestag, Drucksache 17/14600, "Rechtsextremistische Milieus mit Bezügen zum Trio außerhalb Thüringens," pp. 149–89 (p. 163).
100 Ibid.
101 Combat 18, "National Socialist Political Solder's Handbook" quoted in "Rechtsextremistische Milieus … " Deutscher Bundestag, Drucksache 17/14600, p. 164.
102 Combat 18, "*Stormer*—Die Deutsche Fassung Nr. 1" quoted in ibid.
103 There were, however, crackdowns on the use of internet communications for the incitement of racial violence. In late October 2010, the BKA announced that they had conducted a raid against a far-right internet radio station named Widerstand Radio ("Resistance Radio"), which had operated since July of 2009. Twenty-two residences were raided across ten states, with a total of twenty-three suspects between the ages of twenty and thirty-seven arrested "on suspicion of forming a criminal organization, inciting racial hatred and other crimes." Two years later, nine of these suspects were given jail sentences of between one and three years for the dissemination of right-wing extremist ideology and antisemitism. *Expatica*, "Jail terms for German neo-Nazi radio station" (April 11, 2011).
104 BfV report from 2002 evaluated and quoted in Deutscher Bundestag, Drucksache 17/14600, p. 163.
105 Ibid., p. 164.
106 According to an interview with former Combat 18 member Darren Wells for British publication *Searchlight*, Wells had been invited to Germany in 1998 in order to help assemble some homemade bombs. Combat 18 had notoriously been responsible for several bomb attacks in England in the late 1990s. See "Why I turned my back on C18—an exclusive interview with ex-Nazi Darren Wells" in *Searchlight International* (December 2001), p. 5.
107 Julia Jüttner, "Lernen mit Rudolf Heß" in *Der Spiegel* (November 11, 2011).
108 Kapke was able to avoid conviction for his connection to the NSU murders, announcing through his lawyer that he had sustained memory gaps as the result of an accident. He has, however, been convicted of other crimes in which Wohlleben was also implicated, including the "grievous bodily harm" and "coercion" of two young girls in 1999. See Julia Jüttner and Georg Heil, "The Agitator" in *Spiegel Online* (November 24, 2011); *Thüringer Allgemeine Zeitung*, " Tarnidentitäten und ein Thüringer Neonazi beschäftigen in dieser Woche den NSU-Prozess" (February 2, 2014).
109 *Die Zeit*, "Netzwerk des NSU war größer als angenommen" (March 24, 2013).
110 Koehler, *Right-Wing Terrorism*, p. 136.
111 Ibid., pp. 135–41.

112 Court testimony of witness Tom T., Protokoll 228. Verhandlungstag der NSU-Prozess (September 16, 2015), accessed via NSU-Watch.

113 When asked by Götzl what he meant by "*Ausländerproblematik*," Turner replied: "It was about the foreigners, we saw it that way, that they were to blame for the fact that we couldn't get any jobs and stuff like that, I don't know. No idea." In many ways, Turner proved an unreliable witness throughout his court testimony, transparently concerned about implicating himself in activities for which he might face prosecution. When asked, for example, to recall the lyrics to the songs he had provided vocals for in Vergeltung, he was only able to recall vaguely that they were about "foreigners and drug problems" —nor could he properly recall what political goals he was himself pursuing at the time. Earlier statements from Turner contradict his apparent courtroom amnesia; as Götzl read aloud, in a 1997 police interrogation Turner had stated, quite cogently, "Our aim was to fight the state to the point of overthrowing, ultimately to create a national and socialist form of society." Ibid.

114 BfV, *Verfassungsschutzbericht 2004* (Berlin: Bundesministerium des Innern, 2005), pp. 51–2.

115 Ibid., pp. 33–6. See also *Der Spiegel*, "Rechts-Rock: Einstieg in die Nazi-Szene?" (August 16, 2000).

116 *Antifaschistisches Infoblatt* no. 92, "Hammerskin-Konzert in Lothringen" (September 14, 2011).

117 Röpke, "'Hammerskins'—Elitäre Neonazistruktur ... "

118 In some cases, event organizers guided ticketholders to an initial meeting point from which they would be led to the concert. *Verfassungsschutzbericht 2004*, p. 54.

119 As gleaned from examining the now-defunct website for Festival of Nations, www.f-d-v.de, using the Internet Archive's "Wayback Machine" (www.web.archive.org).

120 Moreover, in some cases the prosecution of band members only increased their popularity—as happened when the members of the band Landser were convicted in 2003 for "membership in a criminal organization" (see *Verfassungsschutzbericht 2004*, p. 54). The legislative possibilities of restricting the neo-Nazi scene are to this day limited and fairly unimaginative; while the Federal Department for Media Harmful to Young Persons (Bundesprüfstelle für jugendgefährdende Schriften; BPjM, est. 1956) keeps an index of right-wing extremist music and magazines, the decision whether to ban such material rests with German law enforcement and depends upon whether the media contains outright incitement of violence, Holocaust denial, or instructions on how to commit crime. By no means does the BPjM focus exclusively on the right-wing scene; it is also concerned with violence in video games and with pornography. Its activities during the 1950s seem extremely quaint by today's standards: the first two works indexed by the BPjM were Tarzan comics.

121 "'Thinghaus' in Grevesmühlen" in *Verfassungsschutzbericht Land Mecklenburg-Vorpommern 2013* (Mecklenburg-Vorpommern: Ministerium für Inneres und Sport, 2014), p. 32.
122 The original poster read "The NSDAP secures the national community. Comrades: if you need advice and help, turn to your local group," while the Thinghaus mural reads "Mecklenburg hearts are loyal—The wind sings of freedom."
123 *Nordkurier*, "Das Thinghaus in Grevesmühlen: Ein Blick in den braunen Abgrund" (October 29, 2014). See also *Vice Magazine*, "Hang Up Your Boots" (October 17, 2011); *Spiegel International*, "Protected by the Constitution: Germany Faces Tough Battle to Ban Far-Right NPD" (December 7, 2011).
124 BfV, *Verfassungsschutzbericht 2013* (Berlin: Bundesministerium des Innern, 2014), p. 32.
125 Wolfgang Bendel quoted in *Antifaschistisches Infoblatt* no. 18, "Die 'Jungen Nationaldemokraten'" (July 21, 1992).
126 *Antifaschistisches Infoblatt* no. 58, "Die braune Elite von morgen. Bestandsaufnahme neonazistischer Jugendarbeit" (December 14, 2002). See also *Verfassungsschutzbericht Land Brandenburg 2002* (Brandenburg: Ministerium des Innern des Landes Brandenburg, 2003), pp. 120–1.
127 Juliane Lange, "Mehr als die 'emotionale Kompetenz.' Mädchen und Frauen in der extremen Rechte" in Sybille Steinbacher ed., *Rechte Gewalt in Deutschland. Zum Umgang mit dem Rechtsextremismus in Gesellschaft, Politik und Justiz* (Göttingen: Wallstein Verlag, 2016), pp. 108–28.
128 The media's trivialization of Zschäpe's involvement with the NSU, for example, demonstrated a broader lack of progress in reckoning with the autonomy and enthusiastic support of the loyal devotees of fascism and Nazism, both historically and in the present: there is something salvatory about the persistent yet demonstrably false idea that women are naturally immune to violent ideas and actions, which is to say that fostered within this view is the implication that far-right ideas are anomalous, pathological, and in no sense normative; that they cannot fit into a domestic framework, cannot be mundane, and cannot become an affective bond between men, women, or entire communities. To be sure these are violent communities, and while Zschäpe certainly relied upon gender norms in her legal defense, her claim that Böhnhardt subjected her to verbal and physical abuse need not be treated with any suspicion—if anything it offers us a glimpse into the fraught and noxious environment of a fascistic domicile. Moreover, as Gabi Elverich pointed out as early as 2007, when the NSU were still committing murders undetected, statistics showing the involvement of women in far-right violence in Germany tend necessarily to be determined only by the number of such cases that end up in police reports—which means that "indirect forms of participation by women" such as ancillary violence or "supportive participation"

have often gone ignored by researchers. Elverich estimated that, at the time of writing, the number of women who belonged to far-right political parties in Germany was around 20 percent, and the number of women participating in far-right social cliques was between 25 and 33 percent—a demographic seldom reflected in media portrayals of the far-right as a mostly masculine environment. Gabi Elverich, "Rechtsextrem orientierte Frauen und Mädchen— eine besondere Zielgruppe?" for Bundeszentrale für politische Bildung, *Dossier Rechtsextremismus* (October 15, 2007). See also Ulrich Overdieck, "Zschäpes Vorgängerinnen" in Esther Lehnert and Heike Radvan eds., *Rechtsextreme Frauen. Analysen und Handlungsempfehlungen für die Soziale Arbeit und Pädagogik* (Opladen: Verlag Barbara Budrich, 2016), pp. 41–4.

129 Figure according to *Der Spiegel*, "Szenekontakte der Terrorzelle: Blut, Ehre, Hass" (December 3, 2011).

130 Quotations taken from the now defunct www.f-d-v.de using the Internet Archive's "Wayback Machine" (www.web.archive.org).

131 Ibid.

132 Chapter 5 will explore this movement in depth.

133 *Der Spiegel*, "Das Rätsel der braunen Bombenbastler" (November 9, 2011).

134 A rise in right-wing extremist crime in 2000, followed by a series of attacks on people with disabilities and foreign residents, had galvanized German legislators and political activists into action.

135 *FAZ*, "V-Mann Frenz: 36 Jahre für den Verfassungsschutz gearbeitet" (January 23, 2002); Josef Hufelschulte and Thomas van Zütphen, "V-Mann Affäre: Fatale Frenz-Connection" in *Focus Magazin*, no. 5 (2002); *Der Spiegel*, "Geheimdienste: Blamiert bis auf die Knochen" (January 27, 2002).

136 *Der Spiegel*, "Geheimdienste: Blamiert … " although Hufelschulte and Zütphen state the year as 1959.

137 As public interest in this story peaked, new and increasingly concerning layers emerged. During subsequent court proceedings, for example, it also came to light that Frenz had published antisemitic articles in *Deutsche Stimme*, the national newspaper of the NPD. A 1998 article of Frenz's, in which he claimed that Zyklon B was not used to gas Jews during the Holocaust, landed him a fine ordered by the Bochum District Court. For this reason, the BfV had decided to terminate their contract with Frenz in 1995—but not before delivering him a severance payment of between 5,000 and 6,000 Deutsch Marks. "After so many years of working with us, he was almost entitled to a pension," one BfV agent quipped to the press (see *FAZ*, "V-Mann Frenz"). Having become "burned" as a result of these revelations in court (i.e., he was now no longer trusted within the NPD), Frenz "disappeared" after his 2002 court testimony, abandoning his naturopathy practice which, given the public revelations about him, patients had begun to steer away from. See Hufelschulte and Zütphen. See also *Der Spiegel*, "Geheimdienste: Blamiert."

138 *Antifaschistisches Infoblatt* no. 55, "Ein Diener wird geopfert" (April 12, 2002).
139 Hufelschulte and Zütphen.
140 Ibid.
141 *The Guardian*, "German Court Rejects Attempt to Ban Neo-Nazi Party" (March 19, 2003).
142 *Spiegel*, "Geheimdienste: Blamiert … "
143 Ibid.
144 According to the testimony of Tom T., Protokoll 228. Verhandlungstag der NSU-Prozess.
145 Martin Debes, "35 erfolglose Ermittlungsverfahren gegen früheren V-Mann" in *Thüringer Allgemeine* (March 16, 2012).
146 Koehler, *Right-Wing Terrorism*, p. 161.
147 *Verfassungsschutzbericht Thüringen 1997*, p. 22; see also Jüttner, "Lernen mit Rudolf Heß."
148 NSU-Watch, "V-Mann-Porträt: Carsten Szczepanski" (February 23, 2015) https://www.nsu-watch.info/2015/02/v-mann-portraet-carsten-szczepanski/.
149 Ibid., see also Deutscher Bundestag, Drucksache 17/14600, "Aktivitäten des Carsten Szczepanski im Zusammenhang mit dem KKK," pp. 188–9.
150 Only two parties have been banned in the history of the Federal Republic: a successor to the Nazi party in 1952, and the KPD (the Communist Party) in 1956. There has long existed in the Federal Republic a deep-seated reluctance to ban a party out of a commitment to parliamentary democracy.
151 According to a list of criteria written up by the Constitutional Court in anticipation of another ban attempt, the courts therefore required to be made aware of "the origin of the material submitted." However, one unforeseen problem that this posed was that the NPD by now communicated largely in text messages sent anonymously and online forum postings written under an alias—a dilemma which, in hindsight, intimated the growing reliance of far-right factions on online and encrypted spaces in which they might remain anonymous. *Spiegel International*, "High Hurdles … "
152 *The Guardian*, "German Court Rejects … " see also *Spiegel* "Geheimdienste: Blamiert … "
153 Such fears were especially stoked when Horst Mahler—one-time defender of the RAF who had since turned to the far-right—launched a private campaign of trying to coax other NPD informers to reveal themselves in order to strengthen a case against the BfV. Far-right figures Christian Worch and Steffen Hupka distributed leaflets offering to forgive all current and former informants on the condition that they spill dirt on the BfV. *Deutsche Welle*, "Merkel coalition blocks NPD ban bid" (April 25, 2013).
154 *Spiegel*, "Endstation Rennsteig"; *FAZ*, "Fromm: Meine Mitarbeiter haben mich getäuscht."

155 *Deutsche Welle*, "German intelligence grants access to files in neo-Nazi probe" (July 3, 2012); *Die Zeit*, "Thüringen wagt die totale Transparenz" (October 8, 2012).
156 *Deutsche Welle*, "The Many Faces of Neo-Nazism" (July 31, 2012).
157 *DW*, "Many Faces of Neo-Nazism."
158 Ibid.
159 BfV, *Verfassungsschutzbericht 2011* (Berlin: Bundesministerium des Innern, 2012).
160 Federal Minister for the Interior Hans-Peter Friedrich, "Vorwort" in ibid., p. 3.
161 Friedrich also characterized clashes between left—and right-wing radicals as a major contribution to rising numbers of violence incidents. Ibid., p. 4.
162 The report did warn of the potential for future "self-radicalized" right-wing terrorists but did not situate these individuals within the broader network of right-wing extremism—i.e., it did not seem to consider this a coherent network but one of disparate persons, again playing into the "lone wolf" misnomer. Ibid., p. 65.
163 This was in a sense a national day of mourning; many public institutions and schools held a one minute silence at midday, public transport in Berlin and Hamburg came to a one minute standstill, and flags were flown at half-mast on government buildings.
164 Angela Merkel, speech delivered at the Central Memorial Ceremony to Commemorate the Victims of Extreme Right-Wing Violence (February 23, 2012), transcription available via the Federal Government's online archive.
165 Ibid.
166 Semiya Şimşek, speech delivered at the Central Memorial Ceremony to Commemorate the Victims of Extreme Right-Wing Violence (Berlin: February 23, 2012), transcribed from video footage reported by *Der Spiegel* (https://www.youtube.com/watch?v=f69-ZlreGSo).
167 Ibid.

Chapter 5

1 As pointed out by Frank Decker, "Warum der parteiförmige Rechtspopulismus in Deutschland so erfolglos ist" in *Vorgänge*, no. 197 (2012), pp. 21–8.
2 Kate Connolly, "Far-Right AfD Wins Local Election in 'Watershed Moment' for German Politics" in *The Guardian* (June 26, 2023).
3 David Bebnowski, "Populismus der Expertokraten. Eine Auseinandersetzung mit der Alternative für Deutschland" in *INDES. Zeitschrift für Politik und Gesellschaft*, vol. 2, no. 4 (2013), pp. 151–9; Robert Grimm, "Germany's new anti-euro party, Alternative für Deutschland, might prove to be a game changer in German and European politics" in *LSE Blogs: European Politics and Policy* (April 22, 2013);

Decker, "The 'Alternative for Germany': Factors behind Its Emergence and Profile of a New Right-Wing Populist Party" in *German Politics and Society*, vol. 34, no. 2 (Summer 2016), pp. 1–16; Rüdiger Schmitt-Beck, "The 'Alternative für Deutschland in the Electorate': Between Single-Issue and Right-Wing Populist Party" in *German Politics*, vol. 26, no. 1 (2017), pp. 124–48.

4   This has also become the premise for new visitations of right-wing extremism during the GDR. See Waibel, *Die braune Saat*. See also Volker Weiß, *Die autoritäre Revolte. Die Neue Rechte und der Untergang des Abendlandes* (Stuttgart: Klett-Cotta Verlag, 2017); Michael Minkenberg, *The Radical Right in Eastern Europe: Democracy under Siege?* (New York: Palgrave, 2018); Jonathan Olsen, "The Left Party and the AfD: Populist Competitors in Eastern Germany" in *German Politics and Society*, vol. 36, no. 1 (2018), pp. 70–83; Michael A. Hansen and Jonathan Olsen, "Flesh of the Same Flesh: A Study of Voters for the Alternative for Germany (AfD) in the 2017 Federal Election" in *German Politics*, vol. 28, no. 1 (2019), pp. 1–19; Steven Wuhs and Eric McLaughlin, "Explaining German Electoral Geography: Evidence from the Eastern States" in *German Politics and Society*, vol. 37, no. 1 (2019), pp. 1–23; Lars Rensmann, "Radical Right-Wing Populists in Parliament: Examining the Alternative for Germany in European Context" in *German Politics and Society*, vol. 36, no. 3 (Autumn 2019), pp. 41–73; Micha Brumlik, "Ostdeutscher Antisemitismus: Wie braun war die DDR?" in *Bundeszentrale für politische Bildung* (April 30, 2020).

5   *Financial Times* reporters, "Germany's election results in charts and maps" (September 25, 2017), and *Financial Times* reporters, "German Voters Have Turned Right—and Left" (October 15, 2018).

6   Anselma Gallinat, *Narratives in the Making: Writing the East German Past in the Democratic Present* (New York: Berghahn, 2016), p. 56. See also Konrad Jarausch and Michael Geyer eds., *Shattered Past: Reconstructing German Histories* (Princeton, NJ: Princeton University Press, 2003); Paul Cooke, *Representing East Germany since Unification: From Colonization to Nostalgia* (New York: Berg Publishers, 2005); Maria Todorova and Zsuzsa Gille, *Post-Communist Nostalgia* (New York: Berghahn, 2010); Stephen Ehrig, Marcel Thomas, and David Zell eds., *The GDR Today: New Interdisciplinary Approaches to East German History, Memory and Culture* (Oxford: Lang, 2018).

7   Adam Serwer, "The Cruelty is the Point" in *The Atlantic* (October 3, 2018). See also Cristina Beltrán, *Cruelty as Citizenship: How Migrant Suffering Sustains White Democracy* (Minneapolis: University of Minnesota Press, 2020).

8   See Jackson Lears' compelling rebuke to Anne Applebaum, whose 2020 publication *Twilight of Democracy: The Seductive Lure of Authoritarianism* sought to explain the appeal of right-wing punditry by siphoning blame onto rural working-class communities. Jackson Lears, "Orthodoxy of the Elites" in *The New York Review of Books* (January 14, 2021).

9 Oliver Decker's recent work has described these trends, in psychoanalytic terms, as a "narcissistic" outpouring of authoritarian attitudes. This latent authoritarianism supposedly underpins the far right's conception of statehood and its calls for sovereignty, above all providing a reserve of narcissistic power supply, i.e., a heady and enjoyable rebuke to the conceits of liberal democracy. Oliver Decker, "Narzisstische Plombe und Sekundärer Autoritarismus" in Oliver Decker, Johannes Kiess, and Elmar Brähler eds., *Rechtsextremismus der Mitte und sekundärer Autoritarismus* (Gießen: Psychosozial-Verlag, 2015), p. 21.34.

10 Marcus Böick, *Die Treuhand: Idee—Praxis—Erfahrung* (Berlin: Suhrkamp, 2020).

11 Michael Wildt, *Volk, Volksgemeinschaft, AfD* (Hamburg: Hamburger Edition Press, 2017).

12 See the final section of this chapter.

13 A phrase repeated *ad nauseum* during the Covid-19 pandemic, used to describe the perception that governments have used the pandemic as an excuse to seize totalitarian levels of power over a largely compliant and overly docile populace.

14 Nassehi has also proclaimed that there is no longer any need for a political left at all, as "the formulas of the critique of capitalism have become empty," and takes his understanding of what counts for conservatism from the works of Neue Rechte grandfather Armin Mohler, leaving him with an extremely skewed understanding of the same political binary he claims is in a state of disintegration. See Armin Nassehi quoted in Volker Weiß, "Neue Rechte: Ab wann ist konservativ zu rechts?" in *Zeit Online* (February 19, 2016); Nassehi, "Eine Linke braucht es nicht mehr" in *Die Zeit* (July 13, 2017).

15 Nassehi, *Die letzte Stunde der Wahrheit: Warum rechts und links keine Alternativen mehr sind und Gesellschaft ganz anders beschrieben werden muss* (Hamburg: Murmann Verlag, 2015).

16 Justus Bender and Reinhard Bingener, "AfD: Die rechten Fäden in der Hand" in *FAZ* (April 16, 2016); Tobias Rapp, "Der dunkle Ritter Götz" in *Der Spiegel* (December 21, 2016); James Angelos, "The Prophet of Germany's New Right" in *New York Times Magazine* (October 10, 2017).

17 Strauß beseeched to his reader that "the only thing you need is the courage to secede, to turn away from the mainstream." See Rapp, "Der dunkle Ritter ... "; Strauß, "Anschwellender Bocksgesang."

18 Sumi Somaskanda, "A New, New Right Rises in Germany" in *The Atlantic* (June 22, 2017).

19 Maresi Starzmann, "Nazi Hipsters: Europe's Identitarians Are Young, Fashionable and Proto-Fascist" in *The Indypendent: A Free Paper for Free People* (December 14, 2019).

20 Ibid.

21 The "*Großer Austausch*" / "*Grand Remplacement*" originates from *Nouvelle Droite* figure Renaud Camus, whose anti-immigration manifesto of the same title is

distributed in German by Kubitschek's Antaios publishing house. See Julia Ebner, "Who are Europe's far-right Identitarians?" in *Politico* (April 4, 2019).
22. Starzmann, "Nazi Hipsters … "
23. Philip Kreißel, Julia Ebner, Alexander Urban, and Jakob Guhl, *Hass auf Knopfdruck: Rechtsextreme Trollfrabriken und das Ökosystem koordinierter Hasskampagnen im Netz* (London: Institute for Strategic Dialogue, July 2018). See also Lizzie Dearden, "Generation Identity: Far-Right Group Sending UK Recruits to Military-Style Training Camps in Europe" in *The Independent* (November 9, 2017).
24. Radicalization is framed here as a process of becoming enlightened to the "reality" of a liberal democratic order that is steadily demoralizing the rightful place of white males at the top of a racial hierarchy. Feminism, "multiculturalism," and all other so-called progressive "agendas" are presented as degenerate influences spread via a corrupt mainstream media as well as by liberal governments. Just as the character Neo, in *The Matrix*, is given a red pill to swallow that will awaken him to the reality that he is living in a simulation powered by gargantuan machines who have enslaved the human race (a blue pill by contrast will return him to the safety of ignorance), those on the far-right who consider themselves to have been "redpilled" feel that they alone are informed of a monstrous conspiracy.
25. Ebner, "Who are Europe's … "
26. See Geoff Eley's argument about the link between competitive globalization and resurgent fascisms since the early 1990s. Geoff Eley, "Fascism Then and Now" in Leo Panitch and Greg Albo eds., *The Politics of the Right* (London: Monthly Review Press, 2015), pp. 91–117.
27. This is both a new tactic in the context of far-right politics in the post-1989 era, and also a familiar tactic used by the Nazis in order to construct an enemy—in that case, Jews—that is at once inferior to Western, Christian culture but also existentially threatening to it. As Farid Hafez observed in the context of the mid-2010s success of the Austrian Freiheitliche Partei Österreichs (FPÖ), the new strategy of anti-Islamic populism "is used for construing boundaries and antagonistic confrontation. Islam is seen as inferior, but also as hostile, aggressive and threatening." Farid Hafez, "Jörg Haider and Islamophobia" in Humayan Ansari and Farid Hafez eds., *From the Far Right to the Mainstream: Islamophobia in Party Politics and the Media* (Frankfurt am Main: Campus Verlag, 2012), pp. 45–68 (p. 49).
28. Sarrazin also argued that Muslims are heavily reliant on the welfare state, are lazy/lacking in work ethic, and have lower IQs. He also calculated that Muslim population growth would overwhelm that of "*Biodeutscher*" within just a few generations (thus the title of his book) and proposed stringent immigration and welfare reforms in order to rectify the problem. See Sarrazin, *Deutschland schafft sich ab*.
29. For an account of the manner in which French Islamophobia directly emerges from the post-colonial period—in particular, the politicization of the hijab in

France—see Joan Wallach Scott, *The Politics of the Veil* (Princeton, NJ: Princeton University Press, 2017).
30 Alternative für Deutschland, campaign poster (2017).
31 Note the manner in which Kubitschek attempted to frame his opposition to the *Wehrmachtsausstellung* as one of scholarly concern, which ultimately reads as tiresome.
32 For example, throughout 2008 KSA ambushed a Berlin convention of socialist students; a speech by former GDR apparatchik Egon Krenz; a public reading by Günther Grass; and a discussion forum with Grün politician Daniel Cohn-Bendit. Karin Priester has summed up the KSA's activities as an "ineffective thirst for action reminiscent of the student happenings" of the 1960s and 1970s. Karin Priester, "'Erkenne die Lage!' —Über die rechtspopulistische Versuchung des bundesdeutschen Konservatismus" in *INDES—Zeitschrift für Politik und Gesellschaft* (March 2015), pp. 84–92 (p. 87). See also Gideon Botsch, *Die extreme Rechte in der Bundesrepublik Deutschland. 1949 bis heute* (Wiesbaden: WBG, 2012), p. 135; Volker Weiß, "Die 'Konservative Revolution.' Geistiger Erinnerungsort der 'Neuen Rechten'" in Martin Langebach and Michael Sturm eds., *Erinnerungsorte der extremen Rechten* (Wiesbaden: Springer, 2015), pp. 101–20 (p. 108).
33 Selected articles from the 19-point PEGIDA "Positionspapier" written in 2014, published as a supplement by *Menschen in Dresden* in "Die Auseinandersetzung um Pegida und die 19 Thesen—eine Auswahl" (December 21, 2014). Emphasis in original.
34 See Samuel Salzborn, "Antisemitism in the 'Alternative for Germany' Party" in *German Politics and Society*, vol. 36, no. 3 (Autumn 2018), pp. 74–93.
35 See Bensmann, p. 139.
36 Matthias Dilling, "Two of the Same Kind? The Rise of the AfD and Its Implications for the CDU/CSU" in *German Politics and Society*, vol. 36, no. 1 (Spring 2018), pp. 84–104 (p. 85).
37 To name a few: The Bund Freier Bürger (League of Free Citizens, 1993–2000), who founded in opposition to the signing of the Maastricht Treaty; the Initiative Neue Soziale Marktwirtschaft (Initiative for a New Social Market Economy), founded in 2000, and the Bündnis Bürgerwille (Alliance of the Citizens' Will) and Wahlalternative 13 (Election Alternative 13), both founded by original co-leader of the AfD Bernd Lucke. See Decker, p. 2.
38 Decker, "The 'Alternative for Germany' …, " p. 9. Die Freiheit (full name Die Freiheit—Bürgerrechtspartei für mehr Freiheit und Demokratie) was a short-lived party founded in 2010 by former CDU MP René Stadtkewitz, who had been expelled from the CDU for inviting Islamophobic Dutch politician Geert Wilders to Berlin. In 2016 Die Freiheit announced its dissolution, stating that the AfD had largely adopted all of the party's objectives.

39 See *Financial Times* reporters, "Germany's Election Results in Charts and Maps" (September 25, 2017), and *Financial Times* reporters, "German Voters Have Turned Right—and Left" (October 15, 2018). Prior to this, the AfD had also experienced success on the basis of its Euro-skeptic agenda alone; the European Elections of May 2014 saw the AfD win 7.1 percent of the vote just a little more than a year after the party's formation.
40 Dilling, "Two of the Same Kind? … " p. 93. See also Decker, "The 'Alternative for Germany,'" p. 2.
41 Ibid., p. 85.
42 Olsen, "The Left Party and the AfD … "; Hansen and Olsen, "Flesh of the Same Flesh … "; Wuhs and McLaughlin, "Explaining German Electoral Geography … "
43 Olsen, "The Left Party and the AfD … "
44 Ibid.
45 It also ignores continuing anti-immigrant trends amongst West German politicians, such as SPD candidate Martin Schulz, who in 2017 ran against Merkel (unsuccessfully) on a campaign platform centered around immigration reform. Isla Binnie, "Schulz Turns to Immigration to Revive Flagging Campaign" in *Reuters* (July 27, 2017).
46 See Gauland's own apologia for populism in the pages of *FAZ*. Alexander Gauland, "Warum muss es Populismus sein?" in *FAZ* (October 6, 2018). For commentary, see Klaus Hillenbrand, "Gaulands Text in der 'FAZ.' Zwei Volksschützer" in *Die Tageszeitung* (October 10, 2018).
47 This does not, Mudde points out, make the populist right merely a "moderate" form of the far-right; the nativism or ethnonationalism at the core of most right-populist parties makes them a threat to liberal democracy, one which envisions national transformation based on a politics of exclusion. Cas Mudde, *Populist Radical Right Parties in Europe* (Cambridge: Cambridge University Press, 2007), pp. 29–31. See also Michael Minkenberg, *The Radical Right in Eastern Europe: Democracy under Siege?* (London: Palgrave Macmillan, 2017), p. 16: Jan-Werner Müller, *What Is Populism? and Contesting Democracy: Political Ideas in Twentieth-Century Europe* (Philadelphia, PA: University of Pennsylvania Press, 2016).
48 Patricia Anne Simpson, "Mobilizing Meanings: Translocal Identities of the Far Right Web" in *German Politics and Society*, vol. 34, no. 4 (Winter 2016), pp. 34–53 (p. 38).
49 Somaskanda, "A New, New Right … "
50 Gideon Botsch, "From Skinhead-Subculture to Radical Right Movement: The Development of a 'National Opposition' in East Germany" in *Contemporary European History*, vol. 21, no. 4 (November 2012), pp. 553–73 (p. 563).
51 Karl Siegbert-Rehberg has argued, therefore, that PEGIDA has "two parents": xenophobia, and disenchantment with the shape that reunified Germany has taken.

Karl Siegbert-Rehberg, "Dresden-Szenen: Eine einleitende Situationsbeschreibung" in Karl-Siegbert Rehberg, Franziska Kunz, and Tino Schlinzig eds., *PEGIDA—Rechtspopulismus zwischen Fremdenangst und „Wende"-Enttäuschung? Analysen im Überblick* (Bielefeld: Transcript Verlag, 2016), pp. 15–50. See also Andreas Speit, *Bürgerliche Scharfmacher: Deutschlands neue rechte Mitte—von AfD bis Pegida* (Zürich: Orell Füssli, 2016).

52 See Florian Gathmann, "DDR-Bürgerrechtler wehren sich gegen AfD-Vereinnahmung" in *Der Spiegel* (August 7, 2019).

53 Gallinat, *Narratives in the Making*, p. 158. Meanwhile psychologist Maaz still searches for a mass-psychological explanation. See Hans-Joachim Maaz, "Zur Psychodynamik von Protest und Gegenprotest" in Rehberg, Kunz and Schlinzig eds., *PEGIDA …* pp. 355–66.

54 Gathmann, "DDR-Bürgerrechtler … "

55 For literature concerning the AfD's use of National Socialist concepts, see Marcus Bensmann, *Schwarzbuch AfD: Fakten, Figuren, Hintergründe* (Essen: Correctiv Press, 2017); Stephan Grigat ed., *AfD & FPÖ: Antisemitismus, völkischer Nationalismus und Geschlechterbilder* (Baden-Baden: Nomos Verlag, 2017); Wildt, *Volk, Volksgemeinschaft, AfD*; Gerd Wiegel, *Ein aufhaltsamer Aufstieg—Alternativen zu AfD & Co.* (Cologne: PapyRossa Press, 2017). See also David Bebnowski, *Die Alternative für Deutschland. Aufstieg und gesellschaftliche Repräsentanz einer rechten populistischen Partei* (Wiesbaden: Springer, 2015).

56 Pádraig Belton, "To Oppose or Ignore? How the German Centre of Gravity Is Shifting Right" in *The Times Literary Supplement* (December 23, 2016).

57 Beltrán, *Cruelty as Citizenship*, p. 23.

58 See for example Martin Schulze Wessel, "Zeitgeistgetriebene Erinnerung" in *FAZ* (November 9, 2021); Dirk Peitz, "Am Rande" in *Die Zeit* (July 29, 2022). This phenomenon was the main topic of discussion at a Summer 2022 conference for Haus der Kulturen der Welt titled "Hijacking Memory: The Holocaust and the New Right" (June 9–12, 2022). See also Svetlana Boym, "Restorative Nostalgia: Conspiracies and Return to Origins" in *The Future of Nostalgia*, pp. 41–8.

59 Identitarian strategy handbook quoted in Lukas Jäger and Miro Dittrich, "Medienstrategien rechts-alternativer Akteur*innen: Die grenzen des Sagbaren verschieben" in *Belltower News* (May 7, 2020).

60 Somaskanda, "A New, New Right … "

61 See Jan-Werner Müller, "Behind the New German Right" in *New York Review of Books Daily* (April 16, 2016).

62 Amanda Taub and Max Fisher, "Germany's Extreme Right Challenges Guilt over Nazi Past" in *The New York Times* (January 18, 2017).

63 Ibid. See also Madeline Chambers, "German AfD Rightist Triggers Fury with Holocaust Memorial Comments" in *Reuters* (January 18, 2017).

64 Roger Cohen, "Return of the German Volk" in *The New York Times* (September 29, 2017).
65 Salzborn, "Antisemitism … " p. 76.
66 See Wildt, *Volk, Volksgemeinschaft, AfD*.
67 A prominent leader of the West German Socialist Students' Union, who in 1968 was severely injured by a neo-Nazi assassin.
68 Rapp, "Der dunkle Ritter Götz … "
69 Botho Srauß, "Der letzte Deutsche" in *Der Spiegel* (October 1, 2015).
70 AfD MP Marcus Pretzell, tweet (December 16, 2016).
71 Merkel's 2015 CDU policy proposals were, moreover, a further concession to the perception that the CDU party may lose ground to the AfD, including a call to ban the wearing of burqas in federal buildings and a reform on the granting of dual citizenship. See Christian Nawrocki and Armin Fuhrer eds., *AfD—Bekämpfen oder ignorieren?: Intelligente Argumente von 14 Demokraten* (Bremen: Kellner Verlag, 2016). See also Will Worley, "German Anti-Refugee MEP Blames Angela Merkel for Berlin Attack: 'Those Are Her Dead!'" in *The Independent* (December 19, 2016).
72 Salzborn, "Renaissance of the New Right in Germany? A Discussion of New Right Elements in German Right-Wing Extremism Today" in *German Politics and Society*, vol. 34, no. 2 (2016), pp. 36–63 (p. 51).
73 A later 2019 poster would lean into the same theme of blonde, heterosexual couples celebrating their offspring as the future of Germany. One poster featuring a woman embracing (presumably) her husband while clutching an ultrasound image reads "For our future, naturally." See Simone Rafael, "In Sachsen gibt sich die AfD jetzt 'natürlich' Völkisch" in *Belltower News* (August 9, 2019).
74 See Nicole Doerr, "The Visual Politics of the Alternative for Germany (AfD): Anti-Islam, Ethno-Nationalism, and Gendered Images" in *Social Sciences*, vol. 10, no. 20 (January, 2021).
75 *Das Grundsatzprogramm der Alternative für Deutschland* (2016), p. 81. See also Inken Behrmann, "D-Mark, Familie, Vaterland: Die AfD nach Lucke" in *Blätter für deutsche und internationale Politik*, vol. 60, no. 8 (2015), pp. 99–107.
76 *Grundsatzprogramm der Alternative für Deutschland*, p. 81.
77 *Wahlprogramm der Alternativ für Deutschland für die Wahl zum Deutschen Bundestag am 24. September 2017*, p. 53.
78 See the website AfD-Kompakt (https://afdkompakt.de/2020/04/01/afd-jetzt-auch-geschlechtergerecht/).
79 Ibid., p. 18.
80 The language in this article combined praise for West Germany's postwar economic success as well as memories of the pro-democratic revolutions of 1989: "The Basic Law is the best constitution we Germans have ever had. It was the cornerstone for West Germany's rise after the war. It enabled reunification after the peaceful

revolution in the east of our fatherland." AfD, "Wir sind Grundgesetz" (https://www.afd.de/grundgesetz/).

81 Katrin Bennhold, "Chemnitz Protests Show New Strength of Germany's Far Right" in *The New York Times* (August 30, 2018).

82 Values commonly taken to encompass the notion of *Leitkultur*. See Mona Schaeffer, "Für die Bundestagswahl nutzt die AfD einen manipulativen Trick, um uns zu verwirren" in WMN (September 12, 2021).

83 Ibid.

84 Stefan Scharf and Clemens Pleul, "Im Netz ist jeden tag Montag" in Rehberg, Kunz and Schlinzig eds., *PEGIDA* ..., pp. 83–98.

85 There is an important distinction to be made between misinformation and disinformation, both of which fuel the proliferation of falsehoods in social media spaces. While misinformation is false information unknowingly passed on, disinformation is false information that has been spread deliberately. What often begins as a disinformation campaign by malicious parties swiftly becomes a misinformation epidemic spread by the hapless.

86 As Shoshana Zuboff has written about at length, social media platforms such as Facebook (now known as Meta) facilitate the spread of disinformation via their ruthlessly profit-driven mining of user data. In a paradigm referred to by Zuboff as "surveillance capitalism," user data is gathered indiscriminately only to generate an aggregate image of what a given user likes to see on social media and will want to see more of as they continue to browse. For example, if a user seems to be reading, liking, or pausing for long periods of time on far-right content, more of this content will be delivered to them via an algorithm that has not been programmed with any ethical concern over the hatefulness or lack of factuality within any given content. Zuboff quotes a leaked memo from Facebook executive Andrew Bosworth, who describes a total disregard for truth or consequences: "We connect people. That can be good if they make it positive. Maybe someone finds love … Maybe someone dies in a terrorist attack … The ugly truth is, anything that allows us to connect more people more often is *de facto* good." See Shoshana Zuboff, "The Coup We Are Not Talking About" in *The New York Times* (January 29, 2021). See also Zuboff, *The Age of Surveillance Capitalism: The Fight for a Human Future at the New Frontier of Power* (New York: Hachette Book Group, 2019); Jaron Lanier, *Ten Arguments for Deleting Your Social Media Accounts Right Now* (New York: Henry Holt, 2018); Martin Gurri, *The Revolt of the Public and the Crisis of Authority in the New Millennium* (San Francisco: Stripe Press, 2018).

87 Video interview with expert Andreas Speit by Daniel Müller, "Update für Nazis" in *Zeit Online* (March 21, 2012). See also from the same day Johannes Radke, "Flashmobs gegen die Demokratie" in *Zeit Online* (March 21, 2012).

88 Simpson, "Mobilizing Meanings," p. 39.

89   Ibid.
90   As reported by the Austrian *Standard*, "Hass im Netz: Angebliches 'Hassposting'—Handbuch Rechtsextremer aufgetaucht" (January 15, 2018).
91   Stefan Lauer, "Infokrieg für die Grundschule: 'Reconquista Germanica' und 'D Generation'" in *Belltower News* (January 19, 2018).
92   Michael Lewis, "Has Anyone Seen the President?" for *Bloomberg* (February 9, 2018).
93   Christopher Paul and Miriam Matthews for RAND, "The Russian 'Firehose of Falsehood' Propaganda Model: Why It Might Work and Options to Counter It" (RAND Corporation, 2016).
94   Jäger and Dittrich, "Medienstrategien rechts-alternativer ... "
95   D Generation, "Handbuch für Medienguerillas" (*c.* January 2018), downloaded from the website of anti-fascist group Hooligans Gegen Satzbau (https://www.hogesatzbau.de), p. 1.
96   Schopenhauer's tactics are not designed to lead toward actually being right, but to deceive and exhaust one's conversational opponent into conceding the argument. Examples include "Generalizing your opponent's specific statements," "Making your opponent angry," "Interrupt, break, and divert the dispute," "Put his thesis into some odious category," and "Bewilder your opponent by mere bombast." Arthur Schopenhauer, *Eristische Dialektik: Die Kunst, Recht zu behalten* (Frankfurt am Main: Insel Taschenbuch, 1995).
97   One section of the manual, titled "Attack the Filter Bubble," proposes infiltrating the supposed echo chambers of left-leaning online users by creating painstakingly elaborate Twitter accounts devoted to topics which seem, at first glance, to be scientifically researched. Only after careful reading might it become clear that the information therein has been twisted to give the impression of a pernicious global initiative. From the manual: "An example would be the UN plans for RepMig ['replacement migration,' aka the Great Replacement]. One could run an acc [*sic*] that only posts graphics and sentences from the RepMig plans. Another possible example would be an analysis of the fake news cluster from ÖR-Staatsfunk, Bertelsmann and Springer—the main reason why Merkel wins the election again, despite her fight against us Germans in favor of the EU. And the trafficking NGOs also deserve more attention. Articles could be collected here, GPS data or eyewitness reports." D Generation, "Handbuch für Medienguerillas," p. 8.
98   *Deutsche Welle*, "Far-Right Trolls Active on Social Media before German Election: Research" (February 21, 2018).
99   *Süddeutsche Zeitung*, "Manipulation im Netz: Wie rechte Internet-Trolle versuchten, die Bundestagswahl zu beeinflussen" (February 20, 2018).
100 D Generation, "Handbuch für Medienguerillas," p. 5.

101 The skewing of common perception of what ideas are "trending" can also be achieved through simple actions like giving high ratings to far-right YouTube videos, and negative ratings to videos uploaded by mainstream news outlets—an effect achievable with one click of the "thumbs up/down" button underneath every YouTube video. This will cause positively rated videos to be given algorithmic priority, and negatively rated videos to be effectively erased from, or buried far down in, search results.

102 Ashley Feinberg, "This Is the Daily Stormer's Playbook" (December 13, 2017). See also Andrew Marantz, "Inside the Daily Stormer's Style Guide" in *The New Yorker* (January 8, 2018).

103 Andrew Anglin's *Stormer* style guide quoted in Feinberg, "This Is … " Emphasis added.

104 As noted by Feinberg, the site takes care not to explicitly encourage acts of violence; however, Anglin is well aware of what his readers are capable of if given the right information. From the style guide: "If you're writing about some enemy Jew/feminist/etc., link their social media accounts. Twitter especially. We've gotten press attention before when I didn't even call for someone to be trolled but just linked them and people went and did it." Quoted from Feinberg, "This Is … "

105 See Zuboff, *The Age of Surveillance Capitalism*.

106 While the term "alt-right" was popularized around the time of Donald Trump's 2016 election to the US presidency in order to denote a particular new generation of far-right youth, the term had been circulating online since the 1990s. The prefix "alt," short for "alternative," originated as a USENET hierarchy ("*alt.**") which grouped together discussion topics considered controversial, or that had devolved into heated argument. "Alt-right" has since come to refer to online campaigns that aim toward the mainstreaming of far-right ideas. As Milton Klein, a former leading member of the US-based neo-Nazi group National Alliance, wrote in a manual titled "On strategy and tactics for USENET" in 1995: "Crucial to our USENET campaign is that our message is disseminated beyond 'our' groups: alt.politics*, nationalization, white, white-power, alt.revolution*, counter, alt.skinheads*, and to a certain extent, alt.revisionism* … We MUST move out beyond our present domain and take up positions on 'mainstream' groups." Emphasis in original. Milton Klein quoted in Michael Whine, "Cyberspace—A New Medium for Communication, Command, and Control by Extremists" in *Studies in Conflict & Terrorism*, vol. 22, no. 3 (1999), pp. 231–45 (p. 238).

107 Jäger and Dittrich, "Medienstrategien … "

108 Anglin quoted in Marantz, "Inside … "

109 Weiß, "Neue Rechte … "

110 For a recent study of these broad alliances that took shape during the Covid pandemic, see the articles in Heike Kleffner and Matthias Meisner eds., *Fehlender*

Mindestabstand: Die Coronakrise und die Netzwerke der Demokratiefeinde (Freiburg: Herder Verlag, 2021).

111   The largest percentage of those interviewed were voters for the Greens, at 23 percent, followed by Die Linke at 18 percent. In addition, unlike political populist movements which tend to attract a "lumpen" following, participants in the Querndenker movement mainly identify as middle-class, with 25 percent of those interviewed being self-employed (a figure disproportionate with self-employment in Germany as a whole, which at the time of the study was at 9.6 percent). See Oliver Nachtwey, Robert Schäfer, and Nadine Frei, "Politische Soziologie Der Corona-proteste" SocArXiv Acrhiv, Universität Basel (December 20, 2020). See also William Callison and Quinn Slobodian, "Querdenker: Der Aufstand des Mittelstands" in *Die Zeit* (April 3, 2021).

112   The term "*Querdenken*" also has a parallel genealogy within "the jargon of marketing and consultancy." As William Callison and Quinn Slobodian note, "For decades, *Querdenken* has circulated in C-Suite PowerPoint argot alongside cognates like 'disruption,' 'thinking outside of the box,' or the dot-com era Apple injunction to 'think different.'" The etiology of the term captures "a politically diverse group of actors united under a piece of formally empty jargon native to the world of media consulting—a world[…] from which many of the movement's organizers came." Callison and Slobodian, "Querdenker … "

113   Callison and Slobodian, "Querdenker … " See also Daniel Hornuff, "Corona-Demos: Querquengeln" in *Die Zeit* (August 12, 2020); Paul Middelhoff in interview with Oliver Nachtwey, "Was die Querdenker denken" (January 20, 2021); Philipp Daum and Marius Buhl, "Querdenker: Radikale Herzmenschen" in *Die Zeit* (March 17, 2021).

114   A recent contribution to Michael Vogt.tv, for example, asks whether vibration therapy can cure diabetes. Another posits that ancient Nordic runes "can be understood as the crystalline structure" of human DNA.

115   Herman and Popp are reported to have lured gullible followers to contribute to the purchase of land in Cape Breton, Canada, where—in an eerie nod to the 1978 Jonestown massacre—they host week-long "Knowledge Factory" (*Wisseinsmanufaktur*) retreats and plan to build a colony of right-wing radicals and ideologues. Martin Doerry, "Rechtes Netzwerk lockt Gleichgesinnte nach Kanada: Elche, Bären, Eva Herman" in *Der Spiegel* (July 23, 2020).

116   See "Burschenschaft Danubia" in Jens Mecklenburg ed., *Handbuch deutscher Rechtsextremismus—Antifa-Edition* (Berlin: Elefanten-Press, 1996), pp. 323–4.

117   The popular conspiracy theory speculates that British Prime Minister Winston Churchill intervened, during Hess's visit, in potential peace negotiations, and therefore bears responsibility for the continuation of the Second World War. Conspiracists also argue that Hess did not commit suicide by hanging/

strangulation at Spandau Prison but was instead murdered. See Richard Evans, *The Hitler Conspiracies: The Protocols—The Stab in the Back—The Reichstag Fire—Rudolf Hess—The Escape from the Bunker* (New York: Oxford University Press, 2020), pp. 121–64. See also Christopher Giesen, "Honorarprofessor unter Rechtsextremismus-Verdacht" in *Der Spiegel* (November 12, 2007).

118 Right-wing esotericism—sometimes referred to in German as *rechte Esoterik*, *braune Esoterik*, or *völkische Esoterik*—tends to blend antisemitic, ethno-nationalist, and conspiracist thought with early twentieth-century theosophic theories concerning Aryanism and Nordic mythology. Vogt has worked closely with prominent *braune* esotericist Jan Udo Holey who, under the extremely hokey pseudonym Jan van Helsing, publishes works that engage in paranoia about secret societies and their machinations within international liberal democratic governments, Germany's Federal Republic included. Outside of Germany, journalists have warned of a "cosmic right" on the rise in places such as the United States and the UK. See Keir Milburn, "The Cosmic Right Is on the Rise in the UK. The Left Must Fight It with Reason" for *Novara Media* (September 20, 2020).

119 Deutscher Bundestag, Drucksache 17/10829, "Kleine Anfrage aus der Fraktion Die Linke, 'Rechtsextreme Tendenzen in der Deutschen Burschenschaft'" (September 25, 2012), p. 1.

120 Simpson, "Mobilizing Meanings … " p. 41.

121 Moreover, Vogt uses his online platform to host interviews with such right-wing extremist figures as PEGIDA's Peter Feist, and the traditional gender role advocate Eva Herman, who was fired from her post at the ARD television network for praising Hitler's family policies. Helga Druxes, "Manipulating the Media: The German New Right's Virtual and Violent Identities" in Simpson and Druxes, *Digital Media Strategies of the Far Right in Europe and the United States* (Lanham, MA: Lexington Books, 2015), pp. 123–39 (p. 125). See also Eva Herman, *Das Eva Prinzip: Für eine neue Weiblichkeit* (Starnberg: Pendo Verlag, 2006).

122 Ina Rottscheidt, "Libertärer Antisemitismus: Hygienedemos verbreiten Mythos einer Neuen Weltordnung" for *Deutschlandfunk* (May 29, 2020).

Epilogue

1 See two articles which still resonate: Paul Betts, "1989 at Thirty: A Recast Legacy" in *Past and Present*, vol. 244, no. 1 (August 2019), pp. 271–305; Jennifer L. Allen, "Against the 1989–1990 Ending Myth" in *Central European History*, vol. 52 (2019), pp. 125–47.

2 An example in the United States which caused much public controversy is the *New York Times* "1619 Project."

3   *Deutsche Welle*, "Berlin Bans Rally by Vegan Chef Conspiracy Theorist" (July 23, 2020).
4   See, for example, Ruth Ben-Ghiat, *Strongmen: Mussolini to the Present* (New York: W. W. Norton, 2020). See also Jason Stanley's *How Fascism Works* (New York: Random House, 2018), which is loaded with presentisms.
5   With the exception of the equally reductive narrative that the rise of AfD was entirely explicable as a response to the 2015 migrant crisis, an interpretation which lacked any historical scope at all.
6   With the result, via the Communications Decency Act of 1996, that it is very unclear whether an online space such as a social media platform exists as a public or a private entity, and what the responsibilities of tech corporations are with regard to hate speech, disinformation/misinformation, and online harassment. See Margaret O'Mara, *The Code: Silicon Valley and the Remaking of America* (New York: Penguin, 2019); Zuboff, *The Age of Surveillance Capitalism*.
7   Daniel Bell, *The Coming of Post-Industrial Society: A Venture in Social Forecasting* (London: Heinemann, 1974).
8   François Hartog, *Regimes of Historicity: Presentism and Experiences of Time* (New York: Columbia University Press, 2016).
9   See Farhad Dilmaghani, "Wann kommt das Antirassismusministerium?" in *Die Zeit* (October 19, 2020); *Zeit* reporters, "Neuer Kabinettsausschuss gegen Rechtsextremismus und Rassismus" (March 2, 2020); Tom Sundermann, "NSU-Prozess: Das Mammutverfahren" in *Die Zeit* (May 6, 2018); *Zeit* reporters, "Aufklärung nach Mordserie: Petition fordert Freigabe von NSU-Akten in Hessen" (February 24, 2020).
10 For two salient challenges to this myth, see Bert Klandermans and Nonna Mayer eds., *Extreme Right Activists in Europe: Through the Magnifying Glass* (New York: Routledge, 2006) and Daniel Koehler, "Right-Wing Extremism and Terrorism in Europe: Current Developments and Issues for the Future" in *PRISM*, vol. 6, no. 2, Institute for National Strategic Security (2016).
11 As Farhad Dilmaghani of DeutschPlus has pointed out, it took almost forty years for the Federal Republic to recognize the 1980 Oktoberfest bombing in Munich as an act of right-wing terror. Dilmaghani, "Wann kommt ... ?"
12 See *The Economist*, "Hundreds of Germans Are Living as if the Reich Never Ended" (November 10, 2016).
13 While the growing appeal of Reichsbürger ideology has been noted by state intelligence services at least as far back as 2012, the movement itself dates to the mid-1980s. Not until 2016 did the federal branch of the BfV begin to mention Reichsbürger in their annual report—a development which tracks with the surge in right-wing populism around this time. See Ministerium des Innern des Landes Brandenburg, *Verfassungsschutzbericht Land Brandenburg 2012*

(Potsdam: Ministerium des Innern des Landes Brandenburg, 2013), p. 90; BfV, Verfassungsschutzbericht 2016 (Berlin: 2017). See also *Deutsche Welle*,"German Police Arrest 25 Suspects in Plot to Overthrow State" (December 7, 2022).

14 Philip Oltermann, "The Reichsbürger Plot: Sinister Plan to Overthrow the German State or Just a Rag-Tag Revolution?" in *The Guardian* (December 10, 2022).

15 Thomas Fischermann et al., "Countdown to the Coup" in *Zeit Online* (May 4, 2023).

16 As journalists have noted, the Reichsbürger movement in recent years has gained significant new membership and social currency owing to the prominence of other conspiracy theorist networks like QAnon and Querdenken. Katrin Bennhold and Eika Solomon, "Far-Right Group Suspected in German Plot Gained Strength from QAnon" in *The New York Times* (December 8, 2022).

17 See one recent example: Samuel Woolley, *The Reality Game: How the Next Wave of Technology Will Break the Truth* (New York: Hachette, 2020).

18 Kavanagh and Rich, *Truth Decay*. See also Omand, *How Spies Think*, pp. 233–72.

Sources

Archival Databases

Antifaschistische Initiative Moabit
Antifaschistisches Pressearchiv und Bildungszentrum
BArch (Bundesarchiv)
    BH 7-1 Abteilung Militärarchiv Wiesentalstraße
Bundesministerium des Innern
    Verfassungsschutzberichten, 1991–2020
Deutscher Bundestag
    Dokumentations- und Informationssystem für Parlamentsmaterialien, 1991–2017
Hessischer Landtag
    Veröffentlichungen der Historischen Kommission für Hessen
Innenministerium des Landes Schleswig-Holstein
    Verfassungsschutzbericht, 2002
Ministerium des Innern des Landes Brandenburg
    Verfassungsschutzberichten, 2003–12
Ministerium für Inneres und Sport Mecklenburg-Vorpommern
    Verfassungsschutzbericht, 2014

Internet Sources

NSU-Watch—http://www.nsu-watch.info

Newspapers

Bild, 2011–2013
Deutsche Welle, 2003–
Financial Times, 2017–18
Frankfurter Allgemeine Zeitung, 1992–2018

The Guardian, 1993–
Los Angeles Times, 1992
New York Times, 1991–
Der Spiegel, 1990–
Die Zeit, 1991–

Select Bibliography

Adaire, Esther. "'This Other Germany, the Dark One.' Post-Wall Memory Politics Surrounding the Neo-Nazi Riots in Rostock and Hoyerswerda" in *German Politics and Society* vol. 37, no. 4 (Winter 2019/2020), pp. 43–57

Adaire, Esther. "Destroying German History: The Work of Heiner Müller as a Challenge to Public Memory" in *Communications of the International Brecht Society* (April 2016), https://e-cibs.org/issue-2020-1/#adaire

Adorno, Theodor W. "Was bedeutet: Aufarbeitung der Vergangenheit" in *Gesammelte Schriften 10.2. Kulturkritik und Gesellschaft II: Eingriffe. Stichworte. Anhang* (Suhrkamp: Frankfurt am Main, 1977), pp. 555–72

Adorno, Theodor W. *Aspekte des neuen Rechtsradikalismus* (Berlin: Suhrkamp, 2019)

Assmann, Aleida. "Transformations between History and Memory" in *Social Research* vol. 75, no. 1 "Collective Memory and Collective Identity" (Spring 2008), pp. 49–72

Assmann, Aleida. *Memory in a Global Age: Discourses, Practices and Trajectories* (Basingstoke: Palgrave Macmillan, 2010)

Assmann, Aleida. *Shadows of Trauma: Memory and the Politics of Postwar Identity* (New York: Fordham University Press, 2015)

Bahrmann, Hannes, and Links, Christoph. *Chronik der Wende. Die Ereignisse in der DDR zwischen 7. Oktober 1989 und 18. März 1990* (Berlin: Ch. Links Verlag, 2009)

Bar-On, Tamir. "Fascism to the Nouvelle Droite: The Dream of Pan-European Empire" in *Journal of Contemporary European Studies* vol. 16, no. 3 (2008), pp. 327–45

Bar-On, Tamir. *Rethinking the French New Right: Alternatives to Modernity* (London: Routledge 2013)

Bartov, Omer. "The Wehrmacht Exhibition Controversy: The Politics of Evidence" in Omer Bartov, Atina Grossmann, and Mary Nolan eds., *Crimes of War: Guilt and Denial in the Twentieth Century* (New York: The New Press, 2002), pp. 41–60

Bebnowski, David. "Populismus der Expertokraten. Eine Auseinandersetzung mit der Alternative für Deutschland" in *INDES. Zeitschrift für Politik und Gesellschaft* vol. 2, no. 4 (2013), pp. 151–9

Bebnowski, David. *Die Alternative für Deutschland. Aufstieg und gesellschaftliche Repräsentanz einer rechten populistischen Partei* (Wiesbaden: Springer, 2015)

Behrends, C. Jan; Lindenberger, Thomas, and Poutrus, G. Patrice. *Fremde und Fremd-Sein in der DDR. Zu historischen Ursachen der Fremdenfeindlichkeit in Ostdeutschland* (Berlin: Metropol, 2003)

Belew, Kathleen. *Bring the War Home: The White Power Movement and Paramilitary America* (Cambridge, MA: Harvard University Press, 2019)

Behrends, Jan C., Lindenberger, Thomas, and Poutrus, Patrice eds. *Fremde und Fremdsein in der DDR: Zu historischen Ursachen der Fremdenfeindlichkeit in Ostdeutschland* (Berlin: Metropol, 2003)

Beltrán, Cristina. *Cruelty as Citizenship: How Migrant Suffering Sustains White Democracy* (Minneapolis: University of Minnesota Press, 2020)

Bensmann, Marcus. *Schwarzbuch AfD: Fakten, Figuren, Hintergründe* (Essen: Correctiv Press, 2017)

Berger, Stefan. *The Search for Normality: National Identity and Historical Consciousness in Germany since 1800* (New York: Berghahn Books, 2003)

Böick, Marcus. *Die Treuhand: Idee—Praxis—Erfahrung* (Berlin: Suhrkamp, 2020)

Böick, Marcus. "In from the Socialist 'Cold,' but Burned by the Capitalist 'Heat'? The Dynamics of Political Revolution and Economic Transformation in Eastern Germany after 1990" in *Sustainability: Science, Practice, Policy. Special Issue: Reform or Revolution?* (Spring 2020)

Botsch, Gideon. "From Skinhead-Subculture to Radical Right Movement: The Development of a 'National Opposition' in East Germany" in *Contemporary European History* vol. 21, no. 4 (November 2012), pp. 553–73

Botsch, Gideon. *Die extreme Rechte in der Bundesrepublik Deutschland. 1949 bis heute* (Wiesbaden: WBG, 2012)

Botsch, Gideon; Raabe, Jan, and Schulze, Christoph eds. *Rechtsrock. Aufstieg und Wandel neonazistischer Jugendkultur am Beispiel Brandenburgs* (Berlin: be.bra Verlag, 2019)

Botsch, Gideon, and Schulze, Christoph eds. *Rechtsparteien in Brandenburg. Zwischen Wahlalternative und Neonazismus, 1990–2020* (Berlin: be.bra Verlag, 2021)

Boym, Svetlana. *The Future of Nostalgia* (New York: Perseus, 2001)

Brumlik, Micha. "Ostdeutscher Antisemitismus: Wie braun war die DDR?" in *Bundeszentrale für politische Bildung* (April 30, 2020)

Bugiel, Britta. *Rechtsextremismus Jugendlicher in der DDR und in den neuen Bundesländern von 1982 bis 1998* (Munster: Lit Verlag, 2002)

Cooke, Paul. *Representing East Germany since Unification: From Colonization to Nostalgia* (New York: Berg Publishers, 2005)

Copsey, Nigel, and Richardson, John E. eds. *Cultures of Post-War British Fascism* (New York: Routledge, 2015)

Decker, Oliver; Kiess, Johannes, and Brähler, Elmar eds. *Rechtsextremismus der Mitte und sekundärer Autoritarismus* (Gießen: Psychosozial-Verlag, 2015)

Doerr, Nicole. "The Visual Politics of the Alternative for Germany (AfD): Anti-Islam, Ethno-Nationalism, and Gendered Images" in *Social Sciences* vol. 10, no. 20 (January, 2021)

Dyson, Tom. *The Politics of German Defence and Security: Policy Leadership and Military Reform in the post-Cold War Era* (New York: Berghahn, 2008)

Eder, Jacob. *Holocaust Angst: The Federal Republic of Germany and American Holocaust Memory since the 1970s* (Oxford: Oxford University Press, 2016)

Ehrig, Stephen, Thomas, Marcel, and Zell, David eds. *The GDR Today: New Interdisciplinary Approaches to East German History, Memory and Culture* (Oxford: Lang, 2018)

Ely, John. "The 'Frankfurter Allgemeine Zeitung' and Contemporary National-Conservatism" in *German Politics and Society* vol. 13, no. 2 (1995), pp. 81–121

Eley, Geoff. "Fascism Then and Now" in Leo Panitch and Greg Albo eds., *The Politics of the Right* (London: Monthly Review Press, 2015), pp. 91–117

Evans, Richard J. *The Hitler Conspiracies: The Third Reich and the Paranoid Imagination* (London: Penguin, 2021)

Feit, Margret. *Die "Neue Rechte" in der Bundesrepublik. Organisation, Ideologie, Strategie* (Frankfurt: Campus Verlag, 1987)

Fetscher, Iring ed. *Neokonservative und "Neue Rechte:" Der Angriff gegen Sozialstaat und liberale Demokratie in den Vereinigten Staaten. Westeuropa und der Bundesrepublik* (Munich: C. H. Beck, 1983)

Florin, Klaus, and Seidel-Pielen, Eberhard. *Rechtsruck: Rassismus im Neuen Deutschland* (Hamburg: Rotbuch, 1992)

Frei, Norbert. *Vergangenheitspolitik: Die Anfänge der Bundesrepublik und die NS-Vergangenheit* (Munich: DTV Verlag, 1999)

Frei, Norbert. *Hitlers Eliten nach 1945* (Frankfurt am Main: Campus Verlag, 2001)

Fuchs, Christian, and Goetz, John. *Die Zelle. Rechter Terror in Deutschland* (Reinbek bei Hamburg: Rowohlt, 2012)

Fulbrook, Mary. *Reckonings: Legacies of Nazi Persecution and the Quest for Justice* (Oxford: Oxford University Press, 2018)

Gallinat, Anselma. *Narratives in the Making: Writing the East German Past in the Democratic Present* (New York: Berghahn, 2016)

Giordano, Ralph. *Die zweite Schuld: Oder von der Last ein Deutscher zu sein* (Munich: Knaur, 1987)

von der Goltz, Anna. *Inventing the Silent Majority in Western Europe and the United States: Conservatism in the 1960s and 1970s* (Cambridge: Cambridge University Press, 2017)

Greß, Franz, Jaschke, Hans-Gerd, and Schönekäs, Klaus. *Neue Rechte und Rechtsextremismus in Europa. Bundesrepublik, Frankreich, Großbritannien* (Opladen: VS Verlag für Sozialwissenschaften, 1990)

Grigat, Stephan ed. *AfD & FPÖ: Antisemitismus, völkischer Nationalismus und Geschlechterbilder* (Baden-Baden: Nomos Verlag, 2017)

Gurri, Martin. *The Revolt of the Public and the Crisis of Authority in the New Millennium* (San Francisco: Stripe Press, 2018)

Habermas, Jürgen. "Neoconservative Culture Criticism in the United States and West Germany: An Intellectual Movement in Two Political Cultures" in *Télos* vol. 56 (1983), pp. 75–89

Habermas, Jürgen. *Vergangenheit als Zukunft: Das alte Deutschland in neuen Europa?* (Zürich: Pendo Verlag, 1991)

Hartog, François. *Regimes of Historicity: Presentism and Experiences of Time* (New York: Columbia University Press, 2016)

Hasselbach, Ingo. *Die Abrechnung: ein Neonazi steigt aus* (Berlin: Aufbau Taschenbuch Verlag, 2001)

Heer, Hannes. *Vom Verschwinden der Täter: Der Vernichtungskrieg fand statt, aber keiner war dabei* (Berlin: Aufbau Verlag, 2004)

Heitzer, Enrico; Jander, Martin; Kahane, Anetta, and Poutrus, Patrice eds. *Nach Auschwitz: Schwieriges Erbe DDR. Plädoyer für einen Paradigmenwechsel in der DDR-Zeitgeschichtsforschung* (Frankfurt am Main: Wochenschau, 2018)

Herf, Jeffrey. *Divided Memory: The Nazi Past in the Two Germanys* (Cambridge, MA: Harvard University Press, 1997)

Hockenos, Paul. *Free to Hate: The Rise of the Right in Post-Communist Europe* (Routledge: New York, 1993)

Huyssen, Andreas. *Twilight Memories: Marking Time in a Culture of Amnesia* (New York: Routledge, 1995)

Jarausch, Konrad, and Geyer, Michael eds. *Shattered Past: Reconstructing German Histories* (Princeton, NJ: Princeton University Press, 2003)

Jones, Larry Eugene. *The German Right, 1918–1930: Political Parties, Organized Interests, and Patriotic Associations in the Struggle against Weimar Democracy* (Cambridge: Cambridge University Press, 2020)

Jordan, Jennifer. *Structures of Memory: Understanding Urban Change in Berlin and Beyond* (Stanford, CA: Stanford University Press, 2006)

Kahn, Michelle Lynn. "The American Influence on German Neo-Nazism: An Entangled History of Hate, 1970s–1990s" in *The Journal of Holocaust Research* vol. 35, no. 2 (2021), pp. 91–105

Kaplan, Jeffrey, and Tore, Bjorgo eds. *Racism on the Internet: Mapping Neo-Fascist Subcultures in Cyberspace* (Boston: Northeastern University Press, 1998)

Kavanagh, Jennifer, and Rich, Michael D. *Truth Decay: An Initial Exploration of the Diminishing Role of Facts and Analysis in American Public Life* (Santa Monica, CA: RAND Corporation, 2018)

Kinner, Klaus, and Richter, Rolf eds. *Rechtsextremismus und Antifaschismus: Historische und aktuelle Dimensionen* (Berlin: Dietz, 2000)

Klandermans, Bert, and Mayer, Nonna eds. *Extreme Right Activists in Europe: Through the Magnifying Glass* (New York: Routledge, 2006)

Kleffner, Heike, and Spangenberg, Anna eds. *Generation Hoyerswerda. Das Netzwerk militanter Neonazis in Brandenburg* (Berlin: be.bra Verlag, 2016)

Kleffner, Heike, and Meisner, Matthias eds. *Fehlender Mindestabstand: Die Coronakrise und die Netzwerke der Demokratiefeinde* (Freiburg: Herder Verlag, 2021)

Kleßmann, Christoph. *Die doppelte Staatsgründung. Deutsche Geschichte 1945–1955* (Göttingen: Vandenhoeck & Ruprecht, 1982)

Kleßmann, Christoph. *Zwei Staaten, eine Nation. Deutsche Geschichte 1955–1970* (Göttingen: Vandenhoeck & Ruprecht, 1988)

Ködderitzsch, Peter, and Müller, Leo A. *Rechtsextremismus in der DDR* (Göttingen: Lamuv Verlag, 1990)

Koehler, Daniel. "Right-Wing Extremism and Terrorism in Europe: Current Developments and Issues for the Future" in *PRISM* vol. 6, no. 2, Institute for National Strategic Security (2016)

Koehler, Daniel. *Right-Wing Terrorism in the 21st Century: The "National Socialist Underground" and the History of Terror from the Far-Right in Germany* (London: Routledge, 2018)

Koehler, Daniel. "A Threat from Within? Exploring the Link between the Extreme Right and the Military" ICCT—International Center for Counter-Terrorism Policy Brief (September 2019)

Koelschtzky, Martina. *Die Stimme ihrer Herren. Ideologie und Strategien der "Neuen Rechten" in der Bundesrepublik* (Cologne: Pahl-Rugenstein, 1986)

Köttig, Michaela; Bitzan, Renate, and Petö, Andrea eds., *Gender and Far Right Politics in Europe* (New York: Palgrave Macmillan, 2017)

Kramer, Jane. *The Politics of Memory: Looking for Germany in the New Germany* (New York: Random House, 1996)

Kreißel, Philip; Ebner, Julia; Urban, Alexander, and Guhl, Jakob. *Hass auf Knopfdruck: Rechtsextreme Trollfabriken und das Ökosystem koordinierter Hasskampagnen im Netz* (London: Institute for Strategic Dialogue, July 2018)

Laabs, Dirk. *Staatsfeinde in Uniform: Wie militante Rechte unsere Institutionen unterwandern* (Bonn: Econ Verlag, 2021)

Ladd, Brian. *The Ghosts of Berlin: Confronting German History in the Urban Landscape* (Chicago: University of Chicago Press, 1997)

Langebach, Martin, and Sturm, Michael eds. *Erinnerungsorte der extremen Rechten* (Wiesbaden: Springer, 2015)

Langenbacher, Eric. *Dynamics of Memory and Identity in Contemporary Europe* (New York: Berghahn Books, 2013)

Laqueur, Walter. "Postmodern Terrorism" in *Foreign Affairs* vol. 75, no. 5 (September/October 1996)

Lehnert, Esther, and Radvan, Heike eds. *Rechtsextreme Frauen. Analysen und Handlungsempfehlungen für die Soziale Arbeit und Pädagogik* (Opladen: Verlag Barbara Budrich, 2016), pp. 41–4

Lipstadt, Deborah E. *Denying the Holocaust: The Growing Assault on Truth and Memory* (London: Penguin Random House, 1993)

Mammone, Andrea; Godin, Emmanuel, and Jenkins, Brian eds. *Mapping the Extreme Right in Contemporary Europe: From Local to Transnational* (London: Routledge, 2012)

Mecklenburg, Jens ed. *Handbuch deutscher Rechtsextremismus—Antifa-Edition* (Berlin: Elefanten-Press, 1996)

Minkenberg, Michael. *The New Right in Comparative Perspective: The USA and Germany* (Ithaca: Cornell University Press, 1993)

Minkenberg, Michael. "The Radical Right in Postsocialist Central and Eastern Europe: Comparative Observations and Interpretations" in *East European Politics and Societies* vol. 16 (2002), pp. 335–62

Minkenberg, Michael. *The Radical Right in Eastern Europe: Democracy under Siege?* (London: Palgrave Macmillan, 2017)

Mitscherlich, Alexander, and Mitscherlich, Margarete. *Die Unfähigkeit zu trauern, Grundlagen kollektiven Verhaltens* (Munich: R. Piper & Co. Verlag, 1967)

Mohler, Armin. *Die konservative Revolution in Deutschland 1918–1932* (Stuttgart: F. Vorwerk, 1950)

Mohr, Tim. *Stirb nicht im Warteraum der Zukunft: Die ostdeutschen Punks und der Fall der Mauer* (Munich: Wilhelm Heyne Verlag, 2017)

Moller, Sabine. *Vielfache Vergangenheit: öffentliche Erinnerungskulturen und Familienerinnerungen an die NS-Zeit in Ostdeutschland* (Tübingen: edition diskord, 2003)

Moltmann, Bernhard et al. *Erinnerung: Zur Gegenwart des Holocaust in Deutschland-West und Deutschland-Ost* (Frankfurt am Main: Haag & Herchen Verlag, 1993)

Mudde, Cas. *Populist Radical Right Parties in Europe* (Cambridge: Cambridge University Press, 2007)

Mudde, Cas. *Racist Extremism in Central and Eastern Europe* (New York: Routledge, 2005)

Müller, Jan-Werner. *Another Country: German Intellectuals, Unification, and National Identity* (New Haven, CT: Yale University Press, 2000)

Müller, Jan-Werner. *What Is Populism? and Contesting Democracy: Political Ideas in Twentieth-Century Europe* (Philadelphia, PA: University of Pennsylvania Press, 2016)

Nawrocki, Christian, and Fuhrer, Armin eds. *AfD—Bekämpfen oder ignorieren?: Intelligente Argumente von 14 Demokraten* (Bremen: Kellner Verlag, 2016)

Neubacher, Frank. *Jugend und Rechtsextremismus in Ostdeutschland vor und nach der Wende. Umwelt, Kriminalität, Recht* (Godesberg: Forum Verlag, 1994)

Neumann, Klaus. *Shifting Memories: The Nazi Past in the New Germany* (Ann Arbor: University of Michigan Press, 2000)

Niven, Bill. *Facing the Nazi Past: United Germany and the Legacy of the Third Reich* (New York: Routledge, 2002)

Olick, Jeffrey K. *The Politics of Regret: On Collective Memory and Historical Responsibility* (New York: Routledge, 2007)

Olick, Jeffrey K. *The Sins of the Fathers: Germany, Memory, Method* (Chicago: University of Chicago Press, 2016)

Olsen, Jon Berndt. *Tailoring Truth: Politicizing the Past and Negotiating Memory in East Germany, 1945–1990* (New York: Berghahn Books, 2015)

O'Meara, Michael. *New Culture, New Right: Anti-Liberalism in Postmodern Europe* (Bloomington: Arktos Media, 2004)

Ramelow, Bodo ed. *Schreddern, Spitzeln, Staatsversagen. Wie rechter Terror, Behördenkumpanei und Rassismus aus der Mitte zusammengehen* (Hamburg: VSA Verlag, 2013)

Ramet, Sabrina P. ed. *The Radical Right in Central and Eastern Europe since 1989* (University Park, PA: Penn State University Press, 1999)

Rehberg, Karl-Siegbert; Kunz, Franziska, and Schlinzig, Tino eds. *PEGIDA—Rechtspopulismus zwischen Fremdenangst und "Wende"-Enttäuschung? Analysen im Überblick* (Bielefeld: Transcript Verlag, 2016)

Rosellini, Jay Julian. *Literary Skinheads? Writing from the Right in Reunified Germany* (West Lafayette, IN: Purdue University Press, 2000)

Rosellini, Jay Julian. *The German New Right: AfD, PEGIDA and the Re-Imagining of National Identity* (London: Hurst & Company, 2019)

Salzborn, Samuel. "Antisemitism in the 'Alternative for Germany' Party" in *German Politics and Society* vol. 36, no. 3 (Autumn 2018), pp. 74–93

Salzborn, Samuel. "Renaissance of the New Right in Germany? A Discussion of New Right Elements in German Right-Wing Extremism Today" in *German Politics and Society* vol. 34, no. 2 (2016), pp. 36–63

Saunders, Anna. *Memorializing the GDR: Monuments and Memory after 1989* (New York: Berghahn, 2018)

Schroeder, Klaus. *Rechtsextremismus und Jugendgewalt in Deutschland: Ein Ost—West-Vergleich* (Paderborn: Ferdinand Schöningh Verlag, 2003)

Schneider, Peter. *Berlin Now* (New York: Farrar, Straus and Giroux, 2014)

Shahan, Cyrus M., Howes, Seth, and Hall, Mirko M. *Beyond no Future: Cultures of German Punk* (New York: Bloomsbury Academic, 2016)

Simpson, Patricia Ann. "Mobilizing Meanings: Translocal Identities of the Far Right Web" in *German Politics and Society* vol. 34, no. 4 (Winter 2016), pp. 34–53

Simpson, Patricia Ann, and Druxes, Helga eds. *Digital Media Strategies of the Far Right in Europe and the United States* (Lanham, MA: Lexington Books, 2015)

Speit, Andreas. *Bürgerliche Scharfmacher: Deutschlands neue rechte Mitte—von AfD bis Pegida* (Zürich: Orell Füssli, 2016)

Steinbacher, Sybille ed. *Rechte Gewalt in Deutschland. Zum Umgang mit dem Rechtsextremismus in Gesellschaft, Politik und Justiz* (Göttingen: Wallstein Verlag, 2016)

Till, Karen. *The New Berlin: Memory, Politics, Place* (Minneapolis, MN: University of Minnesota Press, 2005)

Todorova, Maria, and Gille, Zsuzsa. *Post-Communist Nostalgia* (New York: Berghahn, 2010)

Tooze, Adam. *Crashed: How a Decade of Financial Crises Changed the World* (New York, New York: Viking Press, 2018)

Virchow, Fabian. *Gegen den Zivilismus: Internationale Beziehungen und Militär in den politischen Konzeptionen der extremen Rechten* (Wiesbaden: VS Verlag für Sozialwissenschaften, 2008)

Virchow, Fabian; Langebach, Martin, and Häusler, Alexander eds. *Handbuch Rechtsextremismus* (Wiesbaden: Springer, 2016)

Waibel, Harry. *Rechtsextremismus in der DDR bis 1989* (Cologne: Papyrossa Verlag, 1996)

Waibel, Harry. *Der gescheiterte Anti-Faschismus der SED. Rassismus in der DDR.* (Frankfurt am Main: Peter Lang, 2014)

Waibel, Harry. *Die braune Saat. Antisemitismus und Neonazismus in der DDR* (Stuttgart: Schmetterling Verlag, 2017)

Weidenfeld, Werner ed. *Deutschland. Eine Nation—doppelte Geschichte. Materialien zum deutschen Selbstverständnis* (Cologne: Wissenschaft und Politik, 1993)

Weiß, Volker. *Deutschlands Neue Rechte. Angriff der Eliten—Von Spengler bis Sarrazin* (Paderborn: Ferdinand Schöningh, 2011)

Weiß, Volker. "Die 'Konservative Revolution.' Geistiger Erinnerungsort der 'Neuen Rechten'" in Martin Langebach and Michael Sturm eds., *Erinnerungsorte der extremen Rechten* (Wiesbaden: Springer, 2015), pp. 101–20

Weiß, Volker. *Die autoritäre Revolte. Die Neue Rechte und der Untergang des Abendlandes* (Stuttgart: Klett-Cotta, 2017)

Wiegel, Gerd. *Ein aufhaltsamer Aufstieg—Alternativen zu AfD & Co.* (Cologne: PapyRossa Press, 2017)

Wicke, Christian. *Helmut Kohl's Quest for Normality: His Representation of the German Nation and Himself* (New York: Berghahn, 2015)

Wildt, Michael. *Volk, Volksgemeinschaft, AfD* (Hamburg: Hamburger Edition Press, 2017)

Wodak, Ruth, Khosravinik, Majid, and Mral, Brigitte. *Right-Wing Populism in Europe: Politics and Discourse* (London: Bloomsbury, 2013)

Woods, Roger. *The Conservative Revolution in the Weimar Republic* (Basingstoke: Palgrave, 1996)

Wuhs, Steven, and McLaughlin, Eric. "Explaining German Electoral Geography: Evidence from the eastern states" in *German Politics and Society* vol. 37, no. 1 (2019), pp. 1–23

Young, James E. *The Texture of Memory: Holocaust Memorials and Meaning* (New Haven: Yale University Press, 1993)

Zuboff, Shoshana. *The Age of Surveillance Capitalism: The Fight for a Human Future at the New Frontier of Power* (New York: Hachette Book Group, 2019)

Index

Albrecht, Franco 95–8 (*see also* Day X; Kommando Spezialkräfte [KSK]; Nordkreuz)
Alternative für Deutschland (AfD) 3, 133–5, 139, 140–53 (*see also* Gauland, Alexander; Höcke, Björn; Patriotische Europäer gegen die Islamisierung des Abendlandes [PEGIDA])
Amadeu Antonio Foundation 156, 158, 181 n105
"Anschwellender Bocksgesang" (1993) 42–3, 52–3, 136, 184 n6 (*see also Der Spiegel*; Neue Rechte; Strauß, Botho)
asylum laws (Germany) 13–14, 34–6
asylum seekers
    far-right violence against 11, 21–1, 24–8, 142 (*see also* asylum laws; Hoyerswerda attack; Range, Clemens; Rostock attack)

Balkan wars 79–81, 85–9, 91 (*see also* Bundeswehr; Kommando Spezialkräfte [KSK]; Kubitschek, Götz)
Baudrillard, Jean 1, 54
Beam, Louis L. 4, 101, 116–18, 215 n89, 216 n91 (*see also* Ku Klux Klan [KKK]; Leaderless Resistance; LibertyNet; National Socialist Underground [NSU]; White Power)
Blood & Honour 115, 117–19, 122, 125
Böhnhardt, Uwe 10, 81, 100, 104–5, 111, 115, 128, 211 n32, 211 n43, 219 n128 (*see also* Bundesamt für Verfassungsschutz [BfV]; far-right terrorism; National Socialist Underground [NSU]; Turkish Germans; Mundlos, Uwe; Zschäpe, Beate)
    background 105–7
    suicide 103

Brandt, Tino 126–8 (*see also* Bundesamt für Verfassungsschutz [BfV]; informants)
Bundesamt für Verfassungsschutz 3, 89–90, 97–8, 100
    and historical revisionism 82
    and the Neue Rechte 60–1, 66
    awareness of far-right 122–3, 125–30, 182 n27, 220 n137
    awareness of NSU 104–5, 110–2, 119, 214 n67
    (*see also* Brandt, Tino; Bundeswehr; informants; Kommando Spezialkräfte [KSK]; Leaderless Resistance; National Socialist Underground [NSU]; Neue Rechte; Operation Rennsteig)
Bundeswehr 1, 7, 47–50 (*see also* Day X; Kommando Spezialkräfte [KSK]; Roeder, Manfred; Wehrmachtsausstellung)
    far-right activity in 68–70, 74–9, 83–92, 94–5
    origins 71
    post-reunification 71–4

Christlich Demokratische Union (CDU) (*see also* asylum laws; asylum seekers; Bundeswehr; far-right terrorism; *Information für die Truppe: Zeitschrift für Innere Führung*; Kohl, Helmut; Neue Rechte; Wehrmachtsausstellung)
    and the Alternative für Deutschland (AfD) 143, 147, 229 n71
    and asylum seekers 33, 35–6, 146
    and the Bundeswehr 72–5, 83
    and the far-right 28–9, 31–2, 74–5, 92
    and the Nazi past 46, 50, 64–5, 83
    and the Neue Rechte 61, 62–3
    and Turkish Germans 37
Combat 18 115, 117–20, 125, 215 n87, 217 n106

Day X 1, 70, 96–8 (*see also* Albrecht, Franco; Bundeswehr; Kommando Spezialkräfte [KSK]; National Socialist Underground [NSU]; Nordkreuz; *The Turner Diaries*)
Dead Kennedys (band) 17, 176 n30
Der Spiegel 42–3, 53, 56–7, 85 (*see also* "Anschwellender Bocksgesang"; Bundeswehr; Neue Rechte)
Deutsche Alternative (DA) 21, 35 (*see also* Kühnen, Michael; Worch, Christian)
Deutsche Militärzeitschrift (DMZ) 61, 76–9 (*see also* Bundesamt für Verfassungsschutz [BfV]; Bundeswehr)
Die Linke 93, 95, 111–13, 143–4, 169 n8, 214 n67 (*see also* Alternative für Deutschland; Partei des Demokratischen Sozialismus [PDS])
Die Selbstbewusste Nation (1994) 51–63 (*see also* "Anschwellender Bocksgesang"; Neue Rechte; Schacht, Ulrich; Schwilk, Heimo)
Duke, David 12–13 (*see also* Ku Klux Klan [KKK])

Eichberg, Henning 59–60
Enzensberger, Hans Magnus 42, 51, 53, 56–7, 73, 197 n25 (*see also* Historikerstreit; Neue Rechte; Templin, Wolfgang; Walser, Martin)

far-right terrorism 1–5, 103–10 (*see also* asylum seekers; Bundesamt für Verfassungsschutz [BfV]; Hoyerswerda attack; internet; Leaderless Resistance; Mölln attack; National Socialist Underground [NSU]; Nationaldemokratische Partei Deutschlands [NPD]; Rostock attack; Turkish Germans)
  counterterrorism 7–8, 99–103, 110–15, 125–32
  "lone wolf" myth 3–4, 11, 36–8, 100–2, 118–19, 166
  postmodern 3–4 (*see also* Laqueur, Walter)
  statistics 26–7
Frankfurter Allgemeine Zeitung (FAZ) 32–3, 39, 40–1, 46, 47, 55, 60–6, 147–8, 187 n28 (*see also* Historikerstreit; Neue Rechte; Röhl, Klaus Rainer)

Gauland, Alexander 141, 147–9 (*see also* Alternative für Deutschland [AfD]; Höcke, Björn)
German Democratic Republic (GDR, East Germany)
  and the far-right 20–4
  and the Nazi past 29–32, 180 n99, 182 n105
  skinhead scene in 14–19, 20, 181 n100
Gerster, Johannes 31–2
Gesinnungsgemeinschaft der Neuen Front (GdNF) 20–1, 147 n45 (*see also* Worch, Christian)
"Great Replacement" 137–8, 232 n97 (*see also* Identitarian movement; internet; Neue Rechte; Patriotische Europäer gegen die Islamisierung des Abendlandes [PEGIDA]; Sellner, Martin)
Günzel, Reinhard 69, 92–4 (*see also* Bundeswehr; Kommando Spezialkräfte [KSK])
Gysi, Gregor 33, 79, 83 (*see also* Bundeswehr; Die Linke; Partei des Demokratischen Sozialismus [PDS])

Habermas, Jürgen 40, 73–4
Hammerskin Nation 101, 106, 106, 115, 117, 122 (*see also* Blood & Honour; Böhnhardt, Uwe; Combat 18; Mundlos, Uwe; National Socialist Underground [NSU]; Zschäpe, Beate)
Heitmann, Steffen 41, 42, 56 (*see also* Enzensberger, Hans Magnus; Neue Rechte; Templin, Wolfgang; Walser, Martin)
Historikerstreit 3, 39, 40–1, 47–8 (*see also* Neue Rechte; Nolte, Ernst; Stürmer, Michael)
Höcke, Björn 141–2, 147–9 (*see also* Alternative für Deutschland [AfD]; Gauland, Alexander)
Holocaust (*see also* Historikerstreit; Jews; Neue Rechte; Wehrmachtsausstellung)
  denial of 21, 43, 60–1, 220 n137

memory of in postwar Germany 29–30, 47, 65, 148–9, 186 n22
relativization of by Neue Rechte 39, 43, 58, 66, 186 n23, 197 n25
Hoyerswerda attack (1991) 11, 24–8, 31, 32–3, 74 (*see also* Rostock attack)

Identitarian movement 124, 133–4, 137–9, 148–9, 155 (*see also* Alternative für Deutschland [AfD]; Patriotische Europäer gegen die Islamisierung des Abendlandes [PEGIDA])
informants 36, 125–6, 182 n127, 214 n67, 221 n151
and NSU 110–11 (*see also* Bundesamt für Verfassungsschutz [BfV]; far-right terrorism; Nationaldemokratische Partei Deutschlands [NPD])
"V-Mann affair" (2001–3) 126–7
"V-Mann affair" (2012) 129
Information für die Truppe: Zeitschrift für Innere Führung 48–50, 78, 188 n36 (*see also* Bundeswehr; Schickel, Alfred; Range, Clemens)
internet
early use by far-right 7, 82, 101, 116–17, 217 n103
social media use by far-right 153–61, 167

Jelpke, Ulla 75, 94 (*see also* Bundeswehr; Partei des Demokratischen Sozialismus [PDS]; Wilz, Bernd)
Jews (*see also* far-right terrorism; Holocaust; Wehrmachtsausstellung)
as targets of far-right violence 22, 154
Neue Rechte anti-Semitism 92, 225 n27
Junge Freiheit 58, 66, 85, 87 (*see also* Holocaust; Templin, Wolfgang)
Jünger, Ernst 56, 62, 86

Kiowa, Amadeu Antonio 22 (*see also* Amadeu Antonio Foundation)
Kohl, Helmut 17, 28–9, 37–8, 50–1, 63, 72–3, 79
Kommando Spezialkräfte (KSK) 1–2, 65–70, 72, 91–8 (*see also* Albrecht, Franco; Bundesamt für Verfassungsschutz; Bundeswehr; Day X; Nordkreuz)

Ku Klux Klan (KKK) 4, 12–13, 101, 110–1, 116–17, 128 (*see also* Beam, Louis L.; Duke, David; internet; Leaderless Resistance)
Kubitschek, Götz 5, 66, 69, 84–9, 92–3, 136–40, 149, 203 n82 (*see also* Balkan wars; Bundeswehr; Identitarian movement; Patriotische Europäer gegen die Islamisierung des Abendlandes [PEGIDA]; Wehrmachtsausstellung)
Kühnen, Michael 20–2, 177 n51, n52, 178 n55 (*see also* Worch, Christian)

Laqueur, Walter 3–5 (*see also* postmodern terrorism)
Lauck, Gary "Gerhard" 21, 60, 177 n47
Leaderless Resistance 4, 7, 101–2, 116–19, 215 n89 (*see also* Beam, Louis L; Ku Klux Klan [KKK]; LibertyNet; National Socialist Underground [NSU])
LibertyNet 101, 116–17, 216 n91 (*see also* Beam, Louis L.; Ku Klux Klan [KKK]; National Socialist Underground [NSU])
Lyotard, Jean-François 1, 54

Maaz, Hans-Joachim 30–1 (*see also* Holocaust)
McVeigh, Timothy 4, 102 (*see also* far-right terrorism; Leaderless Resistance; Nichols, Terry; Oklahoma City bombing; *The Turner Diaries*)
Merkel, Angela 93, 130–2, 141, 142, 143, 150–1 (*see also* Christlich Demokratische Union [CDU])
Mohler, Armin 6, 52, 59, 224 n14 (*see also* Neue Rechte)
Mölln attack (1992) 14, 28, 34–7 (*see also* asylum laws; Kohl, Helmut; Solingen attack; Turkish Germans)
Mundlos, Uwe 10, 76, 81, 100, 104–5, 109, 115, 128, 211 n32, n35, n38, n43 (*see also* Böhnhardt, Uwe; Bundesamt für Verfassungsschutz [BfV]; far-right terrorism; National Socialist Underground [NSU]; Turkish Germans; Zschäpe, Beate)
background 105–7
suicide 103

National Socialist Underground (NSU) 2, 10, 15, 76 (*see also* Beam, Louis L.; Bundesamt für Verfassungsschutz [BfV]; Bundeswehr; Böhnhardt, Uwe; far-right terrorism; informants; Ku Klux Klan [KKK]; LibertyNet; Mundlos, Uwe; Turkish Germans; Zschäpe, Beate)
  and the Bundesamt für Verfassungsschutz [BfV] 104, 110–2, 128–9
  crimes committed by 103–5, 110–1
  law enforcement awareness of 104–5, 115
  origins 99–100, 105–10
Nationaldemokratische Partei Deutschlands (NPD) 7, 16, 99–102, 120–5 (*see also* Brandt, Tino; Bundesamt für Verfassungsschutz [BfV]; informants; National Socialist Underground [NSU])
  "V-Mann affair" (2001–3) 126–7
  "V-Mann affair" (2012) 129
Neue Rechte (*see also* Alternative für Deutschland [AfD]; "Anschwellender Bocksgesang"; Bundesamt für Verfassungsschutz [BfV]; Bundeswehr; Deutsche Militärzeitschrift [DMZ]; far-right terrorism; Frankfurter Allgemeine Zeitung [FAZ]; "Great Replacement"; Günzel, Reinhard; Historikerstreit; Holocaust; Jünger, Ernst; Kommando Spezialkräfte [KSK]; Kubitschek, Götz; Querdenker; Range, Clemens; reunification; Schickel, Alfred; Schwilk, Heimo; Strauß, Botho)
  and the Bundeswehr 66–79, 85, 92
  and commemoration 5–7, 47, 148–9
  and German conservatism 6, 42, 50, 62–3
  and memory of the Nazi past 39, 42–3, 47–50, 64–6, 77–83, 149
  and right-wing postmodernism 6–8, 40–3, 51–9, 135–6, 167
  ideas of 3, 44, 52–3, 59–60, 63–4, 136–40, 148–53
Nichols, Terry 4, 102 (*see also* far-right terrorism; Leaderless Resistance; McVeigh, Timothy; Oklahoma City bombing [1995])
Nolte, Ernst 6, 39–42, 52, 61–2, 183 n2, 184 n7 (*see also* Historikerstreit; Neue Rechte)
Nordkreuz 1, 96–8 (*see also* Bundeswehr; Day X; Kommando Spezialkräfte [KSK]; *The Turner Diaries*)
Nouvelle Droite 3, 52, 59, 60, 96, 138

Oklahoma City bombing (1995) 4, 102, 216 n96 (*see also* far-right terrorism; Leaderless Resistance; McVeigh, Timothy; *The Turner Diaries*; Nichols, Terry)
Operation Rennsteig (1996–2003) 111, 125–6, 129 (*see also* Bundesamt für Verfassungsschutz [BfV]; National Socialist Underground [NSU]; Nationaldemokratische Partei Deutschlands [NPD])

Pamyat (Память, "Memory") 24, 44
Partei des Demokratischen Sozialismus (PDS, 1990–2007) 33, 41, 78–9, 50, 75, 83–5, 88, 90, 93–4 (*see also* Die Linke; Gysi, Gregor; Wilz, Bernd; Jelpke, Ulla)
Patriotische Europäer gegen die Islamisierung des Abendlandes (PEGIDA) 3, 134, 137–40, 144–53 (*see also* Alternative für Deutschland [AfD]; Identitarian movement; Kubitschek, Götz, reunification)
postmodern 1–2
  right-wing 135–6
  terrorism 3–4 (*see also* Laqueur, Walter)

Querdenker 3, 42, 57, 135, 159–62 (*see also* Alternative für Deutschland; internet; Patriotische Europäer gegen die Islamisierung des Abendlandes [PEGIDA])
Qurbani, Burhan 9–10

Range, Clemens 48–50 (*see also* Bundeswehr; *Information für die Truppe: Zeitschrift für Innere Führung*; Schickel, Alfred)

Red Army Faction (RAF) 6, 46, 109, 213 n50 (*see also* National Socialist Underground [NSU])
Refugees 24 (*see also* Alternative für Deutschland [AfD]; far-right terrorism; Merkel, Angela)
Reichsbürger movement 94, 158–9, 161, 166–7, 235 n13, 236 n16 (*see also* Bundesamt für Verfassungsschutz; Kommando Spezialkräfte [KSK]; Querdenker)
Republikaner (REP) 13, 20, 22, 34, 81 (*see also* asylum seekers; far-right terrorism; Kubitschek, Götz; Nationaldemokratische Partei Deutschlands [NPD]; Wehrmachtausstellung)
reunification 56–60 (*see also* Alternative für Deutschland; Republikaner [REP]; German Democratic Republic [GDR]; Hoyerswerda attack; Nationaldemokratische Partei Deutschlands [NPD]; National Socialist Underground [NSU]; Patriotische Europäer gegen die Islamisierung des Abendlandes [PEGIDA]; Rostock attack; *Wir sind jung, wir sind Stark*)
  and neo-Nazi scene 9–19
  far-right violence and 19–28
  Memory of German Democratic Republic 134–5, 145–6
Roeder, Manfred 67–9, 81–4, 104–5 (*see also* Bundeswehr; Kubitschek, Götz; Rühe, Volker; Wehrmachtausstellung)
Röhl, Klaus Rainer 32–3, 56, 189 n39 (*see also Frankfurter Allgemeine Zeitung*)
Roma 22–3, 27, 186 n22
Rostock attack (1992) 9, 11, 24–8, 33, 74, 125 (*see also* asylum seekers; far-right terrorism; Hoyerswerda attack; Mölln attack)
Rudolf Hess march 23–4, 43 (*see also* Wunsiedel Committee)
Rühe, Volker 68–9, 81, 83–5, 96 (*see also* Bundeswehr; Roeder, Manfred)

Sarrazin, Thilo 59, 138–9, 225 n28
Schacht, Ulrich 51–3, 55, 56, 64–5 (*see also* Historikerstreit; Neue Rechte; Nolte, Ernst, Schwilk, Heimo)
Schickel, Alfred 48–50, 83, 87, 188 n36, n38 (*see also* Bundeswehr; *Information für die Truppe: Zeitschrift für Innere Führung*; Range, Clemens; Wehrmachtausstellung)
Schmitt, Bernd 36, 182 n127
Schwilk, Heimo 51–6, 64–5, 79 (*see also Die Selbstbewusste Nation*; Neue Rechte; Schacht, Ulrich)
Seebacher-Brandt, Brigitte 51, 56
Sellner, Martin 137–8, 149, 155–6 (*see also* Identitarian movement; Kubitschek, Götz)
Solingen attack (1993) 33, 36–7, 45 (*see also* asylum laws; far-right terrorism; Hoyerswerda attack; Kohl, Helmut; Mölln attack; Turkish Germans)
Stasi 17–18, 31, 58
Strauß, Botho 7, 42, 51, 53, 56–7, 136–7, 149 (*see also* "Anschwellender Bocksgesang"; Neue Rechte)
Stürmer, Michael 43, 46–7, 50 (*see also* Historikerstreit; Neue Rechte)

Telegram (messaging app) 1, 96–7
Templin, Wolfgang 41, 42, 51, 56, 57–9 (*see also* Enzensberger, Hans Magnus; Heitmann, Steffen; Historikerstreit; Neue Rechte; Walser, Martin)
The Turner Diaries (1978, Pierce, William Luther) 1, 2, 117–18, 125, 216 n96 (*see also* Day X; Nordkreuz; Oklahoma City bombing)
Thüringer Heimatschutz 20, 100, 105–6, 120–1, 124–8 (*see also* Brandt, Tino; Bundesamt für Verfassungsschutz [BfV]; National Socialist Underground [NSU]; Nationaldemokratische Partei Deutschlands [NPD])
Turkish Germans 28–9, 34–8, 93, 131–2 (*see also* asylum laws; Kommando Spezialkräfte [KSK]; National Socialist Underground [NSU]; Solingen attack)

Unabomber (Ted Kaczinski) 4, 5

von Weizsäcker, Richard 37–8, 64–5

Walser, Martin 42, 51, 53, 57, 195 n118 (*see also* Enzensberger, Hans Magnus; Heitmann, Steffen; Historikerstreit; Neue Rechte; Strauß, Botho; Templin, Wolfgang; Zitelmann, Rainer)

Wehrmacht (*see also* Bundeswehr, Deutsche Militärzeitschrift [DMZ]; Günzel, Reinhard; *Information für die Truppe: Zeitschrift für Innere Führung*; Kubitschek, Götz; Neue Rechte; Roeder, Manfred; Wehrmachtsausstellung)
  and the Bundeswehr 71, 76–8, 86, 90, 92–3
  memory of in the postwar Germanys 47–9, 66, 76–8, 80–4, 87–8, 90–4

Wehrmachtsausstellung (Crimes of the Wehrmacht exhibition) 68, 79–84, 87, 200 n50 (*see also* Bundesamt für Verfassungsschutz [BfV]; Bundeswehr; Christlich Demokratische Union [CDU]; Junge Freiheit; Kubitschek, Götz; Nationaldemokratischer Partei Deutschlands [NPD]; Roeder, Manfred; Wehrmacht)

White Power 7, 116 (*see also* Beam, Louis L.; Ku Klux Klan [KKK]; Leaderless Resistance; National Socialist Underground [NSU])

Wilz, Bernd 50, 75

Wir sind jung, wir sind Stark (2015 film) 9–10 (*see also* far-right terrorism; Qurbani, Burhan)

Wohlleben, Ralf 100, 104, 106, 120–1, 215 n85 (*see also* National Socialist Underground [NSU]; Nationaldemokratische Partei Deutschlands [NPD])

Worch, Christian 20, 222 n153

Wunsiedel Committee 43, 185 n13 (*see also* Rudolf Hess march)

Zitelmann, Rainer 39, 52, 64–5, 194 n111 (*see also* "Anschwellender Bocksgesang"; Neue Rechte; Nolte, Ernst; Schacht, Ulrich; Schwilk, Heimo)

Zschäpe, Beate 10, 100, 103–4, 114, 128, 211 n32, n43, 212 n44, n45, 219 n128 (*see also* Böhnhardt, Uwe; Bundesamt für Verfassungsschutz [BfV]; far-right terrorism; Mundlos, Uwe; National Socialist Underground [NSU]; Turkish Germans)
  background 105–9
  media coverage 108–10

www.ingramcontent.com/pod-product-compliance
Lightning Source LLC
Chambersburg PA
CBHW071822300426
44116CB00009B/1397